War and
the media

War and the media

Propaganda and persuasion in the Gulf War

Philip M. Taylor

Manchester University Press
Manchester and New York
Distributed exclusively in the USA and Canada by St. Martin's Press

Published by Manchester University Press
Oxford Road, Manchester M13 9PL, UK
and Room 400, 175 Fifth Avenue, New York,
NY 10010, USA

Distributed exclusively in the USA and Canada
by St. Martin's Press, Inc., 175 Fifth Avenue,
New York, NY 10010, USA

British Library Cataloguing-in-Publication Data
A catalogue record for this book is available from the
British Library

Library of Congress Cataloging-in-Publication Data applied for

ISBN 0 7190 3753 0 *hardback*
    0 7190 3754 9 *paperback*

Printed in Great Britain
by Biddles Ltd, Guildford & King's Lynn

Contents

Contents

Preface

This is a book about how the allied coalition and the government of Iraq attempted to influence, utilise and manipulate the ways in which the Gulf War was presented by the media to the outside world between mid January and early March 1991. It is only in part about the media coverage of the conflict *per se* since the book concentrates on the point at which the policy and the presentation, the war and the media, came together on both sides to form propaganda. It also embraces, as far as it is yet possible to do so, a preliminary examination of psychological warfare methods employed during the war. Most of the information contained in these pages, however, is gleaned from the media coverage itself – from the press, television and radio. This should immediately place one on the alert in so far as any study of war propaganda is concerned given that the output of the media managers has provided the main sources of information for this book. An analysis of Gulf War propaganda is thus in danger of becoming an extension of that propaganda, merely reiterating uncritically the themes churned out by both sides during the conflict itself.

How to be on guard against this? Well, of course, not everything is propaganda. That emotive word is defined and explained in the introduction. On the other hand, the point at which information and propaganda merge in wartime is frequently obscured. The degree, for example, to which the flow of information in a war zone is controlled by military and political authorities who wish to see the media adopt a particular perspective on what is actually happening needs to be at the forefront of our minds. The type of questions that need to be asked therefore are: what arrangements were made for the release of information, and why? How much censorship was taking place? What alternative sources of information were open to the news gatherers, and were they used? To what extent did the media coverage simply echo or reflect official sources of information? And how far back did journalists stand from what was being told to them, or were they merely drawn into the media management system?

With these questions in mind, the media coverage has been used as a source both of information and of propaganda. The focus is Anglo-American, reflecting the leading contributions made by those two countries to the multinational coalition operating under United Nations' auspices, although it does need to be remembered that Britain's military involvement totalled only about 5% of the whole. It might therefore be argued that the British were allocated a role in the media arrangements that was favourably disproportionate to their actual military contribution. Nonetheless, because the coalition was unequivocally American-led and the arrangements made for the media were largely dictated by the United States, this book cannot help but recognise and reflect that. Although the Gulf War really began on 2 August 1990 when Iraq invaded Kuwait, this book deals exclusively with the period of January and February 1991 when Iraq was faced with armed confrontation by the multinational coalition. Every effort has been made to consider all branches of the media representatively, although in the three principal case studies around which the story of the propaganda war is told – the battle of Khafji, the Amiriya bunker/shelter bombing, and the battle of Mutlah Gap – particular attention has been devoted to the television coverage. The inadequacy of describing a visual medium without the images is a problem that remains to be overcome in book form.

That what is attempted here is even possible at all is due to the foresight of the Director of the Institute of Communications Studies at the University of Leeds, Nicholas Pronay, who took the decision to carry out what was probably the most comprehensive recording project ever undertaken by an academic department. One week before the war began, he asked the Institute's Television Research Unit to begin comprehensive recording of BBC1, BBC2, ITV, Channel 4, CNN and BSkyB (the last of which carried much CBS and NBC coverage), together with evening scheduling from TF1 (France), BR2 (Germany), RAI Uno (Italy) and the Soviet Gorizont satellite service. This continued throughout the war, ending a week after the cease-fire, although more selective monitoring of news and current affairs programmes continued for some time thereafter. It should also be added that this project was made materially possible by the University of Leeds' decision to equip the Institute with a technically advanced satellite reception system and made legally possible by the terms of the new Copyright Act. Consequently, the Institute possesses a vast and perhaps unique educational archive, consisting of approximately 10,500 hours of videotape, upon which – it cannot be emphasised too strongly – this book has only just begun to draw. The archive is too massive, and the time between the war itself and the book's publication too short, for a definitive analysis to be possible here. Hence the decision to focus the study around three of the war's most publicised and indeed controversial incidents, each conveniently about two weeks apart, which does at least mean that an overall view of the conflict can be given with a substantial degree of continuity.

The archive will undoubtedly provide research students and scholars with an invaluable resource for years to come. But meanwhile a start has been made by the Institute's own staff and students with various aspects of the media coverage currently being analysed, together with a comprehensive study of audience reactions supported by a grant from the ESRC and conducted by the Institute's Research Director, Dr David Morrison, and an examination of the structure and language (visual and otherwise) of the coverage by Dr Brent MacGregor. Their detailed findings, once they emerge in print, will undoubtedly add to the story told here, as no doubt will the testimonies and memoirs of the participants once they start to appear – as indeed they have already begun to do. But in a sense, whereas interpretations will continue and differ and new information will emerge, the media record is already fixed, captured forever in print and on videotape. This book purports only to provide an introductory survey of that record. Its approach is to apply that particular blend of quantitative and qualitative technique which comprises the historical method, with its emphasis on evidence. It is designed mainly for those interested in Contemporary History, Media Studies and War Studies. It should also be of interest to general readers who, thanks to the media, could feel that they were a part of the war. For this purpose I have eschewed jargon and complex theoretical frameworks. Wherever possible, extensive cross-references have been made to the more accessible press record in addition to the television evidence possessed by the Institute to facilitate the work of other researchers.

This raises another point worthy of consideration. The seductive nature of television's capacity for immediacy gives the impression of 'instant history'. The arrival of the video cassette recorder has added a further dimension. Instead of television being an ethereal medium, gone with the wind at the moment it is transmitted, it can now be played back, scrutinised, evaluated, verified and criticised. It has become, provided the VCR's *record* button has been pressed, a record like any other. As such, therefore, it has to be treated with considerable caution. Apart from being an important source for what has been transmitted at a particular moment in time, what is it a record of? How reliable is it as a source of information? How and under what conditions was it made? What was the purpose of making it? What impact did it have? Historians dealing with this brave new world of television as evidence are already familiar with these types of questions. But before they and others can deal with television's particular characteristics as an audio-visual record, they must first understand the medium itself.

It is now possible for audiences to scrutinise television, as a source of information and opinions, in the same way that it has long been possible to do with the press. This is also true of radio, of course, but the sheer social penetration of television in the western world[1] gives it a significance that may have been fully appreciated by wartime media managers but has yet to be fully taken on board outside of a few academic departments. In fact the ramifications of the video-recorder for political systems which entertain notions of accountability have yet to be discussed widely in democracies, although the role of smuggled videotapes in the undermining of totalitarian systems in Eastern Europe has been mooted for some time as a contributory factor in the political transformation of that part of the world. Equally, direct broadcasting by satellite or trans-frontier broadcasting provide television with a significance in international relations which has yet to be widely appreciated in terms of its global implications for diplomacy as we approach the 21st century. The Gulf War, then, was the first major international conflict fought against the background of accessible global telecommunications and domestic video-recorders, and might thus prove to be a watershed in the way states publicly conduct their relations with one another.

The problem is that we just don't know yet, especially from the Iraqi side, what precisely happened. The USA has at least so far proved a lot more open about being secretive. General H. Norman Schwarzkopf admitted to David Frost in his first major interview following the war: 'Nobody knew everything that we were doing except for a very few people in Washington and it was even a limited group of people here in this headquarters that knew everything we were doing. And we were very successful, I might add.' More may have come to light about the coalition effort since the war than about the Iraqi but, before hindsight sets in to shape the way in which the future dictates the perception of the past, this book is offered as a preliminary analysis of the way in which the war was presented at the time.

The question of time raises one final point. For the British and Americans, for example, the war broke out on 16 January 1991, whereas in Iraq it was in the early hours of the next morning. Although the coalition's military people worked on Zulu (i.e. Greenwich Mean) Time, every effort has been made here to adapt the appropriate times and dates of particular events to the situation pertaining to the countries under discussion across eight hours of time difference. General Schwarzkopf himself found this confusing at times, which was why he chose to wear a watch on either wrist throughout the war. As a prelude, however, it is important to note that during the war Eastern Standard Time (Washington) was five hours behind Greenwich Mean Time which, in turn, was three hours behind Riyadh and Baghdad. This might seem a small point to make but it was important during the war when the timing of briefings dictated by the Americans was influenced by considerations of media deadlines and when the media presentation of events occurring at a particular time of day or night was often determined by the timing of those occurrences elsewhere.

ICS, Leeds University,
16 September 1991.

Note

1 In Britain, for example, more than 20 million viewers were regularly tuning in to evening television news broadcasts, as compared with some 15 million newspaper readers. During the first week of the war, 12 out of the top 30 BBC programmes were news broadcasts.

Acknowledgements

This book, like all books, could not have been written without the help and support of numerous individuals. Professionally and privately, I am indebted to my colleagues at the Institute of Communications Studies at the University of Leeds and especially to Nicholas Pronay, David E. Morrison and Brent MacGregor. I am also grateful to Professor Warwick Blood whose time as a visiting scholar in the Institute coincided with the war itself. Every time they walked into my room to be greeted with an angst-ridden colleague, they were prepared to endure irritability in exchange for perspective, invaluable information and, most of all, tolerance with someone who had taken on an unmerciful publishing deadline. It would also be remiss of me to avoid expressing my gratitude to Andrew Thorpe, who was responsible for running the complicated processes involved in the massive recording exercise. Equally, I would like to thank the taught M.A. students in the Institute, together with my research students, for such lapses in providing the expected pastoral services of attention and cheerfulness as I might have been guilty of in my preoccupied state. I am also grateful to Jan Euden of PanOptic and to Nick Cull and Ian Bremner for providing me with invaluable additional materials from both sides of the Atlantic necessary for the writing of this book and without which it would have contained some gaping holes. Fiona Assersohn volunteered her invaluable services to help with the newspaper research.

Books are obsessions which call for demands upon friends and relatives who rarely appreciate the contribution they have made to their completion. Among the people in this category most worthy of recording in print with this particular project are Sandra Billingham and David Murdoch. Dr Geoff Waddington expressed a healthy scepticism for the validity of my dealing with such recent sources without official documents to support my views, which forced me constantly to re-examine my methodology, whereas Professor John Young of Salford University expressed unfailing confidence in my ability to adapt the practices of diplomatic history to contemporary media sources. To all, my sincere thanks.

DEDICATION

For
Suzie Heward

Television is no longer a spectator. You know in physics, in subatomic physics, there is something called the Heisenberg Principle, which basically says that, if you observe a phenomenon, you actually change it. Well we now have the Heisenberg physics of politics. As you observe a phenomenon with television, instantly you modify it somewhat. And I think that what we have to make sure of is that the truth is not modified, and that it's constantly fed to the leaders and to the publics in democratic countries.

(Benjamin Netanyahu, Israel's Deputy Foreign Minister, 1991)

Introduction

Image and reality in the Gulf War

'This is a proud day for America,' declared President George Bush immediately following the allied coalition's successful military conclusion to the Gulf War against Iraq in 1991. 'By God, we've kicked the Vietnam Syndrome once and for all.'[1] Greeted with ecstatic applause, this was a phrase loaded with nuance and meaning for the American government and people, not the least significant of which was the belief – almost even relief – that they had finally fought a war on the information front no less success-fully than they had on the field of battle. Indeed, this 'Vietnam Syndrome' figured so prominently throughout the Gulf War and the crisis leading up to it that it prompted the frequent observation that the United States appeared to be still fighting the trauma of that conflict as much, if not more so, than the war against Saddam Hussein.

But what exactly did it mean? One sardonic American critic stated shortly after the war that it meant 'the press had tied our hands':

It meant the freedom for the administration to wage war as if America were not a democracy, as if the public had no right to know the human cost of the havoc wreaked in their name. He [Bush] means that we are 'winners' – as if the tragedy of Vietnam were that we 'lost' rather than that we sacrificed 58,000 American lives in a war that should never have been fought. In the most revealing but little noticed quote of the Gulf War, on Feb. 1, Bush told the wives and children of airmen downed in Iraq that 'the US has a new credibility and what we say goes'. Now, appar-ently, we know that's true.[2]

This last observation, however, raises considerable difficulties. Appearances in wartime can be, and almost invariably are, decep-

1

tive. The aphorism that 'truth is the first casualty of war', together with the phrase 'fog of war', were perhaps the most overworked idioms of the Gulf conflict, certainly vying with the 'Vietnam Syndrome' as the most convenient media rationalisations for what was going on and why, and, more significantly, for explaining why the media were unable to get the whole story.

Vietnam was important in the Gulf War not merely because the United States had previously been unable to defeat a small Third World communist nation. Vietnam had entered popular perception as the first time the greatest power on earth had actually *lost* a war, something which most Americans were still coming to terms with, still trying to understand. As so often happens following a military defeat, the nation had turned in on itself as it sought an explanation. The erosion of self-confidence which this had entailed was only just beginning to be reversed after almost a decade of Ronald Reagan's Presidency and the 'winning' of the Cold War – despite unnerving suspicions in some intellectual quarters that the United States might just be a superpower in decline. Nonetheless, Middle America and the US establishment alike remained convinced that an explanation for the single remaining blemish on America's illustrious military record had been found: the enemy within had been their very own media.

Vietnam may be widely regarded as having been the 'first television war' – although strictly speaking the Korean War more accurately deserves that description – but television was widely blamed for having alienated American public sympathy and support for that later conflict. Regardless of the rights and wrongs of this thesis (and there is much to question in it), it dominated military public relations planning – in other countries as well as the United States – in wars fought since the 1960s. As Patrick Bishop of the *Daily Telegraph* observed while covering the Gulf conflict:

If there was one 'lesson' the US military learned from the Vietnam war, it was that journalists lost it for them. It was a never-ending refrain from the General's office to the Mess Hall chow line that the networks and the *New York Times* had done for the American effort.[3]

The crisis which erupted in the Middle East following Iraq's invasion of Kuwait on 2 August 1990 was, however, of quite a different nature. It is more than a truism to say that the Middle

East was not South East Asia. Nor, if President Bush and his Vietnam-blooded chief military advisers had anything to do with it, was it going to be allowed to be. As the President stated in his televised announcement on the opening night of the war:

I have told the American people before that this will not be another Vietnam, and I repeat this here tonight. Our troops will have the best possible support in the entire world and they will not be asked to fight with one hand tied behind their back.[4]

A major difference this time, of course, was the multinational nature of the conflict. Thanks to Resolution 678 of 29 November 1990, the Bush administration had secured United Nations' authority for the employment of 'all means necessary' to restore 'peace and security' in the region. Yet although a 'line in the sand' had been drawn to protect Saudi Arabia from invasion, a major military commitment would be needed if the United States wanted seriously to remove Saddam Hussein's forces from occupied Kuwait. Operation Desert Shield in other words was one thing but, for Desert Storm, the US military demanded – and received – minimal interference from the White House and, most important of all, clear objectives: a rapid war enabling little time for public protest to emerge; specific goals and war aims; no body bag counting and preferably therefore authority to control and restrict the media's involvement. The war to expel Iraq was thus to be a lightning strike directed against a clearly identified enemy fought by first a 28 and then a 31 nation strong coalition from five continents with seemingly very clear, simple, comprehensible and demonstrably achievable war aims. The American military was delighted, as Major-General Robert Johnston in Riyadh attested: 'We can measure our success here because our objectives are to get the Iraqis out of Kuwait. That's measurable in terms of real estate somewhere down the road.'[5]

President Bush outlined America's war aims as early as 8 August 1990. These were the immediate, complete and unconditional withdrawal of Iraq from Kuwait, the restoration of its legitimate government, the protection of American citizens abroad, and the re-establishment of peace and stability in the region as a whole along lines consistent with US national security interests. Subsequent resolutions passed by the UN Security Council provided, or were interpreted as giving, the United States authority to adopt any measures necessary to expel Iraq if sanctions failed to achieve this objective after 15 January 1991. Plans were accordingly made for a military strike against occupied Kuwait *as well as* Iraq but when in September news of them was leaked out by the American Air Force's chief of staff, General Michael Dugan, who stated that the cutting edge of the war would be in 'downtown Baghdad', he was fired from his post. Clearly, the public must be prepared more gently for what lay ahead.

A particular concern for the coalition, and particularly for the Americans a mere 15 years after their humiliating withdrawal from Saigon, remained the role which the media, and especially television, were to be allowed to play in any war against Iraq. When the distinguished British broadcaster, Robin Day, had pondered the relationship generally between warfare and post World War Two's most pervasive medium in a famous *Encounter* article back in 1970, he had suggested:

Television has a built-in bias towards depicting any conflict in terms of the visible brutality. You can say, of course, that that is what war is – brutality, conflict, starvation and combat. All I am saying is that there are other issues which cause these things to come about, and television does not always deal with them adequately. One wonders if in future a democracy which has uninhibited television coverage in every home will ever be able to fight a war, however just.[6]

The Americans watched with admiration as the British answered this question as they fought the Falklands War of 1982. Then, the British government had fought and won a short, brutal war 8,000 miles from home essentially within an information vacuum. For a variety of reasons – some technical but mostly as a matter of policy – that conflict had been fought far away from the 'visible brutality' of live television, with most pictures emerging only after it was all over.[7] The British, in other words, had apparently found an antidote to the 'Vietnam Syndrome' and the Americans duly went about applying it in the Grenada and Panama operations of 1983 and 1989 when, quite simply, the media were kept well and truly away from the action even though it was taking place in America's very own back yard.

However, thanks to enormous advances in communications technology and to the multinational nature of Operations Desert Shield and what would be Desert Storm, it was going to be virtually impossible to deny access altogether to the world's media from a region that had often been regarded as a likely starting point for World War Three. Although that potential scenario at least had been eased somewhat by the withdrawal of the Soviet Union from the Cold War equation, the problem nonetheless remained those memories of rows of body bags returning from South East Asia amidst massive media coverage, and which haunted the Bush administration. This would clearly have to be a war fought with as little cost to American life as possible – and as quickly as possible. Small wonder that Roger Ailes, the President's campaign manager, was brought in to advise on the orchestration of the American stance. Besides, this was indeed a crisis of such global implications that, for a war to be fought at all, it was essential for the planet's greatest solely functioning superpower to carry with it not just American public opinion but world opinion as well. Projecting 'the enemy' therefore as a serious military, economic and ideological threat to the New World Order was an essential part of the psychological preparations for sustaining casualties by the only power capable of enforcing that new international system. The lessons of Vietnam, the Falklands, Grenada and Panama were accordingly adapted to the waging of an information war on behalf of an emergent order in which the 'forces of tyranny and oppression' and the 'enemies of democracy' were to be finally routed in the name of 'international justice' and 'world peace'.

During the second half of 1990, then, as America poured as many troops into the Middle East in a matter of months as it had done in a matter of years into South East Asia, preparations were made for a war of words and images in order to secure the moral high ground in advance of any conflict against Saddam Hussein. Iraq was presented as a formidable military power which was striving to achieve nuclear weapons, if it had not already done so,[8] and to dominate the Middle East. Kuwait had been 'raped', Iraqi troops were 'plundering' the tiny and helpless state and 'butchering' its people. Saddam Hussein was a 'new Hitler' who must be further stopped from invading Saudi Arabia and thereby holding the world to ransom through his control of the majority of the world's oil resources. It was even claimed, for domestic consumption, that this would be a war for the American way of life. Saddam must not be 'appeased' as Hitler had been at Munich or else he would go on to dominate the entire region and thus jeopardise vital American interests. All this may have been true, of course, but that did not stop it from being propaganda in the terms defined below.

For its part, Saddam's propaganda machine promised the 'Mother and Father of All Battles' against the 'Devil in the White House' and taunted the Americans with claims that they would be unable to sustain massive casualties in the same way as the Iraqi army had been able to do in its eight-year-long war against Iran.[9] Contemptuous of the western democracies which, he believed, were interested less with morality and more in money gleaned from arms sales to nations like his own, Saddam interpreted American warnings about Kuwait as mere rhetoric and hypocrisy. Iraq, he warned, was prepared to turn itself into a massive cemetery 'with no tombstones for the aggressors' and claimed that an army of 12 million men would be required to defeat Saddam's soldiers. The western hostages, including the unfortunate passengers of BA Flight 149 who were trapped in the initial invasion as their aircraft refuelled at Kuwait's international airport, were not 'hostages', they were 'guests', and Saddam's apparent friendliness and kindness to children were plain for all to see on 23 August as he personally visited them at their hotels and bounced 5–year-old Stuart Lockwood on his knee. 'Guest News' became the autumn programming innovation on Iraqi TV to drive this point home. Moreover, while the Americans attempted to play down the autocratic nature of the Al-Sabah regime in Kuwait, the Iraqis touched a Middle Eastern street nerve by arguing that the oil-rich Gulf Arabs were corrupt and decadent and their wealth should be shared evenly throughout the region. Besides, this was not a struggle for Kuwait; that was now Iraq's 19th Province and renamed Kadhimat. It was about Palestine, which meant it was about Israel, America's 'zionist lackey' in the region. As no less a figure than Henry Kissinger warned: 'The impact on the Arab world of anti-western propaganda from Baghdad and the skillful linking of Kuwait and Palestine must not be underestimated.'[10] Small wonder that Margaret Thatcher, Prime Minister until John Major replaced her after the Conservative Party's leadership election on 28 November, while accusing Saddam of hiding behind the skirts of women, also warned President Bush that 'George, this is no time to go wobbly'.

Throughout the autumn and winter of 1990, thanks to the role which Cable News Network (CNN) had defined for itself as an instant electronic interlocutor between Baghdad and Washington, it became clear that television would play a particularly prominent role in any conflict, with Saddam and Bush frequently exchanging verbal blows via the ten-year-old television network once lampooned by rivals as the 'Chicken Noodle News'.[11] Even though the two Presidents addressed each other's people on Iraqi and American television, one journalist wrote later that 'significantly, back in the early days of the crisis, George Bush was furious that his unconvincing efforts to portray Saddam Hussein as a latter-day Hitler were undercut by live coverage of the Iraqi leader's amicable meetings with Western hostages'.[12] But it was already apparent that, by providing a public forum to the traditionally secretive world of diplomacy, CNN was quite simply changing the rules of international politics and that, as a consequence, it was also likely to alter the way in which modern warfare would be projected onto the world's television screens.

But the propaganda war was not to be confined merely to hyperbole between the leaders of Iraq and the United States. If war should come, it would be a Big Story fought by a Big Coalition and the world's media would not only need to be catered for in terms of news and information, they would also have to be exploited for propaganda purposes and, given Saddam was also known to have personal access to CNN, for sending messages to him – accurate or otherwise. Modern communications technology thus provided both an opportunity and a threat for the media managers. Getting the balance right between informing the media in such a way as to sustain public support at home and prosecuting successfully a ferocious war away from the potentially self-defeating impact of real war fought on-screen while at the same time exploiting the medium for disinformation and propaganda purposes would be no mean achievement in the age of instantaneous global satellite telecommunications.

What was unique about the Gulf War of January–February 1991 was that it was the first television war covered by the medium, sometimes live without pictures, sometimes with, from both sides of the conflict. This was not without its controversies. The high-profile presence of television journalists from coalition countries in Baghdad, for example, led to charges that CNN was

serving the interests of Iraqi propaganda and that its chief correspondent Peter Arnett was an Iraqi sympathiser.[13] At one point,
the BBC was even described as the 'Baghdad Broadcasting Corporation'. However extreme such views might have been, one journalist did liken the situation more realistically to 'the equivalent
of having a reporter in a call-box in Dresden or Berlin'.[14]

That, at least, is how it may have seemed initially, but Baghdad
proved to be neither Berlin nor Dresden in terms of the damage
that was to be incurred by the city from the allied air assault.
Moreover, at first, there were no live television pictures from the
enemy capital, although viewers could be forgiven for believing
that they were in fact 'seeing' the war in their mind's eye by virtue
of the graphic audio accounts, especially by CNN's journalists
under fire in Baghdad on the opening night. When various officials
talked of having 'seen' the war break out on television, what they
really meant was that they had *heard* the reports via their television sets. In that respect, initial reports from the enemy capital
might as well have been on radio, rather like the dramatic reports
of American radio correspondents broadcasting from London during the Blitz of 1940. However, it was not to be long before
television's particular characteristics as a visual medium were to
be both exploited and exposed.

The degree to which television featured so prominently at the
outset of this major international conflict provided an indication
of the central role which the media generally were to play throughout the war. But it is important to stress right at the outset that
there were essentially two wars going on: the war itself, fought by
the coalition's combined military forces against the regime of
Saddam Hussein, and the war as portrayed by the media. The
latter did not necessarily reflect the reality of the former. It will
take some time for an authoritative history of the 'real war' to be
written, a task which will be possible only when the official
records are opened to public scrutiny, just as it will require the
benefit of a broader timespan than that allowed here to evaluate
the wider international significance and consequences of the conflict. But, in the meantime, there is already a good deal of information, and especially about the media's war record, to be able to
draw some preliminary conclusions about the manner in which the
conflict was allowed to be portrayed by both the allied and the
Iraqi authorities.

Television is often regarded as a window on the world and in some respects it is. But, in wartime, its potential to become a window onto the actual battle front is limited, not just by the nature of the medium itself but also by the curtain of darkness which military censorship attempts to draw over it. The window thus becomes a mirror for the images generated by those controlling the information. The existence of this censorship caused considerable friction between the coalition and the media and much debate within the latter (and presumably the former) both during and since the war. We can as yet, however, measure only that part of the media debate which is conducted within the public domain, and it will be some time before the results of even routine secret official enquiries concerning the effectiveness of coalition media policy will become more widely available. Moreover, although an examination of the wartime media record might lead one to conclude that the coalition's media managers were sometimes more at odds with the journalists than they were with the enemy forces, this would be somewhat misleading because in fact military–media relations were in most respects more harmonious than they have been at any time since the Korean War back in the early 1950s. There were on the other hand considerable squabbles within the media themselves, with some journalists who felt that they had managed to keep their distance from the coalition's propaganda line arguing that the majority of their colleagues had not. It was this minority who invariably felt that the media had merely become a mouthpiece for the coalition; it was they who generally welcomed the presence of western journalists in Baghdad to serve as a counterweight to allied propaganda; and it was they who, in turn, were criticised for helping Iraqi propaganda, let alone for being self-righteous. But, like all interpretations – journalistic, political, creative or moral – it depends what side you are on. And, in wartime, sides have a tendency towards polarisation. The fact remains that, at the time, there was comparatively little friction about the media's role in reporting the war. There was admittedly some (assiduously chronicled in this book), but it was not really a major issue. It all happened too quickly for military–media relations to become so soured that they became a *cause célèbre*; it is only since the war that serious recriminations have followed.[15] Furthermore, as this book will attempt to demonstrate, the emerging post-war feeling that the Americans stopped the fighting too soon, before the job of removing Saddam Hussein from power had been achieved *inter alia* by the complete destruction of his armed forces, belies the wartime propaganda record concerning limited and clearly identifiable coalition war aims that was so central to sustaining public support for its actions.

One thing the war did expose was the danger created by live television when speed of reporting seemed to be more important than judgement or accuracy in what was actually being said. As one observer noted with a modicum of truth:

The medium's pathological need for moving pictures delivers it into the hands of those who control access. That is why we have endless footage of what the Allied commanders are prepared to let us film, and no pictures at all of the situation in Iraq. The inevitable result is that our coverage is biased because the story has to be led by the pictures. More importantly, the sheer speed of the communications technology has eroded our capacity to reflect, interpret, sift. The imperative is to get the story on the air, no matter how dubious or uncorroborated it is.[16]

The ability of journalists from coalition countries to transmit live instantaneous reports from an enemy capital under fire had never occurred before in the history of warfare. Yet the journalists, it must be remembered, were in Baghdad because the Iraqis permitted them to be. There were no Iraqi journalists in Riyadh, although in a sense there was no need for them to be because the coalition permitted western journalists there comparatively more open access to what it was doing than Baghdad was ever likely to allow. Besides, the Iraqi government (as distinct from its people) could see and hear what the rest of the world's media were reporting, which, in itself, should immediately raise all sorts of question marks about what the coalition was – or even should have been – allowing those media to relate and portray. The suspicion remains that the coalition used global television for disinformation purposes and for sending signals as well as propaganda to Saddam.

In Baghdad, though, western journalists were allowed to operate because they had the technological capacity to transmit directly around the world and particularly into the living rooms of the public of their chief protagonist. The Iraqis, too, had heard of the Vietnam Syndrome. This provided them with virtually their only opportunity to break the stranglehold which the coalition had secured on the international flow of information concerning the progress of the war. It was naive or tendentious for Ted Turner, CNN's founding owner, to argue that 'if we had had the right technology, you'd have seen Eva Braun on the *Donahue Show* and Adolf Hitler on *Meet the Press*',[17] but it is unlikely that Saddam Hussein was motivated by any desire to defend the American media's rights under the First Amendment of the United States Constitution. As the Washington correspondent of the *Daily Telegraph* warned on the eve of war:

You can be certain that if saturation bombing of the Iraqi capital becomes an American tactic, stomach-churning footage of bombed-out schools and hospitals will find their way on to American screens.[18]

As we shall see, this was not what happened. Although the Iraqi government clearly saw an ideal propaganda opportunity to influence global television, this does not mean automatically that it succeeded in making western journalists and their editors serve its purpose. The select band of correspondents who were permitted to stay in Baghdad were conscious of the role which the Iraqis wanted them to play and their main problem was how to balance this realisation against their desire to cover the Big Story in a unique situation that was, when criticised, often justified in terms of fulfilling the 'right to know' of their audience. Whether or not they managed to get this balance right, this has been the subject of some considerable debate. The few *print* journalists who remained in the enemy capital, interestingly, were not subjected to similar charges of treachery in quite the same way as their electronic counterparts, which again raises all sorts of questions about the role of television in contemporary warfare and, indeed, in modern society as a whole. This book will also attempt to address some of the issues surrounding this debate.

By way of contrast, about 1,000 journalists from all the media were present in Saudi Arabia throughout the war. There, they too were being subjected to a 'controlled information environment' which in many respects made the Iraqis look like newcomers as propagandists – a point that was rarely made during the war itself. This was all the more impressive an achievement in view of the way the pluralistic media from mostly democratic societies were handled in a monopolistic manner that gave an appearance of being open. Yet, as Peregrine Worsthorne noted: 'Iraqi censors in Baghdad are not much more, and perhaps even less, intrusive than

American ones in Dhahran.'[19] Or as TV-AM's chief reporter, Geoff Meade, put it: 'Control is subtler under the Allies, but only a little less effective.'[20] What was different was the degree to which the coalition managed to create a media management system that proved far more effective in projecting 'a desired view' of what was going on than the Iraqis were ever able to do with their totalitarian background, limited resources and experience and far fewer correspondents to deal with. The extent to which those journalists in Saudi Arabia, wittingly or unwittingly, served the interests of allied propaganda throughout the war therefore needs to be examined against the backdrop of the arrangements established for them by the coalition.

Not that the 'desired view' was necessarily always an 'accurate view'. As one reporter stated: 'if the truth is defined as what you see, or what someone who was there told you, then our ability to mine the facts was undoubtedly curtailed'.[21] Moreover, the degree to which journalists in any conflict are actually able to cover war is affected almost as much by the nature of the journalistic beast as it is by the imposition of military censorship. Journalists are, after all, only human beings. They do not expect, nor can they be expected, to see and report everything. They can chronicle only what they do see, or are allowed to see, and even then their judgement of what is important is determined by the same sort of experience, perception, education, even emotions, that affect all human beings in their attempts at 'putting reality together'.[22] In wartime, in other words, any one reporter can witness only a slice of the action. The reports they file are by definition selective and subjective, a representation of reality as they see it. John Simpson, Foreign Affairs Editor for the BBC and one of the first to publish his memoirs about life in wartime Baghdad, put it thus: 'it is rather like an account of a football match written from a seat near one of the goals. Whenever the play was down at my end I had a superb view of it. But when it moved to the far end of the pitch I only knew what was happening when I heard the crowd roar.'[23]

Because journalists are neither sociologists nor historians, their concern is more with the detail than the overall picture. They work for news organisations the role of which is to bring to the public the extraordinary rather than the typical, the 'newsworthy' rather than the commonplace. The pressure therefore to produce competitive stories tends to make them focus upon what they consider to be 'news' which can produce good copy and headlines. But perhaps the biggest casualty of all in wartime news reporting, focusing as it does on the spectacular incident or speech around which the story can be framed, is context.

Before going on to explain this, the point can perhaps be best illustrated by the reminder that, during the Gulf War, there was another crisis of major international importance taking place with the Soviet Union's struggle with the Baltic States, a struggle that was resolved only several months later – amidst a blaze of publicity – following the abortive August *coup d'état* in Moscow. In early 1991, because of the Gulf War and of the media's preoccupation with that story, the Baltics tended to be pushed down the news agenda when, in normal times, they would have been on or near the top. Because of the fiercely competitive environment in which the international news organisations operate, and because of the perceived demand among their viewers, readers and listeners for ever more Gulf War coverage, they poured money into the Middle East at the expense of other parts of the world. Many of the American media's recently established Eastern European news bureaux, for example, were being closed down prior to the Gulf War only months after they had been opened. As a result, comprehensive coverage of events elsewhere also proved to be a major casualty of the war.

This assertion highlights one of the chief difficulties in writing this book so soon after the event, namely the paucity of reliable information about what precisely was going on as compared with an embarrassment of riches concerning what the media had actually reported. Television gave the impression of an open war, fought in full view of world public opinion. In fact, then as now, there was much that remained hidden about many aspects of the conflict. What was released was invariably what each side doing the fighting and controlling the information wanted to see reach the public domain. Television tended to amplify this, thereby distracting attention away from the vast amount of information that was not being divulged. As one anonymous journalist quipped at the time, 'never in the field of recent conflict has so little been disclosed by so few to so many'.[24] One might add, in view of what did emerge about military–media relations, that never has so much useful information about the tensions which existed come from so many anonymous sources.[25] More often than not, however, the media just didn't know what was happening, especially in Riyadh and Dharhan where it was not uncommon for television journalists about to go live on-air to ask their British or American newsrooms to read the latest wire stories to them and then simply reiterate that information when they began their transmission as though it was their own latest information.[26] Even in Baghdad on the opening night, the television history-making CNN reporters were frequently asking Atlanta what was happening in Riyadh or at the Pentagon even though they were the ones who most appeared to be at the centre of the action.

Here is revealed one of the dangers of assuming that television provided us with a live insight into the realities of modern warfare. While subscribers to CNN increased and indeed television viewing figures around the world rose considerably, creating in the process a new species of 24–hour television war 'couch potato' suffering from 'Scudavision',[27] what audiences were seeing or hearing was not necessarily what was actually happening or that which was most significant. Television war addicts were in a sense mesmerised by the live coverage, reducing their capacity to stand back from the images objectively or critically. The expectational levels which this aroused was extraordinary: 'usually nothing happens, but nobody can ever be certain. For this is real-time, the unexpected, the brink of the future, not a repeat or a recording or an edited version of reality'.[28] Yet it has to be remembered that the television war was a major event partly because television made it so. Contrast, for example, the six weeks of coverage with the virtual total absence of footage from the eight-year war between Iraq and Iran. Even Vietnam, which lasted a little longer, was denied the kind of 24–hour saturation coverage which the Gulf War received. This sheer quantity of coverage must not be allowed to detract from the quality of what was being shown, although it often did. Perhaps he exaggerated the point, but David Halberstam was not far wide of the mark when he suggested in the *New York Times*:

Contemporary technology is dazzling, offering rare, almost addictive immediacy. 'We should make our motto "We are the world, we are wired" ', a TV executive said recently talking about his network's capacity for instantaneous coverage. What he meant was this: If we are there, the event if important; if we are not the event is not.[29]

But while simply 'being there' may have given the conflict an importance which really only history will be able to contextualise, the media event does nonetheless beg understanding. For, in a sense, the media were the story of this war, not just because they themselves made it so but also because they were allowed to make it so by political and military authorities which needed the media for particular purposes of their own. As I have already pointed out, the full and real story will eventually be told once the archives are opened. But in the meantime, we do have access to the media version of that story, and this can tell us something about the role of the media in modern society, about their growing global significance as we stand at the dawn of a new world telecommunications order and possibly it can even tell us something about ourselves, the audience. Alas, the media record can tell us only a very limited amount about the war itself.

In another sense, however, the broad outlines of the war are already known, albeit in the most general of terms. Since the conflict, as various details begin to emerge, altering slightly here and fine tuning there the media record of the time, we do not as yet have a vastly different picture from that which was being portrayed while the war was going on. No major event that went unreported during or immediately after the war has since emerged to alter our overall view, and nor perhaps will it until we learn the details of the Iraqi version of events. Conversely, as Channel 4's Nik Gowing has pointed out, once the war ended and the news management systems broke down, enabling correspondents to cover the plight of the Kurds in stark contrast to what had been seen of the Iraqi occupation of Kuwait, 'politicians no longer set the agenda. Television images dictated it for them'.[30] Yet he also reminded us that 'journalists did not emerge from military restrictions in the desert bursting to reveal information which had been suppressed' and felt that, despite a handful of exceptions, the 'information aplenty' filtering out at the time meant that 'the mosaic of war could, by and large, be assembled with an acceptable degree of accuracy within the obvious controls of information flow in a continuous military operation'.[31] It was, of course, the question of what constituted 'an acceptable degree of accuracy' which will continue to exercise media critics and scholars for some time to come.

Conceptually speaking, the medium is *not* the message. It may have become the message for audiences who view it uncritically but, for genuine understanding, it is vital to appreciate the context in which the text, the audio-visual message, is delivered. Television, particularly in the United States, is a consumer industry and, especially today, a highly competitive one. It is rooted in certain technologies, the creative and cost-effective utilisation of which is vital to its appeal and thus to its success. Moreover, television cameras 'see' only what they are pointed at; what goes on behind the camera operator's back can be reported only by words and is not part of the visual record. The angle of vision is in turn determined by either what that operator can point at or which he decrees or hopes will be of interest to his editors. The result is to amplify what is before the camera lens and to minimise the significance of what is behind it.

Live television is another aspect of this phenomenon but with different rules of operation; there is always the risk that the direct point-to-multipoint communicative process of live TV, by-passing the editors, will contain images which require explanation now denied by the instantaneous nature of the transmission. This can be both exciting for audiences and dangerous to authorities wishing to control the context in which the images are presented and perceived, as in wartime. During the Gulf War, the race to get a story first often meant that television companies became victims of their own technology in so far as the normal editorial processes, which involve a cumulative application of judgement and context, were being by-passed owing to the excitement of the event taking place before the camera's angle of vision. With the print media, for example, news passes through a series of editorial processes that takes considerably longer to reach the audience, with the result that the non-visual, what goes on behind the camera if you like, is also incorporated to a greater extent than on live television. The medium of live television as a vehicle for relating news instantaneously thus assumes the potential equally for relating uncontextualised or even false information immediately. As well as conveying, uniquely, a sense of involvement and immediacy, it can thus also amplify and distort. It might indeed be both a window and a mirror, but television is also a flawed microscope.

In some respects, it is possible to draw a wartime analogy between the information front and the battle front. On the battlefield itself, of course, communications are vital to the overall command and direction of a battle, and modern technology is capable of providing vast amounts of information from each of the individual fighting units.[32] Disrupting this communication is essential to defeating the enemy militarily. The trick from an intelligence point of view is how to assess and evaluate correctly these various micro levels of information and come up with a macro perspective. The same is in fact true for journalists. In wartime, however, the simple fact of the matter is that, like the overall strategic battle plan, the desired macrocosmic view has invariably already been worked out in advance by propagandists who want to ensure that a particular perspective is taken of the conflagration by pointing journalists to this microscopic or that particular point. One trick from a propaganda point of view, therefore, is how to expose or counter the peceptions being created by the other side. But the essential point is that, although there appears to be more news and information publicly available in modern warfare, it is subject to a whole host of political and military, not to mention technical, limitations with the result that, in the end, what is allowed to reach the public does not necessarily say very much about what is actually going on but certainly says a great deal about the concerns of those controlling the instruments of communications and the images they wish to see predominate. Thus, when the military are able to set the media agenda, it is then that the medium and the message tend to merge into one. This was the major philosophy behind the controversial news pool system employed by the coalition during the Gulf War. We need I.F. Stone to remind us of the dangers created by the reliance of reporters on official information sources when he said: 'They know a lot of things I don't know, but a lot of what they know isn't true.'[33]

Because television is primarily a picture-led medium, it is at its best when depicting, for example, generalised details of military hardware and action than rather when explaining preparations. As a result, it is again often criticised for its inability to present the wider context of any given issue, especially a war. The Gulf conflict was fought on a wide variety of fronts – economic, diplomatic, psychological, political – as well as military. But it was the military aspects which television most favoured and its coverage thus tended to create a somewhat simplistic impression of the multifarious aspects of warfare as well as an illusion of open

17

coverage that basically lacked hard information beyond the most general of details. When so many processes of selection and omission are taking place – by the media themselves, by the military, by the enemy – it became virtually impossible to distinguish between what was simply information and what was in fact propaganda.

Here, we immediately face another conceptual problem concerning the use of the word 'propaganda'. Propaganda, to most people, means lies or at best half-truths. In wartime, 'they' – the enemy – conduct propaganda, whereas 'we' deal with honest news and information. This assumption lay behind the description of coalition pool reports being 'cleared' whereas reports emanating from Baghdad were 'censored'. If 'we' have to engage in such activity, it is only because 'they' are doing it; because they are telling lies about us, we have to correct false impressions with the truth – which is in itself a convenient way of distinguishing 'our' propaganda from 'theirs' and implies that 'our' propaganda is not really propaganda at all. Yet as it was pointed out in *Newsweek* just before the end of the war:

Propaganda is a broad approach to persuasion that encompasses several disciplines ... the most persuasive propaganda is that which is both graphic and demonstrably true. In theory, reporters in democratic societies work independent of propaganda. In practice they are treated during war as simply more pieces of military hardware to be deployed. While the allies play it straighter than Iraq, much of the information they release has propaganda value, too.[34]

Notions that propaganda is somehow a sinister or evil activity designed to subvert human reason and exploit irrational emotion unfortunately remain firmly entrenched in popular consciousness and greatly hinder our understanding of it as a particular form of the processes of persuasion. In fact propaganda has only become a dirty word since the First World War. Before 1914, it meant simply the means by which the proponent of a particular doctrine (principally a religious one) propagated his beliefs among his audience. But, to reiterate, propaganda is simply a *process of persuasion*. As a concept, it is neutral and should be devoid of value judgements. Propaganda is one of the means by which the adherents of a particular cause seek to engender such views in an audience which would induce a desired perception of what is actually going on, and lead to them acting in a desired way, involving amongst other methods the deliberate selection and omission of accurate information as well as falsehoods – the more effective propaganda being that which is unlikely to be identified as such at the time. Philip Knightley wrestled with this issue during the war, stating:

> On the war front, information – propaganda is, perhaps, a better description – is used to keep the enemy guessing, to sap his will to fight, and to mislead him. On the home front, information – news is a better description – is used to arouse the fighting spirit of the nation, to mobilise public opinion behind the war, to suppress dissent and to steel the people for the sacrifices needed for victory.[35]

This, however, merely perpetuates the popular simplistic view. Largely as a result of their First and Second World War experience, for example, the British and Americans have come to concentrate principally upon propaganda techniques based upon the manipulation of news and accurate information – an approach that Nicholas Pronay has labelled 'propaganda with facts'.

The semantic origins of the word 'propaganda' derive from its religious origins. In 1622, Pope Gregory XV decided to establish the *Sacra Congregatio de Propaganda Fide* (the Sacred Congregagtion for the Implanting and Cultivation of the Faith) in an attempt to combat the growing spread of Protestantism in the Counter-Reformation. Thereafter, it began to be used increasingly in a context of political ideology until the First World War when, owing largely to the excesses of atrocity stories, it assumed its pejorative meaning. Stalin's Russia and Hitler's Germany damaged the reputation of propaganda still further. But these were quite frankly extremely unhelpful developments for our understanding of the process. For example, the notion that it is somehow more acceptable to kill a man rather than to persuade him to lay down his arms and surrender highlights the moral difficulties involved in the study of propaganda and of its components such as psychological warfare. The scenario just outlined is, after all, the triumph of persuasion over violence. Equally, propaganda for a 'good cause' should not be unacceptable simply because it is propaganda.

There are, of course, fundamental differences between a communicative process designed to persuade and one whose intention is to coerce. Historians have been working extensively on the subject of propaganda for at least the past 20 years, yet much of their work has still to penetrate mainstream history textbooks, let alone contemporary mass communications research. The relationship of communications to dominant ideologies is crucial to our understanding of propaganda and helps to explain why channels of news and information are principal targets for interest groups with economic, political, social and cultural ambitions. The French sociologist, Jacques Ellul, pointed the way in the 1950s when he observed that propaganda had become an inevitable political response to the communications revolution 'which pervades all aspects of public life'.[36] This applies equally to democracies, as well as to peacetime, as the philosophers Plato and David Hume, together with such pioneers of modern propaganda analysis as Edward Bernays, Walter Lippmann and Harold Lasswell back in the 1920s, would have recognised.

Media practitioners responding to the needs of modern democracies against the backdrop of the communications revolution appreciated the significance of propaganda as a persuasive process more readily than academics; it was Lord Reith, the founding father of the BBC, who pointed out that 'news is the shocktroops of propaganda'.[37] Similarly, politicians and government officials in emergent democracies, such as Britain between the wars, had realised the role which the new mass media could play in persuading the recently enfranchised electorate to adopt a consensus-based political system rather than taking recourse to the totalitarian alternatives that were springing up to challenge them at around the same time.[38] Yet the idea that propaganda was a sinister activity designed to subvert the human mind by playing upon emotion and human instinct rather than reason and intellect, drawing upon emergent theories of psychology and linked to a post-Darwinian reaction to a humanistic approach to understanding human behaviour, was epitomised by the view espoused by Lord Ponsonby in 1928 that 'the injection of the poison of hatred into men's minds by means of falsehood is a greater evil in wartime than the actual loss of life. The defilement of the human soul is worse than the destruction of the human body'.[39]

The assumption that propaganda and truth were somehow incompatible was rejected by the British and American governments in the Second World War. The British Ministry of Information for example worked on the principle that its work was to tell the 'truth, nothing but the truth, *and as near as possible*, the whole truth'.[40] It was, of course, the italicised qualification which distinguished straight information from propaganda and which underlined the inextricable relationship between propaganda and censorship. Moreover, whether there is such a thing as 'straight information' is open to considerable doubt and debate. As for the relationship between propaganda and other forms of persuasion, such as advertising, the line is extremely thin, delineated mainly by the motive of economic gain. Democracies, interestingly, persistently fight shy of the word propaganda – whether it be in the creation of the Office of War Information and the Ministry of Information in the Second World War or the Joint Information Bureau in the Gulf War – in a way that autocratic or totalitarian regimes do not, for example with Goebbels' Ministry of Public Enlightenment and Propaganda or the Propaganda Department of the Communist Party Central Committee. Due largely to the debasement of the word since the First World War and the excesses of totalitarian activity, however, democracies have adopted a variety of euphemisms in an effort to distance their own persuasive processes from the discredited word 'propaganda', ranging from 'political education' to 'publicity' and 'public relations' and, even more recently, 'media management'.

'Public enlightenment' is of course ostensibly more akin to education. J.A.C. Brown has argued that 'education' teaches people how to think, whereas 'propaganda' teaches them what to think.[41] This simple distinction, as Richard Taylor has pointed out, might also usefully be adapted to distinguish between 'information' or 'publicity' on the one hand and 'propaganda' on the other.[42] Because publicity imparts information that might not otherwise have been available, it provides its audience with opportunities to formulate opinions and to act accordingly. It therefore exploits the skills developed through education. By the same token, propaganda may be said to exploit publicity because it tells, implicitly or explicitly, its audience how to use those opportunities. But again, in practice, the distinctions are not always quite so clear cut. Information might be released to inform or to educate an audience for its own well-being but if, for whatever reason, some information is held back in order to strengthen the message, then the intent is deliberate and may therefore be said to be propagandist. Indeed, it is this question of intent which lies at the root of all propaganda analysis. This applies equally to the study of psychological warfare, a process of persuasion employed in conjunction with military operations which is designed to persuade the enemy to think and behave in a manner desired by the source, usually desertion or surrender. This book, by drawing upon the historical method which has done so much to enhance our understanding of propaganda in the past, aims to apply that same method to an analysis of a much more recent event utilising sources of mass communication.

As a process of persuasion, of course, propaganda had been employed for a variety of purposes long before its modern usages. Indeed, it is worth mentioning that among the earliest recorded uses of propaganda in a wartime context was its use by the antecedents of modern Iraq, the Mesopotamians. Nearly 4,000 years ago in the land between the Tigris and the Euphrates, the cradle of modern civilisation was peppered with monuments to the fighting achievements of the Assyrian Empire. Elongated, rectangular stone monuments, or *stelae*, were erected at strategic points depicting the ferocity of Assyrian kings as a means of warning others not to attack. Other ancient Assyrian propaganda adorned their imperial palaces and religious shrines in an attempt to consolidate the position of the rulers and demonstrate divine support for their warlike activities. Visual representations of charging chariots, marching armies, besieged cities and retreating enemies adorned the legacy of ancient Iraq. On one inscription from the sixth century BC, on the royal palace of Assurnasipal II at Nineveh, the following inscription concerning the treatment meted out to the rebellious people of Suru could be found:

I built a pillar over the city gate, and I flayed all the chief men who had revolted, and I covered the pillar with their skins; some I walled up within the pillar, some I impaled upon the pillar on stakes, and others I bound to stakes around the pillar; many within the border of my own land I flayed, and I spread their skins upon the walls; and I cut off the limbs of the officers, of the royal officers who had rebelled.[43]

This was propaganda by deed, designed to serve as an eternal warning not just to the people of Iraq but to its surrounding neighbours.

Saddam Hussein drew heavily upon ancient imagery and symbolism in his own propaganda directed at the Iraqi people following his seizure of power in 1979. At the entrance to the city of Babylon, for example, rebuilt from scratch by Saddam, there was a modern equivalent of a stelae: a large mural of the Iraqi leader receiving a palm leaf from the city's original architect Nebuchad-nezzar.[44] Iconographic images of Saddam combining ancient styles with socialist realism linking him to the glories of the past were in fact everywhere in modern Iraq. One of the best-known images prior to the war was of the gigantic arch in Baghdad of Saddam's arms bearing crossed swords, an epitaph to his 'victory' in the Iran–Iraq war. In attempting to recreate the glory that was once Iraq, first by that lengthy war with Iran and then through his seizure of Kuwait in August 1990, Saddam also employed modern media of communications, developing in the process a modern radio and television service, to spread his message and consolidate the position of his minority Ba'athist Party within the country. In doing so, his regime began to assume the characteristics of classic totalitarian regimes: a one-party state relying upon indoctrination of the young, the terror of the secret police, militaristic aggran-dizement – and state-controlled propaganda.[45]

The problem for modern totalitarian systems, as the events in Eastern Europe during 1989 had demonstrated, was that they could no longer remain secluded from the outside world as they had in the past. The march of recent communications technology has penetrated such regimes like a knife, revealing to once sealed-off populations a brave new world of alternative points of view, lifestyles, ways of being and believing. For totalitarian regimes dependent for their survival upon coercion rather than consensus, such free-flow of information and ideas proved to be incompatible with notions of enforced unity, nationalism and, perhaps above all, the ability to sustain political power by means other than persuasion.

Value judgements about propaganda being a 'good' or a 'bad' thing, therefore, would more profitably be directed at the cause being advocated or the regime conducting it rather than at the process itself. In so far as the process is concerned, we can legitimately refer only to 'effective' or 'ineffective' propaganda. And because censorship is the Siamese twin of propaganda by virtue of the fact that it involves the exclusion of certain facts and alternative viewpoints which may prejudice the credibility of the case being made, we can see that one of the most effective forms of propaganda is that which either remains hidden or which appears in the disguise of 'news' and 'information'. During the Gulf War, Philip Knightley asked:

So how today can the ordinary newspaper reader and television viewer distinguish the news from the propaganda? The answer is that he cannot. Good propaganda is too subtle to be instantly identifiable. The only protection is to treat all good news of the war with scepticism and to remember that history teaches us that in human affairs it is very rare for all the right to be on one side.[46]

But news is also interpreted within a wider context of understanding, experience and education. It is important therefore to create an overall climate of perception in which specific items of news can be rationalised and understood. Propaganda, in other words, is not confined to the manipulation of news content. It was not just that the BBC decided to issue a list of 67 songs deemed 'inappropriate' for air play during the conflict (including *Killing Me Softly, Everybody Wants To Rule the World* and *We Can Work It Out*) or that other television companies pulled certain potentially offensive programmes which contributed to this overall climate of propaganda. It was the degree to which virtually all information upon which opinions and perceptions, great and small, could be formed about the Gulf War was being controlled or influenced by media managers operating on the Vietnam-inspired assumption that wars may be won on the battlefield but they could also be lost on the domestic front. For critic John Pilger, the connivance of the media in the creation of this climate of consensus was the product of a contemptible culture 'in which vast amounts of repetitive information are confined to a narrow spectrum of "thinkable thought"'.[47] For philosophers such as Plato, it would have been inexcusable for democracies not to have employed some form of cultural and informational control.

One aspect of the way in which debate over this issue has been dodged, including during the Gulf War, was the degree to which censorship by the allies and by the Iraqis was compared. Every hour, CNN carried the following 'mental health warning':

CNN is working to bring you the most complete war coverage possible. However, various restrictions have been imposed on access to information and war locations. Iraq, Israel and Saudi Arabia have imposed restrictions for coverage of war activity in their countries. The US military and the

British military are also restricting certain information and access. The authorities involved feel the restrictions are necessary for security reasons. CNN is respecting these guide-lines and will tell you when the reports you see are affected.

The BBC's own guidelines stated that 'programmes should make it known in general terms that some information will be held back for military reasons and that reports out of Baghdad are rigorously censored'.[48] Similarly, ITN's formula was that 'in this, and other reports from the Gulf, some operational facts are omitted for reasons of military security' but when a Brent Sadler report from the enemy capital came through it was invariably flagged as being 'subject to Iraqi military censorship'.[49] Clearly, therefore, 'they' conducted censorship whereas 'our' military issued reports subject to guidelines of operational security. This in itself was excellent propaganda.

Propaganda known to be such is almost useless; it is dismissible simply as 'propaganda' as it is popularly understood. But if it is disguised as news and information, it is more palatable to the by now traditional western notions of the public's 'right to know' balanced against the essential military preoccupation with the 'need to know'. In Saudi Arabia, the tension caused by these conflicting desiderata of the respective professions was epitomised by an anonymous senior American Air Force official when he opened a briefing to journalists with the words: 'Let me say up front that I don't like the press. Your presence here can't possibly do me any good, and it can hurt me and my people. That's just so you'll know where we stand with each other.'[50]

The arrangements made by the coalition for the release of information to the media during the Gulf War were in fact a highly effective form of allied propaganda. They were all the more so because, during the most high-profile media war in history, the debate over the arrangements tended to focus more on what the military was releasing – the 'video game war' – rather than upon what it was not. Yet it was because the released information was comparatively similar in its overall tone and thrust – 'we are winning and we will go on winning'[51] – that a great opportunity for the armchair generals and strategists was created, with the result that audiences were subjected to a wealth of speculation by an army of pundits that was actually in violation of the very guide-lines issued to the media on the eve of war. But it did have

25

the added advantage that it filled up air-time and distracted attention away from the paucity of hard information emanating from coalition news sources.

Although not much could be done about the speculations of pundits working for independent commercial news organisations, the American military remained determined that what was perceived to have happened in Vietnam, namely a comparatively unfettered press corps roaming in and out of combat zones to report a complicated war out of context with disastrous consequences for domestic morale, should not happen again. General Schwarzkopf was particularly influenced by that experience, as when he admitted to *Life* magazine:

Ordinarily, commanding an infantry battalion is the highlight of a military career. Let me tell you, mine wasn't. It was because of all the stuff going on back in the States. No one wants to go to war, but if you go, you like to think that your country is behind you.[52]

In Saudi Arabia, a country not previously noted for its record of press freedom, the military had certain other advantages absent in South East Asia. It might be thought that technology, especially the arrival of portable satellite dishes and telephones, would give journalists a faster, more efficient means for relaying information not emanating from official sources back to their newsrooms. Paradoxically, this only made it all the more important for the military to ensure a tighter rein over their movements and activities, and how this was achieved is examined in the pages that follow.

A critical aspect of the entire media management operation – for both sides – concerned the likely length of the war. As Congressman Lee Hamilton, Democratic chairman of the House of Representatives sub-committee on European and Middle Eastern affairs, warned shortly after the outbreak of war:

Saddam Hussein does not need to win the war; he doesn't need to win the battles. All he has to do is keep this war going and to create casualties. If he does that over a period of time, then you are going to see an erosion of support for the war. That is a worst-case scenario.[53]

There were in fact many 'worst-case scenarios' discussed throughout the war. For the US military, the most serious was that, having committed itself to Desert Storm, Iraq would suddenly decide to pull out of Kuwait and leave its forces intact and massed on the border, thereby continuing to pose a future threat to the Gulf nations that would require a continued US military presence in the region. Despite its insistence that, unlike Vietnam, there must be very clear objectives and that the military must be allowed to pursue them by virtually any and every means, this did raise the question of what allied war aims actually were. Throughout the war, there were many accusations flying about that the United States possessed a hidden agenda of war aims involving the destruction of Iraq's military capability, the removal of Saddam Hussein from power, American domination of the region or even an attempt to control the world's oil supplies.[54] Of course, there must have been a set of 'peace aims' outlining what the coalition wished to see emerge and operate as a result of the war and to which the military–political directives were geared. Once again, these will not be made known until it can safely be assumed that divulging them will not hinder their achievement. What we do know is that little evidence has emerged in the short time since the end of the war to support some of the specific speculations or allegations as to what precisely these aims might have been – although some of the coalition's 'black' propaganda operations do appear to have been geared towards encouraging an internal revolt against Saddam. As we shall also see, political and military objectives would *appear* to have clashed over the question of war aims right at the very end of the war when President Bush called a halt to military operations perhaps slightly sooner than General Schwarzkopf might have chosen to have done. But before then, despite various diplomatic initiatives proposed by a variety of nations such as Iran and the Soviet Union, neither man appeared willing to tolerate a 'pause' in the military campaign until it had succeeded at least in its avowed objective of expelling Iraq from Kuwait.

One final conceptual point needs to be made about propaganda. To be most effective, it must be conducted hand in hand with policy. President Bush, having decided that his policy could be achieved only by military means and having secured United Nations' approval for those means, appears to have been only too willing to allow the military to define the tone of the propaganda because, from 16 January to 28 February, Central Command in Riyadh was responsible for implementing the policy. Although the President was involved at the critical stages of the decision-making process – initiating the dates for the air war, the ground war and the cease-fire – he apparently chose not to involve himself in the specifics of the campaign, preferring not to 'interfere' because, as his chief spokesman said, 'he's not involved in that kind of micro-management'. And so when General Schwarzkopf declared that 'we have no intention whatsoever of terminating this military campaign until we've accomplished the objectives that we announced at the outset' he could do so confident that this *was* United States policy. He did not, you will notice, simply state 'the objectives'; he stated 'the objectives that we announced'. However, there were various points in the war when political considerations were difficult to keep in harmony – as is invariably the case at time of war – with the practical needs of military policy. It was at these points that the White House, State Department and Pentagon in Washington occasionally appeared to be speaking with slightly different dialects than that employed by the coalition's spokesmen in Riyadh.

As the United States prepared to plan, implement and fight the next war, Saddam Hussein was in a sense preparing to fight the last one. Whereas the coalition was preparing to deploy high-technology, precision-guided 'smart' weapons and the latest developments in air power in order to win the war as quickly and 'cleanly' as possible, Iraq was digging in for a long war of attrition, preparing to tolerate massive casualties and employing weapons from the old Cold War era. That had been the pattern of Iraq's war against Iran when even a stalemate could be defined as a victory. The preparations for the propaganda war were of a similar order. Saddam also demonstrated that he was prepared to conduct a war in what appeared to be a different era by a total disregard for the environment: unleashing a massive oil spill into the Gulf and setting almost 600 Kuwait oil wells ablaze.[55] His violations of international law, whether they related to the treatment of civilians in Kuwait or of allied prisoners of war or even to the violation of human rights against his own citizens, served to reinforce the international community's view of him a man who must be stopped – although it also made him the hero of some parts of the Arab world where he was seen as a man who was willing to wage a real war against the West. Saddam's behaviour itself therefore helped to define the spectrum of moral condemnation around which the coalition could shape its propaganda and demeanour. By way of contrast, for example, the United States went out of its way to avoid 'collateral damage' to non-combatants, eschewed the use of its nuclear weapons and avoided targeting Iraq's historical or cultural sites. The occupiers of the moral high ground were plain for all to see – depending upon which side you were on.

The problem of course was that in attempting to keep coalition casualties to a minimum, by the waging of what has been termed 'hyperwar', what somehow got lost was the physical effect of modern weapons on human beings. People die in war; that much is understood. But how they die does not make for good television in most people's minds. No one except the most ghoulish would want to witness a real motorway or train crash, and the same is probably true for war. On this issue the military (who feared it) and the public (who, in so far as preliminary research would suggest, did not want to see it) were at one. If the media had been willing or able to show the 'visible brutality' of war, they would have found themselves out of step both with their sources of news and with their audience. Saddam Hussein of course was hoping that graphic reports of civilian damage from cities such as Baghdad and Basra would raise doubts amongst western opinion, especially as pre-war polls indicated that large segments of that opinion were unwilling to go to war. If Saddam had been able to get coalition bodies, especially American dead, to display, it is probable that he would have made every effort to escort western TV crews to the scenes. However, even if he could supply only Iraqi civilian dead, as he was able to do following the Amiriya bunker/shelter in mid February, he would have found that this did not significantly affect public support for the war once it had broken out, at least in Britain and the United States. And this in turn merely casts doubt upon the importance given by the coalition to its principal propaganda objectives: namely, to be *seen* to be waging a just war by fair means on behalf of international law against an evil regime and not against the people of Iraq. How far this was in fact necessary is a subject for further research. For now, it is important simply to recognise that both sides appreciated the importance of propaganda in the Gulf War, devoted considerable time and effort to conducting it and revealed contrasting styles and methods in their employment of it. The whole truth was of course a major casualty; that is the first reality of war. But when image and reality merge into one in the eyes and ears of the beholder, it may just turn out to be that propaganda and truth were not that far apart, or even that they had become one and the same thing.

Chapter One

'A controlled information environment': allied media management in the Gulf War

Introduction

The Gulf War broke out on television. Or that at least is how television viewers in many parts of the world will remember it. In the United States, on Wednesday 16 January 1991, it erupted on prime-time evening news bulletins. The ABC network can claim to have broken the story first as viewers of its 18:30 evening programme World News Tonight were taken live to Baghdad for a telephone interview with reporter Gary Shephard on the latest developments in the crisis. In Iraq it was just after 02:30 on a moonless night, more than 24 hours after the expiry of the United Nations deadline for its government to withdraw from occupied Kuwait. Within minutes, at 18:34 EST, as his live voice report was being carried over a map of the region, Shephard interrupted his transmission with the words: 'Something is definitely under way here, something is definitely going on .... obviously an attack is under way of some sort.'

Just over ten minutes later, at 23:47 GMT, British viewers who had settled down to watch ITV's recorded highlights of that evening's Rumbelows League Cup soccer matches had the war introduced to them by sports commentator Nick Owen. He was about to begin the post-match analysis when a message came through his earphone: 'and we also hope to bring you more football to come here on Midweek Sports Special,' he said, 'but first of all it's time for a news flash from ITN'.[1] In fact, ITN was carrying CNN's dramatic first night coverage (which began at 23:36 GMT and which is described in the next chapter) and never returned to the soccer, staying with the war continuously and with

31

CNN intermittently for the next 12 hours in what must have been the longest news flash in television history.[2] Ironically, ABC was only able to scoop the world because Gary Shephard had been using ITN's INMARSAT telephone.[3] The BBC, meanwhile, had finally decided to interrupt its late-night film, *Villain*, at 00:06 when it too went immediately over to CNN.[4] It was indeed CNN's coverage, carried periodically by both ITN and the BBC and by television news stations all around the world, that will forever be inextricably associated with the outbreak of television's war in the Gulf.

Among the hundreds of millions of people watching were none other than President George Bush and Prime Minister John Major. Viewing the outbreak of war on TV was certainly an unusual way for two world leaders to learn of the consequences of their momentous decision to launch Operation Desert Storm. According to one source, the President 'was fiddling with the TV remote control when the bombing was due to start, and showed almost childish delight when the raid on Baghdad came through live on television at the time he had ordered it',[5] although another stated that Mr Major, who had also apparently been channel-hopping, was a little surprised 'as it was slightly earlier than he had expected'.[6] American Secretary of State James Baker had spent the previous afternoon and evening alerting coalition partners that war was imminent.[7] The unreality of it all was apparent to everyone involved. One Downing Street official was quoted as saying: 'It is a strange thing, but at this stage it was simply a television war.'[8]

Politicians and government officials were not used to hearing the news break and develop at the same time as television viewers. Yet all were to contribute to a night of high television drama. At the White House just after 19:00 EST, in words reminiscent of Eisenhower's D-Day 1944 declaration, the chief press spokesman Marlin Fitzwater announced: 'The liberation of Kuwait has begun.' Two hours later, at 21:00 EST, George Bush announced in a 12–minute televised live address to the American people and to the wider world what it already knew from watching CNN: that the allied coalition was at war against Iraq. 'Five months ago', said President Bush, 'Saddam Hussein started this cruel war against Kuwait. Tonight the battle has been joined.' In the United States, an estimated 160 million viewers tuned in, making this the highest-rating event in American television history, pushing the funeral of President Kennedy into second place. In years to come, while recalling the memory of that night's events, it would not be too fanciful to suggest that when people are asked the question 'What were you doing the night the Gulf War broke out?', many will reply: 'Watching it on TV'.

But what exactly had they seen? The unique event of sharing in a moment of world history or a piece of surreal television divorced from the realities of war's horrors? As CNN and other television stations employed global telecommunications technology to shuffle and shuttle instantaneously from Baghdad to Riyadh to Washington to London and to other coalition capitals for an interpretation of what was going on, audiences could indeed be forgiven for thinking that they were participating in historic events as they were unfolding. But the excitement of the occasion, when people not directly involved in matters of life and death felt that they were actually a part of what was going on, raises a number of questions about the relationship between war and the media. Was this a new variation of 'total war' in which the gap which had previously existed between soldier and civilian had been substantially narrowed by television? Or was it something else? Were people 'seeing' a war in which nations resolved their disputes for the benefit of their publics, or were they merely being expected to witness something dreadful – if exciting – and thereby to participate indirectly in actions that were merely the consequence of decisions that had been made in their name? Were they, in other words, being manipulated into believing that they were part of something they were not or was public participation in the war via the medium of television an ultimate demonstration of democracy in action?

The 'video-game war'

On the eve of war, as the United Nations' deadline for Iraq to withdraw from Kuwait by 15 January 1991 drew nearer, a series of official ground rules and guide-lines were issued to the media. Some of these turned out to be more honoured in the breach, especially the British warning that 'publicly-aired speculation about future operations, particularly where it gives the appearance of being well-informed or authoritative, also carries the risk of

33

causing an actual or potential enemy to consider possibilities that otherwise might not have occurred to him'. Following the outbreak of war, television stations in Britain and in America initially went over to 24–hour news coverage (the American networks even taking the unprecedented step of suspending their commercial breaks[9]). Throughout the next night and day, as a portent of things to come, a seemingly endless parade of 'experts' from a variety of academic, political and military backgrounds were wheeled before the cameras to fuel the time-guzzling coverage of what was turning out to be a momentous media event, especially once the coalition began feeding the pundits with seductive video footage over which they could marvel at the accuracy of the air strikes. Yet it quickly became apparent that this speculation – or 'analysis', as some broadcasters preferred to call it – was in effect a substitute for hard information about what was actually going on. This was because, mesmeric though the initial coverage may have been, it was as John Naughton soon spotted 'the journalistic equivalent of candy floss: delicious to consume but devoid of substance'.[10]

This was in fact an ideal situation in so far as a propaganda war is concerned, not least because of propaganda's calculated need for simplification at the expense of complexity and of the exigencies of the coalition's democracies to be seen to be operating in the full view of their publics. As the leading player in the coalition effort, the United States was particularly determined to ensure that its 'information policy' was managed every bit as successfully as the political, diplomatic and military direction of the war. This meant simple themes, easily understood, readily assimilated and publicly aired. As its principal supporter, it was equally important for Britain to ensure that it spoke the same language. The French – as another major European contributor, but whose position within the coalition, at least at the start, was generally regarded as being more ambivalent – adopted an information policy stance that essentially reflected their NATO position: in, but apart from, the alliance. One reason for this, as French Prime Minister Michel Rocard indicated, was the general official nervousness in Paris concerning the impact of the coverage on France's 4 million citizens from Muslim, Arab and African backgrounds.[11] And finally, as the principal Arab partner in the coalition which was hosting the contributing military forces, including the non-Islamic coalition media managers on the spot, it was essential for the Saudis not only to provide the necessary facilities that would enable the world's media to report in accordance with the needs of correspondents from a wide variety of reporting traditions and differing cultural backgrounds but also to balance against this the necessity for allied military censorship and maintaining Saudi Arabia's image and position within the Arab world. It was also essential, as the Americans recognised from the outset, for the coalition's Arab forces to play a high-profile role in the conflict. The coalition's information war, therefore, would be run from four main centres: Washington, London, Dhahran and Riyadh. But television was to the information war what the United States would be for the military conflict; because the coalition would be American-led so would allied propaganda be television-led.

Nearly two weeks before the outbreak of war, when the Pentagon had first proposed a series of reporting restrictions, the American media argued that they would severely jeopardise their ability to cover any potential conflict in a manner befitting an open society. Among the proposed forbidden areas were: spontaneous interviews with servicemen and women in the Gulf; off-the-record interviews with troops in the field; the filming or photography of soldiers in 'agony or severe shock'; and the transmission of 'imagery of patients suffering from severe disfigurements'.[12] There was an immediate outcry from some sections of the American media fiercely protective of their constitutional freedoms to report and still reeling from the *fait accompli* of being excluded altogether from the Grenada expedition in 1983. Since then, the Pentagon had compromised with the establishment of a media pool system in which a small group of designated journalists from the various branches of the media industry (newspapers, magazines, wire services, radio and television) were rotated in news pools so that, if a war broke out, those currently on call would be flown out to the scene of the conflict. There, theoretically, following a 'security review' of their copy by military officials, their reports would then be sent back to Washington by military channels for distribution by the Pentagon to the rest of the news media.

Neither side was happy with these arrangements – although they were grudgingly accepted by the military because it was a more satisfactory situation than having journalists roaming freely around the battle front as in Vietnam, and by the majority of the media because it was better than being excluded altogether as in Grenada. However, when this system was first tested in Panama in 1989, it quickly proved unsatisfactory since the journalists, instead of being attached to military units in the field, found themselves confined to a headquarters building where they, like everyone else, were dependent upon US Department of Defense communiqués and television speculation as to what was supposedly happening. Fearing a repetition, on 10 January 1991 a number of American magazines and wire services filed a law suit in a federal court against the proposed restrictions. A companion suit was filed by the Agence France Presse.

It would be fair to say, then, that at the start of the Gulf War the legacy of military–media relations in the United States was such that it did not bode well for a successful coalition media management operation. In Britain, such relations were marginally better; the Royal Navy's Task Force had, after all, carried 30 British journalists to the South Atlantic in the Falklands War of 1982 – although their ability to report that conflict *while it was going on* was severely hampered by communications and other problems. In the years that followed, however, satellite communications technology had become not only more portable but cheaper. Portable satellite dishes and telephones theoretically enabled an individual reporter to broadcast his or her observations from anywhere in the world (such as Tunis or Tiananmen Square or Tirana) and not to rely upon military or other official communications channels to get reports back to their newsrooms. Yet this merely made it all the more essential for the military to involve itself in the detailed planning of how to control and influence what non-military personnel working for the media might not understand. War was too serious a business to be left to the journalists.

So when, during late 1990, with a war in the Gulf becoming increasingly likely, the Pentagon decided to implement a two-tier system of news pools attached to military units and a headquarters catering for the remainder, it may have felt it had found an ideal compromise to the problems of Vietnam and Grenada via the lessons of the Falklands and Panama. If it did, it was wrong – although this is by no means to suggest that the coalition lost the propaganda war as a result. When the Pentagon's latest ground rules were announced delineating what the pools could – or, more significantly, could not – report, a storm of protest erupted. The Pentagon finally 'caved in' to this pressure on Monday 14 January, issuing instead a less specific and shorter set of guide-lines, which still owed more to the British history of censorship than to the American tradition of freedom of speech.[13] Nonetheless, in London, where negotiations between the broadcasters and the MoD had also been taking place in the build-up to the war, it was already clear to Stewart Purvis, ITN's editor, that 'one [visual] shot from one pool will be objectionable to one army but not another' and that 'it will be difficult to co-ordinate the flow of information'.[14]

The British plan for reporting the war had been devised by Brigadier Bryon Dutton, Director of Army Public Relations, following a visit to Saudi Arabia in October 1990.[15] On 14 January 1991, at the Ministry of Defence in London, Hugh Colver, the chief public relations officer, informed editors that although the release of the guidelines at that time 'in no way implies that hostilities are inevitable or imminent', he added: 'the system envisaged by the issue of this guidance will rely on free co-operation and consultation where appropriate'. The areas to be covered by official censorship were the time-honoured and least controversial ones designed to prevent information about military operations from reaching the enemy that might jeopardise the lives of allied soldiers and disturb the sensibilities of relatives. In the information age of satellite telephones and portable fax machines, this was certainly an ambitious aim on the part of the military authorities and required unprecedented levels of responsibility on the part of journalists. But, as Philip Knightley predicted, 'The MoD guidelines (note the suggestion that compliance is voluntary – but see how long you last if you ignore them) will make it impossible to describe the progress of a battle.'[16]

Also in the British guidelines was the statement that 'it is ... necessary to avoid giving credence to enemy propaganda'. This had been a major concern during the Falklands War when the BBC, starved of instant or 'hot' news by official British sources, had carried pictures from Argentinian television and was sharply rebuked by Mrs Thatcher for being 'unacceptably even handed' as a result. Modern communications technology in the hands of western journalists not only in Saudi Arabia but also in Iraq therefore made their capacity for trouble even more of a danger.

Such technology was a further problem for the military in that journalists now possessed the potential to spread information or impressions (accurate or otherwise) instantaneously around the world, thereby placing considerably more responsibility for checking and verifying information on individual journalists in the field than ever before and begged the question: would they be up to the new technologically inspired responsibilities of their profession, or would they become its slaves? Moreover, the guideline would be almost impossible to implement in light of the fact that war was not formally declared and the Iraqis were thus able to keep their ambassadors abroad with instructions to present their version of events whenever possible in the western media. By the time most were asked to leave following the severance of diplomatic relations in early February, they had already conducted a widespread campaign that frankly could be said to have given the very credence to Iraqi propaganda on television stations around the world that the coalition's military authorities had wished to avoid.

As it turned out, BBC bashers were quickly out of their traps again when, on the very first full day of the Gulf War, Tory backbencher Patrick Nicholls used Prime Minister's Question Time to criticise the BBC for referring to the 'British' rather than 'Our' troops. But John Major did not rise to the bait as his predecessor might be expected to have done. Instead he commended the BBC for its impartiality and its 'remarkable reporting'.[17] That might have been interpreted in some quarters as meaning that the government was already generally satisfied with the media coverage because it could see that its restrictions were being broadly observed and were correspondingly resulting in the desired kind of interpretation and perspective being taken.[18]

Unlike during the Falklands War, however, the Ministry of Defence in London was not to be the focus of the military information system. This was to be an international effort, largely under the direction of the Americans who traditionally operated a far more open system of press relations but who were prepared to impose their media management system upon their allied partners for fear of that dreaded Vietnam Syndrome. Even so, as the United States' closest ally, Britain would have to ensure that its tune was piped in harmony, especially if the kind of acrimonious exchanges that had occurred between government and the media in 1982 were to be avoided this time. Accordingly, Mr Major established the Cabinet Media Committee under the chairmanship of Energy Secretary John Wakeham to coordinate the British government's handling of the war coverage. This body met daily after the War Cabinet had finished its deliberations and, significantly, one of its first acts was to ask the backbench media bashers to tone down their criticisms.[19]

At the Ministry of Defence itself, it was intended to avoid the monotonous, 'speak your weight' machine-like briefings which had given spokesman Ian MacDonald such a high profile and correspondingly made him a much lampooned figure of the Falklands conflict. Now a variety of senior political and military briefers, from Defence Secretary Tom King and Chief of the Defence Staff Sir David Craig downwards, would grace the gatherings.[20] Normally, a panel of officials would address the correspondents below a sign which simply said 'non-attributable'. However, the new-style MoD briefings quickly came under attack: the Daily Star, with its wartime gung-ho slogan of 'Go Get 'Em Boys', described them as 'an upper class Muppet show'.[21] Following a specialist live televised 'teach-in' on the air campaign on Sunday 20 January, Tom King refused to give out figures on the numbers of Scud missiles destroyed to date – as the Pentagon was simultaneously releasing precisely this type of information, which, ironically, turned out to be inaccurate anyway. The missing soundtrack (caused by technical problems) to the video of a two-man RAF Jaguar crew in combat seemed indicative of the MoD's silence or, as Mr King had said wryly only a day or so before: 'I'm glad you asked me that because it is precisely the kind of question I am not prepared to answer.'[22] The 'teach-in' prompted an outcry amongst the press, with a Times leader describing it as 'a fiasco, a mass of jargon accompanied by incomprehensible video clips'. Contrasting the MoD's performance with the 'deft presentations' of the Americans in Washington and Riyadh, the article continued.

The defence ministry in Whitehall is hampered by its distance from the fighting: its spokesmen lack the verisimilitude of their American counterparts in the field. That need not prevent them from producing information that at least appears fresh and complete. The MoD has long regarded public relations as another branch of recruitment and arms selling. This is wrong. The Americans learned in Vietnam that the home front is a real front, where not just battles but whole wars can be lost. The British cabinet should instruct the MoD to draw the same conclusion.[23]

Several days later, the *Daily Telegraph* joined in, unfavourably comparing the MoD briefings with the slicker American presentations and wondering whether anything at all had been learned from the Falklands conflict: 'The fact that the United States is leading the allied war effort need not preclude effective British presentation, which will be essential if public morale and understanding are to be maintained at their present high levels until the end of the conflict.'[24]

It was not, however, long before the Pentagon briefings were also to come under attack. In Washington, daily press gatherings were organised at two locations: at the White House where Marlin Fitzwater served as chief press officer and at the Pentagon where the same task was the responsibility of Peter Williams. Fitzwater was liked for his 'sardonic humour' even though he was capable of the occasional undiplomatic slip, as when he described President Gorbachev as a 'drugstore cowboy'.[25] Williams, himself an ex-television journalist, was also a popular figure with the press. Calm, courteous and expressive of a desire to help journalists, he was the ideal spokesman for Defense Secretary Richard Cheney, himself an intelligent performer, with whom he had served as press officer in Congress prior to their move together to the Pentagon after the 1989 presidential election. Williams was, moreover, prepared to be extremely forthcoming once the television cameras had been turned off. Lastly, the Pentagon had the advantage of two further 'guest star' performers: General Colin Luther Powell in Washington and General H. Norman Schwarzkopf in Saudi Arabia.

General Powell had served as Chairman of the Joint Chiefs of Staff since October 1989. Appointed at the age of 52, he was the youngest ever CJC. As a black American, he had a considerable advantage in presentational terms to the Arab world and his performances were such that the media began to tout him as America's first possible black president.[26] As for General 'Stormin' Norman' Schwarzkopf, the Supreme Commander of the Coalition Forces in the Gulf, his image lived up to his preferred nickname of 'The Bear' and he was to emerge as perhaps the most popular single personality of the war. A Vietnam veteran, indeed a decorated hero, Schwarzkopf was only too aware of the importance of a good media war as a result of that experience, combined with what he had seen in Panama, as he revealed in September 1990:

Listen, I ain't no dummy when it comes to dealing with the press. And I fully understand that when you try to stonewall the press, and don't give them anything to do, then before long the press turns ugly, and I would just as soon not have an ugly press. I don't care if they report the truth, I just want them to be correct. Not everything is going to be right. Every time there is something new for the press to look at, I want them to see it. I want to create opportunities for them so they are kept informed.[27]

On the other hand, he conceded that he was only prepared to do this within the bounds of operational security and military censorship:

why should I, as a military man, volunteer anything to the open press that would assist him [Saddam] in his analysis of what we are doing? ... It's not to preclude you having information. It is because when it gets in the open press, he watches CNN religiously, the Iraqi military ambassador in Washington cuts articles from the [Washington] Post and sends them home every day, and I don't want to give him one damn thing that will help his military analysis if I can prevent it.[28]

This eternal dilemma for democratic regimes which purport to cherish notions of freedom of information while waging war, especially against closed authoritarian or totalitarian states which foster no such aspirations, would appear to suggest that the propaganda advantage would always appear to rest with the latter. That the coalition was able to counter this at all was a significant achievement. But Schwarzkopf's own experience should at least have been a warning for his media managers not to go overboard on the question of secrecy, the source of inspiration for so many media conspiracy theories.

One observer who was impressed by the televisual combination of the principal American military characters expressed his admiration thus: 'In US television terms, Williams plays the dry home-based anchorman to Schwarzkopf, the brilliant though somehow rather dangerous star correspondent'.[29] It was this very capacity for 'danger', namely his willingness to apparently deviate from the prearranged publicity arrangements worked out by the Pentagon, which made the Supreme Military Commander such an attractive media figure. For some, however, the type of media identification with the military which this description represented had removed the distinction between objective and subjective reporting. Yet at

41

times uncoordinated or impromptu statements by 'The Bear' when he was attempting to please the press caused considerable embarrassment at the Pentagon. Harmonising the various official sources of information, their differing styles and personalities, across eight time zones therefore required a highly sophisticated and perhaps unattainable system of media management operated by people who understood the diametrically opposed needs of both the military (secrecy) and the media (publicity). For others, the Pentagon had managed to strike this balance perfectly – that is, very much in its favour.

Nonetheless, the coal face of the information front was in Saudi Arabia. In Dhahran, for the majority of journalists not attached to the pools or for those denied accreditation to attend the Riyadh briefings, the coalition established the Joint Information Bureau (JIB) comprising officers mainly trained in the art of public relations (nicknamed 'Jiblets' by the press). Like the rest of the coalition effort, this too was dominated by the Americans. But there was a price to be paid for this. Since many reporters were in Saudi Arabia where they could be more readily influenced and even manipulated by the JIB, this created an opening for the pundits back home whose speculation was such a deep source of irritation to Schwarzkopf.

Before long, however, the journalists in Saudi Arabia began to realise that they were being starved of really nutritious news. Despite the reassuring introduction to the media ground rules that they 'will protect the security and the safety of the troops involved while allowing you reasonable freedom and access in covering your story', many correspondents found that the first part of that statement was more applicable than the last. The complaints began very quickly. It may have seemed to some people back in the United States and in Britain that the reporters were merely being bloody-minded by their quibbles[30] and that the priority of the armed forces was to deal with Iraq as quickly and as effectively as possible rather than catering for the whims of journalists, but the fact remains that the story was being heavily dictated by the agenda of the military. How could it be otherwise in light of the restrictions that had been imposed?

Even so, the reality was that, after its spectacular start, the war did appear to be progressing remarkably well for the coalition, 'just about exactly as we expected it to go' said Schwarzkopf.[31]

The initial air strikes on Iraq showed a high degree of accuracy in hitting strategic targets – and even the correspondents in Baghdad testified to that in their reports from the enemy capital on the first night and day. Nonetheless, initially, some wildly exaggerated claims did begin to fly around. CNN, for example, stated that the Republican Guard had been 'decimated' by the first night's bombing, in fact picking this word up from a Pentagon briefing where one official had unwisely chosen a word which meant literally the destruction of one in ten. Another Washington source maintained that 100 Iraqi airfields had been immobilised, whereas in Cairo the Middle Eastern News Agency was reporting that the Guard as well as the Iraqi air force had been completely destroyed.[32] General Maurice Schmitt, chief of the French armed forces, announced that Iraq's capacity to launch chemical weapons had been demolished. Yet, despite the wild statements and the absence of precise details, the mood of the media was – quite simply and unashamedly – euphoric.

Coalition pronouncements themselves were largely responsible for this: 1,300 sorties flown in the first 20 hours; 100 tomahawk cruise missiles launched in the most intensive air attack since World War Two; 'if it goes on another day like this we will have won the first phase of the war handily'.[33] By the time 2,000 sorties had been flown, the allies had lost only 8 aircraft, possibly the most impressive statistic in the history of air war. Even so, the military and the media did seem to be at one. A generous way of looking at this would be to say that either much of the language being used by military briefers was not fully understood by journalists or else they were being blinded by a science that all but the initiated could be forgiven for misinterpreting. Words such as 'effective', for example, did not necessarily mean that a target had been destroyed; phrases such as 'collateral damage' and 'interdiction' were euphemisms which distracted attention away from realities of what happened after the bombs exploded. Returning pilots, 'the new knights of heroic warfare',[34] flushed with the success and accuracy of their 'smart' weapons and relieved (if puzzled) by the lack of a concerted Iraqi response, were interviewed fresh from their missions, adding to the overall excitement, and gave the war a human face, a coalition face.[35] Nor could the briefers in Riyadh and Washington barely disguise their initial exhilaration. It might be added that this wave of emotional interviews describing what it was like to be on bombing missions over enemy territory while they were still flushed with excitement and fresh from debriefings was a major innovation of television war coverage. And so, when General Powell announced on the first full day that, of the 1,000 or so missions flown by that time, '80% of them have been effective', it was amidst a climate that in retrospect was almost bound to mislead. Even though he added that this meant 'the aircraft got to its target, delivered its ordnance, and returned', what he meant was that only 20% of the air missions had needed to be called off for technical, weather-related or other reasons. He did not mean that 80% of the bombs dropped had actually hit their targets but, because he made no mention of misses, the impression was of an overwhelming and unprecedented degree of bombing accuracy.[36]

This overall picture of striking success and accuracy was compounded by General Schwarzkopf 36 hours into the war at his first wartime briefing on Friday the 18th when he said in his opening remarks that

As in the early days of any battle, the fog of war is present, but I would tell you ... that we probably have a more accurate picture of what's going on in Operation Desert Storm than I have ever had before in the early hours of a battle. The picture is not perfect, but I think it's pretty good ... .[37]

He then went on to state that, of the 2,000 air sorties 'of all types' being flown each day, 'more than 80% of all those sorties have successfully engaged their targets'.[38]

'BDA', or bomb damage assessment, is in fact a highly specialised science with a terminology all of its own and although coalition briefers said they were reluctant to go into precise details until all their data had been thoroughly evaluated, such statements as those by Generals Powell and Schwarzkopf proved to be hostages to journalistic fortune, especially given the media's predisposition towards finding a snappy 'sound bite'. But as this became more and more of an issue, even President Bush was reported to be frustrated by the inability of the military to provide him with more precise details of the effects of the bombing. As Fitzwater explained:

He thinks people are getting as full a picture as we have. He just wishes we had a better one. I mean, President Bush has asked for the same kind of damage reports that you have, and it's just not there.[39]

But it was not hard to find other military officials describing how certain aircraft types had performed 'stunningly well' or how cruise missiles were performing 'exceptionally well' and even 'beautifully'.[40] The problem was that the coalition policy implemented from Day One of releasing spectacular but selective videos of precision attacks tended to create the impression that the military knew everything about what was going on when in fact it didn't.

Not that the media can be completely excused for failing to keep their distance from all this terminological fog. The sophistication of the weaponry was undoubtedly blinding, as when a *New York Times* reporter marvelled at the 'technology that guides cruise missiles so precisely that one fired from a battleship in the Red Sea clipped a communications tower in Baghdad neatly in two'.[41] In the United States, the media watch-dog group Fairness and Accuracy in Reporting was constantly finding examples of how journalists appeared to have become, wittingly or unwittingly, mouthpieces of the military line – from the 'brilliance' of American laser-guided bombs to the Scud as 'a horrifying weapon' (ABC's Peter Jennings) – or how the initial bombing of Iraq was a 'marvel' (CBS's Charles Osgood) following 'two days of picture perfect assaults' (CBS's Jim Stewart). Nor was this simply a matter of terminology. When NBC's Tom Brokaw later announced that 'we must point out again and again that it was Saddam Hussein who put these innocents in harm's way' or when *Time* magazine was defining collateral damage as 'a term meaning dead or wounded civilians who should have picked a safer neighborhood' it might appear that official coalition propaganda not only had successfully dictated the overall picture but had even permeated the language of the media.[42] The phenomenon, as Norman Solomon pointed out in the *New York Times* after the war, was tantamount to 'linguicide':

When a dictatorship like Saudi Arabia, which imprisons and tortures dissenters, is called 'moderate', that's linguicide. And when a few missiles fired at Tel Aviv are called weapons of terror while thousands of missiles fired at Baghdad and Basra are called marvels, that's linguicide too.[43]

Or, as a British commentator noted:

Rarely has it been so obvious that language is volatile stuff, that it succumbs easily to manipulation, to the sedulous distortions of propagandists and censors. In the Gulf War, words have been used to salve the conscience, to cordon off the truth, rather than to communicate it.[44]

On the other hand, it did seem that each day was almost miraculously bringing a major coalition story around which all interpretation could be framed: Day One revealed positive news of the success of the initial air strikes and the first military videos; Day Two saw Iraq firing its first Scud missiles and the successful performance of the latest technological marvel to be unveiled from the coalition's high-tech armoury: the Patriot anti-missile missile.

The Scud attacks were actually a very serious political menace for the coalition, especially with their potential ramifications for bringing Israel into the war. Although initial reports that the Scuds had been carrying chemical weapons (NBC and ABC) or that Israel was retaliating (CBS) were both incorrect as facts, they remained serious fears. But a timely piece of news management deflected their severity. At the Riyadh briefing on the first Friday, General Schwarzkopf and Lieutenant-General Charles 'Chuck' Horner, the US air commander, showed video film taken through a Stealth F-117A's laser target designator of a bomb travelling down the roof ventilation shaft of buildings including 'my counterpart's headquarters'.[45] 'General Horner knew what he was doing,' wrote John Naughton, 'for the video footage proved irresistible to the Western networks'.[46] It was to be the start of some spectacular video imagery released in what became known as the 'Norm and Chuck Show' implying a level of bombing accuracy the likes of which had never been seen before. And a major player in this techno-warfare was to be the Patriot missile, batteries of which, complete with trained American crews, were despatched over the first weekend to protect Israeli citizens from further attacks – and it was hoped to protect the coalition from potential disintegration.

In the *New York Times*, Leslie H. Gelb described the effect of all this as 'Iraq, the Movie' with 'glamorous stars, non-stop virtual action and thus far not a single dead body on screen'.[47] But, noted the television critic of the *Observer*, 'in the process what somehow got lost was the kind of scepticism that serious journalism demands':

Nobody seemed interested, for example, in knowing whether this dramatic footage was statistically representative of the aerial assault. And, of course, nobody asked whether it was the genuine undoctored article. If it's good enough for Stormin' Norman, then it's good enough for us.[48]

'Fortunately', said Schwarzkopf on the first Friday, almost as if to prove this point, 'the seven missiles that were fired against Israel I would characterise as having yielded absolutely insignificant results'.[49] Nonetheless, even as he spoke, major high-level behind-the-scenes negotiations were going on between Washington and Tel Aviv to prevent the Israelis from doing what everyone (including Saddam) expected them to do in accordance with their recent history of military retaliation, just in case further attacks proved to have slightly more significance than the General had suggested.

The initial media euphoria in fact deeply worried President Bush, who feared the ramifications of an 'it will all be over by the first weekend' attitude for what might turn out to be a long war. Within less than a week, when Richard Cheney joked about an American newspaper headline that 'War Drags On', he was engaged in a campaign to dampen down the view that the war would be fought and won quickly and easily, reminding journalists that there had been – and would be more – casualties. He had said this before, in his first briefing of the war. 'I don't mean to be critical of our friends in the press corps,' he said, but 'it's very, very important for people to remember a number of key things: that this is a very serious business, that we are in the very early stages of an operation that may go on for some considerable time'.[50] President Bush had already decided to invite cameramen into the White House cabinet room on Friday 18 January to warn against unwarranted optimism.[51] Both Bush and Cheney admitted that, on the first night, they had been glued to CNN[52] and Cheney even stated his view that 'the best reporting that I have seen on what transpired in Baghdad was on CNN'.[53] By pointing to the reports coming out of Baghdad, some observers could be forgiven for thinking that this was merely deflecting attention away from the paucity of real information emanating from Riyadh, Washington and London.

The American high command was to continue monitoring the television coverage throughout the war, itself a reflection of how significant the Bush administration believed the medium's role would be.[54] In Britain, John Major took the opportunity of war's outbreak to make his first national television broadcast as Prime Minister on the Thursday evening. It was the first time a British

Prime Minister had broadcast live to the nation since before Margaret Thatcher had come to power in 1979. His calming tone suggested as good an antidote as any to the wildly optimistic views of the tabloid press. Nonetheless, as coalition leaders began to prepare public opinion for a longer struggle than that anticipated by some sections of the media, by the first weekend early public opinion polls in America and in Britain revealed overwhelming popular support for the war.[55] The question which therefore begs to be asked concerns the degree to which the media coverage had helped to create this public support, or was simply a reflection of it. This in turn poses the question about the media coverage being simply a mirror image of coalition media management.

It may well be, of course, that popular support emanated from a gut reaction to the fact that people were happy to see some concrete action being taken against an aggressive dictator who had occupied a foreign country for five and a half months in open defiance of UN resolutions. The media are indeed often accredited with an exaggerated power to mould public opinion. British television, especially BBC2's current affairs programme Newsnight which had constructed a gigantic sand-pit of the Gulf region for presenter Peter Snow to take viewers through the ramifications of the crisis since the previous August, was nonetheless criticised by such public figures as Tony Benn for helping to create Britain's war fever. Mr. Benn also criticised the terminology used by CNN's reporters in Baghdad for describing the first night's bombing as 'a firework display'.[56] The war was undoubtedly proving to be a major television event, with audience figures soaring for several days until saturation coverage prompted a return to near-normal scheduling.[57] Yet because the coverage was providing a particular view of a war without corpses – a clinical, clean conflict in which impressive footage of 'video-game' type images stood out and, in Baghdad, blackened skies were illuminated by the patterned tracer fire of 'Triple A' which resembled an electrical storm – one could be forgiven the impression that a 'real' war was not being fought at all: again an ideal situation for coalition propagandists operating with the Vietnam Syndrome at the forefront of their minds when the ugliness of war predominated.

The absence of context was however something which worried coalition leaders as they tried to dampen down the initial euphoria with reminders that Iraq possessed the fourth largest military force in the world and might just prove to be a formidable opponent capable of inflicting considerable casualties. But television is primarily a medium of entertainment and opponents of war were worried that the conflict was being portrayed in precisely this sense. As Mark Lawson wrote at the time: 'You have to at least ask whether television has turned this conflict into voyeurism: the Middle East theatre of war as a European cinema of war'.[58] He went on, however, to suggest that intensive television coverage of the crisis since August had in fact made the task of the wartime media managers more difficult:

Television has been accused of many terrible things in its short life, but the Gulf coverage has, I think, demonstrated one small moral victory for the medium. Television gives faces and histories and fears and weeping wives and children to troops ... This is bad news for generals, who have always depended upon the anonymity of the dead, the inability of even the most well-meaning human being to identify too closely with those blown up. In this conflict, the latest airman posted missing might be someone who has just been speaking to us. In giving biographies and blood to soldiers, in independently questioning the claims of generals and politicians, it has helped to undermine the military assumption of human disposability. The concept of cannon-fodder is harder to sustain.

That, at least, would be true of 'our boys', and certainly pool reports since August had tended to focus on the human aspects of the conflict in anticipation of serious casualties. But what about, opponents of war argued, enemy civilians? This issue was confused by the unprecedented presence of western journalists in the enemy capital. Yet, as we shall see, the initial failure of the Iraqis to produce for them the kind of images which dissenting voices might have felt would improve the credibility of their arguments came as something of a relief for the coalition.

It has to be said that the American media, by comparison with their pre-war position, had largely decided to suspend their more usual antagonistic stance towards the US government. Even the 'Why the rush?' pre-war *New York Times* was prepared to defer its qualms and throw itself behind the war effort in 'the national interest'. Charles Bremner's observation for *The Times* was that the American media 'have followed a line of subdued loyalty reminiscent of reporting from Korea or during the Second World War'.[59] Generally speaking, the mood was highly patriotic, although this indeed may well have been because, as a *Washington*

Post columnist put it, the Pentagon 'controls the news as it controls the skies over the desert'. In Britain also, the predictably jingoistic tabloid press found that the quality newspapers (with the marginal exception of the *Guardian*) reflected their mood of support if not their style. The *Sun* came close to equalling its Falklands War performance with its full-colour front page that carried only a Union Jack flag with the face of a soldier in the middle and its appeal to readers to display it in their windows.[60] As a result, the anti-war demonstrations which erupted throughout the world during that first weekend and which continued throughout the war received scant media attention when compared with the massive coverage being given to the coalition's video-dominated agenda. Dissenting individuals such as Vanessa Redgrave were lambasted in the press, while in Hollywood several actors and actresses testified to the prevailing fear of unemployment if they came out against the war.[61] On the other hand, given that western anti-war groups were in a minority when compared with the overwhelming public support for the conflict even in countries such as Germany, it might be argued that the peace groups were receiving too much media attention. Once again, it depended which side you were on, although a study by Fairness and Accuracy in Reporting discovered that, of the 878 broadcast sources employed by ABC, CBS and NBC during their wartime nightly news programmes, only one represented a national peace organisation.[62]

As it turned out, it did not take long for the military necessities of secrecy to clash with journalistic aspirations. The official briefings were soon recognised to be giving out very little beyond the most general of information, while many of the pool reports consisted largely of library footage taken earlier in the crisis. 'Relative freedom of information before the war', said one journalist subsequently, 'helped overcome the lack of it once it started'.[63] Interviews with troops and returning pilots helped to disguise this situation. But as for the action itself, the release of the official videos of air strikes could not for long hide the fact that 'not only do we not have pictures, but we don't have words'.[64] At a Pentagon briefing in the first weekend of the war, one journalist was so dissatisfied with the reluctance of his briefers to provide hard evidence verifying allied damage reports that he said 'I'm disinclined to believe both of you'.[65]

To a large extent, the initial media exuberance was punctured by Iraq's first Scud missile attack on Israel, 'and I'm not sure', said CBS's ill-fated Bob Simon, 'that's at all a bad thing'.[66] By the first weekend, politicians and military officials alike were sounding cautionary notes, stating that, although the war was going well, it was not by any means over or won. 'A massive amount of damage has been done but the nervous system has not been severed from the brain', said one US official.[67] Moreover, within a week, the media were full of stories about the media coverage of the war. This, according to Cheney, was a sure sign 'that they've run out of things to say about the story',[68] which in turn leads us back to the question whether 'the story' was being adequately or accurately represented by the media, who were essentially at the mercy of the coalition's arrangements for the release of information.

The newspool system

There were essentially three strands to the system established by the coalition forces for releasing information to the media actually present in Saudi Arabia: the Joint Information Bureau in Dhahran; the arrangements made for daily press briefings in Riyadh; and the news pool system for journalists attached to the armed forces at the front.

The pool system was supposed to work as follows. With the troops at the front, journalists were formed into Media Reporting Teams (MRTs). The Americans were to be supervised by censors from the Public Affairs Office (PAO) and the British by the MoD's public relations officers (PROs). There were eventually about 200 places in the pools for the 1,500 or so journalists who had flocked to the region, although in the first half of the war there were only about 50 correspondents with the troops, and most of those were at sea – in more ways than one. The pools consisted of reporters from all the media whose reports were to be made freely available to all news organisations. In an attempt to negate recent developments in satellite communications technology, however, American television companies were refused permission to operate satellite dishes with the US military, which not only slowed down the transmission of their taped reports but sometimes forced them to use British TV pool reports emanating more rapidly from the 1st Armoured Division which did permit portable dishes. The need to provide rapid progress reports from American units for American audiences remained a constant problem, although from the British point of view this provided the further advantage of reminding American viewers that troops other than those from the USA were also part of the coalition. Or at least it served as a reminder that British troops were part of the coalition. There were no pool places made available for journalists from countries other than Britain, the USA and France.

There were six British MRTs. Attached to the British 4th Armoured Brigade, for example, were ITN reporter Paul Davies, two ITN cameramen and journalists from the *Daily Telegraph*, the *Daily Mail* and the *Southern Evening Echo* together with a correspondent from the Associated Press news agency. A second MRT including Kate Adie and a BBC crew and Colin Wills of the *Daily Mirror* was attached to the 7th Armoured Brigade, the 'Desert Rats'. Further MRTs were attached to the Air Force at Tabuk, Dhahran and Bahrain, while another was attached to four ships in the Gulf. This meant that the British media were more favourably represented in relation to the number of their troops in the region than any other country, including the Americans, although this should not detract from the situation that there were still only four television crews covering the 35,000 strong UK contribution.

Journalists were supposed to rotate, but this was rare at first because, for example, the American 'sacred sixteen' (reporters from the *New York Times, Washington Post, Wall Street Journal* and other US papers and the major television networks) voted to keep the pool slots assigned to them before the war to themselves, resulting in bitter fights with newcomers. 'All told,' wrote one, 'reporters seemed to spend more energy fighting each other than fighting pool restrictions.'[69] Having signed the guidelines, accredited reporters agreed to submit their reports for 'review to determine if they contain sensitive information'.[70]

Censorship practices varied widely in the different pools. Photojournalist P.T. Benic found the American arrangements more satisfactory than the British for his requirements.[71] Deborah Amos of American National Public Radio found that the most frustrating aspect of the pool system was the arbitrary nature of being allocated to various PAOs: 'you could get an angel or a devil'.[72] In the American arrangements, it was stated that copy would be examined 'solely for its conformance to the ... ground rules, not for its potential to express criticism or cause embarrassment'. [73] Yet an example of what precisely constituted sensitive or embarrassing information on the part of one American PAO emerged when military censorship deleted a report that navy pilots aboard the American aircraft carrier *John F. Kennedy* 'had been watching pornographic movies before flying bombing missions'.[74] Another indication of American hypersensitivity occurred following a story about a desert disco organised by some of the troops with a DJ called Scud B and a dance called The Gas Mask: 'when the stories appeared, the general was furious, and the PAO was given a serious rollicking'.[75] More usually, it was the offending journalist who was penalised, as when Douglas Jehl of the *Los Angeles Times* filed a story about how 50 US military vehicles had gone missing, had the report passed by the censor only later to be told that it was contrary to the 'best interests' of the military, whereupon he was ordered to leave the pool.[76] Other examples occurred when an American reporter described returning Stealth fighter pilots as 'giddy', only to have the word changed to 'proud', or when the British military informed reporters from *The Times* and the *Daily Mirror* that it would be 'unhelpful' to report anti-Islamic feelings expressed by the troops.[77] The American journalist who complained most bitterly that his copy had been altered was Malcolm W. Browne of the *New York Times* whose view on the system was that: 'Each pool member is an unpaid employee of the Department of Defense, on whose behalf he or she prepares the news of the war for the outer world.'[78]

An important footnote to all this must be made however. Many of these incidents were gleaned from media sources printed *during* the war. This was because nearly every 'censored' report which American journalists protested about was, after being referred back to the Pentagon, printed as originally designated. This was often 'forgotten' and certainly underplayed in wartime media sources, which frequently made an issue of censorship only when the Other Story was not providing sufficient or exciting copy. This was especially true of the American media, which might argue in their defence that speed is of the essence to successful journalism and that any delays in publishing a story defused its news value. If so, the media would appear to have been out of step with public opinion which, according to most polls and surveys, was more than willing to accept military censorship if it was necessary to defeat the enemy. Moreover, some elements in the media might protest about the slightest interference with their 'duty to report', but the fact remains that this often disguised the high degree of cooperation which existed in many strands of the military–media chain. Even when attempts were made to keep certain things secret, as when Whitehall attempted to suppress the news that all British front-line troops had been inoculated for bubonic plague because it would either help Saddam's propaganda or indicate to western publics the seriousness of the conflict which lay ahead, the news still managed to leak out.[79]

According to Kate Adie, British reporters had received assurances on two major issues of censorship, namely that

> any censorship would only be done in the field, by senior officers in close contact with those running the military operation, and that military censorship would be confined to strategic and tactical matters: matters of taste and tone would be the responsibility of the media.[80]

She did, however, admit that the exceptions to this rule involved religious matters and subjects which might offend the Saudi authorities (the Americans called this 'host nation sensitivity'). This resulted on at least one occasion in an absurd pool report by the BBC's Martin Bell who, with British soldiers singing hymns in the background, stated that this was 'an event which I can only call a welfare meeting conducted by a welfare officer whose services are much in demand'.[81] Colin Wills confirmed that there had been rows about this issue and particularly a story of army chaplains conducting Christian services on the eve of battle: 'we kicked up a fuss and eventually won, but it was such a nonsensical issue to have a fight over'.[82]

Many pool reporters appear to have been positively welcomed by the troops in the field. Kate Adie said that 'few military personnel – if any – were hostile to open reporting; most thought it democratically correct to have the media alongside'.[83] Her experience, however, was by no means universally shared. Indeed, there are numerous examples of journalistic testimony to the contrary, and it is important in this regard to distinguish between the troops in the field and the minders drawn from the officer corps, and indeed between the British and American troops whose attitudes towards the media appear to have differed widely. Robert Fox of the *Daily Telegraph* for example encountered a platoon of

B Company of the Royal Scots Guards:

While lounging about on the sand, I asked the soldiers how they liked life in the desert (and I thought to myself what a feeble question I had put). The response was wonderful. 'I like the freedom, it beats jail anyway', said a Jock immediately. 'Yeah, we're just one big happy family', said another with a grin which showed previous battle honours – all front teeth were absent without leave. All but two of the platoon had been inside prior to departure for the Gulf. I duly reported this, but the paragraph was removed before it reached the presses.[84]

Nonetheless, again to keep this in some kind of balance, it needs to be said that, although there were such examples of micro-censorship, the remarkable facet of this system was not the number of pool pieces which were censored but the number which were not. Whether that was due to the phenomenon of 'bonding', whereby journalists dependent upon troops for protection develop with them a sense of identification and mutual understanding,[85] or whether it was due to enlightened self-interest on the part of the military varied from reporter to reporter and from pool to pool.

British censorship therefore took place primarily in the field performed by the information officer in consultation with the unit commander. This at least meant that the pool journalists were having to accept decisions made by military officials who were present with them on the spot, rather than by soldiers divorced from the action. 'At no time,' said Miss Adie, 'were we prevented from filming anything ... and only that considered of use to the Iraqis strategically was deleted; footage that might embarrass or discomfort the army was not.'[86] The journalists would then edit and cut their stories before showing them to their censors, who might occasionally check back with Field Headquarters. Thereafter, anyone could use this material, including the army of journalists left behind in Riyadh and Dhahran.

It was indeed from those centres that serious criticisms of the pool system began to emerge, not least because many experienced journalists and major news organisations were being forced to take copy from some pool journalists who clearly had little experience or specialised knowledge of military matters or who worked for 'small town papers and obscure magazines'.[87] This reveals another source of press frustration with the pool system, namely that the normally competitive world of journalism was suspended by arrangements which forced journalists not in the pools to utilise reports produced by people who would ordinarily be their rivals. Moreover, news tends to be slanted at, as well as by, the source, and the exclusion of news organisations from countries other than Britain or the United States tended to produce an overwhelmingly Anglo-American perspective, while the focus of some pool reporters' interest, such as the determination of one lady reporter to ascertain whether female American troops had taken their vibrators into the field, seemed to others to miss the point of the entire exercise.[88]

Once journalists in the pools had filed their reports and had them cleared by the field censors, the reports were then supposed to be taken to the Forward Transmission Units (FTUs) located to the rear of the MRTs, usually at the JIB in Dhahran. The FTUs had direct satellite links with London and Washington. For months before the war and in the weeks leading up to the ground offensive, everyone who had anything to do with the pool system was anticipating the arrival of the day the armies clashed for the first time, G-Day. It was then that all these arrangements would really be put to the test. Paul Majendie of Reuters, attached to the American 1st Armored Division, subsequently described his assignment as a 'total disaster'.[89] He, like many of his colleagues with the British forces, felt that the problem did not rest with the field censors; 'we were able to get all we needed to write our stories. Military censorship of the content was never heavy-handed'. But, he continued, 'the problem was the totally inadequate method of getting the stories back'.

This was indeed, as we shall see, the major problem once the Ground War started, but it was also the most consistent source of media discontent throughout. Field censorship arrangements, on the other hand, appeared to be working efficiently, and from a military point of view they were. However, as Falklands military war veteran, Patrick Bishop, reporting on the conflict initially with the US Marines for the *Daily Telegraph*, warned:

The army regard a journalist mainly as a propagandist ... the control was pretty well absolute from the outset ... It was deliberately arranged so that once the war proper began it would be virtually impossible to get material out.[90]

His colleague on the same newspaper, Robert Fox, who had actually reported the Falklands conflict, felt that all the lessons of that war had been 'forgotten or ignored' in the Gulf:

The rules were over-elaborate, and vitiated by distance and technical problems of communication. Many of the escort and censor staff gave a good impression of not wanting to do the job, and ill disguised their feelings of animosity to the journalists. Some seemed unclear about their main responsibility and the normal role of a reporter.[91]

Clearly, his experience differed from that of Kate Adie and Colin Wills. Indeed Fox told of how, after the war, a Major escorting the pool with the 7th Armoured Brigade had told him that 'my main intention was to teach the journalists how to live in the field like soldiers' while his counterpart in the 4th Armoured Brigade 'accused me of 'always trying to fish for information''. Fox added: 'What else was a journalist supposed to do?'.[92]

Virtually all the journalists quickly discovered that the system was indeed riddled with delays. Edward Cody of the *Washington Post* felt that the problem was that 'you turn over control of your copy to them [the military dispatchers] and they don't care whether it gets there [to the FTUs] or not. It's not part of their culture. We, the newspapers, did it by buying into this stupid system of take-me-along'.[93] Print journalists especially felt aggrieved as their written dispatches were carefully checked, whereas radio and television correspondents in Riyadh and Dhahran were often able to transmit live and answer questions without pre-scrutinised texts.[94] In most pools field information officers did not have the appropriate equipment to scrutinise 8mm television tape.[95] Even so, television pool reports were rarely transmitted live but examined first by the censors at the FTUs – putting paid to any belief that this was an instantaneous television war in so far as the front line was concerned, let alone the assertion that field censorship was the sole point of scrutiny.[96]

Problems of coordination between the various authorities at the front, in Saudi Arabia and in London and Washington also occurred. For example, when the *New York Times* reporter at a secret airbase filed a pool dispatch concerning the role of the F-117A Stealth bomber in launching the war against key targets in Baghdad, it was cleared by the information officer on the spot but then was delayed by the unit commander who re-worked the report. The reporter agreed to the changes to meet his deadline only to discover the next day that the entire piece had been

suppressed on the instructions of the Stealth bomber unit headquarters at the Pentagon.[97] It took several days for it to emerge
that Stealth bombers had taken part in the first night attacks. In
London meanwhile, John Wakeham's Cabinet Media Committee
was being subjected to a series of requests from the Foreign Office
to provide greater coverage for the Saudi war effort, whereas
information officers in the field were irritated and frustrated by
London's requests to censor reports of coalition prayer meetings
and other facets of their everyday life that were deemed potentially
offensive to the Saudis.

The arrival of the INMARSAT satellite telephone was another
potential headache for the military censors. Though highly expensive, the use of these devices in Baghdad was, as we shall see in the
next chapter, a source of great controversy. Although Kate Adie
felt that they were 'clearly engineered for hotel balconies rather
than desert trenches',[98] journalists with the news pools were
warned that if they used them 'they could radiate signals to the
Iraqis'.[99] This highlights another important factor in the whole
philosophy of the newspool system. No journalist attached to
military units wants to give their position away to the enemy; not
only would it risk the lives of the troops, it would be risking their
own life. In such circumstances, the military thus becomes the
protector and the protected. The extent to which such symbiosis,
let alone mutual identification, affects coverage was not always
fully appreciated by journalists in the pools who, after all, were
most directly affected by it. But just in case the system was
violated, the military kept a watchful eye on the journalists, with
one British television crew even being arrested after their calls to
London were monitored by an airborne AWACS aircraft.[100]

Robert Fisk best highlighted the risks for objective reporting
which this system produced:

Most of the journalists with the military now wear uniforms. They rely
upon the soldiers around them for advice and protection. Naturally (and
justifiably) fearful of the coming land war, they also look to the soldiers
around them for comfort. They are dependent on the troops and their
officers for communications, perhaps for their lives. And there is thus the
profound desire to fit in, to 'work the system', a frequent absence of
critical faculties ... The American and British military have thus been able
to set reporters up against reporters, to divide journalists on the grounds
that those who try to work outside the pool will destroy the opportunities

of those who are working – under military restriction – within it ... The unquestioning nature of our coverage of this war is one of its most dangerous facets. Many of the American pool dispatches sound as if they have been produced by the military, which, in a way, they have. For the relationship between reporter and soldier here is becoming almost fatally blurred. Reporters who are working independently of the military have been threatened not just with the withdrawal of their accreditation, but also with deportation from Saudi Arabia ... This is supposed to be a war for freedom, but the Western armies in Saudi Arabia – under the guise of preserving 'security' – want to control the flow of information.[101]

Or, as P.T. Benic of Reuters put it, 'we were there to cover the war, not become part of it'.[102]

The unilaterals

When an exasperated Carl Nolte of the *San Francisco Chronicle* decided to find out what was happening at the front for himself and drove north from Riyadh in a rented car, he eventually encountered some American troops who complained to him about a wide variety of issues not being covered in the pool reports such as inadequate supplies and late pay-cheques.[103] Several other print and broadcast journalists, including Patrick Bishop and Robert Fisk, decided to reject the pool system altogether and joined the self-appointed 'unilaterals'. Basing themselves in Hafer Al-Batin in north western Saudi Arabia, they were following Richard Dowden of *The Independent* who was among the first journalists to go and live there. Getting to a town which a few reporters would like to present romantically as something out of *Apocalypse Now*, sneaking through military road blocks, living off their wits and disguising themselves as soldiers was by no means easy. Con Coughlin of the *Sunday Telegraph* described the extraordinary lengths to which these journalists were prepared to go to evade official scrutiny.

To avoid detection ... it was necessary to indulge in probably the most outrageous exercise[s] in subterfuge undertaken by journalists in a war zone. Military uniforms of various shades and sizes were acquired, as was any paraphernalia which might lend itself to the general aura of authenticity. Car hire firms in Dhahran were inundated with demands for the model of four-wheel drive jeeps used by allied commanders which, once acquired, were covered with the various markings used to denote participation in Operation Desert Storm. The more adventurous even managed to purloin camouflage netting which made their vehicles indistinguishable from the genuine article. As a final touch, the Filipino barber shops in downtown Dhahran did a roaring trade providing the western media with a variety of military-style haircuts.[104]

Some journalists venturing out on their own found 'more often than not' that they were given every co-operation from units which they encountered along the front, 'most notably the non-American forces'.[105] When one reporter did stumble across some US Marines, he found his car surrounded for six hours by the soldiers who threatened to shoot him if he moved: 'we have orders from above to make this pool system work', said one of them.[106]

Outside Saudi Arabia, it was frequently thought that it was the unilaterals' copy which provided the most objective coverage of the war, with rare insights into the human side – the fear, the boredom, the confusion, even the lack of maps – all of which might appear to have been at odds with the official line, and which might have become a more serious problem for the authorities had the war dragged on.[107] Yet as another unilateral, David Beresford of the *Guardian*, wrote after the war:

The authorities were fully aware of what we were doing but – although many threats were passed on – no serious attempt was made to stop us. This leads one to the suspicion that the unilaterals were a phenomenon at which the allied authorities connived; that they realised the 'pool' system would so discredit journalists under their command as to make them useless as conduits of disinformation with which to feed the Churchillian 'bodyguard of lies'.[108]

If this was correct, it does indeed reveal a highly sophisticated appreciation of the needs of propaganda. On the other hand, as one writer pointed out after the war: 'Telling of loneliness and boredom, cold nights and bad food, their [the unilaterals'] stories offered moving glimpses of soldiers preparing for battle. Unfortunately, they added little to our understanding of the war itself.'[109]

Those journalists who decided to go it alone frequently testified to the risks of losing their passes and possible deportation by the Saudi authorities. Fisk was threatened with his pass being withdrawn on at least four occasions in the first fortnight of the war.[110] Various Associated Press reporters were held for several hours by coalition forces only to be lectured before release.[111] Worse still, there was the early lesson of Bob Simon and his CBS crew, who went missing after straying across the Kuwait–Saudi border on Monday 21 January and who spent the next 40 days in Iraqi captivity (although at first the Iraqis denied that they held the crew) mindful of the fate of a previous journalist who had gone investigating by himself inside Iraq – Farzad Bazoft of the *Observer*, hanged by the Iraqis for spying only a year earlier. The Saudi Defence Ministry issued a communiquè which described the missing crew as having been on 'an unsponsored and unescorted trip, a direct violation of US–Saudi media ground rules' and reminded other journalists in the region 'that travel into restricted areas without official escort or written permission is strictly prohibited'.[112] Colonel William Mulvey, the head of the Joint Information Bureau, supplied the Saudi authorities with a list of journalists who had been arrested or detained and the Saudis considered withdrawing their visas altogether.[113] Going native with coalition forces may have appeared to some to have been infinitely preferable to being captured by an enemy which regarded journalists as possible spies. The risks were even greater for unilaterally minded journalists wearing uniforms and behaving like military personnel to evade coalition detection.

After his release, Simon maintained that 'we weren't after the story of the war. We weren't after an enormous scoop. We just wanted to check out what was going on'.[114] Even so, within days of war's outbreak, the hazards of straying away from allied military supervision were plain for all journalists, no matter how frustrated, to see within days of war's outbreak. From the military point of view, this helped the pool system to hold remarkably well until almost the very end of the war when another CBS crew raced to enter Kuwait City ahead of the advancing troops.

Before then, an incident had occurred which illustrated the extent to which the outside world was dependent for its information about what was actually happening in the war on a controlled, if admittedly somewhat punctured, information environment. On 13 February, the Iraqis launched a Scud attack against Hafer Al-Batin. No mention of this attack was made by the coalition. But the unilateralists managed to get reports of the incident back to Riyadh. As CNN's Charles Jaco reported live from there: 'it has to be said ... that we would not know probably that any of this had happened' had it not been for the violations of the pool system. He added that 'the Saudi Ministry of Information sent

61

some people up there early this morning to try to find out who those journalists are, round them up and bring them out of there'.[115] Ironically, this example illustrates the problems caused by the unilaterals for their audiences, let alone for the military; when their copy clashed with official versions, as it often did, the result was not a clearer picture of what was happening – as the unilaterals had intended – but an even more confused version of events that made it even more difficult for television viewers and newspaper readers craving for information to ascertain what precisely was going on.

The unilaterals certainly had some triumphs. One of the most celebrated was when four Iraqi conscript soldiers surrendered to *The Independent*'s Richard Dowden, *Life* magazine's Tony O'Brien and photographer Isabel Barnes on 6 February. Two of them were carrying an allied propaganda leaflet telling them how to surrender safely.[116] Knowing that if they handed their captives over to the Americans they would be unlikely to receive permission to interview them, they handed them over to the Egyptians 'who found the whole affair so hilarious'.[117] The amused Brigadier General even wrote Dowden a personal note that greatly facilitated access to other Arab forces in the region. But when the story was published, Hafer Al-Batin was suddenly inundated with journalists from a wide variety of nations who all wanted to find some prisoners. Instead they encountered the infamous Major John Koko, an ex-Special Forces ranger and insurance executive who saw his mission as doing everything he could to make it difficult for the journalists. 'The first time I showed up at Hafer Al-Batin,' he said, 'it was like turning the light on in a tenement building with cockroaches scurrying everywhere. Reporters were everywhere.' He arrested some and drove more off:

It was a game. We didn't have the ability to actually take a lot of them back so we didn't want to actually catch them, we just wanted to make their life miserable in Hafer Al-Batin.[118]

Major Koko also described his role as 'rumour control'. One journalist who encountered him said that 'he controls rumours by spreading them himself ... He dutifully, if reluctantly, stops Americans, but truly gets a charge out of busting French and especially Italian reporters, because, in his view, neither country is contributing enough to the war effort'.[119]

The Riyadh briefings

The media's problems did not end there. Because there were in fact more journalists in the region than troop contributions by most of the allied countries, the coalition had to ensure that they were regimented into a manageable force. Husbanded in Riyadh, the non-pooled press corps were virtually totally dependent on the series of daily briefings organised for them in the Hyatt Hotel by the American, British and Saudi military authorities. The French, who held their briefings in a separate hotel next door and initially allowed no journalists other than French ones, not even French-speaking Belgians, failed to release any of their initial bombing footage until the first Saturday, the day after the Muslim holy day, for fear of offending Algerian, Tunisian and Moroccan viewers who had access to their domestic coverage.[120] In Dhahran, the Joint Information Bureau was often known to re-examine and re-censor reports already reviewed by military information officers in the field or gleaned from the Riyadh briefings, often holding up dispatches for several hours after they had supposedly arrived for immediate distribution to the rest of the news media. When the military was able to retain such virtual total control over the flow of information, it could shape the overall view of the war. The revealing irony was that, when it wanted to, the JIB could move quite efficiently, as illustrated by the arrangement of a pool visit to Dhahran airbase for reaction from military personnel on major developments, such as President Bush's speech on Wednesday 27 February – in which he announced a halt to offensive allied operations and a successful end to the war.

It was generally thought however that the briefing system operated quite smoothly, at least after a somewhat shaky start when the officers were felt to be too low level. As the BBC's Mark Laity wrote:

Once you got senior officers, in other words generals, with the authority, knowledge and confidence to interpret what really needed keeping secret, the briefing system started to work. The number of backgrounders, especially on overnight developments, also transformed the amount of info coming out. In fact, in the end, journos started talking about 'death by briefing' and getting 'heavily attrited by US hot air power'. Inevitably this made you wonder whether your judgement was also being signifi-cantly degraded by over-dependence on these official briefings, whether on or off the record. In the end such considerations were irrelevant, because getting it unofficially was so hard.[121]

Even so, the same sort of criticisms levelled against the pool reporters started to be made against those attending the official briefings: they had been sucked in to the official version; they were too prepared to accept official statements uncritically; they were not asking the right sort of questions; they were being led by the nose. 'But in reality', wrote Laity, 'it was the sometimes self-righteous reporters who steered clear of the official system who frequently got it wrong – usually by being over-pessimistic.' Moreover, as he went on to point out, 'official truthfulness was aided because the war was going their way – there isn't much temptation to lie when the truth is mostly good news'.[122]

In Riyadh and in Dhahran, therefore, the allies 'evolved a fairly sophisticated system of news management'[123] based on a series of briefings throughout the day, culminating in an American briefing in time for European and American newspapers and television. As in the pools, there was a price to be paid for this. David Fairhall of the *Guardian* wrote:

In Riyadh, the relationship between press and military was a familiar one, in which one traded operational information and access for the opportunity this inevitably gave the military to present their own version of events.[124]

The American briefings were deliberately timed to begin normally at 18:00 (local time) to avoid any insidious comparison with the infamous 'five o'clock follies' of Vietnam. Yet here also, although not subjected to censorship in quite the same way as the pooled journalists, the press came up against the military's preoccupation more with the 'need to know' than any media aspirations to the 'right to know'. As one journalist put it:

The sober tone of the Riyadh briefings is on the personal instructions of Schwarzkopf, who knows about the perils of misinformation from his experience as a battalion commander in South Vietnam ... The fact that these briefings are beamed live around the world adds a dimension not present in Vietnam. There is immense pressure on the officers not to make any slip that might assist the enemy and jeopardise allied lives. Television's demands for live broadcasts have not met with universal approval, particularly from the print journalists. The military are so afraid of giving away anything that they withhold information they could reasonably disclose. 'If in doubt, we leave it out', said an American briefing officer.[125]

The American briefings were also regarded by some attending journalists to be too full of jargon, too short on hard information and too crude in their attempts to impose 'the White House spin of the day'.[126]

The British briefings on the other hand were felt – by American reporters at least – to be more lively, accessible and informative, owing largely to the presence of Colin Mason, a Lieutenant Colonel in the Territorial Army, who was also Managing Director of Chiltern Radio, and of Group Commander David Henderson who eschewed jargon and was renowned for his wit.[127] General Sir Peter de la Billiere, joint commander of the British forces, was also liked for his frankness, as when he informed briefers in mid February that a ground war was 'inevitable' while his American counterparts were still equivocating on the subject.[128] Even so, John Naughton, TV critic for the Observer, still felt that 'we know very little beyond what the military public relations boys want us to know, and we have no idea if they are levelling with us'.[129] James LeMoyne wrote in the New York Times: 'In the early days of the deployment, Pentagon Press officers warned reporters who asked hard questions that they were seen as 'anti-military' and that their requests for interviews with senior commanders and visits to the field were in jeopardy. This dampened critical reporting.'[130] He suggested that a venturesome article meant the postponement of his interview with Schwarzkopf and that when he broke away from his minders to visit troops in the field the soldiers seemed pleased to see him, welcomed him and chatted openly to him, only to be told two hours later to leave following an instruction from headquarters.

As for the overall impressions left by the briefings, it is indeed difficult to avoid the assessment that many journalists had indeed been absorbed into the one-sided perspective that was being offered to them. At the start of the war, for example, the initial euphoria generated by the media was in part due to military briefings informing journalists that so many sorties had been flown with such and such a percentage of accuracy and that x numbers of mobile Scud launchers had been destroyed or that y number of Iraqis were deserting. On the other hand, bombarded with statistics about the numbers of sorties flown and blinded with science and jargon, the journalists could not really help giving the impression that they were being told a great deal when in fact they

were being told remarkably little. As Sir William Deedes so elo-
quently pointed out in the *Daily Telegraph,* 'the ceaseless sound,
the plethora of voices, round the clock, sheds extraordinarily little
light on what is actually going on'. He noted the effect of this on
soaring equity prices and tumbling gold and crude oil prices and
added that it 'is the power of the mass media in such times to
exercise more influence than the events themselves'.[131]

Two incidents in particular occurred in the first week which
helped to re-create some distance between the military and the
media. The first came as a direct result of the reluctance – or
inability – of the briefers to provide detailed damage assessments
even though the coalition claimed it had achieved 'total air superiority' all over Iraq. By Tuesday 22 January, the chief Pentagon
spokesman Pete Williams was saying that General Powell's statement in his first briefing about an 80% effectiveness in air strikes
had been misunderstood by journalists: this did not mean that
80% of targets attacked had been destroyed. He also had to
explain that other military jargon might have given a false impression, especially the distinction between 'air superiority' and
'air supremacy': the allies, despite earlier statements, had achieved
only the former.

Robert Fisk of *The Independent* earned a reputation during the
war for being one of the few journalists to keep his distance from
the official coalition line and, indeed, it was he who was one of
the first to express scepticism concerning the coalition pronouncements. He noted how much more forthcoming the briefers were
once 'the notebooks have been put away and the recorders
switched off'. He was among the first to point out that 'the
American assessment of 80% accuracy does not mean that targets
are destroyed. The 80% is the statistic for the number of times
aircraft unload their bombs *over* the target – not the accuracy of
the hit'. He added:

It was Winston Churchill who spoke of the need for a nation at war to
surround itself with a 'bodyguard of lies'. It is inconceivable that the new
Gulf War is the first conflict in history not to use such a shield. 'Lies' may
be an unfortunate word to use; misinformation may come nearer the
mark.[132]

Quite often, it was simple ignorance. Intelligence from a wide
variety of sources took time to assimilate, check and evaluate

before it could be filtered out to the public via the briefings. The briefings themselves, by their very existence, provided an illusion of coalition omniscience but, as so often happened in response to questions, the official briefers simply had to say that they didn't know the answer. Undoubtedly quite often they did, but then they would usually say why they could not disclose a particular piece of information, and it was invariably on the grounds of operational security since they knew that Saddam's intelligence service would be watching. Yet this fact also made the briefings an ideal channel for sending out messages to the enemy, and it was this public conduct of censorship and propaganda which made the live televised briefing system such a unique event in the history of warfare.

There was a further aspect of this which needs to be raised. In a sense the journalists were being by-passed as conduits for official information since the military could now speak directly via television cameras to the publics in whose name they were operating. The public could thus judge for itself about the rights and wrongs of a case, without the assistance of reporters to interpret the news for it. It was, in other words, no longer the sole responsibility of journalists to determine whether the coalition was sending out a particular message or whether it was designed for the enemy. This may help to explain why some journalists were so keen to criticise the system. The public seemed far happier with the fact that they were being involved in the conduct of the war and polls indicated greater confidence in the workings of the military than in the media. But the press could not, would not, accept a redundant role and some journalists saw themselves as the keepers of the public's moral conscience and as the watchdog of military veracity. And so, when figures were given out that did not quite make sense, journalists pounced upon discrepancies almost as if to justify their presence. Hence the emergence of an even more serious gap in credibility which was to open over the question of Iraq's ability to launch Scud missiles.

The 'Scudfest'

As we have seen, the clearest manifestation of the coalition line that the war was going well thanks to superior technology was through the release of the military videos. But this, for journalists, was second-hand footage supplied by the military. What the media really needed was their own first-hand material. Television reporters would thus themselves then be able to feel much more directly involved, especially once they were able to report first hand on what it was like to be near the receiving end of an incoming Scud missile. The pictures they were able to take from the moment Iraq launched its psychological terror weapons against Israel and Saudi Arabia from Thursday 17 January (GMT and EST, Friday the next day local time) onwards provided them with an opportunity to describe war for themselves rather than relying upon the testimony of pilots or military audio-visual wizardry. This in turn led to the extraordinary phenomenon, lasting about a week, of what was really media over-indulgence in the Scud–Patriot duels which were in reality but a small facet of the overall conflict.

The 'Scudfest' began, like the war itself had done, on American prime time. CBS was quick off the mark when at 19:12 EST on 17 January, Tom Fenton in Tel Aviv reported that a 'huge blast' had been heard in the city. He was telephoning from inside a sealed room. Then at 19:23 EST, CNN went over to Wolf Blitzer at the Pentagon who reported the news that the first attacks against Israel had taken place, although it was unclear whether the missiles were carrying chemical warheads. CNN then went over to Alex Claude of JCS Radio in Tel Aviv who gave a live audio report saying that they had been told to put their gas masks on. He could hear explosions as he spoke. It was well after midnight in Israel on the 18th. For the rest of the night, there was speculation as to whether the explosions had been caused by Scud attacks and whether chemicals had been used and whether the Israelis would retaliate, although on NBC Martin Fletcher was at first giving a much calmer account to Tom Brokaw in which he stated that the first explosion was not chemical. At 02:33 (local time) CNN carried its first pictures of its *Jerusalem* office where bureau chief Larry Register was seen on the phone in the office surrounded by people wearing gas masks. A wobbly shoulder camera enhanced the tension as Register looked nervously out of the windows: 'And I thought I heard the explosions about 20 minutes ago.' Crew members donned their gas masks ostentatiously before the camera. 'Don't open the window, please', said the anchor as Register put his mask on. Register then transmitted his report through the muffled gas mask and microphone. At 02:46 on NBC, Martin

Fletcher in Tel Aviv joined in when he was interviewed wearing his gas mask: 'at least one gas warhead, at least one conventional warhead, we know that .... we have confirmation that the victims of chemical war have been taken to that hospital.' Brokaw replied: 'It is a very bad situation, getting much worse moment by moment. It seems to me absolutely unavoidable for the Israelis to stay out if that is the case.' Meanwhile, for several hours of dramatic television, CNN's cameras were pointing at the wrong place. In fact it was all in a sense a non-event; Jerusalem was not attacked. Some 25 miles away Tel Aviv was, but not with chemicals. It had certainly not been turned into a 'crematorium', as Baghdad radio maintained.

On 20 January, NBC was able to do slightly better. Reporter Arthur Kent was about to start transmitting a live rooftop report from Saudi Arabia when the air raid sirens sounded as an incoming Scud attack was taking place. Live before the cameras, he was seen dashing around in an agitated and excitable manner:

Get us up on audio. Please, get us up. Hello, New York? This is Saudi Arabia. This is not a drill. Hello, New York? [Holding up gas mask] This is Saudi Arabia. This is not a drill. New York? OK, let's go. We're firing Patriots. We've got flares and we've got sirens. Let's go – focus! [Explosion in distance; Kent ducks] There goes a Patriot, let's go![133]

It was a melodramatic moment as Kent appeared to be performing above and beyond the call of journalistic duty to get his live report started. In fact, all these histrionics were being carried live and the studio rose to the occasion, pleading with Kent to go below to the safety of the air raid shelter and the reporter saying that he and his team felt they should stay at their posts. This incident earned Kent celebrity status in America and various nicknames such as 'Scud Stud' and the 'Satellite Dish' were coined for the new reporter-as-star. Again, on 25 January, NBC news carried a dramatic report from Dhahran during which a Scud–Patriot duel was caught live on air. Well, it was more really a question of the journalists describing the attack as they ducked and weaved and the camera rocked from side to side trying to find its performers.

One man who was reportedly impressed by all this coverage was President Bush. Fitzwater described how the President 'thinks it's extraordinary. When a guy's standing underneath a Scud and it gets hit by a Patriot, baby, there's nothing faster than that.

There's no diplomatic pouch in the world that can keep up with that'.[134] The success of the American Patriot missiles in intercepting the Scuds provided, in microcosm, a televisual symbol of the conflict as a whole. It was a technological duel representing good against evil: the defensive Patriots against the offensive Scuds, the one protecting innocent women and children against indiscriminate attack, the other terrifying in their unpredictable and brutal nature. The very resonance of their names implied it all. Here was beneficial high technology, a spin-off of the American SDI ('Star Wars') programme, being utilised against comparatively primitive weapons of mass destruction from the old Cold War era: the Patriot was the 'Saviour of the Skies' and the 'Darling of the US Arsenal'. Moreover, the political dangers which the Scuds represented in their attempts to provoke Israel into retaliation created a further anxiety which Saddam's propaganda attempted to exploit. But no matter how effective the Patriot anti-missile missile was proving, it was not infallible, especially when one launched unnecessarily in Turkey almost hit a returning American aircraft. Nor, it was felt, was Israel's patience. An urgent allied objective, therefore, was to knock out the Scuds' fixed missile sites and the mobile launchers – not necessarily from a military point of view but more for political and psychological purposes.

The major American networks, momentarily denied access to Baghdad by the Iraqi expulsion of most western journalists (see Chapter 2), shifted to Tel Aviv and Riyadh as a major scene for their competitiveness. One network actually displayed a detailed city map of Tel Aviv pointing out bomb crater sites, which prompted a stern warning from Brigadier-General Nachman Shai, responsible for Israeli censorship, that 'if you wish to commit suicide, gentlemen, please be so good as to do it outside the country'.[135] NBC was so keen to broadcast casualty figures prematurely after one attack on Tel Aviv that the Israelis decided to cut the network's satellite link. Anchorman Tom Brokaw had to apologise on air for the 'inadvertent' violation before the line was restored.[136]

Although the first Scuds caused comparatively little damage to Israel, the attacks prompted President Bush to state: 'Maybe this will help everyone realise why this guy [Saddam] must be stopped.'[137] It might have done in some places but not in others, especially in the Arab world. The Saudi and Kuwaiti newspapers completely ignored the first Scud attacks on Israel, even though the Palestinian and Lebanese press carried the story in almost jubilant front-page stories. Only the Egyptian press seemed prepared to debate the issues and ramifications of the attacks.[138] In Jordan, however, where King Hussein had to balance his official neutrality against considerable popular pro-Iraqi sentiment, the *Jordan Times* wondered how the Scud attacks could have happened given initial coalition statements about the success of their air onslaught: "The answer could be that the Bush administration had deliberately disinformed the American people about the result of the first wave of massive bombardment against Iraq or that the Western media had chosen to present only what their governments said.'[139]

It would appear that the allies vastly underestimated the number of Scuds available in the Iraqi arsenal, believing they had no more than between 50 or 60. Because of their psychological and political significance, they had been a primary objective of the initial phase of the allied air campaign. In his opening wartime briefing General Schwarzkopf had stated that all of the fixed launchers had been destroyed. Then, in a satellite interview with NBC's Meet the Press on Sunday 20th, he repeated that, of the estimated 36 fixed Scud missile launchers, he was 'very confident' that all had been 'neutralized'. Of the estimated 20 mobile launchers, about 16 he said had been destroyed.[140] Given that Saddam had chosen to make his second wartime radio address to the nation that same day, during which he claimed that 150 allied warplanes had been knocked down (the coalition conceded 14), the propaganda initiative appeared to be shifting momentarily in Iraq's favour. Undoubtedly the 'fog of war' – that often quoted phrase – was clearly thickening.

Later that day in Dhahran, CNN almost captured live on television dramatic footage of an incoming Scud missile at 00:50 (local time on the 21st). Crew member Chris Turner turned reporter as he pointed to a black horizon and described what had happened moments earlier, before CNN had gone over to him. The studio asked him to put on his gas mask because 'CBS is reporting that chemicals were used in that'. Fortunately the attack had been captured on tape and this was played back 5 minutes later. When CNN again replayed tape of the Dhahran attack an hour or so later, civil defence organisers who were watching thought it was a live report and even ordered the air raid sirens to be sounded.[141] Simultaneously, a Scud attack was launched against Riyadh which was captured live as reporter John Sweeney described the flashing lights in the night sky.[142] Moreover, the Saudi authorities were reported to be so incensed at the coverage – which showed the precise location of the Patriot battery which shot down the incoming Scuds – that they threatened to pull CNN's plug by military means.[143] The next day would see a visibly frightened and nervous Charles Jaco describing for CNN viewers a daylight Scud attack on Dhahran as the air raid sirens sounded in the background.

However, as the Scuds kept coming over the next few days, press scepticism concerning coalition claims about strikes against Scud launchers began to mount. There was considerable confusion about how much damage had actually been inflicted on the launchers, about how the allies could be sure they had achieved air supremacy when the Iraqi air force was refusing to come out from beneath intensive cloud cover or from hardened shelters, about why the coalition was reluctant to substantiate its claims with hard data. Moreover, it soon emerged that the impressive number of sortie figures also needed qualification; nearly half the missions were support, refuelling or reconnaissance missions. A credibility gap was beginning to open up.

On Wednesday 23 January, Dick Cheney and Colin Powell responded to growing press criticism that very little hard news was being issued by giving a full-scale briefing at the Pentagon – the most informative of the war to date, even though video footage was noticably absent. They conceded that Iraq possessed hundreds of missiles in its arsenal and that, said Cheney, 'obviously, we've still got a ways to go'. He explained the various discrepancies that had been exposed between Washington and Riyadh by saying: 'I think we're working off different sets of numbers here'.[144] After the war, in an interview with David Frost, General Schwarzkopf admitted in response to a question about how many Scud launchers Iraq possessed:

One of the figures I read recently is they had 15 battalions of 15 launchers each, and that multiplies up to 225 – and that was a *lot* more than we thought because the maximum estimate that we had prior to the beginning was 48 and in fact, at one point right before we launched hostilities, we had pretty good intelligence that they had a maximum of only 18. So, by the time we had destroyed 16 of them, I was feeling pretty confident ... that we were really doing a job on them and I think that night deliberately [laughs] they launched a whole salvo of them to prove me wrong.[145]

Moreover, the fallibility of the Patriot was exposed or at least dented when, on Tuesday 22 January, two of them failed to knock out an incoming Scud fired at a middle-class residential district of Tel Aviv. Three elderly citizens were killed ('apparently from shock or heart attacks'[146]) and nearly 100 people injured. By 25 January, when a Patriot again failed to catch its target, 21 Scuds had been launched against Israel, killing 4 and injuring nearly 200 people (and 26 at Saudi, killing 1 and injuring 30). Fears of Israeli retaliation mounted as, almost as if on propaganda cue, another daylight Scud attack against Saudi Arabia occurred and the heroic Patriot missiles were captured on film successfully coming to the rescue. Of the six Scuds fired against Saudi Arabia on the Tuesday, an American spokesman said all were knocked out by Patriots or had fallen harmlessly into the desert or the Gulf.[147] In fact it would appear that only one had been intercepted by Patriots; the others had missed their targets. By the early hours of Saturday, however, following the fifth Scud attack on Israel in eight days, the first Israeli citizen had been killed directly by a missile on the Jewish Sabbath.[148]

As the war entered its second week, growing tension between the military and the media was becoming increasingly evident. The war was not over quickly and indeed, following its spectacular start, it was entering a phase that was likely to frustrate journalists as the air campaign 'dragged on' necessarily as part of its preparations for what would undoubtedly prove a spectacular final phase, namely the Ground War. From a journalistic point of view, the stories that would occupy the middle phase had already been told: the air war, Scuds versus Patriots, the ground preparations, even the role of the media. Bad weather also caused difficulties in assessing damage to the enemy. It also affected the infra-red censors of the precision-guided bombs, which began to raise doubts about the accuracy of these weapons. Moreover, the Pentagon then on 22 January admitted that the Patriot's initial alarm system was triggered not by the crews on the ground, to whom much media attention had been given as the 'heroes' of the high-tech duels, but by the launch flame of the Scuds detected via

73

satellite by the Woomera monitoring station in Australia, whereupon the information was passed on to the US Defense Support Program in Colorado, 7,000 miles away.[149] Often, it emerged after the war, the Scuds broke up as they re-entered the earth's atmosphere and an unnecessary number of Patriots had been fired at their debris as pieces of the missiles fell to the ground. It also emerged that, even when the Patriot had successfully intercepted its target (which apparently it did 45 out of 47 times), the debris was often responsible for deaths on the ground – something which the crews could at least advise upon as they learned from experience.[150]

After a week of war, the press was showing distinct signs of irritability. Bob Woodward of the *Washington Post* summed up the discrepancies. Although the Pentagon stated initially that 100% of Iraqi airfields had been 'neutralized', after 10 days it was admitting that 65% were still operational. Although it was claimed that nearly all of Iraq's air defence radar system had been destroyed in the first week of the war, about 20% of it was back in operation within 10 days. Despite General Schwarzkopf's statements about the number of Scud launchers that had been taken out, only 8 of the fixed launchers had been fully disabled after a week and there was no picture evidence by then of any mobile Scud carcasses. Saddam Hussein still appeared to be in contact with his military commanders, despite apparently successful attacks on his communications systems. Although his nuclear capability had seemingly been destroyed, about 50% of his chemical and biological weapons capability survived. Many of Iraq's runways had been restored and, despite the destruction of about 50 Iraqi aircraft and the flight of a hundred or so other planes to Iran, about 700 remained.[151]

Marlin Fitzwater conceded that 'we'd all like to see better damage assessment' but denied that detailed information was being withheld either to dampen down the initial euphoria or to avoid a public Vietnam-like reaction.[152] Both the *New York Times* and the *Washington Post* ran leaders which pointed to the undermining of coalition credibility by recent statements. The former stated under the headline 'Tell us more, please':

The Pentagon has nurtured disbelief by its relentless boasting about the historical dimensions of the air war without yet documenting its effectiveness ... There is thus no way to trust the truthfulness of even the most basic claims. The Pentagon risks erosion of public support if the situation is not corrected ... This secrecy is driven by recollections of Vietnam. Many in the military still believe that unfavorable news coverage made the war unpopular at home and ultimately lost it. This misrepresents history. Americans lost faith in that war because they gradually realized that the government had misled them. The Pentagon, under its current policy, risks a similar collapse in American sentiment – and at a very early stage of the war.[153]

In fact, early public opinion polls suggested that this was far from the case. On 30 January, a *New York Times/Mirror* poll in the United States asked: 'Should the military exert more control over news reports on the war?' with 57% saying 'yes' and only 34% saying leave it up to news organisations. Further, 80% said the military was not hiding bad news and 72% believed news organisations were trying to present an objective picture.[154]

Even so, the *Washington Post* perhaps helped to explain this by what it described as the 'Nintendo issue'. Americans were being presented with a view of the war that 'portrayed, perceived, underestimated and/or disparaged' a conflict 'as a kind of electronic board game'. It agreed

that the early days of the conflict did create a kind of illusion of perfection and ease and safety in the conduct of combat, and that this is exactly the wrong thing for a public expected to support the war to be encouraged to believe ... It is not a game, electronic or other, and it will not be without its toll in casualties on both sides. The very nature of the 'war viewing' experience – a kind of channel-to-channel kaleidoscopic adventure infused with a heavy dose of whatever the conventional commentators' wisdom is that day – tends to induce fickleness, restlessness, impatience, a compressing of time so that it seems at the end of only a couple of days as if the thing has been going on forever.[155]

In Britain, Max Hastings, Editor of the *Daily Telegraph,* on the other hand pointed to the dangers of being suddenly over-sceptical about official statements:

The problem for the media, in this and almost any war, is that in our collective enthusiasm not to become the puppets of government, we fall over ourselves to seek out evidence of failure and incompetence in the conduct of the campaign. This is made apparent in the lines of questioning pursued by reporters at official briefings in London and Washington. How can we say we are doing well if Scuds have hit Israel? Why are the

Tornados suffering higher casualties than American aircraft? Why can the military not be precise about damage inflicted on Iraq's air force? What precise level of civilian casualties is being inflicted upon Iraq by bombing?[156]

Although such questions were perhaps unanswerable in the 'organised confusion' of warfare, they did nonetheless provide an invaluable antidote to the previously unchallenged assertions of the military for journalists caught up in the initial excitement.

Part of the problem for the coalition damage assessors was not just the weather but Iraqi deception. The degree to which the weather was causing a problem was revealed on 21 January when the MoD imposed a security blackout on weather reports and forecasts from the Gulf and asked the Meteorological Office to stop the sale of its forecasts.[157] As for deception techniques, Soviet-trained Iraqi camouflage experts had perfected the art of disguising damage during the Iran–Iraq war. It was known for example that the Iraqis burned tyres under bridges and at other sites to fool allied satellite and aerial intelligence-gathering systems.[158] Even General Powell admitted that 'they have a long history of using dummies to confuse the enemy. They're quite good at it'.[159] Decoy missiles, tanks and aircraft, faked radio emissions, even dummy bomb craters, were all employed to confuse the enemy and divert attention away from genuine targets. As we shall see in subsequent chapters, such deception and disinformation techniques may have had costly propaganda consequences for the coalition, especially with dual-purpose installations such as factories and bunkers.

Of crossed wires and cormorants

As the war approached the end of its first week, then, spokesmen in Washington began to undertake a campaign of psychological preparations for a longer war than that anticipated by the media. The Iraqis, they maintained, were digging in and had showed an impressive resilience to the early onslaught; they were still likely to have some surprises up their sleeves and set-backs were inevitable; the war might indeed last months. On 24 January, Marlin Fitzwater admitted to high-level concern about the role which the media had played in fuelling extreme swings in public mood:

I think we all have a great fear that because of the way the media is covering this thing that if they shoot down one of our planes everybody is going to say, oh, the tide has turned, or something like that. I'm just saying get ready for a longer conflict than just a few days.[160]

Fitzwater also expressed his concern at what he called the unwillingness of the 'American psyche' to face the possible ups and downs of a long campaign:

There are going to be enemy victories, there are going to be enemy surprises ... we need to get into a frame of mind that allows us to accept those reverses and surges but still keep track of ... our conviction ... that in the final analysis we will prevail.[161]

This shift in emphasis prompted the *New York Times* to state that Iraq's strength, as now being emphasised by official spokesmen, should not have come as a surprise to anyone and that, if reporting restrictions were eased, 'self-induced American jitters' might be avoided. 'The United States needs hard reporting in the war,' wrote one analyst. 'What the country does not need, from the press or military, is astonishment that Saddam is in fact as strong as we made him'.[162]

It was in this climate of media and public anticipation, with more of the same type of stories being punctuated by news of oil slicks being released into the Gulf or of fleeing Iraqi planes landing in Iran, that a wave of rather odd stories – possibly disinformation – gained some notoriety. The case of Saddam's wife fleeing to Mauritania (or Zambia or Algeria or even Switzerland, according to various reports) was one such example, a story which possibly originated from coalition sources that was designed to foster discontent amongst ordinary, less fortunate, Iraqis unable to spirit their own families to safety.[163] Reports that Saddam had had his top air force commanders executed on 24 January was another.[164] This latter story, which came via the newly formed independent Soviet news agency Interfax, was denied by the Iraqis, with their attaché in Moscow saying 'it is part of the psychological war against Iraq', and even the coalition admitted that it could not verify the report.[165] But by that time the story had been flashed around the world and Saddam's reputation for ruthlessness and brutality had been reinforced in the Gulf War's nearest equivalent to a Stauffenberg plot.[166]

It was also during this period that the dearth of big new stories led to the exaggeration of smaller ones into a prominence they might not otherwise have deserved. A good example of this came on Thursday 24 January when western newspapers announced that the first Kuwaiti territory since the 2 August invasion had been retaken. The island of Qurah, 22 miles off the Kuwaiti coast, was liberated amidst a splash of publicity that gave the impression that a full land, sea and air operation had been successfully completed with no loss of coalition life against 3 Iraqi dead and the taking of 51 Iraqi prisoners of war. It was described as 'one of the war's fiercest naval engagements', including in a pool report by ITN's Michael Nicholson who was aboard HMS *Gloucester*, and was compared in its psychological significance by other media sources to the recapture of South Georgia during the Falklands Campaign.[167] In fact, the island was not much larger than Trafalgar Square and, although it might have been strategically significant as an Iraqi forward command post monitoring coalition ships in the Gulf, Baghdad radio poured scorn on the emphasis being given to the victory in the West: 'The infidel American aggressors are desperately trying to blind public opinion by claiming to have liberated a small, rocky island, whose name is not even known to Iraqis, by firing shells at it from a single helicopter at great distances.'[168] It later emerged that the tiny island was in fact an object of dispute between Kuwait and Saudi Arabia, with Saudi troops even having briefly occupied the territory in 1989 and that, only weeks before the invasion of Kuwait, Saudi Arabia had renewed its claims to the rock, even though great play was being made of the Kuwaiti role in its recapture.[169]

Coinciding with this story came the news on 24 January that a Saudi Arabian pilot flying an American-built F-15 aircraft had shot down not one but two Iraqi F-1 Mirage fighters in a single engagement, the first Saudi 'kills' of the war. It was in fact to be one of the war's comparatively rare dogfights, but the media prominence it was given was confined largely to the West; Arabs killing Arabs was a much more delicate issue in the Middle East. When the pilot was interviewed on CNN saying that 'I think this was a very strong message' to the Iraqis, Saddam may have been watching but his people were not. Nor indeed were the Saudi population. Although CNN had been brought to Saudi Arabia by the war largely to service the American forces, it was not transmitted live to a general audience but rather delayed by several hours so that all potentially offensive references could be deleted by the Saudi Ministry of Information.[170] Despite congratulations issued in the Saudi press, nervousness at killing fellow Muslims was revealed by the local media's refusal to print the name of the pilot being celebrated as an Arab hero in the West.[171] But at least this was a timely reminder that Arab forces were playing a 'significant' role in the coalition and allayed fears that they might not be up to the professional standards of western forces.

Not that 'psychological war' was confined to the coalition. As we shall see in the next chapter, the Iraqis were quite prepared to deploy a Vietnam-style weapon in the form of parading captured coalition pilots on television in an attempt to undermine morale in western countries. But they were also trying the same sort of terror campaign against their Arab enemies. On Friday 25 January came the first news that Iraq was engaging in a massive act of local 'environmental terrorism' (as Fitzwater called it) by releasing millions of gallons of crude oil into the Gulf. Saddam had apparently ordered the taps of Kuwaiti oil fields to be opened, thereby releasing millions of gallons into the Persian Gulf (or Arabic Gulf, as coalition briefers preferred to call it for 'host nation sensitivity' reasons) for no apparent military purpose. The slick was said to be 15 times larger than the one caused by the 1989 Exxon Valdez disaster. Iraq insisted that the spillage had been caused by allied bombing of two tankers but, after checking all the raids to date, Schwarzkopf maintained: 'I can tell you that we saw absolutely no indication at all – no indication at all that any US military action caused this to happen.'[172]

Whether Saddam was attempting to demoralise opinion in Saudi Arabia (whose desalination plants were threatened by the resultant slick) or the wider world (where ecology pressure groups might renew their calls for a halt to the war) or whether it was simply a diversionary tactic to shift the emphasis away from his recent set-backs, the move dominated media attention in the second week of the war, securing top billing over the Scudfest. Certainly here was an ideal counter to any suspicions that the allies were fighting a war solely for oil; if they were, here was an example not of Saddam's contempt for the commodity – in fact he was as much motivated by controlling the resource as anyone else – but of his contempt for the environment, an issue which united all sensible and concerned people world-wide. Moreover, for the coalition, here was an excellent opportunity to focus media attention on the Gulf waters from which a sea-borne assault might take place when in fact no such thing was being planned. Perhaps Saddam had already fallen for that disinformation, which is why he may have released the oil in the first place. By keeping up the profile of what was happening in the waters of the Persian Gulf, the allies could continue to send a message to Saddam that they were still considering an amphibious assault as a likely possibility, thereby tying down large numbers of his forces on the Kuwaiti coast which would mean more coalition freedom to manoeuvre elsewhere.

The image of pathetic, shivering, gaping-eyed birds drenched in oil was flashed around the world on the weekend of 25–27 January, to be followed by alarming television pictures of crude oil lapping the Gulf coastline and of dying cormorants and other migrating bird life. In Germany, where anti-war sentiment was more prominent than in any other European country and where the environmental lobby was as influential as anywhere, the coverage was said to have changed attitudes and its government immediately offered to send personnel and practical help to deal with the slick. Foreign Minister Genscher said: 'this shows the dictator in Baghdad will stop at nothing to achieve his aims,' while, back in Saudi Arabia, coalition spokesmen were having a field day. General Walter Boomer, Commander of the US Marine Corps, described Saddam as a 'moral pygmy'[173] while Saudi officials described him as the 'lord of death' and the 'father of destruction', a monster who had violated international as well as Islamic law which stressed respect for the environment.[174]

But the way the story emerged was unusual, especially with one of the war's most enduring iconographic images: the dying, oil-smeared crested cormorant that was supposedly the innocent victim of Saddam's environmental terrorism. Days later, however, it transpired that the first photographic and filmic images had been taken from an earlier, smaller oil spill caused by an Iraqi raid on a Saudi refinery about which hardly anything had been heard. Moreover the latest, much larger, oil slick had yet to reach any coast. This was admitted by General Thomas W. Kelly, operations director for the Joint Chiefs of Staff. Needless to say, his statement was afforded nothing like the publicity already given to the oil-smeared birds.[175] Philip Knightley spotted the incident and asked:

What raid was this? How could Iraqi planes successfully raid a Saudi refinery at a time when the allies were claiming total mastery of the air? And, most intriguing of all, who had decided to release pictures of the dying bird and link it to the spill from Kuwait, thus creating a powerful propaganda image of special appeal to environmentalists – who, until then, were among the leading opponents of the war?[176]

Although Knightley recognised the difficulty of identifying the engineers of this story, he added that 'today, propaganda is so much a part of our society that it seems to occur almost spontaneously, as government and media swing behind the war effort'. To complicate matters further, it then emerged that there was a third slick caused by the emptying of five Iraqi oil tankers moored inshore near the Mina Al-Ahmadi crude oil tank farm.[177] This was suspiciously close to the Iraqi version of events. On 25 January, the Pentagon reported that 'at least half' of the oil then in the Gulf came from these tankers: 'Long before Operation Desert Storm began, five tankers took their oil down to the occupied Kuwaiti port of Mina Al-Ahmadi. They've been there, holding their oil, since last October. The oil the Iraqis are now dumping into the Gulf is coming off those tankers'.[178] All three slicks threatened to merge into one.

Oil storage tanks from a refinery at the Saudi border town of Ras Al-Khafji had been hit by Iraqi artillery fire (not by Iraqi planes as Knightley had suspected) on the first day of the war. ITN managed to get Jeremy Thompson up there with a film crew to report on this, which had been transmitted on 17 January. Several days later, another freelance team working for ITN managed to secure pictures of the resultant oil slick two days before any pool footage arrived. The second ITN report, by Peter Sharpe, ran:

It was the cormorant stumbling across the highway near the beach that signalled something was wrong. And behind the sand dunes we discovered an environmentalist's nightmare ... The first victims of the disaster struggling to free themselves from its grip [over pictures of drenched birds] ... This morning it looked as though the sea had turned to treacle. It even sounded different: Kuwaiti oil gurgling ashore along miles of coastline.[179]

When this report was shown on CNN, it prompted the angry Pentagon and world-wide reaction. Ironically, the unilaterals had not only found a scoop but also provided another opportunity for the coalition to present the war in a particular light and to distract media attention away from some of their more controversial recent pronouncements.

ITN reporter Sandy Gall explained after the war:

Peter Sharpe of ITN had broken the oil story, but without going through the Ministry of Information and had his pass removed for his pains. So I tried, through the Saudi-manned ARAMCO desk [the state-owned Saudi Arabian oil company], but could find no-one to take a decision. Luckily, I had an important Saudi friend in Jubayl, half way up the coast between Dhahran and the Kuwaiti border. As he was extremely anxious for the world to be alerted to the impending ecological disaster, he gave me every possible help. Even then, because of Saudi red tape, getting to the story was extremely difficult, although oiled birds were dying in their hundreds.[180]

But the question of which cormorant was affected by which slick remained extremely confused in the media coverage. The point from a propaganda perspective was that a massive environmental disaster was being extrapolated from pictures of a relatively minor spill. Nor was clarification helped by ARAMCO's reluctance to release its 'top secret' file on the oil spill and its referral of all journalistic enquiries to the allied briefings. Even oil and pollution experts responding to the disaster were reportedly denied access to the region.[181] The impact on marine and bird life was meanwhile being exploited to illustrate Saddam's 'general meanness' (Fitzwater) whereas, as late as 3 February, the second slick was reported to be still 10 miles off the Saudi coastline.[182]

To put the record as straight as it can be put at this stage, what appears to have actually happened is as follows. On the opening day of the war, the Khafji oil terminal was hit by Iraqi artillery fire and probably started to leak oil into the Gulf then. It was this comparatively small slick which Peter Sharpe encountered a week later at Khafji beach and which prompted the world outcry after it was shown on CNN and other networks. A second, much larger, slick was formed when the Sea Island terminal started to release oil on 19 January after the Iraqis opened the valves at the Mina Al-Ahmadi refinery complex in occupied Kuwait. The tankers probably started to leak oil on 24 January, as evidenced by air reconnaissance missions which showed they were very high in the water compared 16 January when they were low.[183] None of this, however, was clear at the time; the impression was that there was only one gigantic slick which the coalition claimed had been deliberately caused by the Iraqis and which the Iraqis claimed had been the result of coalition bombing of its tankers.

Nonetheless, intense media attention continued to be devoted to the disaster, to the even greater threat to Saudi desalination plants and to the international relief effort being made to protect them and the wildlife from Saddam's latest act of ruthlessness. The coalition then grasped the opportunity to be seen to be doing something on behalf of the world community. Eight miles off-shore, the Sea Island terminal slick had already been set ablaze – accidently, though beneficially – on the night of Thursday the 24th when allied air forces had attacked an Iraqi mine-laying vessel moored next to it. Then, on the night of Saturday 26 January, allied bombing raids stemmed the oil flow from the Mina Al-Ahmadi complex by attacking the manifolds with electro-optical glide bombs.[184] It was another example of how 'beneficial' precision bombing could prove and General Schwarzkopf himself duly produced the videos taken through the noses of the precision-guided bombs as they plunged towards the manifolds. By 28 January, the Pentagon claimed that this oil flow had been stopped by pointing out that the previously bellowing black smoke was now a different colour, indicating that the oil was low in the water.

It subsequently emerged that the slick was nowhere near as large as implied at the time, with some sources estimating it to be 'perhaps one-half to one-fifth of the original estimates'.[185] Even by June 1991, the slick had still not reached the Al-Jubayl desalination plant in Saudi Arabia. That said, its environmental impact cannot be minimised; it does appear to have been at least the same size as the Exxon Valdez spill, although subsequent investigations into its size and impact, together with the inadequate post-war clean-up operation, remained clouded in Saudi Arabian secrecy.[186]

The next strange story came with the reports that first 7, then 39 and then more than 100 Iraqi planes were fleeing to Iran. Saddam had tried a similar ploy before, when he had sent some of his air force to Jordan for protection during the Iran–Iraq war. Although the real purpose of this latest exodus was unclear, the whole implication of coalition interpretations was that Iraqi planes were fleeing in desperation, possibly from Saddam himself following the execution of top air force commanders and possibly from the allies, who at last declared 'total air supremacy' on 30 January. Just to be on the safe side this time, General Kelly explained what he meant by this: 'Every time they send an aircraft up ... it gets shot down' or, according to Schwarzkopf, 'it's running away'.[187]

The first week of the war had undoubtedly been, as the *Independent on Sunday* put it, something of an 'emotional roller coaster ... and during the week we have been more down than up'.[188] Much of this depression had been caused by the parading of the captured pilots. Yet however much this, together with the firing of Scuds indiscriminately at civilians in Israel and Saudi Arabia, may have concerned the coalition from a presentational point of view, the incidents also served to clearly identify Saddam's position on the West's spectrum of moral condemnation. Then, on 28 January, Baghdad radio warned that Iraq would carry the war well beyond its borders through terrorist attacks; more than 20 such incidents had already occurred, especially in Greece and Turkey, although without serious casualties. But Saddam's 'strong arm capable of reaching all places', including the threat to make President Bush a 'hostage in his black house'[189] and his call for a holy war fought by all Moslems against the international coalition, was matched by President Bush's speech to the National Religious Broadcasters' convention on the same day. Speaking after a weekend which had seen some of the largest anti-war demonstrations to date in America, he proclaimed that the United States and its allies were fighting not 'a religious war *per se*' but a 'just war' to stop the rape of Kuwait. Once again pledging that this would not be 'another Vietnam', Bush stated that 'naked aggression' must not be allowed to go unpunished. He reiterated that the US was not fighting the people of Iraq and added that he did not wish to see Iraq so destabilised that it might itself become the victim of future aggression. 'We seek nothing for ourselves', he said, and promised that American forces would leave the region as soon as Kuwait was liberated.[190]

In his opening address to the troops at the start of the war, General Schwarzkopf had told his men that 'our cause is just. Now you must be the thunder and lightning of Desert Storm. May God be with you ... .'[191] President Bush had also been keen to emphasise his religious credentials since the start of the war when he had been comforted by the evangelist Billy Graham on the first night and when he gone to church to pray the next day. Iraqi propaganda depicted the struggle as a war between technology and faith: 'The historical movement of the Arab and Islamic nation is our weapon, while the computer and electronics are theirs'.[192] The war was a *jihad*, although Saddam himself, critics pointed out, was not a religious leader but a secularist and thus in no position to incite a holy war. The quasi-religious theme was again reiterated by President Bush in his State of the Union address on Tuesday 29 January: 'Our cause is just. Our cause is moral. Our cause is right.' This tended to clash somewhat with the Pope's noticably under-publicised view that the war was 'unworthy of humanity' and in fact prompted an unresolved debate about the mysterious ways in which God appeared to be moving.[193] For its part, Baghdad radio responded by describing Bush as an 'evil butcher' with a 'sick mind'.[194]

Not that Washington was without its mysteries. At the end of January, Secretary of State James Baker and his Soviet counterpart, Alexander Bessmertnykh, issued a joint statement in which they declared that an end of the Gulf War could be achieved if Saddam made an 'unequivocal commitment to withdraw from Kuwait'. Neither the White House nor the Pentagon claimed to know anything about this. Rapid efforts were made to smooth over the cracks which this conciliatory statement appeared to reveal, espe-cially in the aftermath of the series of morale-boosting speeches by President Bush declaring America's moral obligation to deal with ruthless dictators by force. The Israelis feared the spectre of link-age to the Palestinian issue being raised again and protested. The White House put out reassurances that the statement revealed nothing new, either about America's stance or about its determi-nation to pursue the war to whatever means were necessary to expel Saddam. As for the Iraqi leader, he showed no signs of budging.[195]

There is some evidence to suggest that the Iraqis were astonished at the emphasis being given to the damage caused to bird life at the expense of that being inflicted upon civilians inside Iraq. The oil smeared cormorants and the rescue operation that followed could certainly be monitored in Baghdad via CNN. If Iraq was therefore to stand a better chance of influencing the western media's agenda, it had become essential for its government to reconsider its propaganda policy concerning the presence of western journalists in Baghdad. CNN, thanks largely to the con-troversy which its exclusive position and its coverage of the cap-tured pilots had aroused, was now suspect in the eyes of some in

85

the wider world and thus less valuable than it had been from Baghdad's point of view. And so, at the end of January, permission was granted to allow western journalists and film crews from other news organisations back into Iraq in the hope of providing the kind of images that could serve the interests of Iraqi propaganda and refocus world attention on the issues which Baghdad considered to be more important.

Chapter Two

Reporters under fire: Iraqi media mismanagement in the Gulf War

Introduction

Both before and during the Gulf War, it was often said that Saddam Hussein was a master of propaganda. It would perhaps be more appropriate to state that it was the master of him. When April Glaspie, the former American ambassador to Iraq, testified before the Senate's Foreign Relations Committee in its first post mortem on the Gulf War, she spoke of Saddam's 'total isolation and ignorance' of the outside world.[1] Herself a victim of Iraqi attempts to discredit her by the 'deliberate doctoring and editing' of documents relating to her conversations with Saddam prior to the invasion of Kuwait, she was highlighting an important point about Iraq's approach to propaganda, at least in so far as the western world was concerned. It lacked subtlety, sophistication and substance. As a totalitarian state, the emphasis was anyway always on secrecy at the expense of publicity. Defensive in nature, Iraqi propaganda more often than not assumed that by not mentioning something the issue would simply go away. Even when it attempted to seize the initiative and go on to the offensive (in more ways than one), it usually contained more shadow than substance. It was a propaganda of the threatening word more than of the delivering deed. If it had any skill at all, it was confined to exploiting coalition mistakes. Yet even on the one issue which the coalition most feared might provide Saddam with his greatest propaganda opportunity, namely 'collateral damage', the Iraqis invariably failed to provide watertight, verifiable and incontrovertible evidence to support their claims. Even when they occasionally did, they were unable to overcome two fundamental further prob-

87

lems: the coalition's skill at counter-propaganda and the resolve of public opinion in the West to see Saddam defeated.

Saddam tried a number of propaganda ploys against the coalition, virtually all of which were distinguished by their failure to convince anyone except the already converted. He promised, but in the event could not deliver, chemical warfare, whereas only substantial military success with such weapons could have justified the enormous public relations cost of openly embracing such threats. Right to the end, he promised the 'Mother of All Battles' – and that pledge was exposed as the allies sliced through Iraqi military forces at the end of February. He did manage to deliver dozens of Al-Hussein missiles (or Scuds as the coalition preferred to call them) but these were, as General Schwarzkopf recognised, more psychologically than militarily significant (ironically and tragically taking their greatest toll on a United States barracks in Dhahran on the day Kuwait City was liberated). But, again, the Scuds failed in their primary propaganda objective, namely to force Israeli retaliation and thus split the Arab members from the coalition. Besides, if anything, Israeli restraint tended to produce a groundswell of popular admiration and sympathy for that country's plight not apparent since long before the Intifada and which in turn tended to undermine any sympathy which western opinion might have felt previously for the Palestinian cause – the exact reverse of Saddam's intentions.

Other ploys backfired with similar aplomb: the release of the 'world's greatest oil spill' into the Persian Gulf and other acts of 'eco-terrorism' such as the firing of Kuwait's oil fields, gestures which merely confirmed western opinion of him as a ruthless and cynical tyrant who was a menace to the entire world and not just to Kuwait. The parading of captured, apparently battered, coalition pilots on Iraqi television caused even more outrage and was dropped by the Iraqi Ministry of Information after less than a week. Then there were the claims that 20 Israeli aircraft had taken part in air raids on Iraq (denied, significantly, by the Saudis and Syrians) or that religious shrines had been attacked in the south (not taken up, again significantly, by the Iranians). These were clearly attempts to influence Arab and Islamic opinion but, again, despite significant street support for Saddam throughout the Arab world which envisaged him as a new Nasser, the anti-Iraqi governments of the region held firm in their support for the coalition's objectives.

Iraqi propaganda directed at the Middle Eastern masses was nonetheless considered by the coalition to be a potentially dangerous and potent weapon and it was indeed here that some measure of Iraqi success could be ascertained, certainly by comparison with that directed at the West. Iraqi radio and television transmitters thus became a priority on the coalition's target list. Meanwhile, thanks to CNN, Saddam could keep trying to sow seeds of doubt amongst western opinion, as with the 'baby milk factory' episode (see below pp. 111–18), the claims that 160 coalition aircraft had been shot down after five days of the war (the allies released the figure of 17) and, perhaps most significantly of all, the question of civilian casualties.

Iraq, journalists were informed throughout the war, provided a 'target rich environment' for allied war planes. Conventional bombing, however, as any modern historian would have testified, is a notoriously inaccurate weapon. The Iraqis sided with the historians. They believed that the lessons of the Blitz and particularly of the televised war in Vietnam were twofold: the consolidation of domestic support for the war amongst their own population, as had happened in London in 1940, but, more importantly, there was now a real opportunity to undermine the will to fight amongst western public opinion about the rights and wrongs of the war, as had supposedly happened following the Tet Offensive of 1968 in Vietnam. Because the first truly global television service provided a unique opportunity to influence public opinion throughout the world, the Iraqis therefore gave priority to CNN reporters in Baghdad, who were expected to report on the inevitable horrors that would result from coalition bombing raids, which in turn, it was supposed, would result in a weakening of western popular resolve. And because CNN thus enjoyed a special position, other stations would have to use its footage – which they did – even if the price to be paid by the Atlanta-based network was the allegation of serving Iraqi propaganda interests.

The clues to a fundamentally crude approach to propaganda were evident before the war started, especially if one recalls the way Saddam attempted to use the 'guestages'. He subsequently accused the West of duping him into releasing those hostages prior to war's outbreak. But, then again, throughout the war he repeatedly insisted that Iraq was winning. A further indication of his approach to propaganda came with the broadcasts of 'Baghdad

Betty' to the US troops suggesting that their sweethearts were dating Tom Cruise, Bruce Willis and even the cult cartoon character Bart Simpson, broadcasts which were said to have 'actually helped morale' among the listening American servicemen before the war started.[2] But because his own propaganda was ill-conceived and badly researched, this increased the criticism of those who were felt to be doing it for him, with allegations in some quarters that Peter Arnett was turning out to be the Tokyo Rose or the Lord Haw Haw of the Gulf War.

The controversy surrounding the role of CNN in Baghdad can in fact be said only to illustrate Iraqi clumsiness still further. By drawing attention to the circumstances under which its reporters were allowed to operate, the Iraqis were merely placing audiences on their guard about what could, and more usually could not, be said. Censorship and propaganda tend to operate most effectively when they are kept hidden. Censored reports from the Iraqi capital, especially when reminders were made about reporting restrictions prior to, during and after each transmission, merely drew attention to the existence of both, undermining their credibility as purely objective information. The debate surrounding the question of whether or not CNN should even be present in the enemy capital emphasised this situation even further. Yet too often was it assumed that western audiences were incapable of spotting propaganda when they saw it. And too often were the critics revealing more about their own nervousness concerning the message than they were about the role of the messenger.

On the other hand, it was a ploy worth trying in that it probably did induce considerable nervousness amongst the coalition's public relations people. Day after day, after all, western television audiences were being subjected to images of well-stocked Iraqi markets and shops, even though pre-war this had prompted a counter-offensive using those same images to suggest that sanctions were not working and that other means would be necessary to deal with Saddam. During the war itself, images of loyal Iraqis repeatedly pronouncing their support for Saddam and his cause in Kuwait were attempts to undermine the coalition's claims that the Iraqi leader was isolated and unpopular and provided western audiences with the face of the Iraqi people against whom the war was not allegedly being fought. And in the Middle East, the sheer defiance of resolute, loyal Iraqis, for the most part calm under fire, could only have induced an element of Arab pride amongst those sections of the audience who admired Saddam for standing up to the West. In a propaganda war, anything which has the slightest hope of touching a nerve or a chord amongst targeted audiences is worth trying. However, although letting the western journalists into Baghdad might be construed as a bold and innovative propaganda initiative, the Iraqis' subsequent failure to exploit the opportunities which their presence offered was the result of basically two factors: the media literacy of sophisticated western television audiences, with their critical capacity to examine audio-visual texts, and the Iraqis' own lack of subtlety in dealing with media practitioners from different cultures.[3]

CNN and reports from the enemy capital

CNN was able to sustain its unique initial position thanks to an exclusive rental of a 'four-wire' communications system, negotiated in the previous November with the Iraqi government at a rate of $15,000 a week. This was a highly reliable, independently powered, two-way overseas telephone connection requiring no operators or switching connections and which functioned even when local power lines were cut. With two dedicated channels in each direction occupying a band width twice the size of the conventional, CNN was thus able to deliver a reliable high-quality signal between Baghdad and Atlanta. From the roof of the Al-Rashid hotel where the international press corps was stationed, the signal travelled down hardened gulleys occupied by Iraq's military communications network to a relay station in Amman, Jordan, and then on to the wider world via satellite.

It was certainly a more effective system than that used by all the other western correspondents, who had to rely on operator-assisted calls and local power supplies. The 'four wire', for example, gave CNN the edge over ABC, which actually scooped the all-news network by two minutes on the opening night of the war on American prime-time television but which was unable to transmit after Baghdad's communications tower was hit by a cruise missile In the first air strikes against the city and after the local electricity supplies were cut off. CBS was affected likewise, despite the decision already made earlier in the day to pull out of Baghdad following a tip-off to its producer that 'his children all have colds', a coded message relayed to him by the network's Pentagon correspondent three hours before the first air strike. Similar messages had been delivered to other journalists on 16 January by White House spokesman, Marlin Fitzwater,[4] 'so we knew', said one, that 'something was about to happen'.[5]

It also looked as though the American government feared the presence of western journalists in Baghdad for precisely the same reason that Saddam wanted them to stay. Or, given their knowledge about the likely accuracy of their smart weaponry, even though most of it was admittedly untried in combat, did they? As John Simpson has written:

Saddam Hussein's strategy was dependent upon having American television in Baghdad who could see – and transmit – the terrible scenes he expected would take place. This was why he anticipated only two air strikes on the city: CNN would show the results to the American people, who would put such pressure on George Bush that the air war would be called off.[6]

Perhaps so, but the circumstances which prevailed as the first attack took place turned out to favour the allies more than the Iraqis from a presentational point of view. One journalist described the scene as the first bombs fell:

I was in the NBC office around 2am when reports came from Washington that war would begin very soon. Then, at about 2:30am, the skies lit up. Many of us felt Baghdad would be destroyed in a few hours. The hotel, a very strong building, was being buffeted by the explosions. You could feel the impact of the bombs going off. The lights went out in the hotel and people were screaming and panicking. We went to the hotel bomb shelter in the basement. There was chaos.[7]

Forewarned, John Simpson and his crew were actually driving around the city looking for their best photo-opportunity, but, as the first bombs fell, their terrified Iraqi driver panicked and returned them to the hotel whereupon Simpson was bundled into the basement bomb shelter. There he joined the ITN crew and numerous other journalists, although Simpson's rival and counterpart from ITN, Brent Sadler, had managed to stay above ground to watch the action. But so did CNN, which was the only news organisation with the ability to communicate live to the outside world as the bombs rained on Baghdad with unprecedented accuracy. Ironically, therefore, in the chaos of the opening night, with most of the journalists downstairs and with those that remained above unable to transmit any live pictures, the Iraqis were serving the American cause more than their own.

CNN anchorman Bernard Shaw, who had arrived in Baghdad the day before hoping to interview Saddam, joined reporters Peter Arnett and John Holliman in their suite of rooms at the Al-Rashid hotel. Shaw was apparently 'one of the first down the shelter and was one of a handful allowed to go back to broadcast'.[8] John Simpson was also among the escapees and he was later able to tape a recorded report to camera, as was Brent Sadler once his crew rejoined him. Their next problem would be how to smuggle out their reports the next day. Meanwhile, as the bombs fell around them, neither was able to use their INMARSAT telephones until much later in the morning; even if they had been prepared to go outside to the small farm of satellite dishes located near to the outside swimming pool, they were without power until portable emergency generators could be set up to drive their satphones. With the communications tower knocked out, CNN's four-wire system came into its own, enabling Holliman, Arnett and Shaw to report exclusively throughout the night as they chatted away on their telephones and joked nervously amongst themselves as they scrambled around their hotel room on their hands and knees.

As other journalists in the shelter below remonstrated for nearly four hours with armed Iraqi security men who would not allow them to return, CNN had scooped the world – which caused some resentment amongst the other networks. NBC reporter Tom Aspell complained that CNN had been given 'preferential treatment'[9] while others accused the station of bribing Iraqi officials, although such allegations were strongly denied by the network. When CNN in America refused to allow other journalists the use of its four-wire system but offered them the chance to talk to its own people in Baghdad via Atlanta, only NBC took up the offer. Tom Brokaw, NBC's anchorman in New York, duly interviewed Bernard Shaw, while some CBS stations in the United States even decided to drop their own coverage in favour of CNN's.[10] CBS in fact had a disastrous start to the war, with its ratings plummeting after failing to sustain any kind of first night reporting from Baghdad.[11] This may help to explain why its correspondents in Saudi Arabia, such as Bob Simon and Bob McKeown, were subsequently under such pressure to produce a spectacular coup (see below pp. 243–5).

CNN's entry into media folklore began with anchorman David French interviewing Caspar Weinberger when, at 18:36 EST on the 16th, it went over to Bernard Shaw in Baghdad who was heard to say: 'this is, er, something is happening outside ... The skies over Baghdad have been illuminated. We're seeing bright flashes going off all over the sky.' He then handed over to a breathless Peter Arnett:

'Well, there's anti-aircraft gunfire going into the sky. We hear the sound of planes. They're coming over our hotel. However we have not yet heard the sound of bombs landing but there's tremendous lightning in the sky ...'

Shaw: '...this is extraordinary ... we're getting starbursts in the black sky ... We have not heard any jet planes yet. Peter?'

Thus, after an initial contradiction, they were then cut off after just under two minutes as Arnett was saying 'the Iraqis have informed us ...' Extraordinary service from Baghdad was resumed shortly after, at 18:41 EST. The broadcast included various episodic wranglings with Iraqi officials as they left their room and their microphones on, and some of the following most memorable moments were as follows:

(03:00 local time) John Holliman: ' ... It looks like a 4th of July display at the Washington monument. The sky is just brightly lighted with all these tracer rounds – some are red, some are white. We can see explosions, you know air burst explosions from these weapons. Oh, whoah, now there's a huge fire that we've just seen that is due west of our position. And we just heard – whoa! Holy Cow! That was a large air burst that we saw. It was filling the sky ...' [over the sound of anti-aircraft fire]

Peter Arnett: '... And I think, John, that air burst took out the telecommunications tower ... If you're still with us, you can hear the bombs now they're hitting the centre of the city ...'

(03:10) Arnett: 'I think what is most interesting to me, John, is that these bombs seem right on target ... Tonight every bomb which we've seen land seems to have hit something. They hit the refinery directly, they hit a communications tower directly. They have these laser-directed, guided bomb systems now which are certainly proving very effective here tonight ...'

(03:31) Bernard Shaw: '... it was like the fireworks finale on the 4th of July at the base of the Washington monument. Peter, you're chuckling, but that to me is not an exaggeration.'

Arnett: 'I'm chuckling with nervousness, Bernie, not with derision ...'

(03:48) Shaw: 'Gentlemen, does it occur to you that it is not accidental that we are still reporting to the world?'

Holliman: 'It may not be, Bernie. I'm sure the Iraqis could pull the plug on us, I'm sure the Americans could pull the plug on us ...'

(03:54) Holliman: 'It looks like a million fireflies off to the southwest of our location ... as another wave of anti-aircraft fire goes up into the air.'

(04:21) Shaw: 'Just one comment. Clearly I've never been there, but this feels like we're in the centre of hell.'

(04:52) Shaw: 'We've got to run. Somebody's knocking on the door. John and I are going to hide. Peter.'

Arnett: 'This is Peter Arnett signing off for a minute and I'll see what the action is outside.'

Network rivalry and the sheer high drama of the event may have forced all the stations to go over to 24–hour news coverage but with thrilling moments such as these CNN had stolen the march on its older rivals.

Television viewers world-wide, especially the estimated 100 million with access to CNN in 103 countries, were mesmerised by this historic presence of journalists in an enemy capital under fire. The fact that there were three of them, chatting nervously amongst themselves as they described what they saw and felt, enhanced the drama. But as coalition authorities in Saudi Arabia were simultaneously attempting to control the media's freedom to report, here was precisely the kind of presentation from a battle front that the coalition had feared most. And, initially, the voice reports from Baghdad were uncensored, standing out in sharp contrast to the arrangements made for the media in Riyadh.

The coalition may or may not have been able to do anything about global satellite communications from Iraq, but at least the march of technology had also provided it with the facility to hit targets with unprecedented accuracy. Saddam, in attempting to utilise CNN to fuel anti-war sentiment in the West, had miscalculated again. While in Riyadh the next day journalists were quickly subjected to military videos displaying 'smart' weapons hitting their intended *military* targets through the cross-hairs, Saddam's propagandists were unable – or, for intelligence purposes, unwilling – to escort western journalists to damaged *civilian* areas in Baghdad. Or, at least, not at first.

During the initial wave of air and missile attacks, the Chairman of the Joint Chiefs of Staff, Colin Powell, said that one way his officials had been able to gauge the effectiveness of the raids was by listening to CNN reporters 'who were watching it unfold'.[12] The value to coalition intelligence of CNN's highly descriptive accounts of explosions occurring around them probably prompted the Iraqis to pull the network's plug in Baghdad on 17 January. That occasion was once again pure theatre. While talking to its reporters, CNN was simultaneously transmitting live Iraqi television pictures of Saddam praying, which the reporters could not see. Then an air raid warning sounded in the background: silent pictures from Iraqi TV, voices from the Al-Rashid and an interlocutor in Atlanta. Then CNN cut to live pictures of President Bush entering a church at Fort Myer, Virginia, before shifting back to Iraq. It was, as the anchor pointed out, 'surreal'. Two minutes before 19:00 (Iraqi time), CNN viewers then heard the network's reporters wrangling with an Iraqi official, 'Mr Allah', who had come to their room on the ninth floor of the hotel to tell them to cease their audio reports from the city. They were entering their 17th consecutive hour of broadcasting. 'We have unfortunately been ordered to cease transmitting,' said CNN producer Robert Weiner. 'We have been told that we may no longer transmit live to our audience, and that in the future, taped reports will be subject to censorship.' 'So, that's that,' sighed correspondent John Holliman. 'Obviously this is something that is just abhorrent to all of us, and we'll talk to you as soon as we can', said Shaw. 'I hope we can resume our communication with you in the very near future,' added Peter Arnett. On the east coast of the United States it was 11:00 (16:00 GMT). Then the signal went dead, followed by a hum and a buzz. CNN held its map of Baghdad on the screen for a few moments, 'as if it were a memorial to the suspended despatches'.[13]

As the Iraqis reconsidered their policy, their domestic propaganda campaign was stepped up to provide an image of unity behind Saddam, with Iraqi television showing pictures of their leader in overcoat and black beret surrounded by chanting and applauding citizens in a back street. It was difficult to tell when the pictures had been taken. There was certainly no sign of damage in the street – even though in Baghdad the telecommunications tower, the Ba'ath Party headquarters, the security ministry, the presidential palace and various other government buildings, including command and control facilities, had all been targeted with pin-point accuracy. Iraqi authorities forbade filming outside the Al-Rashid the next morning and so audiences were still reliant on mainly voice and print reports.[14]

Baghdad radio, which took several hours to announce war's outbreak, had carried Saddam's first wartime speech to the nation at 04:15 in which he proclaimed that the 'Mother of All Battles between triumphant good and doomed evil' had begun.[15] Subsequent broadcasts that day declared that Iraqi morale was high and that Saddam's own son, Udai, had joined the call-up to military service of all men between 34 and 36. Udai's message to his father, according to one transmission, was that 'we sacrifice ourselves to you, symbol of Iraq and its leader … I am on my way to southern Iraq to join the brave lions and men of Iraq who will sacrifice themselves in defence of their beloved country'.[16] Baghdad radio also claimed that 60 allied aircraft had been shot down in the first strikes (the coalition announced the loss of 3). Marie Colvin of the *Sunday Times* made the interesting observation about that morning, when the damage caused to the city by precision weapons was nothing like as extensive as most Iraqis had anticipated:

People had even begun to listen for the first time to Iraqi radio, and to believe its propaganda, because they felt that the BBC and Voice of America had lied about allied successes against the air force and missile sites in the first attack.[17]

Simultaneously, Iraqi ambassadors stationed abroad began to launch into their own 'positive information campaign', utilising television as an arm of their 'public diplomacy'.

Unusually, the main diplomatic spokesman for the Iraqi line and its most senior diplomat abroad, Dr Abdul Razzak Al-Hashimi, the ambassador to Paris, was at first conciliatory when ABC's Ted Koppel interviewed him.[18] He was soon to fall into line with his colleagues elsewhere. The Iraqi ambassador to Britain, Dr Azmi Shafiq Al-Salihi, vowed that his country would fight 'to the last child, to the last blood of the Iraqi and Muslim martyrs' and charged western television with presenting too one-sided a picture of how the war was going.[19] At the United Nations, the Iraqi ambassador, Amir Al-Anbari, suggested that 'the US has done this inhumane aggression mainly to protect Israel, not to protect Kuwait'.[20] In Belgium, ambassador Ziad Haidar warned in a radio interview: 'The attack on Israel is coming. The decision has been taken.'[21]

By the second day, following the first Scud attacks against Israel, Baghdad radio was reporting that scores of Israeli aircraft had joined the coalition forces in Saudi Arabia, a move which would only 'heighten the determination of the struggling men of the armed forces and Iraq's people to continue *Jihad*'.[22] The propaganda intention was clear. As the world was admiring Israeli restraint over the Scud attacks, the Iraqis were trying to 'prove' that Israel was in fact retaliating. When questioned live on BSkyB News, the Iraqi ambassador to Paris stated: 'Israeli planes today participated in the raids over Iraq using the Saudi bases and the Saudi airports. So, we have evidence, and we will quote this evidence in the future: Israel is part of this war.'

Question: You say you have evidence. We have no evidence of that. What evidence are you talking about?

Answer: Evidence that Israel participated today in the raids over Iraq by Israel planes. This evidence will be released later, but not now because of military reasons.[23]

Needless to say such 'evidence' was not forthcoming. Al-Hashimi, described by one French journalist as 'a man you love to hate', continued his impression of a man divorced from reality (and possibly severed from communicating with Baghdad) in a Jeremy Paxman interview on BBC's Newsnight several days later by saying that Iraq would treat the captured coalition pilots in accordance with the Geneva Convention but only if the allies actually admitted that the men were missing.[24]

CNN was allowed to resume transmissions from Baghdad with censored voice and taped reports later on Friday 17 January. It was to be a virtual monopoly, as the majority of other journalists were told to pack their bags and get ready to leave. Before he was cut off from delivering his telephone report that day, ITN's Brent Sadler described how the Iraqis 'are beginning to impose a form of very strict censorship. They decided our reports were helping allied aircraft pin-point sites in the city ... I expect very soon to have someone breathing down my neck'.[25] Other journalists were told they had to submit their reports to Sadoun Al-Janabi, a Scottish-trained journalist appointed to serve as chief censor by the Iraqi Information Ministry with the title 'head of protocol'. His role was to read all the copy before it was sent out, make the necessary deletions and then monitor the journalists as they dictated their stories 'to make sure that the censored text was filed unaltered'.[26] 'Dealing with him', wrote one print journalist, 'was like handing an essay to a teacher rather than giving a dispatch to the censor'.[27] Another described how methods were quickly developed to circumvent the system: 'among the favoured techniques is putting into reports particularly offensive decoy paragraphs, which will undoubtedly be deleted, in the hope of saving less contentious passages'.[28]

Restrictions on reporting certainly tightened as the Iraqis suspected the media were helping coalition targeting. Reuters photographer Patrick de Noirmont described how he and two European colleagues were beaten up with rifle butts and accused of spying by Iraqi guards as they tried to leave for Jordan. Al-Janabi was both surprised and relieved when they were momentarily returned to the Al-Rashid prior to the mass departure of western journalists.[29] As that exodus continued, one radio reporter travelling with a party from the American ABC television network was recording a description into his tape machine of an air raid by B52 bombers at Rutbah when the group was arrested and accused of guiding the planes to their targets. Although they were quickly released, the incident did reveal Iraqi nervousness about the precise role which foreign journalists were playing – especially with the Barzoft incident barely a year behind them.

Back in Baghdad, when John Simpson of the BBC managed to transmit his voice-only reports via his satellite phone on the first Friday and Saturday, he attempted to evade the scrutiny of the Iraqi minders. On one occasion he spoke live to the BBC's David Dimbleby back in London as follows:

There's a security policeman standing about 10 yards away from me and I'm just fiddling with the buttons pretending I'm trying to make it work ... We get no information whatever. The people who deal with us are without any instruction themselves – the only information is what we can get from talking to people and straying out when we can.[30]

Herein lies the real reason for the enforced exodus. The war had imposed enormous strains on the highly bureaucratic Iraqi state. It was likely that the normal order of command had broken down below the level of Saddam because the bureaucracy was so tightly geared to a one-man dictatorship. Pending further instructions from Saddam himself, no one knew quite what policy to adopt, least of all in the Ministry of Information. Richard Beeston of *The Times* said after the war:

For those of us who remained in the Iraqi capital after the war began, the first two days were the least restricted because the authorities appeared to have been taken by surprise. Most government institutions, including the Ministry of Information which handles the foreign media, broke down temporarily and western reporters were able to travel unsupervised around Baghdad and file their copy uncensored.[31]

This was not to be the last time that the Iraqis were caught by surprise and raises all sorts of question marks about their ability to evaluate information in the public domain let alone their own intelligence reports.

Within a day or two, however, some order was brought to the chaos. But CNN's problems in justifying its continued presence in Baghdad were just beginning, especially when, on 19 January, the last 38 foreign reporters, including Bernard Shaw, John Holliman and Gary Shephard, made the 350-mile journey to the Jordanian border. 'It's not worth dying for a story you can't really cover,' one American newsman was reported as saying.[32] The official reason for the expulsion was a lack of water, electricity and sanitary facilities, but Arnett said the Iraqis were dismantling the satellite communications used by the media. Bob Simpson of BBC radio was also with the convoy: 'When I suggested it might be because of what we'd been broadcasting, this was very strongly denied.' However, a Palestinian journalist working for the *Financial Times* confirmed that the Iraqis 'grew worried about reports that gave details of the damage to bombed targets, saying that if word got out the bombers would come back again',[33] while George Watson, ABC's Washington Bureau chief, was convinced that Iraq had pulled the video plug because 'the losses being inflicted on their installations and forces make it less appealing to have reporting of any sort coming out'.[34] At least by keeping CNN on the air, the Iraqis had a direct line to Israel in the hope that the same sort of intelligence they feared would benefit the coalition's military planners could assist the targeting skills of their own Scud missile commanders. That at least was the case with the first Scud attacks on Israel on Friday 18 January as CNN's Tel Aviv bureau carried the story of an incoming missile live as the weapon exploded.

This was precisely why the Israelis had to impose a strict censorship of their own.[35] By the end of January, following the first Israeli casualties caused by Scud attacks, censorship was tightened even further, with the government revoking the press card of *Newsweek*'s bureau head Theodore Stanger for violating local censorship restrictions, while the Israelis also monitored the use of domestic telephones by foreign correspondents.[36] However, the fact remains that the Iraqis failed to appreciate the degree to which modern weapons could actually hit their intended targets, especially when compared with their erratic Scuds. At first, therefore, because they were unable to escort the allied journalists to bombed sites strewn with the mutilated corpses of 'innocent women and children', the journalists could serve only coalition interests. In one early censored report from Baghdad, Arnett described the allied bombing raids as 'remarkable. I can't go into detail about what targets are being hit, but there don't seem to be any civilian casualties. Buildings are being taken out in populated areas without damaging adjoining structures'.[37] Another journalist who surfaced from the shelter at the Al-Rashid after the first night of bombing was also startled not to see any devastating after-effects when she returned to her hotel room the next morning: 'it was a strange sensation to see no damage after the storm the night before. After much difficulty finding a driver, I took a car to go "target hunting" ... .'[38]

It proved a comparatively fruitless exercise. Nigel Baker, ITN's news editor, who was with the convoy of departing journalists and who smuggled out Brent Sadler's first taped report, also found little or no evidence of anything other than precision hits.[39] Even a British member of the Gulf Peace Team, which was asked to leave the region at the end of January, commented when she was taken first to Baghdad that the Iraqis had to 'hunt about a bit' to find appropriate sites: 'It didn't look like Portsmouth when I lived there in the Second World War.'[40]

From Riyadh, meanwhile, the Iraqi government was able to

witness on CNN the enthralling military videos showing bombing of unprecedented accuracy of what were clearly military or strategic targets. And because they *were* military sites the Iraqis could hardly escort allied journalists to them for fear of providing their enemies with more invaluable intelligence about how much damage, including 'collateral damage', had actually been caused because it might possibly invite further air strikes. Having been denied their propaganda opportunities by the coalition's high-technology weapons, the Iraqis thus realised their mistake and, with the exception of CNN's Peter Arnett, a Jordanian cameraman working for WTN and an NHK crew from Japan, all the television journalists had left for Jordan by the end of the first weekend. Some print journalists, mainly Arab, stayed behind to see a cruise missile shot down on the third day, with part of it falling on the Al-Rashid's servants' quarters. Although no one was hurt, fragments were gathered as souvenirs.[41] A leader in *The Times* commented:

Information is a liquid that can seep out through the tightest censorship. The Iraqis have evicted virtually all foreign news media. They have unwisely failed to realise the impact that uncensored newsreel of bombed civilians can have on non-combatant publics abroad. Censorship is no substitute for this. Iraq's public relations is now at the mercy of the rumour factories.[42]

For just over a week, most journalists had to observe events from neighbouring Jordan, while the Iraqis tried to conduct a propaganda campaign of sorts by transmitting unverifiable pictures on domestic television services which could be picked up in Amman. But the Iraqis had miscalculated again, this time concerning western journalistic criteria. Standard media scepticism raised all sorts of doubts about these pictures, for example whether the damage had been sustained during the Iran–Iraq war. The blue skies over Baghdad evident from much of the footage certainly alerted the observant at a time when Iraq was suffering its worst seasonal weather for 14 years.

Other than Peter Arnett, there was only one other western journalist left in Baghdad: Alfonso Rojo of Spain's *El Mundo* who also filed reports for the *Guardian*. There appears to have been considerable tension between the two men. Peter Arnett had maintained on air on 20 January when reporting the departure of other journalists that 'CNN has been invited to remain to cover the developing story, leaving the three CNN man team the only western journalists still in the country'.[43] But Rojo was also there and when he tried to use CNN's phone link Arnett refused, causing a row. Arnett said after the war: 'if he had been in any way reasonable, I probably would have accommodated him. But you know, if you're dying to use someone else's communications, you had better be nice about it.'[44]

As for his own working conditions, Arnett elaborated on these at length on 23 January when he transmitted a voice report at 18:20 (local time). He described how his satellite phone was powered by a portable generator at the Al-Rashid, that it could be assembled in minutes, whereupon his minder sat with him as he read out his pre-censored dispatch and answered any questions from Atlanta. CNN's lap-top computers were no longer working since their batteries had expired and he would occasionally get to use a typewriter. When he was not transmitting, he spent most of his time lobbying for information and learning how to wash and shave on one bottle of water a day. Every morning a taxi left for Jordan carrying videotape: 'There is no censorship, so far, of any of the videotape we are sending.' He also said that the only information which he was told to leave out was about military or strategic matters. 'Of course we're under a controlled environment; we're nowhere near the front ... But conditions here are probably more relaxed, say, than when I was in Hanoi in 1972 or in some other locales where there has been pretty strict supervision. I think the fact that I can sit here and talk with you for 10–15 minutes means that ... they probably feel I haven't had access to the kind of information which could be detrimental to them'. He said he could leave at any time if he wanted to, but he had not done so because 'I have been in much more dangerous situations in my career ... I haven't left because the story is quite do-able ... This is an air war that is targeting strategic installations. I am not sitting in a strategic installation. I am with officials who are interested in getting their point of view across, who believe that they have a point of view that the world should hear about ... I don't see any reason in the world, Bob, to leave here ... I guess I'm doing what war correspondents have done certainly for a century that I know of.'

Parading the captured pilots

Peter Arnett also suggested on another occasion that CNN had been allowed to remain in Baghdad because the Iraqis deemed its reporting to be 'impartial and balanced'.[45] He might as well have stated that the Iraqis regarded CNN as an ideal world-wide conduit for their propaganda. The fine line which CNN had to walk between providing straight reports of what was actually happening behind enemy lines and projecting Iraqi propaganda was rarely drawn more clearly than during the episode in which captured coalition pilots were paraded by Iraqi television on Sunday 20 January.

The Iraqis were presumably attempting to play a Vietnam card by evoking memories of an era in which Hanoi regularly released film of American airmen confessing to their 'crimes' and denouncing a criminal war and their own reluctant participation in it. Iraqi television showed the pictures on the evening of Sunday the 20th and CNN transmitted them to the world the next day. ABC, however, issued the following statement after deciding not to air the first pictures:

It is our assumption based on evidence during the Vietnam war and in various hostage situations, that statements by, and interviews involving hostages or prisoners of war are often made under duress. ABC News will be careful not to do anything that either endangers the well-being of Americans in captivity or furthers the aims of those holding them.

Altogether, in the days that followed, footage of 13 captured pilots – 8 Americans, 2 Britons, 2 Italians and 1 Kuwaiti – was released showing them delivering what appeared to be carefully prepared answers to predetermined questions and anti-coalition statements. Many of them looked to have been brutalised.

This behaviour certainly seemed to stand out in sharp contrast to the first published photograph of Iraqi PoWs captured following an attack on an off-shore oil rig over the first weekend: a dozen or so Iraqis sitting with their backs to the camera. The American guards supervising the captives informed Reuters photographer Charles Platiau that they were not 'exhibits in a zoo'.[46] As P. T. Benic, another photographer with Reuters, said after the war:

The film ... was red-flagged at site, meaning the Dhahran JIB officials had to review the negatives. They were unclear on the Geneva convention rules so they asked for help from the Defense Department in Washington. The ruling came quickly: PoW pictures shot by military personnel showing the faces or the soldiers in bad light were not allowed. The key was military personnel. Platiau worked for Reuters; the picture moved. Total delay was an hour.[47]

This careful distinction might help to explain why so many surrendering Iraqis were shown later in the war as the ground offensive began; because most of that footage and film was taken by pool reporters it was left up to the media themselves to decide whether or not they were violating the terms of the appropriate Geneva Convention.

According to one reporter, public anger in Baghdad at the initial bombing prompted threats from ordinary people 'to grab pilots who are shot down and chop them into pieces'. The same journalist also 'heard of one pilot being stoned before he was taken away by guards'.[48] Not even the Iraqi government could afford such a possibility and when an official appeal to keep the pilots alive seemed to have little impact, a reward of 30,000 Iraqi dinar (£15,000) was offered for any pilot handed over alive to the authorities. When the Iraqi government also announced that the 20 pilots in its possession would also be used as human shields at 'scientific and economic targets as well as among other selected targets', it said it was doing this because the allies had been targeting Iraqi civilians.[49] This did not quite make sense. If the allies had been bombing civilians, it would surely have been the Iraqi ploy to place the pilots in residential areas. That, after all, is where the Iraqis maintained the allies were bombing and where, the coalition suggested, many of the Iraqi high command, including Saddam himself, were subsequently reported to be sheltering. And when a coalition pilot was reported on Baghdad radio to have been killed in an air raid on 29 January, it was said to have been the result of a bomb hitting a government building.[50]

Nonetheless, the pictures did produce a mixture of both depression and anger in countries from which the pilots had come. Many blamed the messenger, CNN, for carrying the pictures, although Walter Cronkite stated that: 'if we are capable of voting our boys into combat ... round the world, then we have the responsibility to share their experiences in combat'.[51] President Bush, on the other hand, captured the popular mood when he declared that 'America is angry about this' and described how:

I watched, along with all of you, that repulsive parade of American airmen on Iraqi television: one more proof of the savagery of Saddam. But I knew, as they read their prepared statements criticising this country, that they were false words, forced on them by their captors.

Similarly, in Europe, the mood was one of disgust, with Mr Major describing Saddam as 'a man without pity'. When ambassador Al-Hashimi was interviewed live from Paris on BSkyB News, after explaining that the pilots were 'well looked after and very well treated, that's for sure', the exchange went as follows:

Interviewer: That is clearly not the picture that we saw, Mr Al-Hashimi. They looked bruised and battered. They looked dazed. They said their statement mechanically.

Answer: Well, if you can really tell how a pilot fell off a plane, his plane was shot down, and ejecting from that plane, the plane [had] either fire in it or flying maybe in the speed of sound, you expect that pilot's going to fall on the ground without a scratch, or without being injured or without being affected?

Question: In that case, why are they on Iraqi television and not in hospital?

Answer: Well, er, do you have any evidence that they were not taken to a hospital afterwards? They were taken to a hospital to be treated, that's for sure.[52]

Although it was a slithery performance that did the Iraqi case no good at all, it did emerge after the war that, although the pilots had been beaten and badly treated, some of their injuries were in fact sustained during ejection. One of the American pilots had even smashed his own nose in an attempt to avoid being paraded.[53] And although all of the pilots experienced inhumane treatment – one was apparently just saved from summary execution by an Iraqi officer while another had his head shaved, was blindfolded and regularly threatened with execution – and some were systematically tortured, it was the appearance of brutalisation combined with the very fact that the Iraqis would resort to such tactics on television which caused the fury aroused in Bush, Schwarzkopf and other coalition leaders. Moreover, rarely for the Gulf War, television's ability to signify if not quite the whole truth but as near as possible to it earned considerable credence by post-war revelations.

In Britain, especially because the RAF was beginning to suffer more than its fair share of downed planes owing to the dangerous low-flying raids of its Tornado aircraft, the tabloids screamed at the 'Bastard of Baghdad'.[54] After the early euphoria, the mood had now turned gloomy. 'It's a bit like a roller coaster,' commented one Whitehall official to the press. 'At first everyone was over euphoric and we tried to dampen you down. Now you've gone too far the other way.'[55] When the Iraqi ambassador to London was summoned to the Foreign Office, which protested that the Geneva Convention had been violated because it was forbidden to display PoWs for 'public curiosity', he defended himself by pointing to television film showing a US Marine with some of the first Iraqi PoWs. The Foreign Office replied: 'The British Government has not made a deliberate attempt to parade prisoners of war. The Iraqi government has done. There is a clear difference.'[56] Nonetheless, it was a nice point and one which, interestingly, was later avoided by French television coverage of Iraqi PoWs crossing the lines to surrender which employed graphics to cover their faces.

After the war, General Schwarzkopf admitted that he had been angered when he had first seen the pictures on CNN in his Riyadh headquarters but that 'I also knew at that time that they [the Iraqis] were paying a terrible price':

It was a combination of anger at them for doing that because it was such a blatant violation of the Geneva Convention and at the same time compassion for not only the pilots but their families because you just didn't know what the pilots were going to have to go through and there was great concern for them too ... And I didn't like the idea that I was seeing them on CNN. I will have to state that openly. I did resent, you know, CNN aiding and abetting an enemy who was violating the Geneva Convention by putting, you know, that's a a clear violation of the Geneva Convention. Yet CNN was broadcasting them to the world; that bothers me.[57]

If Saddam had been attempting to exploit the Vietnam Syndrome to create public disaffection with the war effort, the apparently brutalised nature of the pilots merely caused fury and resentment and prompted calls for Saddam's treatment as a war criminal once the conflict was over. Asked on his return from Camp David if Saddam would be held accountable, Bush snapped: 'You can count on it.'[58]

CNN was certainly beginning to attract more and more criticism, especially with charges that the showing of the PoW 'interviews' was itself a violation of that section of the Geneva Convention which forbade the undignified exposure of captured troops. The retransmitting of Iraqi television pictures around the world was once again revealing how modern communications technology had stolen the march on the established rules of warfare. One *Daily Telegraph* journalist in Dhahran, Robert Fox, wrote:

The sad fact that no amount of notices of 'passed by the censor' labels can conceal is that the service is now to be a conduit of the propaganda of Saddam's men, for they have the final say now about what comes over the ether from Baghdad. Such is the confusion of emotion and intention in the race to be first at all costs that rumour and propaganda can easily slip into the garb of information.[59]

CNN of course denied this, but the PoW issue had so angered western political and popular opinion that the station found mounting criticism was replacing the early praise for its first days of reporting.

Meanwhile, Radio Baghdad continued to pour out its stream of invective and propaganda against the allies. Throughout the war, two or three times a day at unpredictable times, it carried what it described as 'military communiqués' (*'bian aaskarri'*) which in fact contained the official propaganda themes to be pursued. Many broadcasts were designed specifically for Arab audiences in the region, although western agencies were monitoring it for intelligence purposes. Despite the obviously propagandistic broadcasts, Baghdad radio also served as an invaluable source of information to the coalition for ascertaining Saddam's intentions. The Iraqi leader frequently used the medium for telegraphing his aims, which he would then attempt to follow through by actions to increase his stature amongst Arab listeners. By doing what he said he would do on the radio, it was felt he could assume almost heroic qualities. For example, on 11 January, six days before the war began, Saddam told Islamic fundamentalists that his strategy was to keep his forces entrenched in a defensive posture until the allied bombardment was over and 'when the enemy tanks and ground forces advance, the boys will come out and fight'. He had also warned numerous times that, if war should come, he would launch Scud missiles against Israel, and that he would blow up Kuwaiti oil fields. 'Even now', one military analyst was quoted as saying on 29 January, 'Saddam hasn't done anything he hasn't told us he was going to do days, weeks or months ago.'[60]

Radio, with its far higher degree of social penetration in the Middle East than television and with a longer broadcasting tradition, was a particularly effective form of penetrating other Arab regimes which might more readily censor unpalatable television pictures in accordance with their own political, religious and cultural traditions. Despite the initial allied attacks which knocked out Iraq's telecommunications tower, Baghdad radio was able at first to continue transmitting on a dozen short wave radio frequencies from unknown or well-protected locations. The two principal domestic services, the Voice of the Masses and the Radio of the Iraqi Republic, had been amalgamated on 17 January and some reports suggested that both the radio and television stations had been moved to new buildings outside Baghdad. The signals were much weaker but the service was able to continue transmitting descriptions of civilian damage, news of western anti-war demonstrations, invective against the United States and its allies and paeans of praise for Saddam Hussein. During, and sometimes for a short period after, allied air raids, the station went silent altogether. Allied policy was originally to allow Baghdad radio to keep functioning as a source of intelligence 'and partly in order to allow an open channel for an Iraqi surrender'.[61]

Iraqi television was also able to continue regular broadcasting for a week or so after the war began, although its international range was significantly reduced owing to its inability to utilise the ARABSAT satellite which was run by a consortium of Arab countries but was controlled from Riyadh. For the most part, therefore, Iraqi television was limited to reception inside Iraq's borders, with some spillage of the signals into neighbouring countries such as Iran and Jordan. Yet Iraqi radio propaganda remained a problem. By 11 February, Pete Williams at the Pentagon revealed that a change of policy had occurred and announced that henceforth all transmitters would be targets:

It's not part of our operational theory that we should leave their radio stations on the air ... We have done a lot to take their radio off the air ... there are some low power radio and television stations around the country that come on and off the air. We try to get those as we can.[62]

One can only presume that the dangers of Iraqi radio and television propaganda were beginning to outweigh their value as intelligence sources. This meant that the Iraqis had to rely heavily upon CNN to carry their pictures for them to the wider world. Until 30 January, this was done by CNN sending videotape taken by its crew or from Baghdad TV overland by hired taxis in a hazardous 10–hour journey to Jordan and then on to Atlanta by satellite. This was, for example, how the first footage of the opening night's raids and of CNN's PoW pictures reached the outside world. One other option was for the television news agency Visnews (owned by Reuters, the BBC and various Commonwealth broadcasting authorities) to pick up the weaker signals in Iran and then transmit them to its subscribers, although the picture quality of that material was poor and often deemed unusable from a technical point of view, or for WTN (owned by ITN and ABC), another picture news agency which employed a Jordanian correspondent in Baghdad, to get its footage overland to Amman.[63]

When the Iraqis stopped parading the PoWs on 25 January they said that it was because the number of 'interviews' screened so far was 'considered sufficient' to make their point.[64] There is however some evidence to suggest this entire episode, together with the transmission of collateral damage on Iraqi TV, prompted the coalition to make a primary target of Iraq's television transmitters. On 25 January, Major-General Robert Johnston, chief of staff for Central Command, said at a Riyadh briefing that 'we are able to shut down his radio and television capability for internal communications, and I'm not guaranteeing we can shut it down all the time but I guess you probably haven't seen TV Baghdad for a while'.[65] Baghdad radio also announced that day that another British pilot had been captured – which may have been the pilot of the sixth Tornado announced to have been lost by the coalition earlier – although the real purpose of the broadcast was to launch into a tirade against the British Prime Minister who was described as 'an ally of the devils': 'did Mr Major believe he had sent his forces on a pleasure trip to the Arabian Gulf or that they would be conducting aerial acrobatics?'[66] The Iraqis held the British in particular contempt for their past imperial record in the region and for determining the destiny of Iraq until 1958. Britain, according to some Iraqi propaganda, was also portrayed as the post-colonial puppet-master of the USA. Later in the war Baghdad radio was to have another go at the British in similar tones:

May God fight malice when it becomes utter, comprehensive stupidity, such as the stupidity prevailing today in Britain and its statesmen, machines and minds. It is the stupidity of base criminals who have inherited baseness one generation after another and have been pursuing aggression against peoples to plunder their wealth. We tell the stupid statesmen of Britain: You know the Iraqis better than your accomplices, the Americans, do. You are aware that the Iraqis are known for their iron will and their clinging to their freedom and independence. Perhaps you remember that they never remain silent when they are done injustice, and that they never let criminal aggressor get away with his deed.[67]

Although the Iraqis stated that they might resume parading PoWs, in fact Iraqi television itself was no longer able to transmit after the end of January, which presumably indicated that the coalition air forces had at last succeeded in identifying the location of its transmitters. It was left subsequently to Baghdad radio to sustain the threats and invective against the pilots, calling them war criminals: 'in other words they should be dealt with on the basis of their being killers of defenceless women, children and old people, not as soldiers waging a war against other soldiers'.[68] This was much the same line adopted by the Germans, in both world wars, against Anglo-American 'terror bombers'.

Baghdad radio continued to play on two particular aspects of the allied air offensive, namely the amount of civilian damage sustained and the number of coalition aircraft shot down. For the first week, broadly speaking, the figures were always low for the former and high for the latter. At the start of the war, Iraqi military communiqués reported far fewer allied air raids than the coalition was admitting it had undertaken and claimed far more aircraft had been shot down than the coalition conceded, sometimes ten times more. The reliability of Iraqi claims again became an issue on Saturday 2 February when the Iraqis reported that no allied planes had been shot down, whereas the coalition admitted to having lost two.[69] This, wrote one observer, 'tended to support the belief that the aberrations of Iraq's official war reporting stem, at least in part, from disrupted communications rather than – or perhaps as well as – fluctuating policies on what to tell people'.[70]

The 'baby milk plant' episode

Chemical weapons received a very high propaganda profile

throughout the war.[71] Though never used, Iraq made constant threats and Saddam, of course, had already demonstrated his willingness to employ this particular weapon of mass destruction against the Kurds and in the Iran–Iraq war. Whether or not Iraq possessed the capability actually to deliver such weapons in warheads mounted on its Al-Hussein missiles, it was vital for the coalition to destroy the source of manufacture as well as stores and delivery capabilities. For this reason, early priority in the air war was given to finding the Scud launching sites and to attacking the NBC (Nuclear, Biological and Chemical) plants Iraq was known to possess.

On 22 January, reports began to filter through that Czech chemical protection units forming part of the coalition had detected toxic agents in the air along the Saudi–Kuwaiti border, which was assumed to be the result of attacking chemical factories or stockpiles, or both.[72] Basra was thought to be a particulary high activity centre in this respect. On the following day, the Iranians reported that explosions had been heard across the border 'so powerful that buildings in the Iranian port of Khorramshahr, 25 miles south east of Basra, were severely jolted'.[73] This was followed by Iranian reports that 'black rain' was beginning to fall in that country. Given the emphasis placed by the coalition pre-war on Iraq's chemical and nuclear capacity, the one provable, the other possible, it was essential for the coalition on the one hand to play up its success in destroying Iraq's NBC capability while playing down the environmental consequences of that action. At a military awards ceremony on 23 January, President Bush declared that 'our pinpoint attacks have put Saddam out of the nuclear bomb building business for a long time to come'.[74] But given the number of real unknowns in the Iraqi nuclear argument and the coalition's own self-professed difficulties in assessing BDA, it was far better to concentrate on the provable chemical issue.

The most celebrated media incident of this phase of the war was the alleged attack on a 'baby milk plant' which CNN's Peter Arnett announced on 23 January. Arnett described how the previous day he had been taken to what his Iraqi escorts described as an 'infant formula factory' in the region of Abu Ghurayb on the main highway to Jordan, the only such source of manufacture in Iraq for babies under the age of 1 year, which had allegedly been attacked on the 20th when Iraqi television had first carried the news with pictures. The reporter described how the machinery inside was a 'molten pile' and pointed to the sign which read 'Baby Milk Plant' in English and Arabic. His broadcast was prematurely cut off, although he was able to speak more a little later. It was the first time Arnett had been able to report on damage to allegedly civilian installations that he had seen. As his report was repeated over the next few hours as America woke up to the news, among the viewers was President Bush himself.

CNN's honeymoon with Washington was over, with the White House stating that Iraq was using the station to serve as a conduit for propaganda 'that hurts our government'.[75] Within hours of Arnett's first report at 11:38 (local time), the coalition's information officials launched into their counter-offensive, with Lieutenant-Colonel Mike Gallagher actually interrupting their routine briefing that day with a statement that the facility had military guards around it, a barbed wire fence and a military garrison outside. The factory, his intelligence sources stated, had in fact been 'associated with biological warfare production', utilising the growing theme that the Iraqis frequently doubled up on the military and civilian uses of their sites.[76] When CNN subsequently went back to Arnett to comment on this, he replied that 'it looked innocent enough from what we could see'.[77] At the Pentagon later, Marlin Fitzwater stated that the Iraqis had hidden the true purpose of the installation 'as a form of disinformation', adding: 'they have fake buildings, they have fake weapons, fake production plants ... It's a well known tactic and they have used it throughout the country.' General Powell added: 'it is not an infant formula factory, no more than the Ratba chemical plant in Libya made aspirin. It was a biological weapons facility, of that we are sure – and we have taken it out.'[78] He wondered how it could be interpreted otherwise in view of the high military fence, the guard posts on all four corners of the installation, its camouflage paint and it being a heavily guarded facility. Several days later, General Schwarzkopf himself pointed out that the Iraqis had begun moving their aircraft into residential areas because they knew the allies were not targeting those sites. He also added another point:

We knew, in fact, that this particular facility we attacked was in fact what it was. We also used precision munitions on it to make sure that we destroyed that part of it ... So I reject the argument that it was only a baby formula plant, but I would also clearly state that when we went after that facility, we went after it in a precision way, damaged only that part of the facility that we knew or had a very high assurance as given to us by the intelligence community, that it was in fact a research facility for biological warfare.[79]

Fitzwater also took the opportunity to remind journalists that all CNN reports coming out of Baghdad were subject to Iraqi censorship and control and 'are in effect coming from the Iraqi government'.[80]

Peter Arnett responded later by stating that, when he had arrived at the site, workers were indeed bringing out 'a cart full of powdered milk from Britain' for display to his crew. But a great question mark remained, especially when different journalists who returned to the country at the end of January reported conflicting opinions, as when Reuters correspondent Bernd Debusmann claimed to have found evidence that 'appeared to indicate the plant was everything the Iraqis said it was'.[81] The French contractor who built the factory in the late 1970s subsequently stated that it was a purpose-built infant formula plant and could not have been converted to make chemical products.[82] New Zealand technicians who had visited the plant as recently as May 1990 said they had actually seen it 'canning milk powder'.[83] Other correspondents pointed to the freshly painted sign in English, the barbed wire fence and the obviously carefully arranged milk urns. File footage showed products bearing the name 'Guigoz', an affiliate of the Swiss chocolate company Nestlé which, when consulted by New York's *Village Voice*, quoted a spokesperson as saying: 'we know that this was a state-built infant-formula plant'.[84]

It was the story that would not go away. Clearly the coalition had been targeting Iraq's chemical capability. On 30 January, General Schwarzkopf revealed that 31 of Iraq's NBC plants had been bombed, including 10 specific biological facilities.[85] Further reports of toxins detected in the air as a result of bombing continued to cause some concern. From Riyadh, General Robert Johnston was quick to allay resultant fears:

I would say to that report that we have, in attacking those targets, attacked them in such a way – and I can't give you all the technical aspects of it – to minimize the potential for that, for any of those toxins to go into the air. It's not to say that it couldn't happen, but certainly with a view to minimizing, if not eliminating any possible contamination of the surrounding areas. It's been done very carefully. I can't say that some may not be in the air and the immediate surroundings, but I suspect there would be no serious damage to any community.[86]

Despite this admission, however, Washington remained adamant that the baby milk plant was connected with germ warfare and had been converted for this purpose the previous autumn – after the New Zealand technicians had last seen it. Even CNN's file footage of the factory, showing bottles of milk being filled, was flagged September 1990.

On 8 February, Iraq asked the United Nations to send a fact-finding mission to determine the truth – the first and only request made by Iraq to the UN to investigate collateral damage since the start of the war.[87] By then, official coalition statements had contradicted each other, with one White House official stating that the plant had been converted to germ warfare purposes as recently as the previous autumn while another intelligence community official stated that it had originally been built as a biological weapons facility, while still another said it could produce items useful in the production of biological weapons. Clearly, the US was attempting to conceal its intelligence-gathering methods but, in doing so, it had undoubtedly got itself into a muddle. The New Zealand technicians had pointed out that a 'nearby' garrison was in fact 4 kilometres away, but that there was a pharmaceutical plant in the same complex a little further back from the highway, the implication being that this was the more likely target of the bombing raid.[88] In addition, there may have been the possibility that the allies were targeting the Abu Ghurayb 'Presidential Grounds' listed on their targeting documents. As for the UN fact-finding team which finally went in after the war: 'its reports in response to the requirements of the cease-fire stated that no biological capabilities existed'.[89]

Indeed, the sum total of the evidence would appear to point either to an intelligence mistake in misidentifying the plant or to a targeting mistake in hitting the wrong building. After the war General McPeak would only say that 'time will tell what kind of factory that factory was. There is no doubt that we made some mistakes about what we bombed',[90] although a former Director of the Defense Intelligence Agency, Lieutenant-General Leonard Perrots, was prepared to go further when pointing out that the giant milk vats had been mistaken for devices for mixing chemical and biological compounds. 'We made a mistake,' he said.[91] Journalists who visited the factory at the end of war 'took a package from the site and mixed it with their coffee [and] said it seemed like the real article'.[92] But perhaps the most telling piece of evidence was circumstantial. Given the proven reluctance of the Iraqis to escort journalists to military installations damaged by the bombing, both before and after this incident, why break from this practice now?

The common denominator to all interpretations to date is indeed the word 'mistake' and, if the Americans had been a little less sensitive to such errors and a little more open about their frequency, public opinion would probably have been able to accommodate them without altering substantially its views of the rights and wrongs of the war and to be less suspicious of coalition propaganda as a result. Right to the end, however, General Powell was sticking to the official line:

Even after it was destroyed, some of the so-called baby powder that was around could not have been made there. We saw the packages and read the labels. It was made by a company that was not, to the best of our knowledge, doing business in Iraq. There was a body of evidence to suggest we knew what we were doing.[93]

The incident did at least reveal that the air war was being extended to areas of Iraq's infrastructure. What remained confusing, despite the impression given by the parading of captured pilots, was why the Iraqi air force was offering so little resistance. Was it because Saddam was holding it back for use in the future, as Iraqi propaganda maintained? Following the Interfax report that senior air commanders had been executed, there followed stories that dozens of Iraqi planes were landing in Iran from Monday 28 January onwards. Were they fleeing to search for safe haven or had a deal been made with Iraq's former enemy? Coalition spokesmen were baffled: 'all we know is that they are clearly out of the conflict,' said one official in London. An Arab spokesman was quoted as saying that 'if Saddam somehow hoped to influence the domestic political rivalries in Tehran, with some idea that the planes' arrival would bolster hardline Muslim groups, it is another miscalculation'.[94] It was certainly so from a propaganda point of view as it gave the impression that Iraq's air force was running away. Baghdad radio did not deny the incident; its listeners were too close to any Iranian broadcast version of the events. But it did say that the planes had been 'obliged' to land in Iran and that 'contacts are under way regarding the return of the aircraft and the pilots to their homeland'.[95] Just to make sure that Iraqis were exposed to an alternative interpretation, leaflets were prepared by coalition propagandists suggesting that Iraqi planes had deserted their ground troops, leaving them even more vulnerable to sustained bombing.[96] And, as we shall see in the next chapter, allied 'black' propaganda reinforced this impression still further.

What exactly the Iranians would do with the planes specifically and with the war generally, especially once the allies began bombing the Shia areas in southern Iraq, remained a worrying point for the coalition. Despite the fact that almost 200 Iraqi aircraft eventually sought refuge in Iran and were not to be returned, it was the measure of uncertainty about Iranian intentions and the possible re-entry of the planes into the war which caused some concern. It was not that the allies could not have dealt with them – their sheer aerial superiority would have ensured that – although further casualties and captured pilots would have been inevitable. It was a more a question of Iran's political position vis-à-vis its neighbour and worries that it was playing a double game. Rumours of a secret deal and reports that thousands of Republican Guards were camped near the border dressed in Iranian Revolutionary Guard (Pasdaran) uniforms and that considerable smuggling of food and medicine was taking place over the border may just have been Iraqi propaganda attempts to play a possible Iranian card and thus force the coalition to think again about its attacks on that region, but any such efforts to salvage something from what was clearly a blow to Iraq's air defence system were worth trying, and the line adopted for domestic consumption was that clever Saddam was once again lulling the Americans into a false sense of security whereupon he would unleash another of his surprises. When one western journalist asked his minder why the Iraqi air force was not retaliating, back came the reply: 'The Americans want that, but ours are waiting. President Saddam knows what he is doing.'[97]

Some observers indeed believed that Iraqi propaganda was gradually improving. Having realised the counter-productive impact of the PoW episode, the decision had been made (or was made for them) to stop broadcasting further similar footage. The question of civilian damage was creeping up their propaganda agenda and more and more footage of alleged damage was seeping out. The baby milk plant episode had caused some concern in the West and pro-Iraqi sentiment appeared to be increasing in Muslim countries. On Saturday 26 January, footage of a distressed Roman Catholic congregation praying in the ruins of their Iraqi church was transmitted in Britain which, according to a *Daily Telegraph* leader appealing for more concerted allied propaganda, 'was calculated to touch Western public opinion in a way that, say, film of a bombed mosque could not'.[98] Yet the fact remained, as the same leader pointed out, that 'in war, every item of news has propaganda value'. Because the coalition media managers were getting themselves into trouble over damage assessment at a time when the war was entering a phase of attrition that journalists found less exciting than the initial air strikes, Saddam was thus provided with an opportunity to exploit the lull in the western media's view of the war to score what successes he could. When Iraqi propaganda succeeded, in other words, it was due largely to coalition mistakes.

It did, however, frequently backfire as when, on Monday 28 January, the Iraqi news agency reported that a captured airman being used as a human shield had been injured and another had been killed 'as a result of the enemy air raids on populated areas and civilian targets'.[99] In Nicosia, Baghdad radio was monitored as stating:

We declare to the world public that the United States bears the results of these ugly crimes committed against our citizens and the prisoner pilots whom Iraq is hosting. Let the voices of the peace advocates, good people, and the families of the prisoners rise up to denounce Bush's crimes.[100]

As we shall see in Chapter 4, if the pilots had been located in such targets, they were less likely – according to coalition statements – to have been in danger. And, as we shall see below, Saddam himself was to give an interview to Peter Arnett that very same day in a civilian bungalow.

'They murder children'

Nonetheless, the most fertile area for Iraqi propagandists to exploit remained the issue of real 'collateral damage' as the allies extended their bombing raids to destroying Iraq's infrastructure. Iraqi propaganda directed particularly at Arab audiences in the

Middle East was busily exploiting emotive pictures of 'innocent civilians' killed and injured in the air raids. One Iraqi TV programme, 'They Murder Children', depicted graphic images of dead and injured young people and, to get an idea of the full flavour of such propaganda, it is worth quoting from the commentary *in extenso*:

Cursed are the filthy hands of the killers. Cursed are the hateful hands of the savages who endeavour to murder the tender childhood, who stop the smiles of the children, those beloveds of God ... History would record with letters full of pain and patience that a horrible crime is being carried out against the innocent Iraqi children. History would record that shame will befall all the assassins for committing such an ugly crime and will befall all those who brag falsely about human rights. But God the Almighty has exposed them and they prove themselves to be enemies first of human rights, enemies of humanity and to be first grade assassins. The barbarians of the late 20th century who failed in tackling a decent confrontation against justice, dignity and righteousness have turned their shameful mean acts against children. The children of Iraq are the dear treasure of the nation. They are the future. They are the symbol of innocence and free life, full of dignity and honour. All free people of the world must witness these acts and memorise these scenes which expose the barbarity and ugly face of the alleged civilisation of the United States, of Zionism and of their allies. The free world must know that the innocent Iraqi children, with their wide hearts and unfulfilled dreams, have withstood the rockets of hatred and the war planes of arrogance and of aggression. The free and honest world must know the false allegations of the Americans and their untrue allegations of honesty and values or any respect to human rights. History will never forget this barbaric crime led by Bush against the innocent people and innocent children in Iraq. Shame be on those arrogant, evil forces who must understand that real power is not in demolishing schools or killing children, women and aged civilians ... Glory be to immortal Iraqi civilisation, to the Iraqi children. Words can say no more when the pictures are so expressive.[101]

It has to be admitted that it is extremely difficult to verify the accuracy of the images over which this commentary was made – a problem which undoubtedly prompted many news editors to omit from their programmes many of the pictures emanating from Iraq. As with 'They Murder Children', it is virtually impossible to determine whether footage was shot during the Iran–Iraq war or even whether the shots of dead Iraqi children were filmed as a result of the gassing of the Kurds. Even so, the motivation of the

Iraqis was clear enough. 'They Murder Children' displayed graphic shots of badly burned or maimed children, often filmed in slow motion, against a backdrop of emotive music and a loaded commentary. One irony of this film was that segments of it were shown on Britain's Sky News in the aftermath of the Amiriya bunker/shelter incident because BSkyB at the time had no access to pictures of the incident itself and in fact compiled its story from various library shots.[102]

When ambassador Al-Hashimi appeared via satellite on CBS's Face the Nation on Sunday 27 January he insisted that 'a lot of civilian damage is taking place in the city of Basra and believe me ... when these pictures come out, the world opinion will be the judge of who is going to be tried for war crimes'.[103] Even though Iraqi TV pictures from Basra shown on BBC1's Six O'Clock News two days later were accompanied by the commentary 'despite the destruction, Iraq has not reported any civilian deaths in the area', what Saddam really needed at this point was to allow western television journalists to return to Iraq and provide them with greater freedom to visit areas to the south where there was growing evidence of civilian casualties, particularly from Iranian sources.

As the necessary arrangements were being made, the few journalists still in Iraq continued to be escorted to 'suitable' sites. Alfonso Rojo was among those taken to the Shiite holy city of Najaf, significantly with two Iranian reporters, where, he wrote, raids had apparently been taking place since 20 January and where 23 people were said to have died. Rojo pointed out that they were all encouraged 'to see every building, to photograph every corner ... the whole trip has been planned to show that the Americans are intentionally attacking civilians'. Even so, he continued:

There are no chemical plants or nuclear installations in the area. There are not even reserve military barracks. Here was not a case of a missile off-course or deflected by anti-aircraft fire and crashing into a residential neighbourhood. The only explanation is that someone got the wrong city.[104]

This was just what the Iraqis needed, especially as no mention was made of the failure to escort him to military sites in other places they visited. On the other hand, it would be better still to have camera crews there too. As a propaganda state, pictures issued by the Iraqis were automatically regarded as suspect in the free world. Film shot by western crews was likely to be regarded as less dubious, although the insistence of the Iraqis that their minders should accompany foreign journalists everywhere only served to undermine the dependability of even those reports.

When film crews from coalition countries were allowed back into Baghdad at the end of January, it certainly looked as though there would be plenty of damage for them to shoot. Almost as soon as they had arrived, they were able to film six Tomahawk cruise missiles flying above them and travelling down a street,[105] compelling footage that added to the drama and was an early indication of what lay head: the damage incurred when the Tomahawks *missed* their intended targets. As the journalists entered the Al-Rashid, one of the first to greet them was Al-Janabi who gathered them together in the Sherezade Bar of the hotel, where he told them:

The more you co-operate with us the easier it will be for you. Point number one, no information on damage inflicted on strategic installations can be given. Point number two, no important logistic data can be included. Point number three, you must show us your stories before sending them.[106]

Among the party of 15 correspondents was Richard Beeston of *The Times*, who stated after the war:

It became clear from the moment we arrived in Baghdad that the Iraqis had devised a comprehensive system designed to maximise the international propaganda value of civilian casualties of allied bombing, while limiting access to the Iraqi people in order to prevent the outside world from gauging domestic attitudes towards the war and the regime.[107]

In the days that followed, journalists were taken to sites which had clearly suffered civilian casualties: a school playground in rubble, badly maimed and burned children being treated in hospital.[108] On 2 February journalists, including a Japanese NHK television crew, were taken to Diwaniya, south of Baghdad – pictures of which were transmitted around the world.[109] But the journalists tried not to play the Iraqi's game wholeheartedly. In Brent Sadler's report of a visit to Najaf, for example, he stated that 'it cannot be overstressed that these sort of Iraqi press tours are one sided. They fail to give a picture of the military situation'. Sadler also pointed to some buildings in rubble, and said that these pictures had been shown on at least two previous occasions. Further, local residents had told him that there had been no attacks there for about two weeks.[110] In Hillah, 60 miles south of Baghdad, the Iraqi Ministry of Information took reporters around residential areas, a children's clinic and a secondary school. Reuters correspondent Bernd Debusmann wrote: 'Blackboards in the school and sheets of medical reports in the clinic left no doubt that these buildings were what the Iraqis said they were.'[111] It was this type of report, combined with a discernibly greater amount of filmed coverage of civilian damage, which began to cause some alarm in the West. President Bush, annoyed by the mounting campaign, insisted the bombing was 'fantastically accurate' and was quick to point out that Saddam was relocating his command and control centres into civilian buildings, 'such as schools'.[112] Then, in Nasiriyah in southern Iraq, up to 180 civilians were said to have died in a single raid on a bridge – the highest such death toll claimed by the Iraqis to date. The bridge across the Euphrates was said to have been packed with cars and pedestrians when it had been bombed in mid-afternoon and journalists who were taken to the scene realised at least 47 people had died there, an incident which gained widespread publicity, not to mention notoriety.[113] ITN's coverage of the hospital nearby contained some of the most graphic images of the dead and wounded it had shown to date.[114] Needless to say, no precision video, if one existed, was released by the coalition of this incident for public consumption. Yet, as one source in London had already pointed out:

You can't orbit the targets and wait for a two mile gap in traffic before hitting the bridge. If a line of communication is still being used by civilian vehicles, unfortunately one or two people will get killed.[115]

Beeston was only too aware of what the Iraqis were up to, noting at the time in his secret diary:

The Iraqis seem finally to have mastered the careful manipulation of the press through a system of censorship and control which leaves journalists unable to get the full picture of what is going on in the country. Coaches wait like commuter buses every morning outside the hotel for the daily 'civilian destruction' trips which take journalists to all areas of the country in search of demolished houses and witnesses with tales of wanton killing by the allies. Although these stories do make up an important part of the coverage of the war, journalists are unable to address the key questions of what is going on in the minds of the Iraqi leadership, and the capability of the armed forces.[116]

Beeston felt that although this system 'worked well initially', with the Iraqis organising trips to bombed sites across the country and providing ample publicity,

it became harder for journalists to justify their work, when it consisted exclusively of one topic, which served the interests of the Iraqi war effort but failed to address the central questions of the war, namely Saddam's survivability, the morale of the Iraqi people and military and the country's fighting capability.[117]

Indeed, Beeston was highlighting an important point about propaganda in general. To be successful, it must be able to operate within a wider context of war aims, moral justification and popular support. Plugging a line without this wider perspective merely identified the line as a propaganda ploy, and therefore dismissible simply as 'propaganda'. The trick is to conduct an information campaign across a broad front, in which all the strands are woven credibly and inextricably into the overall impression – something which the Iraqis consistently and, worse still from their point of view, ostentatiously failed to do.

Most journalists in Baghdad stayed in the capital and travelled to other cities and towns only when they were given permission to do so by the Iraqis, who inevitably escorted them. The very fact, therefore, that the Iraqis were directing journalists to this or that site rather than allowing them to roam freely about the country, combined with the constant reminders issued by anchormen and women that the footage that was being shown could be done so only because it had been cleared by Iraqi censors, reduced and even undermined the propaganda impact which the Iraqis hoped would result. As Beeston noted in his diary,

what we are not allowed to report are the increasingly regular sightings along the route of squadrons of tanks and armoured personnel-carriers and ammunition dumps camouflaged in palm groves, frequently located next to farms and villages.[118]

Various other tours were subsequently arranged, but by this time the western journalists had been subjected to so much criticism from home that they were even more on their guard than usual when filming 'evidence' provided by the Iraqis. Moreover, there was growing scepticism that the footage was of purely civilian damage when it was claimed by the coalition that there were so many dual-function installations in Iraq that it was impossible to tell which was civilian and which was military. Therefore, if bombs were missing their 'civilian' targets, why were there no pictures of 'accidental' hits on nearby military sites?

On the other hand, as a *Times* leader stated, 'reports from Iraq are becoming progressively harder to dismiss as mere propaganda or the relics of the Iran–Iraq war'.[119] It became harder still given that also amongst the convoy of journalists who returned to Iraq at the end of January was a truck with the letters CNN painted on its roof. This contained a portable satellite 'flyaway' dish that would enable the station to start transmitting live pictures from the enemy capital. Called 'flyaway' because they are essentially small enough to be carried on an aircraft as excess baggage, these mobile broadcasting units were capable of transmitting live and video-recorded images up to either the INTELSAT or EUTELSAT satellites and then on to the Goonhilly receiving station in Cornwall and, via British Telecom's London tower, to television stations around the world.[120] In addition, CNN possessed two INMARSAT telephones. These highly expensive satellite telephone systems beamed their signal up to a satellite over the Indian Ocean and then on to several earth stations, including Goonhilly, where they were plugged into the world telephone system at $10 a minute. Such technology had only become available to journalists in the past five years. Two phones were needed to co-ordinate the transmission of pictures together with commentary. Five other news organisations, including the Associated Press, Agence France Presse, ITN and BBC, also brought these INMARSAT telephone systems with them, together with portable electrical generators, to overcome the problems of transmitting from a country which had had most of its communications and electrical power supplies largely knocked out by allied bombing. But, before long, some of these organisations were being criticised for allowing Iraqi Ministry of Information officials to use the telephones to communicate with the outside world. CNN strongly denied the charges, stating that the phones were constantly supervised and dismantled when not in use, and claimed that the only time they had been used by their Iraqi minders was to sort out visa details for other journalists wishing to enter the country from Jordan. The phones had also been used for 'humanitarian' purposes, such as trying to trace missing journalists like Bob Simon or for notifying relatives and employers that other journalists were safe. Following the criticism, CNN had asked all Iraqi officials using the phones to speak in English so that what they were saying could be monitored by the now six strong CNN team. And finally, Arnett added:

One factor overrides all in our use of the phones. We believe that our conversations are being monitored by the eavesdropping resources of the US defence establishment. None of us want to become targets so we are careful about what we say and who says it.[121]

And, of course, the Iraqi minders themselves were ever-present when the phones were in use.

CNN was thus able to start transmitting live pictures from Baghdad on 30 January, the day of all the confusion concerning the battle for Khafji and the day on which General Schwarzkopf announced that air supremacy had at last been achieved after two weeks and that a new phase in the air war was about to begin. This came several days after Saddam had granted Peter Arnett an exclusive interview from a bungalow in a suburb of Baghdad – the first with a western journalist since the war began. In that 90 minute interview, Saddam blamed the United States for the oil spill in the Gulf, dodged the question about the Iraqi planes in Iran, stated that his Scuds were capable of carrying chemical and biological warheads and that he might be forced to use them, that Iraq was justified in using captured pilots as human shields and that Iraq would win the war.[122]

A storm of protest erupted over the interview. 'Standard propaganda,' said Fitzwater. 'The only real truth that emerges is that he must be stopped.'[123] Max Hastings, for example, wrote:

thanks to Iraq's generosity in granting facilities, cameramen and reporters in Baghdad are allowed to film damage to civilian life and property. Acres of film and newsprint are being daily exposed on this theme. Yet no foreigners in Baghdad can perform the function of the proper journalist – to search for information and report this in context – because they are being granted no access whatever to news or pictures of the effects of bombing on military objectives. Saddam is thus successfully exploiting the media to place injury to innocent civilians on the world's front pages ... we, the media, should do our utmost to ensure that we are not addressing the agenda of Saddam Hussein.[124]

Sean Maguire of Visnews also made an important point about this after the war, saying that he felt the main reason why he and his colleagues, and especially CNN, were allowed back into Baghdad was that 'they represented the Iraqi government back to itself; in that way "global" television gave the regime an external electronic validation'. He continued:

the greater the access the less was discovered; the interviews were so hedged by restrictions, the interviewers so mesmerised by the occasion, that little of substance ever materialised. The event was the story: the end result of gratification of a television network and Saddam's self-import-ance.[125]

Jeremy Bowen of the BBC also testified that 'the photo-oppor-tunities were designed to stop us getting near the real story':

When there was fighting in the south, they [the minders] suggested a trip to the north. When we wanted to see an oil refinery that had been bombed, they suggested a return visit to some minor civilian damage. But they were, at least, a source of pictures. There was also a chance, too, of an encounter that might provide a grain of information.[126]

This would appear to suggest that the main purpose of the Iraqis in permitting western journalists to return was not necessarily to utilise them as a conduit for propaganda; merely allowing them to be there was sufficient propaganda in itself. If the allies began to tear themselves apart as a result of the debate concerning TV coverage, so much the better. It might also have been the case that the Iraqis feared the intelligence value which television pictures might provide for their enemies. Perhaps they simply assumed that western audiences were as incapable of spotting propaganda as their own people – who dared not.

Bowen described how on one occasion, on a routine visit outside Baghdad, the car in which he, his crew and their minder was travelling started to be followed by a transporter carrying a Scud missile. 'The horrified minder at first pretended not to notice the weapon, which was loosely covered by a flapping tarpaulin. He only relaxed when he remembered that the BBC would not be allowed to report seeing the Scud, or the base at which it stopped.'[127] It would appear, then, that everything was geared up to short-term propaganda, with little consideration given to the long-term consequences of inadequate or misrepresentative repor-ting. Requests to interview leading members of the regime, to visit Iraqi troops in Kuwait, to interview people on the street – all were 'received with an ironic smile and then forgotten'.[128] As Bowen pointed out:

The restrictions on movement were the Iraqis' best weapon against the journalists – far more effective than the mere censorship of words and pictures which happened before any material could be transmitted. If you stop a reporter gathering news, you save yourself the bother of having to cut his story.[129]

The editor of *The Times,* Simon Jenkins (who in fact took a different view) encapsulated this argument when he described the two freedoms essential to journalism: freedom to move and see and freedom to write about what has been seen. 'If both are curtailed, reporters are worse than propagandists; by their professional status, they validate propaganda.'[130] Regardless of CNN's privileged position, what was the point of having journalists stay under these circumstances? Jenkins put the case thus:

Every war is a casualty to censorship. Few journalists see military action. If they do, they only see a microcosm of it ... Reporters who plead for an 'uncensored' war are naive. War reporting does not start pure and become tainted by censorship. It starts censored and is an act of de-censoring ... In war as in peace, the task of a newspaper is simple: to make the best possible stab at the truth in the time available.[131]

The difficulties of reporting objectively were illustrated by an occasion on which Richard Beeston managed to interview some Iraqi citizens critical of Saddam's regime out of earshot of his minders. He included the criticisms in his article, only to have them deleted by the censor. But then Naji Al-Hadithi, the director-general of the Ministry of Information, ordered an enquiry into who precisely had passed on these comments to the press. Beeston filed the story – without the names of his informants – from Jordan several days later, only to be told by colleagues that he would not be allowed a visa to return to Iraq as a result. He said:

Journalists who did not file this story were allowed to return to Iraq again and so the Iraqis managed to impose a level of self-censorship even over correspondents who had left the country but were concerned that critical articles would jeopardise their chances of return.[132]

Sean Maguire of Visnews elaborated further on this point:

The Iraqis quickly realised the western media's obsession with 'being there' and played the visa game quite deliberately. Since the physical process of getting a visa was so difficult many journalists released from captivity by the poolside of international hotels in Amman were subconsciously grateful to the Iraqis. Once in Iraq the Ministry of Information could rely on journalists' desire to have their visa extended to introduce an element of self-censorship into their work.[133]

He added that he had some difficulty in persuading the Iraqis that Visnews pictures were in fact seen by more people than CNN's. Although this was potentially true, a great deal of the footage of civilian damage taken by Visnews cameramen was not managing to penetrate the news bulletins of its subscribers in Britain and the United States.

As the allies stepped up their bombing raids, so the Iraqis stepped up their propaganda. But if the pictures were having little impact in the West, Baghdad radio attempted to employ words as weapons, especially against Arab listeners. It continued its stream of invective against allied bombing, describing pilots as the 'spiritual inheritors of colonialism' and even charging them with machine-gunning civilians in the street. On 7 February, the station exhorted Arab and Moslem regimes to join 'the mother of battles' and stated that there was no place left for neutrality in the Gulf conflict. The war was portrayed as an anti-imperialist crusade to liberate Islam's holy shrines, Palestine, the Golan Heights, south Lebanon and 'Moslem wealth from the oil sheikhs'.[134] It was a war between 'faith and justice on the one side and atheism and injustice on the other'.[135] But a noticeable absence from such statements was any claims about massive civilian damage which the Iraqis had supposedly sustained. UN Secretary General, Perez de Cuellar, felt that the Iraqis had become prisoners of their own rhetoric: 'They don't want to say there are more than a few hundred casualties, but there appear to be thousands. Yet they won't allow the Red Cross to certify the situation in Iraq.'[136] Despite considerable evidence to the contrary he, like millions of others in the Third World, was beginning to assume that allied bombing was indiscriminate, prompting the fear that 'the impact of a carefully executed and potentially successful military strategy may begin to be eroded by external perception'.[137] Perez de Cuellar, however, was soon being lambasted by Baghdad radio as 'dishonest and incompetent', 'a dirty criminal and a conspirator who has played his role in a hypocritical and discreet manner' and 'America's slave and protector'.[138] No one, it appeared, was free from this type of invective, but the mistreatment of the Secretary

General of the United Nations had been Saddam's mistake before the war, as it was again now.

It just so happened that, in the aftermath of the Khafji incident, General Schwarzkopf had decided to reform the briefing system in Riyadh to pre-empt mounting press disaffection with the allied information policy (see Chapter 3). But Khafji was momentarily being hailed by the Iraqis as a significant military and moral triumph – and even the allies conceded that it 'merely a propaganda victory'.[139] With the air war entering its third week, and as every day which passed without defeat being trumpeted as another Iraqi victory, it was essential for the coalition not to lose the propaganda initiative. The lesson was clear: official briefers would simply have to become more forthcoming.

In the United States, this fear prompted renewed attacks on CNN from people who accused Peter Arnett of being a Saddam sympathiser. Public opinion polls indicated that most people wanted to see even tighter controls over the press as President Bush's personal ratings soared and support for the military was almost omnipresent. Abroad, however, Saddam's ratings were also soaring, especially in the Arab world after the 'victory' at Khafji. As one White House analyst stated: 'Saddam is fighting a political war and we're fighting a military war.' Defense Secretary Cheney may have insisted that 'I don't buy the argument that Saddam is winning by losing'[140] but the fact remains that long as the war went on without a comprehensive coalition victory, the Iraqi dictator could parade his achievement of having taken on the world and, with every day which passed, had won another battle. This was precisely what such figures as the PLO's Yasser Arafat picked up on, stating on 11 February: 'The West said at the start he would last three days. He's already into his fourth week and I believe his resistance will last at least three years.'[141]

The first two weeks of February, then, saw a concerted Iraqi propaganda campaign surrounding the question of collateral damage, with numerous tours being organised for the journalists who had been allowed back inside Iraq (see also Chapter 4). This revealed an important point about Iraqi censorship policy which differed from coalition approaches. Military escorts with the allied pools were similar in function to the Iraqi minders, monitoring what journalists – and interviewees – said and informing them of what could not be reported. It might indeed appear that the Iraqis had developed their own version of the coalition's pool system with the small band of western journalists allowed to return to Baghdad. But it was important to remember that there was no equivalent in Iraq to the unilateralists in Saudi Arabia. Many pool reporters even in Saudi Arabia testified to the comparative freedom to film anything they liked and encountered field censorship only immediately prior to the point of transmission. Journalists in Baghdad encountered this also but it was mainly therefore at the news-gathering stage that most Iraqi censorship took place. No journalists were allowed to visit Kuwait, for example. What information was being allowed out in other words was what the Iraqis wanted to be allowed out – which merely made it propaganda in some people's eyes.

Providing that 'propaganda' with the aura of credible 'information' was something which the Iraqis gradually realised was essential. Bernd Debusmann insisted that the outside perception of Iraqi information control was false and that 'despite the curbs, reporters can have access to a wealth of information, both official and unofficial – and while the latter often cannot be reported, it helps balance the correspondent's assessment'. He went on to describe an incident in which the chief Iraqi minder, Al-Janabi, demonstrated an appreciation of the importance of credibility concerning the Nasiriyah bridge story:

Scrolling up the story [on the computer screen], he came to a paragraph that made him frown. It gave conflicting figures on civilian casualties caused by an allied air attack on a busy bridge in Nasiriyah. 'You say here figures on the death toll ranged from 47 to 180', said Janabi. 'And the way you put it implies that you doubt the higher figure. So why not just say "at least 47" ?'[142]

Although reporters in Iraq were clearly sensitive to mounting criticism at home about their presence, taking refuge in such notions as 'there are two sides in a war and if a news organisation does not report both, it is falling down on the job' (Peter Arnett),[143] there remained the essential doubt caused by their inability to go where they liked when they liked.

The extension of the coalition's air offensive from finding mobile Scud launchers in western and southern Iraq to encompass supply lines feeding the Iraqi army on the two main roads south from Baghdad to Kuwait led to increasing attacks against road and rail bridges. This in turn led to greater risks of causing civilian damage and, correspondingly, to more propaganda opportunities for the Iraqi Ministry of Information. At the point of transmission, despite the presence of official minders and listeners, journalists were finding at the start of February that the Iraqis were easing up on what the reporters could say. Following the destruction of the first of several of Baghdad's bridges over the River Tigris (the Jumhouriya bridge), the rules concerning the identification of bridges, roads and government buildings were relaxed somewhat.[144] But there was still a limit to what could be said. When Debusmann left Iraq for Jordan, one of his first uncensored reports included a statement by a local resident about the Jumhouriya: 'the Iranians tried this for years. The Americans did it in one second.'[145] Indeed, the Reuters correspondent testified to considerable disquiet within Iraq, with slogans such as 'Down with Saddam' beginning to be daubed on walls (and quickly removed) and suspicions that he might have miscalculated in taking on the Americans.[146] Free from Iraqi controls, Debusmann continued:

The number of civilian victims appears to be relatively small considering the 50,000 plus sorties the allies have flown. That may be one explanation for the astonishing absence of anti-western feeling in Iraq. Even in areas devastated by bombs, Iraqis treated foreigners courteously.[147]

Even so, this did not stop the television pictures desired by the Iraqis being shown around the Arab world. From the city of Basra came footage of a little girl who was said to have lost her leg in an air raid, prompting further outrage and further statements by the likes of Yasser Arafat who described the war as representing 'glorious days for our Arab nation'.[148]

In the coalition's attempts to isolate the Iraqi army from the rest of the country, which began in earnest during the second week of the war, major air attacks were launched against supply routes, described by briefers as 'interdiction'. On 12 February, General Kelly elaborated on the reasons for attacking bridges across the Tigris and Euphrates:

We said in the past that linear things are difficult to interdict, so if you cut a road or a railroad or a pipeline or things of that nature, they can be repaired relatively easily. You can get a bulldozer and repair a road. It might not be a smooth ride, but it's workable, whereas if you can take out a bridge, you have created a much more serious interdiction problem.

The theater of operations is dominated by the Tigris and Euphrates rivers. Therefore, the Iraqis have to cross those rivers in order to provide war materiel to their forces at the front. What we would like to do is see those forces at the front atrophy ... If you take out the highway bridges over the river, it has ... the bonus effect of causing traffic back-ups at the bridges. When those traffic back-ups are military in nature, they make lucrative targets for our aircraft to attack.[149]

Iraqi statements concerning casualty figures, however, remained erratic and misleading. By Day 28, they claimed they had killed 53 coalition troops while the allies admitted to 47, and had lost 90 of their own men, while the allied figure was 79 – which wasn't so wide of the mark. Yet in other areas there was a much wider discrepancy. For example, they stated that 27 Iraqi planes had flown to Iran (the allies claimed 147), they claimed that they had shot down 309 aircraft and missiles (the allies announced 36 planes lost) and that 867 civilians had died (the allies at no point during the war put a precise figure on this). But the greatest hole in the statistical war was the numbers which the Iraqis were not releasing. By mid February, they had released no figures for the numbers of missing or captured Iraqi troops (the allies claimed 1,087), for the number of Iraqi planes shot down (138) or for the number of Scuds fired (61).[150]

That aside, the Iraqis did manage to punctuate their civilian damage campaign with other incidents, not altogether without success. At the end of January, about 70 terrorist acts against largely American and other coalition targets were conceded to have been detected, chiefly in the Third World in such places as Thailand and Tanzania.[151] On 3 February Baghdad radio warned that it was about to renew world-wide terrorist attacks against especially American targets: 'There is a difference between terrorism and struggle. This is a legitimate act.'[152] The very next day, six bombs described as 'pretty sophisticated sabotage weapons' were found attached to two chemical tanks in Norfolk, Virginia – the site of America's largest naval base.[153] But the point is that they were found. By mid February the Iraqi Voice of the Masses Radio (see Chapter 3) was still maintaining that 'we tell Cheney that Iraq's surprises will continue, and we promise him that these surprises will multiply and grow. They will be devastating'.[154] What these were to be was anybody's guess, not least because of Baghdad radio's occasional sudden bursts of cryptic messages without introduction or explanation, such as 'From the headquarters to Urwah: implement the last meeting' or 'Call from Mahyub to 301: report to the bank'.[155] Whether they were actually messages to terrorist agents abroad appears less likely than their being another effort at psychological warfare, and one borrowed from the techniques adopted by Britain's Political Warfare Executive in the Second World War. But an indication of what Saddam may have had in mind came at the end of the war's third week, with reports that 50 Kuwaiti oil-field fires had been started by the Iraqis.

Iraqi propaganda abroad, therefore, placed great emphasis on threats, but the problem with that strategy was that its effectiveness ultimately depended upon the ability to fulfil its promises. It was not just that Iraq felt that its actions would speak louder than its words; rather it needed words and images to publicise the deeds. It was almost a classic terrorist approach to publicising any gesture, no matter how insignificant militarily, to invoke fear and caution. Unpalatable incidents undermining the argument were simply omitted. Hence the low casualty figures not just amongst civilians – which might adversely affect domestic morale – but also amongst the troops. That would undoubtedly affect civilian morale as well but it was more important to present an image of near-invulnerability against the high-technology weapons being employed against its armies. As we shall see, the coalition was employing mainly 'conventional' bombing techniques against Iraqi troops, although that was not the impression that was being given by briefers in Riyadh and Washington. Again, the degree to which coalition bombing was eroding the Iraqi army's will to fight was also exposed during the battle of Khafji. Yet no amount of words, spoken by Baghdad radio or, better still, by western correspondents, could compensate for a propaganda gesture of the deed. The challenge for the Iraqis, therefore, was how to make their actions speak louder than coalition words.

Chapter Three

War on the mind: preparing for the ground offensive

Introduction

The early media emphasis on the air offensive not only created an optimism that air power was a clinical, clean and casualty-free weapon but also reinforced the impression that the war against Iraq might be won by air power alone. Spectacular though air power is, as at the end of the First and throughout the Second World War, military strategists recognised that in the last resort wars are essentially won or lost by the troops on the ground. Despite hopes that the high technology of modern air power might just bring Saddam to his knees without the need for a bloody ground war, more realistic appraisals suggested that one was inevitable. In the Gulf War, however, the fears surrounding heavy troop casualties and the memories of returning body bags from South East Asia combined to prompt especially American military planners to allow air power to do as much preparatory destruction of enemy positions as was possible. The overall purpose of the air war, stated Rear Admiral McConnell on 1 February, was to 'degrade the war-fighting infrastructure in the country, to eliminate the ability to wage war'. The sheer ferocity of this campaign was rarely captured by the media. 'We flew as many combat missions in one day as he [Saddam] experienced in eight years of war with Iran,' said General Horner after the war.[1]

In fact, as General Schwarzkopf also admitted after the war, coalition troops had begun moving into forward positions in readiness for a ground war as allied bombers were attacking Baghdad on the first night – movements which were actually picked up in some of the world's media but which tended to be subsumed in the initial euphoria of those early first days. The offensive against Iraq was to start with a massive air strike followed by a short, sharp ground offensive. The former had been worked out as far back as October, 'executable right down to a gnat's eyelash,' said Schwarzkopf.[2] This involved altering previous American military organisational thinking 'to create a single joint Air Force commander [Horner] who wrote a single air tasking order from which all air forces operated'.[3] Schwarzkopf added:

We knew that we were going to establish air superiority immediately so, on 17 January, whoosh, it started. I mean because we needed all of that time ... So the day we launched the offensive campaign, that was the day we started moving west.[4]

The reference to moving west was of course an indication of where the major coalition thrust would be, by-passing Iraqi front lines on the Saudi–Kuwait border and swinging left into southern Iraq round the back of the enemy in a one-sided enveloping movement. Deceiving the enemy into thinking that something else is on the cards is a standard part of modern military doctrine, a well-known World War Two example being Operation Fortitude in 1944 by which the Germans had been misled into thinking that the Allied landings in Normandy would take place elsewhere. Given that the allies had just about decided on their Gulf War plan of ground attack as far back as November 1990, it was essential not to give the game away to the enemy. As allied troops moved their supplies nearer and nearer the front lines in a logistical exercise of historic proportions, an elaborate disinformation campaign was conducted to confuse the Iraqis about where precisely the main attack would take place. Although General Schwarzkopf occasionally worried that he might not be able to keep his promise to the American people 'that I would try to achieve the absolute minimum number of casualties on our side', nonetheless 'minimum casualties was my intention all along – and we did it'.[5]

Saddam Hussein was, of course, working on the assumption that American public opinion would be unable to tolerate massive troop casualties. He had said this to April Glaspie as long ago as July 1990 and it had recurred in Iraq's taunting propaganda ever since. Polls conducted in Britain immediately before the war suggested otherwise,[6] but Britain had not fought a Vietnam. Iraq, by way of contrast, had been able to accommodate hundreds of thousands of casualties during its eight-year war with Iran. The different approaches to the loss of life were a major part of the propaganda campaign placing each side on a simplistic moral spectrum, which the warring parties delineated by Judeo-Christian values concerning a just war at the one end and the Islamic concept of a *jihad* at the other. Small wonder that the war occasionally prompted comparisons with the Crusades.

Again siding with the history of conventional warfare and the American experience in Vietnam, Saddam seems to have believed that despite the United States' superior technology he could actually win a land battle when it came to the coalition's attempt to physically expel the Iraqi occupying forces from Kuwait. He made much of his Republican Guard, and the western media invariably added for him the word 'elite' to preface any story concerning Iraq's 140,000 or so professional troops, most of whom were anyway in southern Iraq rather than in Kuwait itself. As for the conscripts, the remaining four-fifths of Iraq's perhaps half million strong army located in the region, they were placed in the forward line – presumably to absorb the coalition's first wave of ground attacks whereupon the Republican Guard would be able to inflict heavy casualties against already battle-weary troops that had been forced to break through his front-line minefields and fortifications: the much vaunted 'Saddam Line'.

Coalition assessments tended to create an impression that, though large in numbers, the vast majority of the Iraqi army was poorly trained, badly led, ill-equipped and capable of fighting only a static defensive campaign. Though this impression was to be confirmed at the end of the war, before then it was only really the Republican Guard who were trumpeted as formidable opponents capable of giving NATO-trained forces a run for their money. The battle for Al-Khafji threatened initially to burst this bubble, even though artillery skirmishes had been taking place for over a week before it made front-page news, resulting, *inter alia*, in the first of the celebrated oil spills.[7]

Cock-up at Khafji

On the night of Tuesday 29 January, the largely abandoned Saudi coastal town of Ras Al-Khafji was occupied by the Iraqis for 36 hours and was only liberated by Saudi and Qatari troops, backed up by American artillery and air support units, by about noon on Thursday 31 January. It subsequently emerged that the Iraqis had begun crossing the border further to the west at about 22:25 (all times hereafter are local unless otherwise stated) on the Tuesday, but were repelled successfully with the loss of 13 tanks by allied forces. About half an hour later, the Iraqis launched another thrust down the coast with armoured personnel carriers quickly overrunning Saudi border positions, and were in full control of Al-Khafji by midnight. The ease with which what was estimated to have been an initial Iraqi force of only 45 vehicles and 400–800 men had entered the town was something of an embarrassment to the Saudi High Command, which very quickly latched on to a story as its chief explanation that the enemy tanks had approached Saudi positions with reversed turrets as if planning to surrender.[8] As the tank turrets turned to point at the town and opened fire, the defending Saudi and Qatari troops had been forced to abandon their positions, leaving two US reconnaissance Marines in hiding to fend for themselves as the Iraqis overran the town. It was only after American forces, using heavy artillery, ground attack Cobra helicopters and fixed-wing aircraft (and with the trapped Marines acting as spotters for them), were able to block the Iraqi advance, that sufficient time and support were provided for the Saudi and Qatari troops to launch a counter-offensive. Initially, they failed to dislodge the defenders but by 07:30 on the Thursday morning they were able to move in and begin retaking the town.

None of this was clear at the time, and indeed much remains unknown about what precisely happened in what is still one of the most confusing episodes of the war. Clearly the incident was difficult for the coalition on a variety of levels. For a start, given the impression of jubilation and the mood of inevitable victory by air power in the first two weeks of the war, how was it that the Iraqis were suddenly able to launch an *offensive* against allied positions, especially when they had been supposedly pounded by bombing and their morale was said to be lowering? Inter-coalition politics were also threatened. It was imperative, for example, that the Arab forces should be seen to perform successfully for appearances' sake and pool reporters noticed how the US Marines appeared to be deliberately taking a back seat in the final liberation. Moreover, the whole allied information system was tested for the first time in the reporting of a land battle, and found wanting. In

137

Dhahran, the Saudi High Command announced that 160 Iraqis had been taken prisoner (the eventual figure was 400) while in Washington, General Kelly announced that 41 enemy tanks and 35 other enemy vehicles had been destroyed – primarily by American air attacks. Chris Hedges of the *New York Times* wrote after the war:

It is worth remembering that during the first twenty four hours of the fighting in Khafji ... the allied commanders insisted that only Arab forces were battling the Iraqis. They changed the story after an AP reporter climbed into a US armoured personnel carrier and drove into the city, where he witnessed marines engaging Iraqi troops. The US wanted to build the confidence of the Arab forces, but at the expense of the truth.[9]

Because it was apparent that this was what was happening, this realisation in itself tended to take the gloss off the Saudi–Qatari achievement which the coalition was so keen to emphasise.

Border clashes had been occurring on the Saudi–Kuwaiti and the Saudi–Iraqi border on Monday 28 and Tuesday 29 January. Early reports indicated that clashes were occurring at Ar'Ar, nearly 400 miles to the north west of Khafji. It was not yet clear whether this was the first phase of a full-scale Iraqi assault, news of which began to filter through only on the Wednesday. Coalition briefers in Riyadh, Washington and London meanwhile gave conflicting reports and assessments which only added to the confusion. By the weekend, it had emerged clearly that Al-Khafji was merely a small fragment of the overall picture. Across the entire Kuwaiti–Saudi border, Iraqi forces had been testing the strength of the coalition's frontier defenders to find a weak point and, at Al-Wafra, a force of 60,000 Iraqi troops, backed up by a 10 mile long supply column, was attempting to break through. This was eventually repelled by allied air power, an encounter famously described by one pilot as a 'turkey shoot', although an AC-130 transport plane was also reported missing behind enemy lines.[10] Incidentally, it was Washington, not Riyadh, which released this last piece of information, adding to the growing tension between the military and the media on the spot. The major confrontation at Wafra was the 'hidden' battle, fought ferociously but far away from the television cameras which were focusing on the comparatively small skirmish at Al-Khafji.

News of the Iraqi assault against Khafji was broken more than

12 hours after it had begun. At 13:16 on Wednesday 30 January, CNN picked up a report from the French news agency, Agence France Presse, citing Iraqi military communiqué No. 31 announced on Baghdad radio that a 'massive land offensive has been launched against Al-Khafji'. That the news was broken first by Baghdad radio, claimed *The Independent*, 'must have given Iraqi broadcasters considerable credibility among their listeners'.[11] It took a further 15 minutes for the Pentagon to admit that a clash between Iraqi and coalition troops had occurred but at an unspecified point. CNN's sources in Saudi Arabia then reported that the battle had been at Al-Khafji. Fifteen minutes after that, at 13:45, an Associated Press report confirmed that allied forces had beaten back Iraqi troops from the town. This was inaccurate. Throughout the rest of the afternoon, conflicting pool reports clashed more with Pentagon and JIB statements than with Iraqi reports about whether the battle had been fought and won or whether it was still going on. Unilaterals roving around the border added to the confusion still further. One US Marine colonel was quoted as saying the fighting had been 'hellacious'. His job had been to call in the air strikes: 'it was a joint operation and it worked like clockwork ... it really felt good. We kicked their asses.'[12] But once again, it was by no means over yet.

It just so happened that on that very day CNN was able to start transmitting live pictures from Baghdad, thanks to the arrival of its flyaway satellite uplink, and news from the enemy capital was more at variance than usual with coalition statements. Despite the event being in the immediate aftermath of the disappearance of the CBS news crew led by Bob Simon, now thought to be in Iraqi hands, several unilaterals were prepared to risk their lives by trying to find out what was going on for themselves. Sandy Gall of ITN encountered the enormous difficulties of cutting through Saudi red-tape when he tried to get official permission:

ITN had upset the Saudi military press officer, and he flatly refused on two occasions to take us on a facility to Khafji. When I asked to be allowed to go on a third occasion, he said 'I have been there twice in the last two days. I'm tired and I don't intend to go there again'. Without his permission we could not go officially.[13]

Meanwhile, Baghdad radio was having a field day, presenting the occasion as a massive ground attack with reports stating that the

Iraqis had penetrated at least 12 miles into Saudi territory across a wide front. On hearing the news, a demonstration was quickly staged in Jordan of about 3,000 people who chanted: 'Forward, forward Oh Saddam, from Al-Khafji to Dammam [200 miles further down the Saudi coast].'[14] US State Department officials attempted to draw some 'modest comfort' from the fact that support for Saddam reflected by other demonstrations in pro-Iraqi states 'seemed strongest where it mattered least', namely in Islamic countries distant from the area such as Algeria, Morocco and Pakistan.[15]

Throughout the next confusing 36 hours, however, Baghdad radio attempted to keep up its momentum, stating that the offensive had been personally planned by Saddam during his recent visit to the front lines (at one point it actually claimed that Saddam was directing the battle himself on the southern front[16]). It warned the Saudis that 'Our entry into your land is not occupation' but that 'all of us are in one line – against the line of atheism, crime and corruption, the line of Fahd and Bush and their failing collaborators'.[17] Another of their military communiqués, now coming thick and fast, stated that the 'heroic men' of the Iraqi air force had shot down three of the coalition's 'rats'. Not that this type of language was confined to the Iraqis; at a Riyadh briefing on the Thursday, Lieutenant-Colonel Dick White described how the Iraqi move provided a perfect opportunity to hit targets from the air that had previously been dug in. 'It's almost like you flipped on the light in the kitchen at night and the cockroaches start scurrying there, and we're killing them.'[18]

Throughout the battle the overall tone of Baghdad radio was epitomised by the statement:

Oh brothers! The good omens of this splendid victory over the enemies of God, the enemies of the Arabs and Muslims, have appeared. It is the banner of Iraq, the banner of Allahu Akbar [God is Great] under which the swords of the faithful are brandished to tear apart the corrupt bodies and turn the soil of the pure earth into fire that will burn the cowardly remnants fleeing in the face of the determination and might of the Iraqis.[19]

And as for its impact on Iraqi public opinion, that was evident to the western reporters whose return to Baghdad at the end of January coincided with the battle. Alfonso Rojo, who had been there all along, asked the manager of the Al-Rashid why he was so relaxed and back came the reply: 'Bush said he was going to finish us off in three days. We have come to the end of the second week of the war and we have just occupied part of Saudi Arabia.'[20]

Early coalition statements were at pains to downplay the significance of the Iraqi attack and when Lieutenant-Colonel Mike Gallagher made the first official pronouncement about it in Riyadh at 14:30 on Wednesday the 30th, all he would say was that clashes had occurred at three border positions during the previous night and that Iraqi casualties had been heavy. One source maintained that even this brief announcement was only prompted after an Egyptian journalist discovered the Iraqi presence in the town by telephoning the Khafji Beach Hotel, where two Iraqi soldiers had apparently answered the call, stating 'See you in Jerusalem' in Arabic before hanging up.[21]

It soon transpired that there was a great deal more to this story than the coalition was admitting. When CNN's Rick Sallinger gave a live progress report from Riyadh at 15:00 on the Wednesday, he stated that the fighting had begun at 23:30 the previous evening. It was an Iraqi probing attack which had been countered successfully but with some coalition casualties. By 03:00 that morning, he said, the fighting had ceased. This was also inaccurate and his source was presumably the Joint Information Bureau. At 15:45, CNN reported that American sources were admitting that casualties had been sustained but that Baghdad radio was claiming that Iraqi forces were still in Khafji.

At 16:00, CNN transmitted a report by WTN/ITN correspondent Geoffrey Archer stating that Iraq had launched a series of probes, one the previous day being mounted as far west as Ar'Ar and one in the early hours of that morning at Khafji. Some pictures were shown to illustrate his report, but they were old library footage of the town taken earlier in the previous week when ITN and other crews had gone up to Khafji to discover the oil spill. When Peter Arnett in Baghdad was consulted live at 16:13, he was able to report that the Iraqis were still claiming an 'astounding victory' at Khafji. In the hours that followed, the first pool reports began to filter through. Most were conflicting as to the real situation. As CNN's Charles Jaco speculated live at 16:01, 'somebody knows, but they're not talking right now' because 'they're probably pretty busy'.

It was in fact unlikely that anyone had a clear picture at that stage of what was actually happening. Trying to piece together various intelligence reports from the front was as difficult for the military as it was for the media. Nonetheless it was apparent that although the military was trying to state that a battle had occurred but was over, one was actually still going on. Some pretty bizarre events occurred as journalists tried to penetrate the fog of war. Robert Fisk, for example, encountered a news pool attached to the 1st US Marine Division and was told by one American network reporter: 'You asshole: You'll prevent us from working. You're not allowed here. Get out. Go back to Dhahran.'[22] After the war, Fisk stated:

Of all the things you don't need in a war, you don't need your own colleagues trying to get you out of it, which is ridiculous. If this person really thought for example that my presence was going to break the pool system, what was the pool system worth?[23]

A French TV crew was reportedly forced at gun point to turn over footage of soldiers wounded at Khafji to US Marines,[24] although they and a team from Visnews did manage to get into the town before the pool reporters. In fact the pool reporters were not allowed into the town until 18 hours after the fighting had started and so, in the meantime, it was left to unilaterals operating on their own to provide what accounts they could. Ironically, their reports only added to the confusion back in Riyadh and Dhahran.

It was only in the Saudi briefing in Riyadh, transmitted live on CNN at 17:32, that it was officially confirmed that the abandoned town of Khafji was part of an 'ongoing operation' although the situation was 'under control'. In fact, it was far from that, with the main Iraqi thrust having moved south of Al-Wafra to Umm Hujul where the American 1st Marine Division was engaged in fierce fighting. All that was conceded at the time, however, was that Saudi and Qatari units had been involved in the operation and casualties had been sustained. The US briefing at 18:00 added only that four Iraqi border incursions had been launched, including those at the Khafji and Al-Wafra locations. It was not until 19:43 that CNN was able to transmit any pictures from the battle itself, with Wolf Blitzer at the Pentagon delivering a live voice-over to the pictures as they came in via the satellite. It transpired that these pictures of daylight American artillery fire bombarding

Khafji had been taken some 10 hours earlier. Interestingly, they appear not to have been viewed in advance of their live trans-mission by the station as, when a soldier was being questioned by a reporter as to what his artillery battery was doing, he was interrupted by his commanding officer, who had spotted some vehicles on the horizon, with the words 'What the fuck is going on?' and, turning to the camera, 'Can we do this later, please'. Needless to say, the expletive was deleted later when these pictures were repeated, but it does reveal that matters of taste and decency in language at least were being left to the journalists rather than the military censors to decide.

But the officer was right to ask. It was still not clear beyond the sketchiest details what had transpired nearly 24 hours earlier, or indeed what was still going on. Even General Schwarzkopf, in his now famous 'bovine scatology' briefing that evening, was unable to provide anything other than the most cursory of details, although he did state that the fighting was not yet over despite the early loss of 12 Marines. 'I expect a lot more fighting will occur tonight; the Iraqis have a lot more fight left in them.' Even this, however, was buried beneath a bombardment of other details on the progress of the war and subsumed amidst the most detailed briefing – complete with spectacular videos – to date. It was at this briefing that General Schwarzkopf announced that the coalition had at last achieved air supremacy after 30,000 sorties. As CNN's John Holliman, now back in Atlanta, pointed out: 'if the General's goal was to take the media's attention away from the first day of double digit American deaths in the war, he apparently succeeded: there were no questions about how the marines died'.[25] Or, as a *Guardian* leader put it concerning Saddam's boasts: 'if this is propaganda, so are the evasions of the allied briefers'.[26]

There was another way of looking at Schwarzkopf's perfor-mance, according to Max Hastings. The general, by mentioning Khafji only at the end of a business-like briefing about the overall progress of the war, was placing the battle in its proper perspec-tive:

Even for those watching on television in an office several thousands of miles away, the tension was apparent between the host of journalists and onlookers aching for the commander-in-chief to 'get to the point', and General Schwarzkopf himself, determined to show what he considered *was* the point.[27]

One thing the incident was clearly indicating was that the recent coalition line – that the Iraqis might just prove to be a tougher nut to crack than had been first suggested by initial air successes – had found some real supporting evidence. Throughout the Wednesday night and Thursday morning, as the coalition forces attempted to repel the invaders and retake Khafji, news of their better-than-expected performance continued to filter through, albeit very patchily. Although there were four newspool cameras in the area of the battle to the east, their pictures were very slow to appear. On Wednesday the 30th, for example, the BBC was still using library footage of the empty town taken before the battle began until the first unspectacular pool pictures of distant artillery firing into the horizon came in just in time for its Six O'Clock News. It then transpired that the Marines who had been killed were further west, near Al-Wafra, where there were no pool reporters, yet where the fighting would if anything appear to have been more ferocious, raging for three nights and two days.

After it was all over, General Schwarzkopf attempted to play down the military significance of the battle for Khafji: 'a mosquito on an elephant'. However, for a time it did appear that something slightly more than that was happening, with the launch of a series of probes and spoiling actions utilising three battalions and with a flotilla of 17 Iraqi naval vessels moving parallel down the Gulf. Although allied air and naval forces, chiefly RAF Lynx helicopters, made short shrift of the latter, there were also reports from US Marine Harrier pilots that a huge column of Iraqi vehicles, 1,000 strong, was moving south far to the west of Khafji, which was part of the 'ongoing operation' for several days after Khafji had been liberated.

On Friday 1 February, coalition briefers were at least managing to project a fairly consistent picture of what was still happening. Not that it was a particularly clear picture. Brigadier-General Patrick Stevens admitted that Iraqi troop movements were still taking place 'but we do not necessarily concede that any major action is about to happen'.[28] Here was clearly an attempt to minimise the significance of what had already occurred, despite Baghdad radio's claims, and the same message was also driven home by General Peter de la Billiere, who described Khafji as 'a clear military disaster' for the Iraqis.[29] Yet, as a veteran American correspondent was quoted as saying:

Whatever anyone tells you on the TV, the script for this war was not supposed to open with the Iraqis taking a town inside Saudi Arabia and holding it long enough for the news to get all around the Arab world.[30]

Or, as a French observer put it: 'I thought these Iraqi troops were all supposed to be starving, lice-ridden and longing only for surrender. If that is the case, I hope the allies do not come up against any in proper shape.'[31]

The fact indeed remained that Iraqi troops had crossed into Saudi Arabia and, even though they were repelled, it was regarded as a significant propaganda triumph for Saddam. Within Iraq, the state-controlled media were jubilant at their greatest victory of the war so far, with the Ba'athist newspaper *Al-Thawra* declaring that 'our valiant forces crushed the armies of infidelity in a lightning attack'.[32] Well not quite, perhaps, but BBC Radio had remarked that 'the day belonged to Iraq'.[33] On the Thursday, Baghdad radio was still claiming it had beaten off the allied counter-attack with great losses, to be followed by a total silence until late on Friday when the briefest of announcements declared the battle to be over and that Iraqi forces were withdrawing to base. Thereafter, Khafji – even 'the memory of Khafji – had been erased from news and propaganda broadcasts'.[34]

The credibility of the coalition was further damaged in some media eyes by the discrepancy between the pool pictures taken in Khafji and the official versions offered in the briefings. Despite official statements that the US Marines had provided only artillery and air support, for example, most of the pictures coming back depicted slightly greater involvement than that. This was awkward. A particular perspective of the battle needed to be taken, especially when it concerned the involvement of the coalition's Arab forces. And the Iraqis would also have been able to watch via CNN as the coalition's line was caught at sixes and sevens. One journalist even noticed how General Schwarzkopf appeared to take his cue at his briefing from the CNN cameraman, pointing out that the military knows 'that an estimated 100 million people world-wide (including the Iraqi High Command) watches the broadcast live, as well as 600 million who see the highlights on the evening news'.[35] This does raise a further question about those Khafji pictures shown earlier in the week, namely that because the military controlled the news pools the media could film and transmit only what it was allowed to, and, if Khafji was pictured empty and the footage sent out, it was with allied military approval since unilateral footage could have been stopped at point of transmission. Were the allies trying to use television for disinformation purposes? Because they knew Baghdad would be watching, were the pictures of the empty town designed as a temptation to the enemy to see how strong was Iraqi military strength in the area? Or was it part of the disinformation campaign to suggest the allies were preparing for an amphibious assault? Whatever the truth, the Iraqis proved to be more formidable opponents after their carpet bombing than had previously been assumed, especially as the battle raged across a wide front. A note of concern was discernibly creeping into allied briefings as difficult questions were asked about if that had been the performance of Iraqi's conscript forces, what sort of opponents would the Republican Guard make? And then there was the unfortunate British cock-up at a press briefing on the battle for Khafji which stated that 300 rather than 30 Iraqis had been killed because a typing clerk had added an extra 0![36] As for eventual coalition losses, there were in fact 11 US Marines killed. In addition, at least 15 Saudis were reported killed (although the figure was thought to be considerably higher), many of whom were thought to have died in successful Iraqi ambushes in the Khafji street-fighting as they tried to mop up the town.[37]

Another major problem stemming from the sketchy initial reports of the battle, with political ramifications for the Arab partners in the coalition, occurred over the role of the American forces at Khafji. It was eventually admitted that the 11 US Marines killed had been as the result of 'friendly fire' in the 'hidden' battle to the west.[38] These were the first American troop losses in the ground fighting, yet official statements were at pains to emphasise the role which the Saudi and Qatari troops had played in the battle. On 31 January, BBC1's Six O'Clock evening news stated that the liberation of Khafji had been under the personal leadership of Prince Khalid bin Sultan and that 'no other allied ground forces were involved'. John King of the Associated Press managed to sneak into the city on the first night of fighting and watched as Arab forces attempted unsuccessfully to retake the town:

The pools did not get an accurate view because they didn't see it. They wrote that the Saudi and Qatari troops liberated the city, but they had no realistic view of how long it took, what happened or how many Iraqis were in there.[39]

Later, on the outskirts of Khafji, he joined some American Marines who were listening to a broadcast by General Schwarzkopf in which he also stated that no US forces had taken part in the liberation of the town. He continued:

'Tell him that!', said a Marine officer, pointing to an exhausted Marine who had escaped from the frontier town just minutes earlier, carrying with him a charred AK-47 he took from an Iraqi armoured personnel carrier.[40]

Nor did the official version match the pictures that eventually emerged, which showed that the Americans had been heavily involved in important roles but whose military contribution was being underplayed for political purposes. And when the post mortem began about why the Iraqis had managed to get into a town 12 miles into Saudi territory, there emerged the story about how the Iraqi tanks had approached Khafji with their turrets turned backwards as if to surrender. This story helped to dispel the suspicion in some quarters that the coalition had been taken completely by surprise, which would have raised doubts about the efficiency of allied intelligence, let alone their supposed air superiority. Even though the border areas were kept largely free of troops to deny Iraqi artillery any profitable targets, the fact remained that, as John Keegan wrote: 'The Iraqis may not have held Khafji for long, but the damage was done. Saddam got his headlines – banner ones in the Islamic world – and the Allies got into a stew.'[41]

Part of the reason for this was the extent to which the media were being regarded as a central player in the overall conflict. The prominence given to media management by both sides encouraged the belief that the media were possibly more important in the outcome of things than they were. Certainly, if public opinion polls in the United States were anything to go by, the media were perceived to be more of a nuisance to the business of getting on with the war and winning it than they were serving the public's right to know. A *Washington Post* survey conducted just before the battle revealed that 85% of respondents had 'a great deal' or 'quite a lot' of confidence in the US military, as compared with only 29% for newspapers and 33% for television. In a separate poll conducted by the Times Mirror Centre, 78% stated that they supported the Pentagon's restrictions on media coverage of the war, with 59% saying that it should exert 'even more control'.[42] Nonetheless, Martin Walker of the *Guardian* wrote from Washington that Khafji had already 'sobered the US public, unprepared by Pentagon briefings on the success of their hi-tech weapons for this evidence of the ability of the Iraqi troops to counter-attack and hold ground for 36 hours even after weeks of allied bombing',[43] while President Bush decided to tour military bases in America, it was said, 'to rally a public morale jolted by the first news of US ground casualties'.[44]

In Britain, also, public opinion appeared to be more in step with the military than with the media. As Charles Laurence pointed out in the *Daily Telegraph*:

Journalists argue that their task is to reveal as much information as they can gather; this is in the public interest and justifies their work. They argue that at Khafji, for instance, it was essential to dispel question-marks over the efficiency of the Saudi forces to deflect any damage to their fragile partnership with Arab allies. That, they insisted, was where the overriding public interest lay.[45]

But it was the power of the media to mould opinion which politicians feared and which some critics felt was creating an arrogance on the part of journalists. Peregrine Worsthorne wrote in the *Sunday Telegraph* that

the Gulf War has seen the media getting more and more out of step with public opinion. 'Media opinion', useful to impress the politicians but for little else, has replaced (or at any rate rivals) public opinion. An exception might be made for the tabloids which, on the Gulf, have been forced by the need to keep their readership to follow public opinion more closely than do their 'quality' colleagues ... What they point to is a self-absorption and a threatened disconnection from the realities of public opinion which might turn the media into at best a simple branch of the entertainment industry or, at worst, a representation of interest groups and well organised minorities (see the disproportionate amount of attention now focussed on the British 'peace movement').[46]

It was certainly true that, as the war 'dragged on', more and more attention was being given to attitudes towards the war which had not been fully represented before, when the initial optimism had pushed all but the spectacular start of the air campaign down the list of priorities. Even General Schwarzkopf admitted that 'perhaps in the euphoria of the high-technology weapons and this sort of thing, we had lost sight of the fact that lives are being lost'.[47]

Psychological warfare

Lives were indeed being lost: Iraqi lives. The coalition had begun to step up its bombing of enemy troop positions in Kuwait and southern Iraq as part of its preparations to soften up the opposition before the ground war. Nonetheless, the conscripts were considered to be a prime target for one aspect of the propaganda campaign which might just save their lives: psychological warfare operations. The need essentially was to convince them of how they were being used as cannon-fodder by Saddam, to demonstrate that further resistance was futile and to show them how to surrender safely.

On 21 January, the *Daily Telegraph* reported that, according to the CIA and other agencies conducting psychological warfare operations against the Iraqis, morale among the Iraqi troops could be a deciding factor in the length of the anticipated ground war. Senator Sam Nunn, chairman of the Senate's Armed Services Committee was quoted as saying: 'I certainly think it's possible there could be a psychological breakdown there and if that happens, it could go very rapidly.' Apparently President Bush had issued three secret directives between August and December outlining the Psy Ops campaign incorporating increasingly organised Kuwaiti resistance groups inside the occupied country with a combined use of 'black' radio stations and leaflet propaganda. As part of the preparations for this, thousands of transistor radios had been smuggled into Kuwait and southern Iraq with the help of nomads so that the enemy troops could listen to coalition broadcasts.[48]

One of the coalition's problems was that the government of Bahrain refused to allow American broadcasts in Arabic from the Voice of America's medium wave transmitter in that country. Short wave transmissions in Arabic, with their far greater range, were doubled to about 15 hours a day when the war began but receivers were too expensive and too few and far between in Iraq. If the coalition wished to penetrate the medium wave receivers possessed by the majority of Iraqi troops they would need access to the Bahrain transmitter. The obstacle was that the Bahranian government believed the Voice of America's Arabic service was too *friendly* to Saddam, with its information minister revealing to VOA director Bruce Gelb on 28 January that he was unwilling 'to take the risk of allowing others to talk on your behalf in a language you cannot monitor or understand'.[49] This was felt to be a reference to Palestinian and other Middle Eastern journalists working for the VOA whose loyalties were considered dubious. It was therefore left to the BBC's World Service, broadcasting in Arabic from its medium wave transmitter on the island of Masirah, to bear the brunt of the coalition's 'white', or overt and information-based, propaganda broadcasts.

'Black' propaganda, on the other hand, gives the appearance of coming from somewhere it is not. In the Gulf War, black broadcasts appeared to be emanating from disaffected groups inside Iraq and Kuwait, when in fact they were coming from transmitters within coalition-controlled areas. Given the vast desert landscape and what we know now about special operations forces roaming behind enemy lines, it was also possible to set up portable transmitters very close to Iraqi troop emplacements and even near to cities and to start broadcasting voices of disaffection in the hope that soldiers and civilians alike would eavesdrop.

We still know very little about this aspect of the propaganda campaign in the Gulf War but it was a tried and tested method in World War Two. Then, Britain's Political Warfare Executive and especially Sefton Delmer's unit, broadcasting in fact from Britain, ran a series of 'stations' (called Research Units) which gave the impression of conversations between underground cells of disaffected soldiers. Inside occupied Europe, allied agents would also risk life and limb transmitting rumours ('sibs') designed to sow seeds of doubt in the minds of any eavesdroppers. The latitude given to such propagandists, not only in their choice of language but in their actual content, was considerable; they did not need to worry about lies, for example, because they were not obviously coming from allied sources. The main criterion was credibility, and if that involved graphic language and gossip by seemingly ordinary people expressing their private reservations about their rulers then so much the better from the point of view of authenticity. Moreover, because the broadcasts seemed to be coming from inside Germany it was also possible to express views that ran counter to the official line. In the Second World War, for example, following the Casablanca Conference of 1942, allied policy was one of unconditional surrender, which implied that no amount of negotiation would be possible, not even if the German people rose up against their Nazi rulers. Black propagandists, on the other hand, could suggest that 'we' get rid of 'Hitler's gang' and 'our' situation might then well improve.[50]

Psychological warfare radio stations presumably transmitting from Saudi Arabia, such as the allegedly CIA-run Voice of Free Iraq and Radio Free Iraq, called upon the Kurdish and Shia Iraqis to rise up against the 'Saddam Hussein gang'.[51] Cleverly, coalition black propaganda blamed Saddam for bringing the forces of the 'Great Satan' into the area and insisted he must be punished for this.[52] The official coalition line was that this was a war to liberate Kuwait and not to overthrow Saddam Hussein. Allied leaders stated repeatedly that the coalition was not fighting the Iraqi people, which meant that, officially at least, the coalition would not be able to utilise dehumanisation propaganda against the enemy population as a whole. Instead, the coalition chose to separate out the Ba'athist Party and its storm-troopers, the Republican Guard. These were the people that were holding the Iraqi people back from peace and prosperity. And these were the people that must be overthrown – not by the coalition, but by the Iraqi people themselves.

The Voice of Free Iraq (*Sawt Al-Iraq Al-Hurr*) started broadcasting from a clandestine location on 1 January, although test transmissions had been picked up by the BBC Monitoring Service at Caversham since 21 December 1990. Claiming that its facilities had been donated by the Syrians, Egyptians, Saudis and other members of the Gulf Co-operation Council, the station was unashamedly anti-Saddam. From 26 January, the station identified itself as the 'Radio of the Iraqi Republic *from Baghdad*, the Voice of Free Iraq', the first part of this identification being identical to that of the official Iraqi national radio service.[53] Yet it remained unclear who precisely was running this operation.[54] On 30 January, it was broadcasting the following statement:

After all this destruction you are seeing around you, you Iraqi brother, you must be wondering: what did we gain, what did we reap in the Saddam Hussein era? ... And was it good for Iraq? Who is going to rebuild Iraq which was rich with its resources and great with its wealth, after all this destruction you are seeing around you ... As soon as he finishes a war, he takes us into another war, and as soon as he finishes with a problem, he creates another problem for our country, and as soon as he finishes a massacre, he initiates another massacre.[55]

The message was clear: the Iraqi people should rise up against Saddam Hussein so that the country could return to the peace-loving community of nations.

Nor was such an appeal confined to the civilian population. On 31 January the Voice of Free Iraq broadcast an appeal by the 'National Committee for the Salvation of Iraq' to the troops in the field:

Our heroic army! O sons of our brave armed forces! The tyrant has issued the order for the destruction of Iraq and its brave army, and has escalated his threats. By bragging about his missile capability, air defences and aircraft, our army has now become exposed not just in Kuwait but also in Iraq, and is being subjected to air bombardment which, God forbid, may lead to a great catastrophe liable to blow away Iraq, its people and army ... Onwards to revolution, O fearless soldiers and on to rebellion, O heroic officers. Aim your rifles at the tyrant's heart and at the heads of his filthy myrmidons. Hasten to the salvation of Iraq.[56]

On other occasions, opposition groups (fictional?) transmitted messages in tones similar to those heard on Iranian broadcasts by Shiite clerics in support of fundamentalist viewpoints. A spokesman for the 'Islamic Call Party', for example, maintained that

It has transpired that, behind this aggression, America is aiming at destroying Iraq for the benefit of Israel. If the declared objective of America is the liberation of Kuwait, then why all this destruction of Iraq we are witnessing. Is this meant for Israeli security through the breaking of the Iraqi military machine. We say to the Iraqi people that American law does not permit the planning for the assassination of a foreign head of state, but this law permits the destruction of a people and removing of a country like Iraq from the political map. This would seem strange to wise minds.[57]

Another clandestine station was The Voice of the Gulf (*Idha'at Sawt Al-Khalij*) which began transmissions on 5 February on both medium wave and FM, occupying some of same frequencies as those used formerly by Kuwaiti radio (now the Iraqi 'Mother of All Battles' station). Interspersed with readings from the Koran and patriotic music were direct appeals to the troops to surrender, such as the following:

Why don't you save your life and that of your colleagues by coming to the Kingdom of Saudi Arabia as the war is going to finish soon and then you will be able to return to your homeland and your family? And when you come, dear Iraqi soldier, it will be at the invitation of the command of the joint forces and operations theatre. You will be a guest of this command ... while enjoying the usual Arab generosity, security, safety and medical care.[58]

This was all a fairly one-way process. Holy Mecca Radio, a black Iraqi station targeted at anti-Saudi listeners, was not heard after 18 January. The Iraqi Voice of Peace station, which had accused Bart Simpson of sleeping with the wives of American troops prior to the war, was not heard after 20 January – to the lament, no doubt, of many troops. The Mother of All Battles station, which took over Kuwaiti radio and began transmitting in Arabic from 25 January and was joined by Voice of the Masses two days later, would also appear to have been knocked out by 5 February. Because these stations had all used powerful short wave frequencies, their appeal was clearly to the wider Arab world. It was the Mother of All Battles station, for example, which gave full play to Saddam's pronouncement that every Iraqi, Arab or Moslem who engaged in terrorist activities against coalition interests would be considered a martyr[59] and which boasted of its triumphs in the holy war against the infidel. The degradation of Iraq's capacity to spread propaganda both inside Iraq and beyond by means other than via western journalists would appear to suggest that the coalition considered this a significant part of their overall bombing campaign. One can only speculate as to the feelings of the planners concerning reporters in Baghdad who were undermining this effort, especially since reports from Iraq provided faces to the enemy people and bombing victims which coalition propagandists would sooner have remained anonymous.

A further problem for the allies was how to supply the Iraqi people with alternative sources of reliable (i.e coalition) information about what was going on. Accordingly, the Voice of America began transmitting in Arabic on the same frequency as Radio Baghdad, which became harder to pick up as the allies extended their bombing; by mid February only one transmitter was operational on the short wave and jamming (about three times more expensive than broadcasting) made this even more difficult to receive.[60]

The main focus of the coalition's psychological warfare activities was, however, designed to encourage Iraqi troops to defect. Before the war, the American Psychological Operations Group (POG) had experimented with leaflets scattered by balloon along the Kuwait–Saudi border.[61] Drawn up in consultation with Arab psychologists, a common form of leaflet was the 'invitation card', illustrated with cartoons and designed 'to play on the feeling of Arab brotherhood that we hope will survive this conflict'.[62] One highly effective method was to drop leaflets by aircraft prior to an air strike, announcing precisely when the raid would take place, and then again after the bombing saying 'we told you so'. Others depicted Saddam riding a bedraggled barefoot soldier like a horse or depicted anxious Iraqi parents worrying about the safety of their sons.[63] On the back of many were the following instructions:

CEASE RESISTANCE – BE SAFE

To seek refuge safely, the bearer must strictly adhere to the following procedures:

1 Remove the magazine from your weapon.

2 Sling your weapon over your left shoulder, muzzle down.

3 Have both arms raised above your head.

4 Approach the MULTINATIONAL Forces' positions slowly, with the lead soldier holding this document above his head.

5 If you do this, you will not die.

Reports suggested that, by the start of February, 5 million leaflets had been dropped about how to surrender.[64] By the end of the war, something like a total of 30 million leaflets would be dropped over Iraqi lines, an astonishing figure which meant nearly two for every member of the Iraqi population and about 50–60 for every enemy soldier estimated to be within the theatre of operations.[65]

Paper promises were one thing, but their credibility depended upon the ability of the coalition to deliver what it said it could do. Accordingly, immediately after war's outbreak, the coalition air forces began to concentrate on pounding the Republican Guard positions in southern Iraq and northern Kuwait. It was here that B52 bombers, some of which would soon be flying from Fairford airbase in Britain, concentrated their fire-power in their indiscriminate 'carpet bombing' of the well dug-in, heavily protected and privileged 'elite' units. Similarly, thanks to immediate achievement of air superiority, allied planes were targeting front-line Iraqi conscript troops. Poor weather often hampered the ability of precision-guided planes to hit strategic targets inside Iraq and so combat missions were frequently diverted to attacking positions inside Kuwait, 'so there was no time, from day one on, that the Iraqi ground forces were not under heavy air attack'.[66] As General Schwarzkopf had insisted: 'I can assure you that when and if we have to fight a ground war, I'm not going to fight his [ie Saddam's] war. He's going to fight our war.'[67]

Psy Ops were to play an integral part of that bombardment. On 6 February, leaflets were dropped stating that 'Tomorrow if you don't surrender we're going to drop on you the largest conventional weapon in the world'. The next day, a BLU-82 bomb was dropped on the target area. At 15,000 pounds, this weapon (also known as a 'Daisy Cutter') was the size of a Volkswagen Beetle and its massive explosion resembled an atomic bomb detonation. A British special operations team in the area radioed back to headquarters that 'Sir, the blokes have just nuked Kuwait', while Colonel Jesse Jackson, Schwarzkopf's special operations commander, informed his superiors that 'We're not too sure how you say "Jesus Christ" in Iraqi'. Subsequently, more leaflets were dropped stating: 'You have just been hit with the largest conventional bomb in the world. More on the way.' A major success of this characteristic example of a psychological warfare operation was the defection of an Iraqi commander and his staff who raced across the border to surrender before the second bomb could be dropped on their positions. One of them brought with him the maps of the Iraqi minefields along his section of the Saddam Line – an invaluable intelligence coup that was to greatly help coalition troops once the ground war started.[68] In the weeks that followed, almost three-quarters of the defectors crossing the Saudi border stated that their decision to give themselves up had been influenced by allied leaflets and broadcasts. But the bombing itself must have played the major role in their decision; prior to the war, there was nothing like the same number of desertions even though the Psy Ops campaign had barely got under way.

The absence of any real aerial resistance on the part of the Iraqis nonetheless still fostered the illusion in some quarters that a ground war might be averted. Although Iraq's nuclear capacity was said to have been destroyed at the outset of the air war, and much of its chemical and biological manufacturing capability undermined, there was still a fear that Iraqi troops in the field possessed chemical weapons. As this anxiety increased, coupled with a growing media impatience about the lack of information coming out of Riyadh and Washington, on Wednesday 23 January General Colin Powell made a timely declaration that coalition strategy was to 'cut off and kill' the Iraqi army. In the most forthcoming briefing of the war up to that point, Powell and Cheney reiterated General Schwarzkopf's point about fighting the war on their own terms and that the aerial bombardment would go on: 'time is on our side,' said the Defense Secretary.[69] The major questions, therefore, were when and where.

As for the latter, it should have come as no surprise – to the Iraqis least of all – that the attack eventually took place where it did. A careful examination of the informed western media would have provided ample clues. As early as 27 January, for example, *The Independent*'s correspondent Phil Davidson travelled across the 300 mile allied front and his observations left him in no doubt that 'in the battle to free Kuwait, US armour and infantry will thrust forward across southern Iraq'. While Baghdad may or may not have been reading *The Independent*, a similar strategy had been outlined more than once by military strategists interviewed on CNN, which was certainly avidly watched there. That the location of the attack still came as a surprise, therefore, was a tribute to the overall military deception operation (see also Chapter 5).

As for the question of when, on Sunday 27 January Dick Cheney elaborated on his position in a televised interview. He said that the United States had 'always assumed' it would need a land war to expel Iraqi troops from Kuwait, 'but we don't want to do it any earlier than we have to', by which he meant 'after we've done enormous damage to his ground forces – after they've been significantly weakened'.[70] Apart from the carpet bombing of the Iraqi entrenchments in Kuwait and southern Iraq, this was to be achieved by cutting supply lines and, as the war approached the end of its second week, the coalition turned its attention to attacking bridges and supply columns. On Monday 28 January, allied war planes were reported to have caught an Iraqi military convoy moving across the open desert in Kuwait, destroying 24 tanks, armoured personnel carriers and supply vehicles – in fact the largest known single success against Iraqi armour since the start of the war.[71] It was also at about this time that some pool reporters noted that something had changed in the field:

the usually hypersensitive US censors have permitted information to be released about the unpreparedness of sections of the American force, leading to the suspicion that a full scale disinformation may now be under way to try to fool Saddam about the date of any attack.[72]

This would appear to reinforce the suspicion voiced above about Khafji. That battle was not only an invaluable lesson for the military, providing important information for the ground war to come, but it also exposed many of the problems which the media managers were becoming increasingly aware of, which, in turn, would enable them to get things right well in advance of any ground offensive.

Storm in the desert

Dhahran, quipped one journalist, was 'a news free environment' while, after Khafji, others complained that they were frequently threatened with the withdrawal of their credentials 'if we try to find out what really happened'.[73] In the recriminations that followed over the confusion which had prevailed owing to the coalition's version of events there were essentially two stages. First, the media blamed the military for not telling them that the liberation of the town was going on and that they had heard it first on Radio Baghdad; then, many military analysts blamed the media for letting the Iraqis know that Khafji was empty by transmitting pictures of the deserted town during the previous weekend.[74]

General Schwarzkopf had become increasingly dissatisfied with growing acrimonious exchanges between media and military, reminding him a little of Vietnam. On Thursday 31 January and Friday 1 February, he watched the mood turn so sour as Brigadier-General Pat Stevens fielded questions about discrepancies over Khafji that he decided to summon press representatives, to listen to their complaints about sanitisation and access and to reform the system. Henceforth, the televised portion of the briefings was to be limited normally to 30 minutes, with time for more off-the-record, and therefore supposedly more forthcoming, question-and-answer sessions afterwards. Three American briefings per day would take place, but normally only one would be in the presence of television cameras. The 'witty and telegenic' Major-General Robert Johnston was appointed to conduct the press briefings in future. Schwarzkopf also started to grant more personal interviews.[75]

On Sunday 3 February, the new arrangements were announced. In addition to the nightly televised briefings, it was decided to add a morning background briefing and a further question-and-answer session after the cameras had been turned off in the evening. These sessions would allow greater latitude in the answers given out because military officers would not be identified, 'in theory allowing them freedom to give information they are unready or unwilling to give at the televised briefings where every word is recorded'.[76] Promises were also made to get information to the media more quickly than had happened previously. This, however, seems not to have satisfied everyone and perhaps even served only to encourage unattainable aspirations. As one journalist observed subsequently, 'Frustration abounds. The US military pretends to be perplexed about journalists' complaints.'[77]

A further consequence of the Khafji incident was the expansion of the size of the allied pools by mid February. This followed a series of rows which indicated that military–media relations were continuing to deteriorate despite the modifications to the system. First came a request by the US military to the Saudi government to expel four French unilaterals.[78] Tension also persisted concerning the absence from the pools of any journalists other than Anglo-American reporters. Eventually, on 12 February, an open letter was written by 300 journalists from 23 different countries (but none from Britain and America) to King Fahd and the allied commanders in the Gulf which threatened 'direct action' unless something was done, by which was meant a concerted attempt to break through road-blocks erected to keep non-pool journalists away from the troops. 'Frustration about the system is reaching crisis point among international journalists,' the letter warned, and further stated:

Our understanding of this military conflict is that it is carried out under the auspices of the United Nations. However, the clear impression here is that Americans and the American military are in total command of the situation, including the movement of foreign nationals on sovereign Saudi territory.[79]

Although the Pentagon subsequently announced that 5 new pools would be created, comprising 7 members each, adding to the 15 currently in existence, it failed to alleviate tension amongst the non Anglo-Americans. The expansion was explained to be 'a response to the complaints of the press corps, who have brought to our attention the inadequacies of the current system'.[80] The actual operational rules within the pools, however, were to remain unchanged. The mounting tension within the French camp was to reach flashpoint on 19 February when, following TF1's screening of an interview with several French soldiers who claimed they did not know why they were there but it might have been to fight for oil, French TV crews were banned from the front, whereupon they began a boycott of coverage of the war in protest at the refusal of the French military authorities to permit a news pool to accompany the Foreign Legion and other forward units in the impending ground war.[81] The row was quickly settled, with the army agreeing to ferry journalists to the French forces at the front.[82] It was, after all, vital for it to have been done so. The last thing the coalition wanted or needed was undue media attention being afforded to the position of the French forces as they moved secretly into position for the ground war, given that the French Daguet Force was in fact to spearhead one of the main western thrusts into southern Iraq.

Another consequence of the Khafji incident was for the allies to step up B52 bombing raids flown from Britain, Spain and Diego Garcia against Iraqi troops stationed in forward positions in Kuwait. Avoiding a repetition of Khafji was essential, especially from a propaganda point of view. There was still clearly a long way to go before a ground offensive could begin, especially when spy satellite intelligence data from the Basra area indicated that only about 10% of the Republican Guard's heavy armour had been destroyed despite more than a fortnight of intensive bombing.[83] General Schwarzkopf cautioned against impatience: 'we're only two and a half weeks into a very, very major military enterprise, and we've cautioned all along against false enthusiasm'.[84] Iraqi propaganda meanwhile continued to taunt the coalition forces, accusing them of being afraid of hand-to-hand combat, itself a reflection of some confidence despite the eventual defeat at Khafji.

This did indeed prompt General Schwarzkopf and other briefers to warn of the difficulties his troops were likely to face once Desert

Storm moved into the ground attack phase. America's first ground casualties prompted an escalation of the psychological preparations directed especially at the American public for the land offensive and for more deaths to come. This was an extremely delicate campaign because of the need on the one hand to sustain public support by realistic appraisals of how many were likely to die and, on the other, not to alienate that support by suggesting that the figure was likely to be too high. This in turn was used to justify an intensification of the aerial campaign against Iraqi troop positions and to 'soften up' the Republican Guard.

The growing number of Iraqi soldiers crossing their own mine-fields to escape allied bombing of Kuwaiti positions, not to mention alleged murder squads employed by Saddam to deter deserters,[85] were in fact providing vital intelligence that Iraqi morale was gradually being worn down. In Riyadh, General Neal described the wretched conditions of these men. They were badly fed, lice-infested and in poor physical and mental health.[86] 'Some', said General Michel Roquejeoffre, commander of French forces in the region, 'are very happy to have been captured.'[87] Of those taken prisoner in the battle for Khafji, it was said that, although they had fought well, once captured they admitted to being demoralised, hungry and happy to be out of the war. Many were carrying coalition leaflets. Those to the north who had managed to cross into Turkey spoke of shortages of food, ammunition, fuel, water and clothing. It was to exploit such conditions and to drive home the futility of their plight that the allies stepped up their broadcasts while simultaneously stepping up the air bombardment of Iraqi troops in Kuwait.

Reluctance to be drawn into precise casualty figures, either actual on the Iraqi part or potential on the coalition side, was, said General Robert Johnston, because 'we did that during Vietnam. That was a mistake. Our ability to count, to give you a body count, is so imprecise that's its not a good way of measuring an enemy engagement'.[88] Added to this was the element of disinforming the enemy as to where a likely assault would take place, which meant a stepping up of naval activity and the bombardment of the Kuwaiti coastline by such visually impressive vessels as the USS *Missouri* and USS *Wisconsin*, described as 'target practice, getting ready' for the Marines.[89]

The clearest indication for the media of the impact of all this came when four Iraqi soldiers gave themselves up to a group of unilateralist journalists on 6 February.[90] After handing them over to the Egyptians, the journalists were able to gain their best picture to date of what life for the front-line troops was like. Hungry, surrounded by minefields and policed by Republican Guard units, the deserters described how they had listened to the BBC's Arabic Service and other stations before their battery-operated radios had expired. They said the war and Saddam were 'stupid' and 'crazy' and that 'everyone wants to come like us'. It is, of course, a well-known phenomenon that captured soldiers tend to tell their interrogators what they think they want to hear, but here at last was tangible evidence from journalists rather than official briefers that much of what had been claimed about the state of morale within the Iraqi front-line forces was not far wide of the mark – which was extremely useful for the coalition so soon after Khafji. By speaking so explicitly, the enemy soldiers were placing their own lives in danger if they returned to Iraq after the war. Besides, on this occasion it was the press who were interviewing them, not troops who were interrogating. Other clues also began to leak out. From Baghdad, Richard Beeston of *The Times* had recently visited a hospital in which the doctor had pointed to a body and stated: 'This is one of the marchers from Kuwait. They do not normally bring them here; usually they take them to a hospital across town.'[91] Further references to this mysterious march were deleted by the Iraqi censors but, in the weeks that followed, journalists in Iraq were testifying to the increasing number of troops returning from the front at the Baghdad bus station – but cameras were forbidden to film and journalists to interview any of these people. 'Were Saddam to give a body count, if that were possible,' wrote one analyst, 'he would risk alarming his own people.'[92]

Although on 8 February Tom King dodged a question in London about whether more Iraqi troops might be deserting but for the fact that they had no option except to stay put, the delicate issue for intra-coalition politics of pounding members of the Arab brotherhood was taken up incessantly at the Saudi briefing that day. The commander of the Saudi forces, Lieutenant-General Khalid bin Sultan, confirmed that the Iraqis had created a special execution squad to deal with deserters.[93] But no matter how sympathetic coalition opinion was being encouraged to be by portrayals of reluctant Iraqi conscript soldiers as part of the 'we are not fighting the people of Iraq' propaganda line, the fact remains that it was those very conscript troops who were mostly stationed in Kuwait. And Kuwaiti resistance groups were beginning to speak more and more of atrocities being committed by the Iraqi army. These stories, difficult to verify as yet, were given considerable credence – and widespread publicity – when, on 7 February, a report compiled by Physicians for Human Rights in the US and Denmark was published. This report detailed evidence of a systematic campaign of terror against the citizens of Kuwait, with summary executions and arbitrary arrest, and of how prematurely born babies were being removed from hospital incubators and left to die. One doctor was reported as stating:

Uniformed Iraqi soldiers unplugged the incubators and threw the babies on the floor. They took the incubators. The soldiers said: 'These things belong to Iraq now. This equipment belongs to Baghdad. People have to die.' We couldn't even touch the babies. We had to wrap them and send them for burial later on.[94]

If there was a Gulf War equivalent to the famous First World War Bryce Report on Alleged German Outrages in Belgium, this was it. Although most of the stories contained in it were from the post-invasion, pre-war period, the wartime message was clear enough. Moreover, given that the Republican Guard was mainly situated outside Kuwait City, back up on the Iraq–Kuwait border, these stories were clearly referring to those ordinary reluctant conscript warriors who had fought surprisingly well at Khafji and who were now fleeing increasingly across their own minefields in hundreds to desert.

In the days that followed, the media had little new to report. Much was made of comparatively little: the USS *Missouri* firing its shells against Iraqi emplacements on the Kuwaiti coast – the first time it had fired its massive 16 inch guns in anger since the Korean war; the island of Umm Al-Maradim surrender after the letters SOS were spotted from the air (both of which prompted renewed speculation about a possible sea-borne invasion); the oil slick that was moving further down the Gulf to threaten Saudi Arabia's desalination plants and attempts to rescue the wildlife. All these, in normal circumstances, were by themselves big stories but some of the media had been spoiled on the initial air campaign and angered by the Khafji incident. While pool reporters routinely followed the progress and preparations of the troops in the field and the unilaterals attempted to find out whether something out of the ordinary was really happening, attention in some ways shifted to the diplomatic manoeuvring involving Iran and the Soviet Union.

In a sense, these were also non-events. King Hussein of Jordan had already discovered the difficulties of attempting to call a halt to the fighting, claiming that he had secured an Iraqi agreement to withdraw from Kuwait within 48 hours of war's outbreak, but that this had been 'stifled'.[95] The White House also reacted coolly to President Rafsanjani's offer of 3 February to mediate between Iraq and the United States, with Tehran even offering to restore diplomatic links with its former enemy.[96] This cautious American response was not surprising in view of Iran's insistence that Saddam indicate his willingness to withdraw from Kuwait *before* any peace plan could be discussed further and given that Saddam had never shown willing to make such an announcement at any time since the invasion began – unless King Hussein's underpublicised initiative was taken into account. Very little more was heard about the Iranian initiative until the Iranian President denounced Saddam as 'despotic' before a mass crowd of Islamic activists in Tehran on 11 February. In Britain meanwhile, as Foreign Secretary Douglas Hurd was visiting the Middle East, attention shifted temporarily to the harsh winter and whether interest rates would fall and, more dramatically, to the IRA mortar attack on Downing Street on Thursday 7 February. Iraqi radio propaganda attempted to exploit the IRA·attack, together with the explosions at London railway stations, in terms that 'the capital of imperialism – London – has been turned into an arena of confrontation, explosions and acts of violence, revealing the regime's shaky position, weakness, unpopularity and inability to maintain security and solve national problems by democratic means'.[97] Two days later, a slightly more worrying development for the coalition came when President Gorbachev warned that the coalition risked exceeding the UN mandate and dispatched his envoy Yevgeny Primakov to Iraq for the third time since the war began. All these diplomatic manoeuvres in the conflict were building up to the first wartime meeting of the United Nations' Security Council on 13 February.

Given the unattractive nature of diplomacy for television, the problem for the coalition's mood managers was the dearth of

sensational new stories; the old ones were pretty impressive from
a military point of view, but they were nonetheless old stories from
the media's viewpoint. So the slightest hint of a dent in the allied
preparations – whether it be a unilateral report that the build-up
was in disarray or that a Scud attack in a remote area was not
announced – was picked up and given a prominence it might not
otherwise have deserved. As John Keegan wrote, 'the media find
the news famine frustrating', or as Sir William Deedes put it:
'relative inactivity gives the imagination too much free play'.[98]
And indeed it was in this climate that attention shifted to the
question of collateral damage in Iraq (see Chapter 4), which in
turn tended to produce a series of stories questioning the veracity
of coalition statements. In its turn, this resulted in the media
discussing their own role and the effectiveness or otherwise of
Iraqi propaganda.

This did however prompt an interesting debate in the British
press about the nature of 'truth'. Those journalists who appeared
to be hunting for bad news came under attack in Britain by Herb
Greer in the *Sunday Telegraph*, who wrote:

It seems a particularly dangerous form of self-delusion to pretend that a
national quest for 'Truth' allows the media to behave like the most cynical
arms dealer and indifferently supply the weapon to both sides. When
public opinion is a vital arm of any nation's will to fight – especially in a
democracy – the ability of our media to undermine the national will for
combat is (as the Vietnam syndrome showed beyond doubt) simply denied
by the journalist of 'liberal' persuasion.[99]

He went on to wonder what on earth the missing CBS crew
thought they were up to, especially as they might now be subjected
to Iraqi interrogation and thus reveal information which might
jeopardise the lives of coalition troops. Citing T.E. Lawrence's
axiom, he continued:

Our governments, especially America's, have learned a lot about the value
of relative openness, and practise it now, even in wartime. The journalist's
denial of this, supported with simplistic and one-sided generalisations, is
itself a kind of propaganda. It carries the potential of great harm to
journalism, to the reporters themselves ... to our combat troops and to
the nation's ability to fight in a decent cause. It can thus deliver 'the
greatest weapon in the armoury of the modern commander' exclusively
into the enemy's hands.

Two days later, Hugo Young in the *Guardian* addressed the same issue, pointing out that 'truth-in-government' was an elusive commodity anyway, even in peacetime. 'War, in one sense, merely accentuates the conditions of peace, in which truth-telling is destined always to be imperfect.' While conceding that in wartime truth is 'at best fragmentary and episodic', he added:

This time, however, one difference is important and begins to give substance to the discontent. Although the whole truth is no more available than it ever was, the illusion of truth is more strongly present than it has ever been. This is the achievement of wall-to-wall television. Here is this powerful medium, uniquely the medium of the actual and believable, devoting so much time to the war that unwary viewers may be easily lulled into the belief that their picture is complete.[100]

Moreover, because the journalists were essentially at the mercy of the military, 'although one cannot yet call this a total war, it has inspired a regime of total propaganda from which as much evidence as possible of the bloody hellishness of war should be erased'. Christopher Dunkley in the *Financial Times* took this point further:

In the long term, honesty is still the best policy. And if the cumulative honesty of television in a free society (i.e. the tendency of a diverse broadcasting system to provide, collectively, a sort of truth) has the effect of turning us increasingly against war, perhaps that is no bad thing.[101]

In fact, none of this resulted in a waning of either media or public support for the war. In Britain, polls indicated that public support for the government was greater than it was during the Korean and Suez conflicts and at least as strong as at any time during the Falklands War.[102] On the other side of the Atlantic, the *New York Times,* which had argued for the maintenance of sanctions as a means of resolving the dispute before the war, remained (albeit almost reluctantly) behind what it called 'a just, but not a wise war', although it also remained extremely nervous about the likely casualties of a ground war. Indeed, that was where the major debate now focused, with the Vietnam factor once again very much in the forefront of discussions concerning anticipated US casualty figures.

On 6 February, American Secretary of State James Baker warned that expelling Iraq from Kuwait would require military actions which will 'necessarily involve many casualties, great hardships and growing fears for the future'. It was going to be, he said, a formidable task and no one should underestimate Saddam's military capabilities. This came a day after President Bush had warned that it was unlikely that an air offensive alone would be sufficient to expel the Iraqis. Between them, both men were beginning to prepare the psychological ground for a land offensive and indeed for eventual victory, with reminders that a just war was being fought against a brutal dictator and that everything was being done to avoid civilian casualties and with the first indications of American post-war policy. This, according to Baker, was to include the rapid withdrawal of American forces in the area, regional arms control measures, the establishment of new regional security arrangements, renewed efforts to solve the Israeli–Palestine problem and the reconstruction of Iraq: 'we have no quarrel with the Iraqi people,' he said.[103] But, first things first: the war itself would need to be won.

One of the further problems revealed by Khafji and its aftermath was the difference in tone between the more politically sensitive Washington briefings and the more militarily oriented briefings in Riyadh. For example, while one Pentagon official was describing the Iraqi action at Khafji as 'a good performance from ordinary troops, who included conscripts and makes you think how tough the Republican Guard will be', General Schwarzkopf was asserting: 'Any time a significant amount of fire was brought to bear on any place where the Iraqis were, they began to give up.'[104] Other reports suggested that the military wanted a ground attack sooner rather than later, with some predicting a 'Saint Valentine's Day Massacre' for 14 February. Clearly, the military and the politicians would need to get together.

On the weekend of 9–10 February, Cheney and Powell visited the allied Central Command headquarters in Riyadh (known as the 'Black Hole') to assess the situation and establish a possible date for the land offensive. Schwarzkopf urged that it should be later rather than sooner and that at least two more weeks of bombing should take place. Cheney later told the press that he was 'struck' by the sheer size of Iraq's military machine and admitted that there was still a possibility that Saddam could deliver more surprises. This sobering note was echoed by Tom King, who said there was 'still some way to go'.[105] Even though over 1,000 Iraqi prisoners of war were now in allied hands,[106] the air war would need to continue to pound those hundreds of thousands who were not, together with their supply lines, for some time yet.

General Schwarzkopf was soon claiming that attacks on those supply links had resulted in a 90% reduction of Iraqi supplies. The purpose was to minimise allied casualties once the ground offensive began, although a *Guardian* leader suggested also that 'their true mission is to help convince American public opinion that bombing alone can't finish the job'.[107] Despite the risks which the attacks involved of increasing opposition to the bombing among peace groups and in anti-American Muslim countries, they were apparently made on the advice of Schwarzkopf and relayed to Bush via Cheney and Powell. Not only did the allied commander want to keep casualties on his own side down to a minimum, but he was reportedly also concerned by logistical problems in the sea-borne delivery of essential military equipment for the ground war caused by poor weather conditions.[108] Douglas Hurd, still in the region visiting Arab leaders of the coalition, added that those allies were in no particular hurry either. The President said: 'we must continue down this road. We're the ones who are going to set the time for any action that is taken.'[109]

Even so, the President still had to balance military considerations against the political dangers of the various diplomatic initiatives and possible fall-out over civilian casualties, all of which seemed to be increasing. As we have seen, the Iranian move, backed by other non-aligned nations such as India, had failed to receive much of a hearing in Baghdad, let alone Washington, possibly for reasons related to the issue of the fleeing planes. President Gorbachev's envoy, Yevgeny Primakov, had however arrived in Baghdad on 9 February to see what he could do, but the very next day Saddam was still proving defiant when he broadcast to the nation, urging Iraqis to be patient, assuring them of eventual victory – and making no mention of the peace moves. Iraq, he said, was 'a fortress of faith' and that with 'every moment, minute, hour, day, week and month' that passed the allied defeat was made greater. From Amman, Iraq's deputy prime minister, Sadoun Hammadi, was also in defiant mood when, on 10 February, he even invited an international delegation to inspect the civilian damage in Iraq: 'Innocent people, women and children, are dying from the plane and missile attacks by the states claiming to be the defenders of human rights,' he said.[110]

But then when, on 12 February, Saddam suddenly and unexpectedly informed Primakov that he was now willing to find a settlement to the dispute, fortunately for the coalition he said he would do so only in the context of seeking a solution to the wider problems in the region. So the United States could still insist that Iraq must first leave Kuwait under the terms of Resolution 660 before any negotiating was begun. As there was no sign as yet of Saddam's willingness to do this, the protagonists stood firmly at opposite poles of a diplomatic spectrum in which other powers attempted to find some middle ground. This was usually referred to as finding a 'face-saving option' for Saddam, but part of the problem with this was that Bush and Saddam had so personalised the conflict that neither was able to make any concession without the other appearing to have lost face or to have backed down from their public stances. It was precisely at this point, in mid February, that an event occurred which was to dominate the world's media and bring to the fore all of the issues which the war had exposed both militarily and politically: the bombing of the Amiriya bunker/shelter.

Chapter Four

'Collateral damage': the air war and the issue of civilian casualties

Introduction

The issue of 'collateral damage' in general, and of the tragic Amiriya bunker/shelter incident in particular, was a critical aspect of the propaganda war in the Gulf conflict – for both sides. The tragedy at Amiriya created precisely the kind of allied nightmare and the sought-after Iraqi propaganda opportunity which coalition media managers had feared since the outset of the air attacks on Baghdad. On 13 February, in the Amiriya suburb of the city, two allied precision-guided bombs smashed through the roof of an installation killing hundreds of people. By early light, western correspondents, transported to the scene from the Al-Rashid hotel by the Iraqi Ministry of Information, were literally swarming all over the ruins. Here at last, in full view of the world's television cameras, was 'evidence' not only of the horrors of war but also, the Iraqis claimed, of the brutal, deliberate and indiscriminate nature of allied bombing which they said had been going on for weeks.

Significantly, all Iraqi censorship and reporting restrictions were lifted. Charred corpses of mainly women and children, barely recognisable as human beings, were carried out from the smoking rubble on improvised stretchers made from patterned blankets and later paraded in front of the Yarmuk hospital. The shock of the event was all the more severe coming as it did after three weeks of a sanitised, almost bloodless, war – despite the mounting number of uncomfortable indications that civilians were dying as a result of the air campaign. *The Times*, looking back for parallels to the Falklands War in the same way that the Americans searched

169

for points of comparison with Vietnam, likened the event to the sinking of the Belgrano in 1982 when 380 Argentinians had died and which 'had an emotional and psychological impact on the British public since it marked the first heavy loss of life before the ground war began'.[1] Or, as the French anchorman put it on the TF1 television channel, 'that which everyone has feared has come to pass'.[2]

The issue of 'collateral damage'

In many respects from a propaganda point of view, the tragedy of Amiriya could indeed be regarded as having been inevitable. By choosing to launch a massive air strike against Iraq as their preparation for the ground war, allied military planners must have known that the risk of hitting civilian targets was high. It was admittedly nowhere near as high as it had been in wars past, thanks to the possession of sophisticated laser-guided weaponry which could hit precisely what it was aimed at, but accidents do happen, especially at the human (intelligence, programming or pilot error) stage. It later transpired that there was also a limit to the amount of smart ordnance available to the coalition. However, a decision had been taken at the time by the coalition against the area bombing of cities and to make a key propaganda point of this; there would be no Guernicas or Dresdens – and certainly no Hiroshimas – in the Gulf War. Iraqi cities would be targeted only with smart weapons and not carpet bombed. In his very first wartime briefing, for example, General Schwarzkopf had made a point of emphasising that 'we're doing absolutely everything we can in this campaign to avoid injuring or hurting or destroying innocent people. We have said all along that this is not a war against the Iraqi people'.[3] Western correspondents were struck by the degree to which coalition servicemen channelled their feelings of hate not against the enemy population but mainly against the individual persona of Saddam Hussein with slogans being painted on bombs such as 'Hussein, if Allah does not answer, ask for Jesus', 'Saddam: this one's for you' and 'Here's looking at you, Saddam'.[4] The public relations people undoubtedly worked hard to prevent cameras from being pointed at less acceptable or more offensive slogans.

Before the first week was out, however, one London official

pointed out privately that 'we are already worrying that if the bombing goes on for a long time, as we expect it will, people will begin to accuse us of another Dresden'.[5] From a propaganda point of view, this risk was made all the more serious owing to the apparent determination of western reporters to remain inside the target country. Although coalition spokesmen had never denied that collateral damage was bound to happen, the impression created from Riyadh of a smart, clean war by the regular release of military videos depicting clinical bombing accuracy of military and strategic targets nonetheless helped to create an atmosphere in which any accidents to civilian areas were bound to prove highly embarrassing.

The initial reluctance (or inability) of the Iraqi authorities to escort western journalists in Baghdad to undeniably damaged civilian sites had consolidated still further the impression created by the coalition's statements. At first, the Iraqi News Agency, INA, conceded the deaths of only 23 'martyrs' and 66 'others' wounded after two days of allied bombing,[6] which, for what was being described as the greatest aerial assault in military history, was a remarkably low figure by any estimation. The upper floors of an apartment block in Baghdad, for example, were reportedly hit in the initial air strike yet no information was forthcoming from the Iraqis about civilian casualties. 'All that was known', reported the *Guardian*, 'was that 12 survived.'[7] The Iraqi Minister of Information, Latif Nassif Al-Jassem, simply declared that many civilians, mainly old people, had been killed but gave no specific figures or corroborating evidence.[8] Likewise, from Paris, ambassador Al-Hashimi merely asserted to the BBC on the first weekend that 'more civilian targets are being hit and casualties are high'.[9]

In Dick Cheney's first-night statement in which he said that the best damage assessments he had seen were on CNN, he had added: 'It would appear, based on the comments that were coming in from the CNN crew in the hotel in Baghdad, that the operation was successful in striking targets with a high degree of precision.'[10] When CNN was closed down temporarily the next day and Iraqi censorship reintroduced, British Defence Secretary Tom King was accordingly able to tell the press at the MoD briefing on Friday 18 January that the decision suggested that there was little civilian damage to report. 'I do not think', he pointed out, 'that would be the case if they felt there was a situation which could be used for propaganda purposes of civilian casualties.'[11] Or, as John Sweeney wrote in the *Observer*:

In such a totalitarian society, it may be possible to deduce something not from the evidence, but from the absence of it. To date, there have been no pictures of Allied attacks on schools, orphanages or hospitals. Perhaps that is because there have been none: such footage would be too good a propaganda coup for the Iraqis to pass by.[12]

Irritating questions put to military briefers in Riyadh in the first few days about what might have happened once the flash on the screen had faded to black were greeted either with a 'no comment' or with the statement that it was too early to evaluate the precise nature of the damage. There was be no gloss taken off the shining examples of modern technology at work.

Cheney's tacit admission that CNN was as good an intelligence source as any possessed by the coalition for bomb damage assessment clearly proved to be a double-edged sword when Peter Arnett's voice reports over the next ten days repeatedly testified to the impact of allied bombing. As a result, coalition briefers started to change their emphasis. General Colin Powell announced 'that we were very concerned about the collateral damage, making sure that no innocent civilians were killed or injured, and we were very sensitive to cultural or religious sites within the area'.[13] Yet the fact remained that official Iraqi propaganda figures concerning casualties were actually helping the allied case – yet one more example of the failure of Iraqi propaganda to exploit the most obvious of opportunities.

Some Iraqi exiles believed that this situation existed because the bombing had completely disoriented the Ministry of Information in Baghdad, that the war had caught the Iraqis totally by surprise and unprepared. Others believed that Saddam was too vulnerable to a coup for him to risk publicising the real extent of the damage. A Palestinian journalist working for the *Financial Times*, Lamis Andoni, claimed that the Iraqis were initially reluctant to issue any sort of casualty figures because they were worried about demoralising their own public.[14] As to what damage had actually been caused to civilians, in the west supporters of the war pointed to the military videos as 'evidence' of accuracy whereas opponents were forced to guess and presume that such damage 'must have been' caused.

Following the expulsion from Iraq of most of the western journalists on 19 January, speculation concerning the extent of civilian damage if anything actually increased. Even Lamis Andoni, who stayed until 23 January and who saw destroyed apartment buildings in the city centre and heard much talk of civilian casualties, noted that she did not see 'black banners on houses – the customary sign of mourning for a death in the family.' But, she added: 'It may have been too soon for this.'[15] By Wednesday 23 January, however, Iraqi newspapers did begin to publish photographs of damage to civilian areas. Yet because the majority of western journalists had been told to leave several days earlier, there was now even less way of corroborating Iraqi claims, not least because of Baghdad's refusal to allow the International Red Cross to visit the alleged sites. Moreover, even after six days of bombing and nearly 10,000 sorties, the Iraqis maintained that only 41 of their people had been killed and 191 wounded in air and missile attacks.[16] By the next day, the figure of dead Iraqi civilians was said to have risen to 60, including 13 killed when a coalition plane crashed into several houses.[17]

Whether or not the Baghdad regime was disguising the real nature of the damage for the benefit of morale amongst its supporters in the Arab world, such figures were not really the stuff of which atrocity propaganda is made. Furthermore, the Iraqis claimed that 'only 90 martyrs' had been killed in the military theatre of operations – again a remarkably low figure given the number of sorties flown and the carpet bombing which had taken place up to that time. When Saddam Hussein made his first wartime visit to the southern front, he was quoted by Iraqi sources as having said 'the American aggressors and their allies deluded themselves into believing they could carry out an overwhelming attack against Iraq, but they are disappointed'.[18] This may have indeed been designed as much for domestic consumption in that it was an attempt to undermine the credibility of premature coalition claims about having achieved air supremacy. But the message they were putting out was clear: Iraq can take it, a message in fact being carried far and wide by the western media.

In the meantime, a few Palestinian and Lebanese refugees arriving in Jordan spoke of the damage incurred to their homes and neighbourhoods, of coffins on the roofs of cars, of buses that had been hit from the air. One Palestinian teacher was quoted as saying: 'People have started hating these air raids ... They live in constant horror, fearing death in their shelters.'[19] In western terms, the problem with such reports was that the Palestinians had lost a great deal of sympathy by their reported support for Saddam and for his action in Kuwait. In wartime, when lives are at stake and emotional responses are heightened, loyalties tend to take sides at the expense of compassion. Besides, their allegations contained largely second-hand impressionistic data that were difficult to verify by aerial or satellite intelligence owing to poor weather conditions over an Iraq overcast by cloud for most of the first week. As an Arab Reuters correspondent conceded after interviewing refugees, 'none had reliable details of casualties or civilian buildings hit'.[20] Moreover, once all the information from Iraqi, Jordanian and coalition sources was analysed and the speculations sifted out, it was clear only that intensive bombing was taking place.

Back in Saudi Arabia and in Bahrain, journalists who tried to eke out impressions from returning pilots about how they felt about the possible impact of their missions found that their questioning along this line was most unwelcome. It was one thing to get the pilots to talk about their excitement over flying combat missions or their relief at having returned safely but quite another to discuss the consequences of their actions against innocent women and children. As Ben Fenton of the *Daily Telegraph* stated after the war:

An early, somewhat ham-fisted attempt by *The Independent* to write about the way they approached the task of bombing targets hundreds of miles inside Iraq met with such outrage from the aircrew that they ostracised the sizeable press corps, MRT and non-MRT alike.[21]

Cordial relations were re-established only because reporters were sharing the same hotel with the RAF Tornado crews who were sustaining significant casualties in their dangerous low-flying missions. 'By the middle of the air war,' wrote one reporter, 'we treated these people as friends and most of them reciprocated.' The effect of this on distanced reporting was fully appreciated by Fenton: 'many reporters operated such a stringent form of self-censorship to avoid harming or offending their new friends that the Squadron Leader PRO could put his feet up'.[22] There would be little help for Saddam's campaign from that location of the war.

Perhaps sensing the potential of the refugees as vehicles of anti-coalition propaganda, Iraq decided to re-open its frontier momentarily with Jordan on Wednesday 23 January. On the previous Sunday, Iraq had suddenly announced that the considerable number of mainly non-Iraqi Arab refugees on its side of the border would require exit visas and they would therefore have to return to Baghdad on the hazardous highway to get them. Exit visas were not normally required for Arabs. But then suddenly on the Wednesday, 900 refugees, mainly Jordanians, were allowed out bursting to tell stories of their terrifying journey to the border and the hardships they had left behind caused by the bombing. For the first time, the impression created by coalition statements had a credible counter-challenge, especially as it became apparent that, although the allies were not deliberately attacking civilian targets, it was the civilians who were among the people suffering most as a result of the disruption of water, sewerage, fuel and electrical supplies. General Schwarzkopf's response was emphatic: 'I will tell you quite candidly that there are several almost predominantly civilian facilities right now that I would very much like to attack because I know for a fact they're being used by the Iraqis, and we're not doing it for that reason.'[23]

Awaiting the refugees who had fled the country were scores of eager journalists camped in Amman.[24] Although the real reason for attacking this area of western Iraq was to knock out the mobile Scud launchers that were being used to attack Israel – the Americans called the highway 'Scud Alley' – the fact that the region also housed the main refugee exit routes from Iraq to Jordan benefited the Iraqis and alarmed the coalition politically. The more bombing which took place the more likely were accidents to happen, as General Thomas Kelly recognised: 'It's difficult to look at the ground and tell what a civilian target is and what a military target is because, for example, oil trucks out in that area could be carrying fuel for Iraqi aircraft.'[25] State Department spokesperson Margaret D. Tutwiler went further, accusing Jordanian sanction-busting oil trucks of mingling with military convoys.[26] Given that many raids against these convoys were taking place either at night or in poor weather conditions, the risks of hitting civilians were compounded still further, which was why the Iraqis were quite prepared to allow the refugees to do their job for them from Jordan. Eventually, it began to bear fruit. The border was again re-opened on 28 January, releasing another flood of bombing stories. And then came the decision to allow western journalists back into Iraq. Brent Sadler's filmed report of his night time return journey stated that 'Jordanian protests ... were well founded ... This was the first hard evidence of the allied assaults on Iraq's lines of communications and transport routes in the west of the country'. Nor did attacks on the highway diminish. When some of the journalists went back to Amman on Friday 8 February, they counted 28 destroyed lorries and tanker trucks on the same road, 'roughly half of them civilian'.[27]

A further problem for allied propagandists were the statements of Iranian news sources which testified to the intensity of allied air raids in southern Iraq near to their border, especially against Basra. This was a city of almost 1 million people which, according to one western print journalist in early February, had been subjected to a 'hellish nightmare of fires and smoke so dense that witnesses say the sun hasn't been clearly visible for several days at a time' and which had also experienced the levelling of whole blocks of apartment buildings and 'craters the size of football fields'.[28] It was here, the coalition argued, that the likely operational centre for the Kuwaiti campaign was based and it was in this area that the Republican Guard was mainly stationed. But there were no television crews permitted by the Iraqis, perhaps fortunately for the coalition. It took some time for a comprehensive statement about Basra to emerge, following the transmission of CNN's first pictures from the city which showed school playgrounds and children being treated in hospital. General Neal pointed out as late as 11 February:

It's important to understand that Basra is a military town in the true sense. It is described as a major naval base and port facility. The military infrastructure is closely interwoven within the city of Basra itself ... I think our targeteers and the guys that deliver the ordnance have taken extraordinary steps to try and limit collateral damage. But I will be quite frank and honest with you, that there is going to be collateral damage because of the proximity of these targets close to abutting civilian sites.[29]

Before the end of January, however, there was little film to substantiate the various claims although, on Tuesday the 22nd, the Iraqis did begin escorting Peter Arnett to various bombed sites and, two days later, ITN carried some footage from Iraqi televi-

sion of the bodies of children being brought out of ruined buildings in Mosul. Brent Sadler's taped report from Amman over these
pictures added:

It is impossible to analyse from this source alone the extent of civilian
damage and Iraqi casualties. Nor is it possible to be precise about what
allied weaponry caused this destruction. Iraq will doubtless attempt to
exploit it on the humanitarian level to undermine allied resolve in the use
of heavy bombing against targets near civilian centres.[30]

The following day Peter Arnett was escorted to a small town 100
miles from Baghdad with no visible military targets but where 23
homes had been bombed, 23 fresh graves had been dug and there
was a huge crater outside a mosque.[31] It was during this phase
that the 'baby milk plant' episode occurred. When, on 28 January,
the BBC transmitted on its Six O'Clock News still photographs
released by the Iraqi embassy in Amman, the commentary added:
'there's no indication of when or where the pictures were taken or
of resulting casualties' although it later showed pictures from Iraqi
television and injured children 'with their powerful emotional
appeal'. The same thing happened again on BBC1's Nine O'Clock
evening news on 31 January with the words: 'It's potent propaganda and it's touching Arab opinion.' Yet, even on 29 January,
with their own television capacity much reduced, the Iraqis were
still only conceding that 320 civilians had been killed in the allied
air raids which, out of 26,000 sorties flown by that time, remained
a remarkably low figure.

As this issue was given mounting prominence by the western
media, General Schwarzkopf showed some signs of irritability at
probing questions: 'I was bombed by our own B52s in Vietnam,
but I'm sure it wasn't intentional.'[32] But, he admitted, 'it's going
to happen. It's absolutely going to happen, there's no question
about it, but we're doing everything we can to prevent it'. Talk of
mounting 'collateral damage' – an unfortunate phrase which stuck
in the memory – increased markedly as the allies extended their
bombing raids to destroying Iraq's infrastructure. Coalition
briefers remained on the defensive, especially when the press
showed little understanding of the military reasons for attacking
targets that did not appear to fall within the specific objectives of
expelling Iraq from Kuwait or which clearly affected the Iraqi
people indirectly in terms of power and water supplies. On 30

January, General Schwarzkopf stated:

> I think I should point out right here that we never had any intention of destroying 100% of all the Iraqi electrical power. Because of our interest in making sure that civilians did not suffer unduly, we felt we had to leave some of the electrical power in effect, and we've done that.[33]

He also added that 'we didn't want to destroy their oil industry, but certainly we wanted to make sure they didn't have a lot of gasoline for their military vehicles'. Nonetheless, a discernible shift in emphasis was taking place over this issue, moving from the initial line that the coalition was doing everything it could to avoid civilian casualties to one in which it was stated that such casualties were regrettably unavoidable, especially in light of Saddam's cleverness in constructing dual-function installations. Responsibility, in other words, was being shifted onto the Iraqi leader and away from the coalition air force.

The Iraqis, who could watch these briefings, realised their media management mistake and western film crews were accordingly allowed back at the end of January – even though, if anything, the conditions under which they would be operating were actually worse than when they were asked to leave supposedly for their own safety and comfort. When he later emerged from Iraq, Richard Beeston of *The Times* was able to publish his diary of his time in Iraq in which he noted that 'if the standards at the Al-Rashid hotel, Iraq's premier five star establishment, are any measure of the collapse of the country's ability to function, Iraq is in more trouble than most people suspect'.[34] Although this time there was some genuine evidence of civilian damage for them to report, journalists were however being shown only the aftermath of the raids during the previous ten days: bombed out buildings and bridges and hospital patients. And despite the growing number of press reports on this issue that were beginning to appear, what the Iraqis really needed were recent, authentic and verifiable television pictures.

By the end of January and the start of February, coalition briefers in Riyadh became perceptibly more aggravated about civilian damage. Major-General Robert Johnston found that more and more questions were revolving about this issue and repeated 'with total conviction that we are scrupulously avoiding civilian targets'. Nonetheless, he added: 'That's not to say that there will not be some modest collateral damage, and I would not stand here and say that there will not be one single civilian casualty'.[35] Even so, not one public admission had been made of a mistakenly hit target, which provided a real opportunity for the Iraqis if they could only find one. In the first days of February, they took journalists repeatedly to such alleged sites. Western television crews filmed what they could and filed their reports which, combined with the testimonies of refugees in Jordan, at last forced General Kelly to concede on Sunday the 3rd that 'we're not purposely going after civilian vehicles. If one got hit, it was certainly a mistake'.[36]

Moreover, as the Iraqis stepped up their campaign in the first two weeks of February, there was the additional twist of spotting the plant. Several civilian damage items had been transmitted with apparently 'innocent' victims shrieking at the cameras. ITN's Brent Sadler filed a report at the start of February which had not, it was claimed, been altered or cut by the Iraqis. It carried dramatic pictures of cruise missiles passing overhead, investigated the baby milk plant ('it looked, smelt and appeared to be an innocent factory ... but the watch-tower was out of place and it left a nagging doubt') and went on to cover a hospital in which injured civilians were shown and a doctor (Dr Boghossian, who was to figure prominently in the Amiriya coverage) explained how difficult it was to treat the children without electricity. From there, the report went on to a house in ruins where a woman in a white United Nations tracksuit was filmed shouting: 'Westerners are guilty, including you lot ... You are all guilty of killing people for oil ... This is not a game. These are human lives. Enough of civilians ... Remember my eyes.'[37] The report portrayed a defiant and angry people, an observation echoed by Brent Sadler in a live report from the city that followed. It later transpired that the tracksuited lady was a member of Iraqi Foreign Minister Tariq Aziz's staff,[38] but by then the coalition was furious with Sadler's closing statement: 'Tonight the bombers returned ... Tomorrow, more of Iraq will have been destroyed.'[39]

Alfonso Rojo was also a part of this organised trip. His 'eye-witness' column published by the *Guardian* relayed many of the same issues but emphasised an important point of context not always apparent in the war coverage, namely that 'what often happens if they [Iraqi anti-aircraft gunners] hit the missile, is that it loses direction and crashes just anywhere with all its cargo of death'.[40] General de la Billiere confirmed that this was a frequent cause of civilian casualties,[41] while General Schwarzkopf also took up the theme in his 'Guys in white hats don't do that' briefing on the same day.[42] It was, of course, a neat counterploy now that the Iraqis had begun to claim increased civilian casualties.

The guys in the black hats were doing all sorts of things to press home their point. On 8 February, BBC cameraman Peter Jouvenal arrived back in Amman from Baghdad and, free from Iraqi restrictions, reported that the Iraqis had censored his film of destroyed military targets and of a bridge in Nasiriyah to give the impression that only civilians had been injured in an air raid. He did not deny that civilians had been hurt, and some of his pictures were shown, but he claimed the Iraqis were trying to give the impression that they had been deliberately targeted. At the hospital, he had even been prevented from filming wounded soldiers while an official escort covered a soldier's uniform to give the impression that he was a civilian.[43] This contrasted with Brent Sadler's report for ITN from the same hospital which emphasised that they had never before been allowed access to military hospitals and which showed a dead 6–year-old boy and other injured children: 'of all the hospitals I have seen so far, Nasiriyah's casualty room and wards were the bloodiest'.[44] But the incident had put the BBC on its guard and, that weekend, further reports from the Iraqi capital contained few pictures. Alan Little's report from Baghdad on BBC1's 17:10 Evening News on 9 February was a 'voice only' report describing the previous night's raid on Baghdad – with no pictures. Similarly, in the 21:05 News, the BBC only carried Little's report over 'recent pictures' of life returning to normal in Baghdad after the previous week's raids and made great play of the civilian damage caused by Iraqi Scud attacks in Tel Aviv. The same pattern was repeated on the Sunday: no shock, no horror, no mayhem – and no bodies.

Further, as Richard Beeston noted on 11 February:

In some cases the Iraqis have only themselves to blame for the loss of civilian life. Their policy of relocating staff from government offices to schools and other civilian buildings and of moving military hardware out of their barracks to better camouflaged wooded areas in the countryside near farms and villages frequently exposes non-combatants to attack.[45]

This was also the line being taken by the coalition briefers at this point, with General Kelly stating 'if there is an additional effect on the civilian population, it's one that Saddam Hussein has chosen, not one that we did'.[46]

When Iraq decided to sever its diplomatic ties with the USA, Britain, France, Italy, Egypt and Saudi Arabia on Wednesday 6 February, it maintained that the coalition was trying to 'expel Iraq from the Twentieth Century'. Real doubts as to what precisely the coalition was doing emerged the very next day following an MoD briefing in London at which a video was shown of bombs launched by an RAF Tornado that appeared to be aimed at a commercial vehicle travelling over a bridge. The bridge was hit although the vehicle just managed to escape and speed away as the explosion occurred behind it. Journalists found this 'an unnerving experience' even though something not dissimilar had been shown by General Schwarzkopf a week earlier when he had described the driver of a truck who had likewise experienced an explosion in his rear view mirror as 'the luckiest man in Iraq'.[47] On 4 February, ITN carried a Brent Sadler report from Baghdad in which there was footage of damaged buildings just yards away from an undamaged bridge. After several days of silence or evasion about why precisely the allies were attacking bridges which appeared to be unconnected to supply lines to Kuwait but which carried a high risk of civilian casualties, Brigadier Neal finally said on 12 February that many of the bridges carried communications links of various kinds which enabled Baghdad to keep in contact by land line with troops in the south.[48] That may indeed have been the real reason, and, although it was also a highly plausible explanation it was one which had nonetheless taken more than two weeks to emerge.

The Ramsay Clark mission

There was one example of a western television crew that did manage to roam quite freely throughout Iraq. Between 2 and 8 February, an avowed opponent of the war, President Carter's former Attorney General Ramsay Clark, decided to investigate for himself the claims about civilian damage. A freelance 'video-journalist', Jon Alpert, joined him. Alpert's view was that his crew were 'probably the most uncensored and the least watched' by the

Iraqis. They entered Iraq unescorted by night from Jordan on 2 February and there were, he said, other occasions when there were no Iraqi minders with them, about 50% of their time there. They were able to film food vehicles that had been bombed on that road and, once they had reached Baghdad, they were escorted to the 'baby milk plant'. There they filmed the camouflaged building and the barbed wire fence but the rest of the building was 'so badly burned that it was hard for us to tell' what had been going on inside. Back in Baghdad, they filmed the Justice Ministry, which was located next to a market: 'one bomb hit the Ministry, another hit the market.' They then filmed a residential neighbourhood that had been struck by a missile, and a hospital and then, unescorted, they went to the (undamaged) mosque at Najaf. English-speaking Iraqis described the civilian use of these locations. At one site, a bridge near a hospital, the bridge was unscathed and the hospital had been hit. At Najaf, one Iraqi even described the war as 'stupid'.

Alpert's method of filming was to interview people while shoulder-carrying his camera. This gave a direct approach so that the viewer would be staring straight at the faces of the bomb victims. The major American networks would not touch his film. Interviewed just before the end of the war on New York's Channel WNET 13, Alpert said that the 'stupid' remark would have undoubtedly been censored if the Iraqis had got their hands on his film, but he and his crew had been careful not to extract too many private opinions from their interviewees for fear of getting them into trouble if the Iraqi authorities had seized the footage. He realised that the Iraqis were trying to manipulate them and said that he would often wait until his minders were not present and then would interview ordinary people who would thus be prepared to speak more freely. Wherever possible, his crew attempted to corroborate the claims that had been made to them. Alpert was convinced that 'the illusion that was created in the beginning part of this war of a clean war and a bloodless war was a false illusion'. When asked for his opinion about the baby milk factory, he replied:

It seemed to be a Baby Milk Plant. I mean the Iraqis were very heavy-handed. When they thought they had a propaganda advantage, they really tried to press it home. So, for example, you see that crudely hand lettered sign out in the front, freshly painted 'Baby Milk Factory'. Inside, every-

thing was burned to a crisp except for a very convenient stack of powdered milk that was waiting for you to investigate. Everything else was all
soiled and burned. They didn't have to lay it on that heavy and that
created scepticism on the part of reporters. But folks who have investigated this, who have talked to the company that built the factory, the
French company, are certain that it was just making milk, nothing else.[49]

In Basra, which the party visited on 6–7 February, the damage was
even worse. While they were staying at the Basra Sheraton Hotel,
a bomb landed down the street. The next day they investigated
and it appeared that the intended target was a nearby bridge which
had clearly been missed – for the second time, said one local – and
which was very near to a hospital. Alpert said: 'the frustrated
residents want to blow up the bridge themselves to avoid further
attacks.' A Pepsi Cola factory had also been hit, for no apparent
reason that Alpert could see, along with five or six blocks of the
residential area behind. An air raid siren that went off while they
were filming failed even to stir the locals being interviewed. Other
journalists such as Alfonso Rojo were also present on this trip to
Basra, and if anyone still doubts the vividness of television pictures
as compared with newspaper reports, they should contrast his
column with Alpert's film.[50] At the hospital, for example, Alpert
filmed the injured and the medical staff and his pictures depicted
scenes of much more identifiable human suffering than print
journalism, however well done, was able to portray.

In Baghdad, Ramsay Clark informed journalists that what he
had seen in Basra was 'a human and civilian tragedy' and that the
bombing was exceeding the United Nations' mandate. He saw no
signs of military damage and wondered how the the Iraqis had
managed to clear this up so quickly.[51] On their return to Jordan,
the group encountered an angry Iraqi whose house had been
bombed the week before and who they thought was about to kill
them. They did manage to get out safely, whereupon Clark
sounded a rare note of unease amidst the public euphoria about
the bombing when he returned to New York on 11 February,
accusing the US of 'war crimes': 'we are raining death and destruction with our technology on the life of Iraq. And there ought to
be a cessation to the bombing now,' he told a news conference.[52]
He added that the Iraqi Red Crescent had informed him that
6,000–7,000 civilians were estimated to have died in the bombing
so far.[53] The 'Ramsay Clark line' sounded an uneasy note of

discord and reservation against the overwhelming consensus
largely created by coalition propaganda over this issue. Moreover,
that line was given a substantial boost on 11 February by the Iraqi
decision to reverse its previous policy over publicising civilian
casualties. Now they claimed that thousands, not hundreds, had
died. Greater emphasis was also placed on the destruction of
mosques and other holy places.[54]

Despite Tariq Aziz's complaint to the UN Secretary General
about the 'horrendous and deliberate crimes against Iraqi citizens
and their economic, scientific, cultural and religious installations',[55]
General Schwarzkopf had insisted a few days earlier that 'we are
not, not, not, not, not deliberately targeting civilian casualties, and
we never will. We are a moral and ethical people ... and therefore
we're not going to do business that way'.[56] On the other hand,
some sources in Washington were clearly beginning to worry
about the ramifications of having their propaganda line of a smart
war exposed by a sudden tragedy. Congressional contacts and
military analysts close to Pentagon sources began to claim privately that 'only about 60%' of the smart weapons were hitting
their targets, which helped to explain why coalition pilots sometimes had to return to their targets a second time and, more
significantly, why some 'collateral damage' was clearly taking
place.[57]

Such suspicions and admissions were evidently having an impact, if not on public opinion then at least on world leaders,
especially when, on Saturday 9 February, President Gorbachev
appeared to have been influenced by them when he too stated that
the war was threatening to expand beyond the UN mandates.
Following the Amiriya incident, *Izvestia* was to further proclaim
that 'we are siding with murderers in this slaughter in the Gulf'.[58]
Meanwhile, on 11 February, Marlin Fitzwater complained that
Saddam was scoring points in the propaganda battle by the western media's acceptance of his exaggerated accounts of the extent
of civilian damage. Responding to President Gorbachev's concern
about the bombing, President Bush stated: 'This war is being
fought with high technology. There is no targeting of civilians. It
has gone far better in terms of casualties than I had hoped.'[59]
Given that the American President had deliberately avoided becoming involved in the details of the bombing plan,[60] he could be
said to have been tempting fate. The White House implication was

that the Soviet leader had fallen for Iraqi propaganda. 'It is disturbing', said Fitzwater, 'to find evidence that somebody's buying it.'[61]

When British Defence Secretary Tom King visited President Bush in Washington on Tuesday 12 February, a photo-opportunity of the two men chatting captured the President saying that he didn't think the world was believing the 'one sided propaganda machine cranking out myths and falsehoods'.[62] Bush added: 'I think there's a conscientious effort on his part to try to raise the propaganda value of accusing us of indiscriminate bombing of civilians and it's simply not true.'[63] Later that day, in a press interview, King was asked for his views concerning Saddam's recent propaganda ploys concerning civilian casualties. Almost anticipating events of the next day, the Defence Secretary replied:

It's difficult to get the whole picture and it's certainly very difficult in a society like Iraq, where the propaganda is so totally controlled, to know what the situation is. Let me just make clear what our position is. We will do everything we can to minimise civilian casualties. Sometimes if an accident happens, well that is very regrettable and we do regret it. But let us just remember on whom the responsibility lies and how many casualties there were in Kuwait and how also we are dealing with somebody who while we try to minimise civilian casualties is actually himself targeting Scud missiles deliberately at centres of civilian population in Israel.[64]

Both King and Bush were of course right – at least in one respect. The coalition's record in attacking military targets and not deliberately targeting civilians was plain for all to see. No member of the coalition had promised a totally clean war from a civilian point of view; such casualties were recognised as being both inevitable and regrettable. But because the coalition did not *deliberately* target civilians, whereas Saddam clearly did through his Scud attacks, it had placed itself on a lofty pedestal in the propaganda war that was always vulnerable to collapse when such accidents did occur. If Bush was correct and nobody was believing the 'myths and falsehoods' of Iraqi propaganda, he was assuming that the facts of the overall situation would speak louder than either the words or images of specific instances.

He does indeed appear to have been proved correct in this assumption. But again that Vietnam Syndrome – the belief that television was invested with a power to end wars on the domestic front without securing victory on the battlefield – seems to have created a sensitivity on the part of democratic policy-makers accountable to swings in public moods. A considerable amount of insurance against this had been invested in the 'video-game war' approach. As we have seen, those images were so telegenic that they tended to dominate the framing of the story of the air war in the first month. Iraqi efforts to show what happened on the ground after the bombs had exploded were, as we have also seen, largely unsuccessful – at least among members of the coalition. But those same Iraqi efforts had sowed seeds of doubt. Could the bombing really be that accurate? Had American technology really reversed the course of history? Or were there more videos of bombs missing their intended targets? Why weren't journalists allowed to see those? At the start of February, the *Washington Post* had almost anticipated the problems that were to emerge from Amiriya when it stated:

Nor do we know how many of our weapons have slithered through windows and down chimneys, compared to how many have landed in empty fields or on civilian targets. The mistakes too are recorded on tape that is for now, and perhaps forever, unseen. After the bombing raid of Libya in 1986, the Pentagon released a video of a direct hit. That turned out to be one of the few accurate bombing runs. A GAO analysis of the mission concluded that laser-guided weapons were actually less accurate than old-fashioned unguided bombs.

In the 1989 raid on Panama a bomb from an F-117 Stealth fighter missed its target by over 300 yards, despite the Pentagon's initial claims of 'pin-point accuracy'. In an astonishing interview last week on CNN, John Lehman said off-handedly that when he was secretary of the Navy he used to pay settlements 'at least once a month' for damage done when laser-guided bombs hit resort towns in California and Nevada, two or three miles from the target area. Lehman later told Fred Kaplan, of the Boston Globe, that laser-guided weapons were hitting targets in Iraq about 60% of the time. This, Lehman said, was 'consistent with the test performances' – but quite inconsistent with the ratio suggested by the very few videos the Pentagon has shown.

Similarly, we have been told in briefings that Tomahawk cruise missiles, the only truly new weapon used so far in Iraq, have hit more than 90% of their targets. Yet just two days ago CNN ran footage of Tomahawks flying into Baghdad and destroying residential buildings.[65]

From a propaganda point of view, it might be thought that releasing such material might prove counter-productive on the part of coalition. In fact, it might have helped the credibility of the allied line still further. It would be tantamount to an admission of 'reality', an honest approach in an honest cause against an evil regime oppressing its own citizens. If Iraq, in other words, was criticised for its denial of alternative points of view, how different was the coalition proving in its approach to war coverage?

The allies were determined to fight a short war, and short-term propaganda themes took precedence over the possible long-term consequences of discovering how much civilian damage might really have been incurred when the war was over and won. However, because the military was also infused with that Vietnam Syndrome, which created a massive mistrust of the media, a circle had been formed which proved difficult to break out of: the military released comparatively little hard information about bomb damage assessment, which forced the media to seek out information for themselves from other sources, say in Baghdad, and to speculate, which in turn made the military distrust them even more. Right from the start of the war, when CNN reported that the Republican Guard had been 'decimated' or when several American networks reported that Israel had launched a counter-attack against Iraq or when CBS reported that 11 Scuds had hit Jerusalem, the military was concerned that 'media diplomacy' might affect its ability to wage the war successfully. 'I spend more time putting out fires than dealing with real information,' complained Fitzwater at one point. Yet the fact remained that the military believed that if bad news was released, it would be blown up out of all proportion by the media. After all, 'the nature of journalism is that bad news tends to be stressed and good news underplayed'.[66]

Amiriya, 13 February 1991

In the early hours of Wednesday 13 February – ironically on the 46th anniversary of the bombing of Dresden – something happened which could not be simply ignored or glossed over. At about 04:30 (Iraqi time) two allied bombs, some reports said several minutes apart, shattered the roof of a facility apparently containing civilians, mainly women and children. The Iraqis lifted all censorship restrictions as daylight revealed the sheer extent of the horror now available to their propagandists in and around the

Amiriya instillation. According to early reports, possibly 500 or even 1,000 were said to have been killed. Film crews scrambled around the tragic scene as Iraqi minders pointed them towards the charred remains and the grieving relatives. When they returned to the Al-Rashid hotel to transmit their pictures, they found that their minders were happy for them to say whatever they liked about what they had seen. When the pictures themselves were so expressive, words would be superfluous.

Iraqi pictures were transmitted around the Arab world in time for that day's evening news.[67] In Tunisia the headlines screamed 'Shame on Them', 'Carnage', 'Massacre' and 'Barbaric Butchery'. In Lebanon, one read 'The Shelter Massacre: 800 Iraqis killed' and the press ran stories about 'an American massacre in Baghdad'. The *Jordanian Times* called the bombing 'a living testimony to the US-led alliance's cruelty, cynicism and total disregard for human life in conducting this ugly and pointless war against Iraq'. President Chadli Benjedid of Algeria said that war now appeared to be one of 'extermination'.

But in the Arab coalition countries, blame was placed squarely on Saddam's shoulders for leading his people to a 'crematorium' (Syrian radio), for his 'arrogance and megalomania and his fictitious dream of an empire built on the ruins of sister nations and Arab states' (Qatar's *Al-Sharq*) and for a 'catastrophe of his own making' (Bahrain's *Gulf Daily News*).[68] In Saudi Arabia, news of the civilian deaths was played down, with one newspaper simply stating 'Washington confirms: the bunker was a military command centre'.[69] The Arab coalition partners, at least, were holding firm, although Morocco (with 1,300 troops in the multinational force) did pull out of a Cairo meeting of anti-Iraqi Arab states and other secular governments were forced to contain demonstrations whipped up by Islamic militants.

In so far as the western world was concerned, the Iraqis also miscalculated. As the pictures arrived in the news rooms around the world, all sorts of issues erupted which militated against their full use. In Britain and the United States, it revolved around questions of taste and decency. The pictures were so horrific, and the filming of the corpses so graphic, that they would need skilful editing if audiences were not to be offended or alienated – not necessarily from a propaganda point of view, but from a broadcasting point of view. A considerable amount of self-censorship took place, rather in the same way as television editors would treat pictures of a motorway or rail crash. As a result, the true horror was never broadcast into the living rooms of people who might now question the war as a result.[70]

CNN broke the story first. Just after 13:00 Iraqi time (10:04 GMT; 05:04 EST), Peter Arnett transmitted a live voice report from Baghdad on his INMARSAT phone:

We have the makings of a major tragedy here in Baghdad today. We have been taken to the Amiriya district of west Baghdad and there were two direct hits on a civilian bomb shelter. Now this was a large shelter marked as a shelter with street signs leading to it saying it was a shelter. It was in a complex of community buildings. There was a mosque, a school and supermarket in the same large block. Now we were taken through this bomb shelter. Two bombs had entered through the top of the structure. We went inside. Firemen were trying to open steel doors that led to various chambers within this shelter. We saw ourselves a total of 40 bodies that had been removed from this shelter in the earlier hours. They were charred almost beyond recognition. There were women, there were children in this group. There were 30 we actually saw laid out at a hospital, the Yarmuk hospital. While we were actually at the shelter, there were 10 bodies that had been loaded into a truck. This is the worst of the civilian incidents we have seen in Baghdad so far.

When questioned about whether this was just another example of collateral damage, Arnett replied:

To our observation in this particular Amiriya district which is a middle class civilian area. This shelter was a large concrete building ... 100 feet long, 100 feet wide ... From what we could see there was no immediate military target within miles of this place.

The previous night's air raids had clearly seen some of the heaviest bombing of the capital to date; pool reports transmitted from Saudi Arabia and aired on British breakfast time programmes before the Amiriya story broke described a massive combined land, sea and air bombardment that had been launched against the enemy in Kuwait *and* Iraq. But here, for the first time since the start of the war, was an uncensored report of the actual impact on the citizens of Baghdad. Arnett began to describe another building near the Al-Rashid which had been hit but which he couldn't identify when a voice – presumably his minder's – was heard in the background: 'Well, I can say it now,' said Arnett: 'It was a conference centre 200 metres from our hotel door ... That

189

took a direct hit.'

CNN carried its first pictures of the carnage at the 'shelter' half an hour later with a voice-over report by Arnett. They were in fact ITN pictures (with which CNN had a contract) and showed no bodies. ITN first aired the same self-censored pictures in Britain, complete with Arnett's commentary, at 10:55 GMT. This was less than an hour and a half after a live picture report (09:30 GMT) from Riyadh by ITN's Peter Allen about how the focus of the bombing seemed to be shifting away from Iraq to the Kuwaiti theatre of operations. Interestingly, NBC's early morning bulletin at 07:31 EST used different pictures but with an interview with the BBC's Alan Little in which he stated: 'It really is beyond all the ability I think of the Iraqi Information Ministry to stage manage if you like any kind of show for us. As I say, things were very chaotic.' So chaotic, in fact, that one angry woman moved aggressively towards the camera and spat at it, only to be moved back hastily by an Iraqi policeman.[71] With the breaking of one of the major news stories of the war, the global information village was operating in overdrive and feeding off itself.

In Britain, BSkyB News in fact got the story first (at 10:25 GMT) but because it had no pictures the anchorwoman could merely quote extracts from Arnett's first CNN report, which had started 10 minutes earlier. The BBC carried its first coverage of the story at 11:00 GMT with Alan Little's voice-only report lasting less than a minute, stating 'the place was chaotic when we arrived. The rescue and recovery operation, such as it was, was still going on. The area was surrounded predominantly by men, I think because those inside, it seems, were women and children'. BBC's first pictures were shown at midday, with Jeremy Bowen's edited package ('compiled under Iraqi restrictions'). The pictures showed night-time shots of the raids, with a building exploding, and then the bedlam outside the shelter at daybreak, but there were no graphic shots of the human carnage. Bowen ended with a piece to camera: 'It's the worst damage by far that they have taken us to see but they say there have been more serious attacks on civilian areas.' A fuller report, including 'scenes which you may find distressing' – in fact mainly shots of the covered bodies – was carried on BBC's 13:00 GMT News. This report did show distressed relatives and some of the bodies from a distance but, as anchorman Michael Buerk stated after the item appeared to end abruptly: 'Many of the pictures coming from Baghdad of burned civilian bodies are considered too dreadful to show you.' Buerk then ran another interview with Bowen, taped minutes before, and the latter's voice-only report stated:

The mood of the Iraqi officials who accompanied us – we're always with these Iraqi officials – was very different to the mood on other occasions where they say there have been civilian casualties. There they have been quite calm, it's been yet another photo-opportunity. In this one they were genuinely shocked, some moved very close to tears. The crowd outside had gathered, hundreds of them looking very stunned about what had happened. I think all the signs are that this was indeed what the Iraqis say it was – a civilian shelter ... I am as certain as I can be that this was a shelter. The question may be about who was in it, whether it was just women, children and old men, as the Iraqis say or whether other people were in there. We have no proof either way on that. The building itself is a low squat concrete structure. We were told that it was built by Scandinavian engineers and I can't see how it could have been used for any other purpose other than a shelter.

Reaction in Whitehall and Washington, the item went on indicate, was essentially that, if the reports were true, the incident was regrettable but these things happen in war.

ITN, which appears to have had the first pictures, carried a film report by Brent Sadler at 12:47 GMT. Some of the shots were quite graphic, though not gratuitously dwelling, and Sadler said that the building was 'undeniably used by civilians'. From inside, he watched a body being brought out in a blanket: 'I think it was a woman.' He also added over the film that 'no one has survived this', which, as we shall see, clashed with a later CNN report and, indeed, was corrected not long after in an ITN report by Ken Rees which stated that there were eight survivors in the hospital (there were, in fact, about 15).

Being first with the story turned out to be a real problem for CNN. At 14:00 (Iraqi time, 06:00 EST), Arnett had filed another live report, this time over new pictures taken by CNN's own cameraman, Dave Rust. It was a fuller report, stating that perhaps 400 rather than the 1,000 claimed earlier may have died. The CNN team had arrived at the instillation at mid-morning, several hours after the attack had taken place. The Iraqi Minister of Health, Abdel Salam Mohammed Saeed, had given a small press conference for the 20 correspondents who had been taken to the scene, where he had described the raid as a 'criminal, premeditated, pre-planned attack'. The Iraqi Minister of Information and Baghdad Police Chief, Brigadier-General Kamel Zedau, had also been present, although only the latter was interviewed in the report. Showing pictures of rows of bodies covered in patterned blankets, Arnett described the mainly civilian area in which the 'shelter' was located, near to a school, a mosque and a supermarket. He added that an air raid alert had been taking place at the time (later disproved), that he had walked on the roof of the building (later challenged by the coalition) and that his cameraman had gone inside the building (later said by the coalition to have proved nothing). About an hour later, they had been taken to the hospital where Arnett had witnessed 'one of the most grisly sights I'd ever seen' as the bodies of mainly women and children were displayed for the cameras. Finally, under questioning from Atlanta, Arnett said that he did not know whether military personnel had been inside and could not comment on whether the Iraqis had been moving their leaders into civilian areas. He also added the telling point that, in the past, he and other journalists had been taken only to areas of civilian, not military, damage.

Words turned out to be a sore point in the coverage; the pictures may have been self-censored but even the sanitised images were still so shocking that the commentaries of journalists became the focus of ire. People on the East Coast of the United States were waking up to the story as CNN was still piecing together what had happened. Yet scooping the world failed to do CNN any favours amongst critics, not least when it was later claimed by other sources that there was no air raid siren going off at the time of the attack. This was not to be the first time that day that Arnett made statements which inflamed various people and added to the confusion and conflicting reports.

Arnett transmitted several other reports that day, but two in particular helped to finalise CNN's version of the event. Just after 16:00 Iraqi time (08:00 EST, 13:00 GMT, as BBC's Michael Buerk introduced Bowen's early self-censored picture report in Britain), a fuller report indicated that 150–250 bodies had been removed so far and Arnett spoke from inside the building where firemen and rescuers were bringing out corpses. Outside were angry people and grieving relatives. The Police Chief was interviewed saying there were no military targets in the vicinity. Then, outside the hospital, CNN showed the rows of charred bodies in a long shot – the first and only time audiences could get a glimpse on this station of the real carnage caused to human life. Dr Paul Boghossian (ITN later labelled him as 'Borassian'), chief of surgery, gave an interview in fluent English about how young some of the victims were ('a baby, one month old ... it's terrible ... how will it help to liberate Kuwait?'). Then there was a shot of the conference centre that had been hit downtown, a description of Amiriya as a middle-class residential district and shots of the sign marked 'shelter' in English and Arabic. According to *The Times*, the sign was 'weathered',[72] not freshly painted as at the 'baby milk plant' and as was suggested later in the day. Arnett added that the dozen or so television correspondents and the dozen print journalists had that day been allowed to say whatever they wanted about what they had seen, adding

this was pretty good evidence to me that they believe this was indeed a civilian target, that it was at least a mistaken bombing if not what they say is a deliberate bombing. So I am here speaking freely about any aspect of this particular incident that you want to ask me about, Reid [Collins, the anchor in Atlanta], that you want to ask me on.

Arnett admitted that a minder was present with him as he was transmitting, but claimed he was there only to check pronunciations.

Western official reaction was not immediate, although at 06:05 EST (an hour after Arnett's very first report) CNN's Gene Randall reported live from the Pentagon that one official had said there was no way as yet of telling whether the casualties were military or civilian. The unnamed official had added: 'it is not in the American tradition to go after civilian targets and if this attack on a shelter did happen we will feel very bad about it'.[73] In Riyadh, at 15:35 (local time, 12:35 GMT), Group Captain Nial Irving gave an unusual live interview with ITN's John Suchet, well in advance of that day's briefings, stating that until they had all the facts the authorities there were still sceptical. Irving was in fact to be the first and the last of the day's coalition military spokesmen. He was accordingly at a disadvantage on both occasions, the first because he was speaking before the official coalition response had been fully worked out. He stated that it was not possible for British aircraft to have taken part in the raid. Irving then made the point that the Iraqis had previously tried to pass off military casualties as civilians – possibly a reference to the Nasiriyah hospital incident. However, when Suchet informed him that they in London had seen the uncut pictures and they clearly were of women and children, Irving replied in that case, if it was really a shelter, then something had gone wrong and that it was a tragic mistake because it could not have been an *intended target*.[74] Several minutes later, Mary Tillotson reported for CNN live from the White House that Fitzwater had become aware of the reports but would not speculate on whether it was an accident or whether Iraq might be distorting what had happened, but had reiterated the point that the allies targeted only military installations. 25 minutes after that, CNN reported that 'an official from the British Prime Minister's office said it was regrettable' but added that such accidents were 'bound to happen sooner or later'. It then showed another extract from Irving's interview when he pointed out that only the previous day British Tornado pilots had returned from a mission with their bombs because they could not be certain whether they could have hit their bridge targets precisely owing to adverse weather conditions. Clearly, instantaneous satellite television was moving ahead of the ability of the various allied information centres to co-ordinate their response.

The coordinated official reaction was finally worked out by the time the American briefing began in Riyadh at 18:15 (local time), just over five hours after CNN had first flashed the story around the world. Following his update on the overall war situation, Brigadier-General Richard Neal then addressed the incident:

I'm here to tell you that it was a military bunker. It was a command and control facility. It's one of many that has been used by the Iraqi government throughout this operation. We have been systematically attacking these bunkers since the beginning of the campaign. Within the last two weeks this particular bunker became even more active as a command and control facility. It's a hardened centre. Just recently the roof was painted with a camouflage pattern to further try to keep it out of the aviation vision. We have no explanation at this time really why there were civilians in this bunker.

The questions that followed were long and intense; it was, wrote Robert Fisk who was on a rare sojourn to Riyadh amidst his unilateralist activities, a 'question-rich environment'.[75] Neal said that it was 'plausible' that Saddam might have deliberately placed his own civilians in this bunker for a propaganda coup – the interpretation picked up by most of the tabloid press the next day[76] – but added that, from the coalition's point of view, 'we don't feel that we attacked the wrong bunker or that we made a mistake' and that Central Command was 'comfortable' that the right target had been hit. He admitted that they would not have attacked the bunker if they had known civilians were present but that Iraqi leaders were beginning to move into civilian areas because by now they knew that they would not be attacked there. In response to other questions it emerged that collateral damage had occurred before in civilian areas because the Iraqis located their military targets close to them, that the bunker had originally been built as an air raid shelter but had been converted in 1985, that it had been reactivated as a bunker only in the past few weeks and that it was a command and control facility that had been communicating with troops in Kuwait – which is why it was targeted legitimately.[77] 'We are not out to destroy Iraqi people,' Neal repeated, but if Saddam was placing civilians in active military installations it was he who should be held accountable.

Fisk was appalled at the performance, especially by the initial statement in which 'the general uttered not one single expression of regret, a fact that will have been noticed by the Arabs watching his live television broadcast'.[78] Even though Neal corrected this slightly in his subsequent answers ('You're damn right I regret it ... but it was nevertheless a professionally executed strike ... on a legitimate target') Fisk felt by then the 'damage had been done'. It was arguably this repeated insistence upon the infallibility of coalition intelligence and precision bombing which was to create more damage to the propaganda line which the allies had adopted since the start of the conflict than the pictures from Amiriya were ever able to do.

Normally, since Khafji, the coalition permitted only one of the three daily briefings to be televised live by individual stations. Not so that day. But first came another Peter Arnett report from Baghdad, at 18:55 (local time). He said that the known death toll had now risen to 200, mainly women and children, and that, according to the manager of the installation (Abdel Hassan Janebil), 300 more were still inside. Everyone in Baghdad was denying that there were any military personnel present as CNN transmitted a graphic shot of a burned child being brought out, and the blanket folded away for the camera (not to be repeated in later reports when this shot was cropped). Arnett said that local custom dictated that the sexes should not mix and so only women, children and old men had been inside the shelter. When the grieving crowd had learned that he and his team were Americans, they became hostile towards them, although not physically violent. This was one of the first times that western reporters claimed to have experienced personal hostility from local citizens. At the hospital, they were allowed to interview survivors and one badly burned 17 year old was shown talking through an interpreter about his experience. Arnett added that he could not tell whether any of the victims were military people because their clothes had been burned off, but he did repeat that he had seen mainly women and children. Reports had been leaking out of Washington and especially Riyadh that the facility had been transmitting radio signals, but Arnett said that although he had noticed an antenna on top of the building he had merely assumed this was a television aerial.

Ten minutes later, CNN carried the Saudi briefing live. Colonel Ahmed Al-Robayan confessed he was relieved that General Neal had spoken first about the incident and reiterated the point that it was a legitimate command and control centre and that if Saddam had placed civilians within it for propaganda purposes then it was he who was to blame. After expressing regret for the loss of civilian life, he pointed out that there was no air raid warning at the time of the explosion, which suggested that the civilians were already there, possibly as part of Saddam's attempt to lure the coalition into a mistake.

Half an hour after that, at just after 19:40 local time, the British briefing began, but CNN interrupted it within minutes to go live to an unexpected press conference called at the White House by Marlin Fitzwater. Given that it represented the official political response to the incident, it is worth quoting in full:

Last night, coalition forces bombed a military command and control centre in Baghdad that, according to press reports, resulted in a number of civilian casualties. The loss of civilian lives in time of war is a truly tragic consequence. It saddens everyone to know that innocent people may have died in the course of military conflict. America treats human life as our most precious value. That is why even during this military conflict, and with the lives of our servicemen and women are at risk, we will not target civilian facilities. We will continue to hit only military targets. The bunker that was attacked last night was a military target, a command and control centre that fed instructions directly to the Iraqi war machine, painted and camouflaged to avoid detection and well documented as a military target. And we have been systematically attacking these targets since the war began. We don't know why civilians were at this location but we do know that Saddam Hussein does not share our value in the sanctity of life. Indeed, time and again he has shown a willingness to sacrifice civilian lives and property to further his war aims. Civilian hostages were moved in November and December to military sites for use as human shields. PoWs reportedly have been placed at military sites. Roving bands of execution squads search out deserters amongst his own ranks of servicemen. Command and control centres in Iraq have been placed on top of schools and public buildings. Tanks and other artillery have been placed beside private homes and small villages, and only this morning we have documentation that two MiG 21's have been parked near the front door of a treasured archaeological site which dates back to the 27th century BC. His environmental terrorism spreads throughout the Persian Gulf, killing wildlife and threatening human water supplies. And finally, Saddam Hussein aims his Scud missiles at innocent civilians in Israel and Saudi Arabia. He kills civilians intentionally and with purpose. Saddam Hussein created this war. He created the military bunkers and he can bring the war to an end. We urge him once again to save his people and to comply with the UN resolutions.

There were no questions permitted and CNN returned to the British briefing.

BSkyB News, meanwhile, had continued to carry Group Captain Irving's briefing live. No mention of the shelter/bunker incident was made in his initial statement, although press questions afterwards inevitably forced him on to the subject. Irving said that, although there were no British aircraft involved in this particular raid, they were part of the overall coalition effort 'and so all coalition partners are part of this'. He raised the point about the camouflaged roof and the electronic signals as being undoubtedly efforts 'to make this look like a military target' and that minor military targets in civilian areas were 'off the menu' because of the risk of collateral damage. When he was picked up about this, Irving denied that he was attempting to make it seem like a deliberate Iraqi deception. 'Putting civilians anywhere near a structure like that is totally irresponsible.' He was not convinced at that stage that anything had 'gone wrong' and stated that large military installations needed to be destroyed in order to minimise Saddam's military capability. Irving was unfortunate in coming last in the briefings. The journalists by now had all the details of both versions of the event and were eager to pick up on the slightest slip in his choice of words. For example:

Q: Have the allies changed their policy about bombing residential areas? General Neal said that this was in a residential area. You just said that *minor* military targets in residential areas will not be struck. To date, I thought the understanding was that *no* military targets in residential areas would be struck. Has there been a change?

A: I have, er, I am not aware of the statement that it was in a residential area. What I am saying is that significant military targets that can be guaranteed to be hit by precision weapons, as occurred in this case, are legitimate targets and that we have a responsibility to take them out rather than endanger our own people.

So the lines, though blurred at the edges, had been drawn. The media were presenting the general impression of journalists in Baghdad that it was a civilian shelter (which was also the Iraqi view) whereas the official coalition line was that it was a military bunker.

Holding fast the inner lines

So was it a shelter or was it a bunker? Neither side denied that an installation had been hit in a bombing raid by two allied precision bombs or missiles at around 04:30 that morning during one of war's heaviest air raids to date. Neither side denied that there had been significant casualties. The reporters present at the scene within hours were clearly shaken by what they had witnessed. They had seen the charred corpses of mainly women and children brought out of the wreckage and later paraded in front of the hospital, although some were so badly burned it was impossible to ascertain the gender of some remains. The filmed 'evidence' had indicated a sign marked 'shelter', barbed wire around the facility and clearly distressed rescue workers and observers. Reports by both British and American journalists and film crews testified to the hostility of the crowd.

None of this could be denied. They were, in a sense, the 'facts' of the situation. But it was the interpretation placed upon those facts which prompted the official concern. The first, and in a sense the most important, fact that was disputed was whether or not the installation was a military bunker or a civilian shelter. Official coalition reactions throughout the day had been categoric in their assertion that it was indeed a bunker. It had been originally built as an air raid shelter but had been converted to a bunker in the mid 1980s. The sign marked 'shelter' in English raised memories of the 'baby milk plant' episode, although there was no local testimony as to whether this one's paint was still wet; quite the reverse in fact. And there was that barbed wire surrounding the building. Was it designed to keep people out, in which case it could be argued that it was a military installation, although there were no checkpoints posted outside (even Baghdad's television station was normally guarded by military personnel). Or was it designed to keep people in, in which case the point about Saddam's deliberate locating of civilians was given some credence. Certainly, it made access in or out difficult, whereas a bomb shelter would normally require easy, rapid access. Or it might even have been designed to house members of elite families and to keep them safe from the less fortunate Iraqi citizens without privileged access.[79] As for the bodies, an early CNN report quoted a Pentagon official as saying there was no way of telling whether they were military or civilian,[80] let alone rich or poor. The pictures showed the installation to be in a fairly wealthy district of Baghdad and even Peter Arnett had stated earlier in the day that the shelter did indeed look like a huge bunker.[81] But the Iraqi ambassador to the UN later told CNN that the shelter was for poor people, whereas the Amiriya district was an affluent residential suburb comprising houses with walled gardens for wealthy, and well-educated, retired Iraqis. There were certainly plenty of English-speaking Iraqis to interview in the vicinity, who made the point that they would never have placed their families in the building if they had known it was a military installation (which was a good point in the allies' favour that they could latch on to since it confirmed that locals recognised what kind of targets had been predominantly targeted). This in turn prompted some speculation that the shelter was for the exclusive use of senior figures from the Ba'athist Party and their families and that the allies might have thought Saddam himself might have been inside. Many observers in recent days had speculated that the killing of Saddam himself had become a primary allied goal.

Arnett transmitted another live interview at 12:05 EST (20:05 in Baghdad). He said that although a minder was present he could still say what he wanted and understood that his report would not be interfered with. When asked if it was possible that there might have been a military complex underneath the ruins he had seen, Arnett replied: 'Anything is possible in constructing shelters and buildings' but that 'it was not obvious to us'. Clearly he was being asked to clarify matters of detail to substantiate the coalition's claims. There was an antenna, for example, but his technician had told him it was a television aerial. It remained unclear as to when it had been placed there. Arnett admitted that he didn't think to ask whether military personnel had been present in the building because the issue had not arisen at that time when mainly women and children were being brought out. He added that the absence of an air raid siren did not necessarily mean that Baghdad civilians would wait for an alert; shelter life had become a habit in the nightly raids.

The time had clearly arrived for a senior politician to place the coalition's version of events on record and to place the incident in its wider political context. Defense Secretary Dick Cheney addressed the American Chamber of Commerce at just after 13:00 EST and his speech was carried live by CNN. He stated:

We sincerely regret any damage or any deaths caused to the civilian population. We've done everything we can to avoid that. Our forces, I think, have done an excellent job of targeting military targets and avoiding collateral damage to non-military targets. But the facility that was struck yesterday[82] we've gone back and checked very carefully on, and it was indeed a military facility, a hardened bunker, camouflage painted on top, plugged into his military communications system. We did in fact drop two bombs on it. They hit with great precision and there's no question in my mind or in the mind of our key people that what we hit was a military target. Some have suggested this morning on television – some of the talking heads that we have all grown familiar with in recent weeks as we've watched this affair unfold – that Saddam might now be resorting to a practice of deliberately placing civilians in harm's way, of deliberately putting civilians on what he knows are military targets for us. I have no way of knowing whether or not that was the case in this instance. But we do know that he had previously placed hundreds of foreign civilians held hostage all last fall at strategic sites throughout Iraq. We do know that he has threatened to place prisoners of war at strategic targets throughout

Iraq. We do know that he is placing military equipment in civilian areas especially in Kuwait but also in Iraq. And just this morning we received a new piece of intelligence that is interesting because of what it reveals about his practice with respect to his effort to try to blur the lines between military capabilities and civilian areas.

He then went on to cite 'recent satellite imagery' of the Iraqis placing two MiG 21 aircraft alongside a step-sided ziggurat pyramid in the city of Ur – no hollow claim as it turned out[83] – and to remind his (world-wide) audience of Saddam's record in gassing the Kurds: 'So I suppose the suggestion that he may indeed have encouraged civilians to occupy what he knew to be a military facility is possible.'

During General Neal's briefing, it had been mentioned that the roof had been camouflaged and this point was taken up by Lieutenant General Thomas Kelly at the Pentagon's daily briefing at 13:30 EST. Given that Peter Arnett and indeed all the various television crews had been allowed to swarm all over the smoking building, including the roof, this was to be one of those blurred edges that was yet to be resolved. Kelly appeared with Captain David Herrington of the US Navy, equipped with maps and drawings of the Amiriya vicinity which they said had been based upon intelligence photographs. They pointed out that Iraqi strategic command and control facilities had been located in the heart of Baghdad and, because they had been the object of allied raids, the Iraqis had decided to move away from the centre to the suburbs to facilitate their continuation, such as the one seen on television that morning which 'we knew was active'. This was an odd point to make, not picked up in the questions afterwards. It was odd because the conference centre that was hit was in fact downtown and, as it emerged later, was also considered to be active as a military centre. Moreover, reports by western journalists right from the start of the war described how military installations, power stations, refineries and the like had been hit not just on the outskirts of town but also in the suburbs. Just before his expulsion, Richard Beeston of *The Times* described how targets in the city centre 'were largely spared'.[84] Yet, as Peter Arnett later described the previous night's bombing, the attacks were 'closer to the centre of the city than in previous nights'.[85]

In fact, Kelly and Herrington admitted to knowing a 'great deal' about the Amiriya facility. Herrington continued:

Because it was located in the middle of a lot of civilian kinds of facilities, we chose at 04:30 in the morning local time to strike this target. At that time, 2 bombs, laser guided, went right down to the centre of that facility. It's baffling to me as an American and it hurts me deeply to see that apparently civilians were placed in what is clearly a military facility. Saddam Hussein who lives in this city has seen the results of a very strategic and surgical bombing campaign directed against that military infrastructure. He had to know that we knew that this was a military facility, and why he would put innocent civilians in this facility troubles me greatly and is something quite frankly that just mystifies us.

He reiterated that command and control equipment was present in a hardened, camouflaged building with electromagnetic pulse protection that would be sufficient to protect it in a nuclear strike. The reinforced steel roof and the barbed wire surround all pointed to it not being an air raid shelter 'in the classic sense of the word'.

Under questioning about whether, then, a bunker containing civilians was hit owing to a failure of intelligence, Kelly replied:

First, everything we are seeing relative to this facility is coming out of a controlled press in Baghdad ... We don't have a free press there asking hardened questions like you all do here. We didn't know that there were people in there. I think I heard on TV earlier today they were going in there every night, but that was strictly hearsay. They could have been put in there last night. We simply don't know.

There were, Kelly admitted, some 'very strange things' about the television pictures. The shelter sign looked new to him and, when asked to elaborate on the Riyadh statement that signals were picked up coming from the building, he replied:

We specifically do not talk about our ability to intercept Iraqi military communications because that would then allow them to change the way they are doing it and we wouldn't be intercepting that – and I don't agree with what you said, Sir, that silence is helping them. We think we are being very forthcoming with the information.

The key points to remember, he stressed, were that Saddam had fired Scuds at civilians in Saudi Arabia and Israel, he had gassed Kurds and 'pulled the plugs out of incubators in Kuwait'. The antenna may have been moved after the raid to disguise any external signs of military use. Although he conceded that the United States might have been 'sandbagged' by Iraqi propaganda, when asked to comment on the correspondents' observations about the camouflage, Kelly snapped: 'Did they climb up on the roof?' When told they had, he replied: 'Well, then they've got bad eyes because I have seen and I will guarantee you that there is camouflage blotches painted on that roof.' However, as the *Sunday Times* pointed out the following weekend, 'the faded green markings were unlike camouflage painted on other Iraqi buildings in recent months'.[86] Kelly also added that Iraqi military personnel could have gone into the bunker after dark when allied reconnaissance would not have been able to identify them and it would certainly not have been bombed if it was known that civilians were inside. He denied it was hit because of a belief that Saddam might have been there. When asked if it was a sanctuary for privileged Iraqis, Kelly responded by saying that if his family were in that situation, he certainly wouldn't put them in a building with a camouflaged roof: 'no rational man would want to build a [military] shelter like a [civilian air raid] bomb shelter'. The conference centre that was hit was also 'associated with military activity'. One might add that, had there been civilians present in the conference centre just yards away from the Al-Rashid, the Iraqis would undoubtedly have made more of it. Finally, Kelly again pointed out that what had been seen was the product of a controlled press system which did not tolerate the kind of strong questioning that he was being subjected to:

I would also ask you to remember that when we have television pictures coming out of Baghdad and the sirens go off the people continue to mill around. When we have pictures coming out of Riyadh or Tel Aviv and the sirens go off, you see people dashing for air raid shelters and I think that begins to put it in context.

It was a mixed performance under intensive and penetrating questions. Kelly clearly had to be careful not to give too much away for security reasons – he knew Saddam might be watching – but the points about the antennae and the camouflage left nagging doubts as they were the only actual facts which clashed with the journalistic versions from Baghdad.

When Kelly left, Peter Williams, chief Pentagon spokesman and a former TV journalist from Wyoming 'who has the rare distinction of being trusted by the journalists *and* the men in uniforms',[87] took over. He pointed out that the *prima facie* evidence so far was that the United States was not attacking civilian targets deliberately. One journalist said 'trust us', to which Williams replied that it was not a question of trust, just a matter of presenting the evidence. He himself had asked the intelligence people only that morning about how many misses had been recorded and had been told: 'a handful'.

'The civilian deaths in Baghdad hit Washington like a live grenade, which the White House sought to hurl back at Saddam Hussein' was how CNN's Charles Bierbauer put it in a report live from White House.[88] The problem for Washington in a sense was that the image of precision bombing fostered by the constant stream of official videos had promoted an illusion of infallibility which had suddenly been exposed by the Amiriya incident. Patrick Cockburn argued in *The Independent*:

The real lesson of the destruction of the shelter in Baghdad ... is that the allied air forces have become victims of their own propaganda. They have pretended that they can carry out surgical strikes: but mass bombing remains a blunt instrument.[89]

In fact the coalition had never 'pretended' that collateral damage was wholly unavoidable. Besides, officials argued, the bombs hit what they were aiming for.

At the United Nations – the Security Council of which was due to meet the next day for the first time since the outbreak of war and which on Anglo-American insistence was to be held behind closed doors for the first time in 15 years and only the fourth time ever[90] – the Kuwaiti ambassador also made the point that the tragedy had shifted the focus of media attention away from Iraqi atrocities against civilians in his country and invited western correspondents in Baghdad to request permission to travel there.[91]

In Britain, the main early evening news programmes went out before the statements of Cheney and Kelly had been made. ITN's news at 17:30 GMT nonetheless presented both the Iraqi and the American case, first the former with Brent Sadler's report stating:

... Iraq has been continually protesting high numbers of civilian casualties through allied bombing. A grotesque procession of human remains was brought out in what can only be described as powerful and harrowing evidence of large civilian loss. Iraq is already using these disturbing scenes of trauma to attack the allied coalition for the allied bombing campaign ... Since the war began Allied commanders have repeatedly denied that residential areas were targeted. But this carnage inside a shelter undeniably used by civilians, and hit twice, will require a detailed explanation ... Amiriya is a middle class residential area. I could see no military or strategic targets in this vicinity ...

The report lasted 3 minutes and 15 seconds.[92] Anchor Fiona Armstrong then related the American claim about electronic signals emanating from the building 'but some experts say that this time the Americans have made a mistake'. Despite Neal's assertion that it was a command and control facility (showing him speaking at the briefing earlier that day), ITN interviewed Sir John Moberley, former British ambassador to Baghdad, who stated that he found it hard to believe that the Iraqis would deliberately place civilians in a military bunker because of security reasons of their own. A report on the reaction on the streets of Washington was described as 'that's tough, but that's war' as vox pops were shown indicating this feeling. Bill Neely's report concluded with the observation that the American administration's chief worry was about the impact of the bombing on the Arab members of the coalition. The reaction at the United Nations and in Britain was also described. In total, about 5.5 minutes were given over to the coalition version and about 4 minutes to the Iraqi, with the remaining 2 minutes of the story being broadly factual or neutral in tone.

BBC's Six O'Clock News devoted half of its programme to the story. It also began first with the pictures from Baghdad, with a report by Jeremy Bowen – but not before anchorman Peter Sissons had, if anything, given more emphasis to the American, version by way of introduction (13 seconds to the Iraqi version, 36 seconds to the American with the remaining 32 seconds being broadly factual or even-handed). Bowen's report, said Sissons, was 'compiled under Iraqi government restrictions and you may find some scenes in it distressing'. Much of the report had been shown at midday, but there was additional footage and additional observations following on from his statement to camera that the Iraqis claimed there had been more serious attacks elsewhere:

But this is the first time I've seen this level of damage at a civilian location in Iraq. I've seen similar damage, though, at the other targets which the allies have been hitting with great accuracy.

Grieving and angry people were shown and some charred bodies, but the BBC had also self-censored its pictures so that the burned remains were not graphically dwelt upon. Some NHK pictures of the few survivors in the hospital were included in the report.

Bowen added:

There were dreadful scenes outside the hospital [over grieving women, including the one who spat at the camera]. None of this was set up for our cameras. As usual, we were accompanied at all times by officials, but this was not a propaganda stunt. It was real grief and real anger.

Bowen's report lasted 3½ minutes. Neal Bennett's report from Riyadh that followed, including the time given over to that day's briefings, lasted 2 minutes. However, when combined with the first half of Keith Graves's report that followed from Washington and the United Nations on the White House reaction and version (1 minute out of a 3 minute report) and the portion of Martin Dowle's report from Westminster devoted to the British reaction and version (again 1 minute out of 3), we can see that slightly more time was given over to the coalition's interpretation of events.

Then, however, Sissons ran an interview with Bowen which had been recorded a few minutes earlier. Bowen began: 'I've seen no evidence myself that this was a military target, as they [the coalition] have been saying.' He had seen no antennae or other signs of military use but he had seen dead women, children and old men, although he had not seen civilians in this kind of structure before. He would not comment one way or the other on whether Saddam had deliberately placed civilians in the installation, but he did say that the Iraqi censors had adopted an 'entirely different tone' all that day, compared with other sites they had been taken to. Bowen had seen tears in their eyes this time and there was 'real emotion' and the grief and anger of the crowd were genuine, whereas previously they had experienced friendliness from the local citizens. At the end of the programme, however, a segment of Dick Cheney's speech to the American Chamber of Commerce (which was still going on at that time) was run, stating that 'it was a military target'.

If anything, then, both the BBC and ITN had given slightly more time and emphasis to the coalition version of events and they had self-censored the really graphic pictures that were available for them to use. Even so, the event itself was still so shocking that accusations were launched against the 'Baghdad Broadcasting Corporation'[93] for transmitting Iraqi propaganda, while on the other side of the Atlantic CNN was described by right-wing critics as

the 'US Voice of Baghdad'. In America, the Republican Representative for California, Robert Dornan, criticised Arnett's reporting, especially his point about shelter life having become a habit
for Iraqi citizens which, he said, was 'pure speculation'. However,
evidence gathered by other journalists also testified to this, with
The Times quoting one local who had lost 11 members of his
family as saying: 'All the families around here spent the night in
this shelter. We thought it would withstand a nuclear bomb.'[94]

The problem, of course, was that the pictures from the Iraqi
side were far more graphic from a visual point of view than those
available from the coalition side, which were largely a series of
'talking heads': Neal, Irving, Fitzwater and Cheney. No matter
how rational and convincing their arguments, they could not
compete with the sheer visual power of the smoking bunker and
the rows of charred bodies. Iraq, in other words, now appeared to
be the victim rather than the aggressor in this war.

The same pattern of coverage was repeated later in the evening
on both the BBC's Nine O'Clock News and ITN's News at Ten.
On the 'Nine', Bowen's report was concluded with the words by
anchor Michael Buerk: 'You should know that many of the pictures from Baghdad of the burned bodies of the victims were
considered too grim to show you.' Buerk then spoke to Bowen,
transmitting a picture interview from the Al-Rashid, and the reporter was insistent that he had seen no signs of military use – no
satellite dishes, no antennae, no signs of military personnel
amongst the victims. He had not been all through the shelter
because the rescue effort was still under way. He said that the
American suggestion that civilians had been deliberately placed
there for propaganda purposes was being greeted with 'derision
and contempt' by the Iraqis. The attack had 'affected people in a
way that none of the other air raids that have been going on here
now for a month have done'. From Saudi, Neil Bennett then
reported that this had been the most difficult day of the war so
far for the military briefers.

On the 'Ten', anchor Julia Somerville warned that 'some of the
pictures are distressing' – the first time ITN had issued this
warning. She also stated that 'Brent Sadler's reports are subject to
Iraqi censorship though the Iraqis didn't cut or alter anything in
tonight's'. The thrust of the emphasis was that the bunker had
been used by the military and that the attack was therefore

legitimate, although it was regretted by all sides that civilians had been killed.[95] At the end of Sadler's report, Somerville again stated: 'Well, as we said, the Iraqis didn't censor any part of Brent Sadler's report but we at ITN did edit out some scenes because we regarded them as too distressing to broadcast.' Edward Stourton's report on the coalition's case included pictures taken on the previous Monday of destroyed Iraqi bridges.

Many of the pictures of bomb damage that have reached the west support allied claims that targets are identified with care. There have been civilian casualties but nothing we know of on the scale of what happened last night.

Various political figures were interviewed to relate the British political reaction. Paddy Ashdown, leader of the Liberal Democratic Party, talked of the potential impact of the bombing on the Middle East and described Saddam as a 'master of propaganda'. But the allies had formulated their case and the western media had, by the evening, reflected the coherence of the official line that was now being taken. It had become more of a bunker than a shelter, containing civilians possibly because Saddam had placed them there or at least not discouraged them from seeking shelter in a camouflaged military installation that was emitting radio traffic – again, it was suggested, possibly even deliberately in order to encourage an allied attack for propaganda purposes.

If Saddam was indeed a 'master of propaganda', the allied version in effect portrayed him as being not very good at the art. All sorts of propagandist motives were imputed to him, but the upshot of the allied statements, backed up by intelligence 'evidence' that could not in fact be verified, was that he had been found out. The emphasis of criticism therefore shifted to the messengers who had carried the pictures, although as we have seen the main news programmes at least presented the story in a relatively balanced manner and had self-censored the pictures, if anything giving more credence by the end of the day to the coalition's version.

But then, on BBC2's Newsnight that evening, at 22:30, Jeremy Paxman began by saying:

Today was the end of illusions about the Gulf War: women, children and old people killed by allied war planes in our name ... Until today it had seemed such an uncannily sanitised war: clever bombs that wrecked real estate but somehow appeared to leave people unscathed. Now the first mass civilian deaths, unintended though they may have been, present the allies with a potential public opinion and diplomatic nightmare.

Some pretty nasty shots of the dead and grieving were shown as Paxman asked: 'Who can predict the impact of pictures like this being broadcast throughout the world?' Dr. David Manley, Civil Defence Adviser to the Home Office and an expert on military installations, was then interviewed and said it was definitely a civilian bomb shelter, very poorly designed and constructed, whereas Saddam's military shelters were known to be much more capable of surviving bomb attacks. He added: 'I rather think that it was used for civilians to be able to get the propaganda over that civilians are dying in this war.' As for the military signals, Dr. Manley said that communications equipment may have been stored in the building, 'but I don't agree that this was one of his military shelters'.

In a report from Saudi Arabia, Mark Urban suggested that the tragedy may have indeed been caused by a failure of coalition intelligence. Newsnight then ran an item on civilian damage generally, including an interview with Ramsay Clark, who described how he had travelled from Baghdad to Basra with relative inconvenience, with only one small diversion caused by a downed bridge. He said: 'the traffic that gets hit is all civilian'. Ironically, Clark was essentially providing no better military justification for why the bombing of strategic targets such as bridges on the supply routes to Kuwait should go on.

That evening, at 21:02 EST, CNN carried a live interview between Larry King and the Iraqi ambassador to the UN, Abdul Amir Al-Anbari, who claimed to be familiar with the Amiriya suburb of Baghdad. He said that the shelter had been built for the benefit of low-income people. The furthest he would go in support of the American version was to say that B52 bombers could not discriminate between civilians and military personnel and that Americans in their 'normal ordinary life' did not intentionally kill children. He continued:

There is no way of proving that it was definitely intentional. However there is circumstantial evidence – the fact that there is no military installation on that area, the fact that all Arabic signs showed that was a military, er sorry, a civilian shelter, the fact that we saw the victims in that shelter, that they were civilian children, and given the sophistication

209

of all the intelligence instruments of the United States – they should know better.

He also cited Ramsay Clark's statements and admitted that 'we have a lot of things to make propaganda about thanks to the American bombardment of civilian institutions and hospitals'. About 7,000 had died so far, he said. He deflected questions from King about the treatment of Kuwaitis and said that the Scud attacks on Israel were deliberate because 'we believe that the Israelis are the root and branch of this conflict'. He also denied any knowledge of the whereabouts of the missing CBS crew (even though they were in Iraqi captivity at that time[96]). Before the commercial breaks, CNN did run tape of coalition official statements and of the Kuwaiti ambassador to the UN. Anti-Saddam sentiment, as reflected in the phone-in calls, was due, the ambassador maintained, to a concerted orchestrated propaganda campaign waged by the American government and its public relations firms for the past year. The barbed wire was there to protect the shelter from thieves, stray dogs and for security purposes in a low-income area. Finally, when placed on the spot about other Iraqi atrocities committed during the war, he stated that it was an 'open question' whether or not the oil spill in the Gulf had been caused by allied bombing.

By the time the story itself had been well and truly covered, the analysis of its impact began. As the war of words continued, CNN's John Holliman concluded:

If Saddam Hussein's goal was to shake coalition resolve, he probably failed – there is no indication that the bombing will stop. But if his goal was to up the emotional ante in the Arab world with pictures of burned babies, he probably succeeded. And in the Arab world emotions, like politics and regional loyalties, run deep – perhaps deeper than anywhere else on earth.[97]

Certainly, just after Jordanian television had shown pictures of the tragedy, a German student mistakenly taken for an American was stabbed in a street in Amman.[98] The Jordanian government, angry also at news that 30 Jordanian nationals and 30 Sudanese refugees had recently been killed in allied air raids on the sanction-busting convoys between Iraq and Amman,[99] declared three days of national mourning. One day of mourning was announced in Tunisia, the US embassy in Amman was pelted with rocks and the Algerian government called a minute of national silence. 'It was the television pictures that did it,' wrote one correspondent from Amman.[100] The pictures were all the more welcome to the Iraqis in view of the fact that the capacity of Baghdad radio to transmit to the Arab world had been by this time severely reduced, by bombing and jamming. Baghdad radio did manage to put out a call 'to ask every person on earth' to join Iraq in its 'historic mission' against 'American–Atlantic–Saudi aggression' in 'confronting these predatory beasts and groups of infidels who rule the world through vileness, injustice and affronts to human decency'.[101] But Arab members of the coalition were holding firm, despite the UN Secretary General's statement that he was 'dismayed by the magnitude of Iraqi civilian casualties' caused by the bombing of a 'civil defence shelter'. Syria and Egypt blamed Saddam unequivocally for the incident, while the press in those countries downplayed the whole affair.[102] A 15–minute telephone conversation between President Bush and Prime Minister Major giving reassurances of the validity of American military intelligence was no doubt repeated with other coalition leaders.

The fact that this entire event, prompted by the spectacular and powerful television pictures, was the object of so much debate would appear to indicate in itself the unusual nature of the bombing incident. If more civilians had been killed in similar incidents, the promptness of the Iraqis at Amiriya would suggest that they would have been quick to escort western film crews to other scenes. Even Saddam, by granting his interview to Arnett only days before in a bungalow rather than in a bunker, was tacitly admitting that the coalition was not targeting civilian areas. But in a sense, the Americans were expecting their assertions that it was a bunker to be sufficient. The evidence that it was – the barbed wire fence, the reinforced roof, the steel doors – had to be balanced against the graphic shots of women and children being brought out of a building that was marked 'shelter'. The grief amongst the crowd outside shook the reporters – and indeed television audiences. As *The Times* put it:

And it would have been hard to make hundreds of grief-stricken people tell the same story, either in overheard conversations or in answer to journalists that their women and children had gone there every night to sleep.[103]

The issue of camouflage and of the antenna remained unclear. But the journalists were convinced it was a shelter whereas the military remained adamant that it was a bunker. The journalists had the pictures, the military had the intelligence. Because the pictures were public and the intelligence was secret and would have to remain so, the presentation of the issue by the media tended to support the pictures even though broadcasters had gone to great pains to explain the coalition line. For example, one military spokesman was quoted as saying 'those weren't five year old kids on the radio and telephones',[104] but he was obviously unable to reveal how he knew this. Besides, there were 5–year-old kids being brought out of the rubble. Nonetheless, the key point was that the pictures failed to shake public opinion in either Britain or the United States, with around 80% of people surveyed in both countries indicating that it was a legitimate target and that the incident had made no difference to their support for the allied effort.[105]

This did not however prevent some criticism of the coverage afforded to the event. A *Daily Telegraph* leader admitted that newspapers were sometimes jealous of television's power and audience, but claimed that 'the immense air time' given to the Amiriya incident was also 'a case study in the limitations of that medium'. It criticised the 'hushed and frankly accusatory' tone of television reporters in their coverage of the incident and added:

As so often with television, it is not the scale of the horror that shapes the coverage, but the nature and quantity of available visual material ... Many many apologists still seem unwilling to accept, as most of the public believes, that rather than acting as proper journalists, reporters in Baghdad are being allowed to dispense only one commodity: a tightly framed series of snapshots of civilian suffering. They cannot even pursue effective investigations into whether the devastated bunker was a military or civilian installation ... What the media in general, and television in particular, find so difficult to achieve is a sense of proportion and context for events. Television is a marvellous medium of impression, a hopeless medium of analysis ... it is the broadcasters whose coverage thus far threatens their standing and respect from the public which displays more grim common sense about the war than those in the studios.[106]

The essential point that ordinary people accept that such tragedies of war inevitably happen without this affecting their overall view of the war would appear to stand up to analysis. In surveys conducted amongst British audiences, the vast majority of people did not wish to see the uncut footage while still supporting the presence of western correspondents in Baghdad.[107]

By the following day, the Americans were attempting to shift the focus of the debate into the area of Iraqi 'dual function' installations. In Washington, some intelligence information was leaked, on the condition that the sources remained anonymous. For example, it emerged that the raid had been conducted by F-117A Stealth bombers from the 37th Tactical Fighter Wing of the USAF using two GBU27 2,000 lb laser-guided bombs. Public Shelter No. 25 had been clearly identified as a military command centre on the list of coalition targets.[108] It was also claimed that the installation had a military function beneath the civilian sanctuary, following assessments of reports from foreign engineers who helped to construct and modify the shelter into a bunker.[109] It was claimed that only in the past two or three weeks had the converted shelter become an active command and control bunker. American military officials in Riyadh, according to the *New York Times*,[110] further claimed that Iraq was hiding a major military communications centre in a secret basement of the Al-Rashid hotel, from where signals were being sent to Iraqi forces in Kuwait along fibre-optic telephone cables hidden in two of Baghdad's remaining bridges. They said that they had been ordered by Washington *not* to bomb these sites because of the risk to civilian areas even though, by destroying the link, it would force the Iraqis to use high-frequency radio signals that could be more easily intercepted by the coalition forces.[111] 'No comment,' said the Pentagon to this odd claim.[112] The hotel where western journalists were housed as a no-go area for air strikes was a fair enough point to make if the coalition was attempting to emphasise the trouble to which it was going to avoid unnecessary casualties. But if the links across the nearby bridges were, as claimed, the final connection remaining between Baghdad and Kuwait and between Saddam and the Scud missile launchers, the political as well as the military imperative would surely point to them being knocked out by those wonderfully accurate precision missiles that had been knocking out bridges elsewhere without collateral damage. Moreover, the leak suggested that the United States had effectively abandoned any hope of completely cutting off Saddam's communications from the Al-Rashid with his armed forces, so why bother with bombing other subsidiary communications centres such as that alleged to have been in Amiriya? One can only speculate whether this was more disinformation or, pending the release of the official documents, whether this reflected a degree of irritability by the military authorities at Washington's efforts to minimise for political reasons the impression given at the briefings that Central Command in Saudi Arabia was 'comfortable' with the targeting of Amiriya. General Schwarzkopf was reported to have 'angrily denied once again that his forces were purposely striking civilian targets' and that one of his aides had said that there was '"no way, no way at all" the United States would refrain from hitting all urban military targets, even for a brief time'.[113]

The Iraqi Ministry of Information responded by allowing journalists to make an 'unrestricted' tour of the Al-Rashid hotel on the Thursday. According to the Associated Press, the tour provided no evidence of there being a military communications centre in the basement.[114] Later, however, it did emerge that a main command and control bunker possibly lay underneath the road between the Al-Rashid and the conference centre that had been hit just down the street. Both sites may indeed have been secret access points to perhaps Saddam's principal bunker.[115] The presence of western reporters at one and not at the other might one day help to explain coalition targeting policy more adequately.

As the first of the Amiriya victims were being buried – when again hostile crowds were reported by the press – the Iraqis reduced their figure of the total dead to 314. On Friday the 15th, the story was at last pushed down the media agenda by Saddam's sudden announcement that he was apparently prepared to withdraw from Kuwait, a ploy that was dismissed by Bush as 'a cruel hoax' following a few hours of elation – in Washington and Baghdad – at the prospect of the war's victorious conclusion without a ground war.

There is some evidence to suggest that considerable friction was taking place between Central Command in Riyadh and the more politically sensitive centres in Washington. The anticipated fall-out in the Arab world prompted a variety of stories indicating that the Pentagon was considering altering its bombing strategy.[116] On 14 February, General Kelly stated that 'if we wanted to hurt civilians, that's the easiest thing in the world to do':

We could have tens of thousands of them hurt. We could have run this operation the way the Iraqis ran their operation against the Iranians. We could have fired missiles up there that are terribly inaccurate right into the middle of their cities. We've done none of that.[117]

Marlin Fitzwater however denied any friction: 'there's no review, no change of procedures, no change in policy, no change in targeting development at all'.[118]

Aftermath

By the weekend, sources at the Pentagon and in Riyadh were admitting privately that the bombing had occurred as a result of an intelligence mistake. Robert Fisk reported that one senior military source in Riyadh had told him that the raid was 'a serious error' which had caused 'deep distress to America's Saudi military allies'.[119] His source appeared to be part of the row that was going on about the wisdom of continuing to bomb Iraq rather than Kuwait. 'There's not a soul who believes it was a command and control bunker ... We thought it was a military personnel bunker',[120] Fisk quoted him as saying. Elsewhere senior officials were saying – also anonymously – that they were wrong not to check whether the building was being used by civilians.[121] This perhaps should have been the line to take from the moment the story broke, but the continued official insistence that the building itself was a bunker continued to evoke journalistic scepticism until the intelligence 'evidence' that the coalition insisted it had was released. The Pentagon maintained that releasing such proof could jeopardise further intelligence-gathering techniques. Nonetheless, as the *Observer* noted: 'At the week's end, the Baghdad bunker looked like a cock-up: at worst, a total failure of intelligence; at best, a mistaken belief that the bunker was for military personnel.'[122]

The Iraqis, not unnaturally, refused to let up on the question of civilian damage, even if in a sense Amiriya had demonstrated that the issue was not succeeding in dramatically increasing public opposition to the war in coalition countries. If anything, in the USA support had actually increased, with polls indicating that 84% blamed Saddam for the deaths in the shelter.[123] The Royal Air Force were the next to come under scrutiny, with the Iraqis claiming on Thursday 14 February that a bomb had killed between 50 and 130 civilians in an apartment block and market place at

Fallujah, to the west of Baghdad on the road from Jordan to Kuwait. Western journalists were escorted to the scene but could find no trace of the RAF Tornado which the Iraqis claimed to have shot down after the attack. The RAF announced that it had lost such an aircraft on that day but during a different raid on an airfield.[124] An official at the MoD in London stated: 'If hundreds had been killed, wouldn't Saddam Hussein's propaganda machine have got this out sooner? They didn't waste any time on the so-called shelter in Baghdad.'[125] The Iraqi claim, however, appeared to have some substance.

Three different statements were issued to the press as the military checked the story. Then, on Sunday 17 February, the British decided to release a video showing a not so smart laser-guided bomb missing its target in Fallujah and falling into a civilian area.[126] 'If there were any civilian casualties, we very much regret that,' said the British spokesman, Group Captain Irving, but a spokesman at the MoD in London stated that the video was taken on the Wednesday, a day before the Iraqi claim.[127] The next day, Group Captain David Henderson said in Riyadh: 'unfortunately it looks as though, despite our best efforts, bombs did land in the town. If a [laser-guided] bomb malfunctions, then it will go astray.'[128] This was a well thought-out decision. By admitting to an honest and regrettable mistake, it avoided the likelihood of a similar media fuss to that which had built up over Amiriya; it was good propaganda which limited the damage and increased British credibility. There is also the distinct possibility that by admitting now to an honest mistake, the coalition was attempting retroactively to enhance the credibility of its Amiriya interpretation, ie that it was most definitely *not* a mistake. Publicly, the Americans maintained their official stance over bombing accuracy and Saddam's disingenuity to the last, with Admiral McConnell stating at the Pentagon on Saturday 16 February that an allegedly bombed mosque in Basra had in fact had its dome removed by the Iraqis themselves under the cover of darkness earlier in the month. A military source in Riyadh said he had seen photographs of the mosque taken on 4 and 11 February: 'somebody took the dome off, but it wasn't us ... it was very surgically removed'.[129] Then, on 22 February, the *Washington Post* reported that Defence Department officials 'suppressed a film showing a U.S. smart bomb early in the war accidentally striking a civilian building in downtown Baghdad, across from the Interior Ministry'.[130]

The Iraqis attempted to drive home the Fallujah mistake by stepping up their anti-British diatribes whenever Baghdad radio could transmit, even on reduced power:

The heinous crime committed by the aggressive Britons against defenceless citizens is to be added to the British criminal record and to Britain's crimes that have been committed in Iraq since the turn of the century ... Since the Americans committed their abominable crime that embodies all their feuds, racism and enmity for the Iraqis in the Amiriyah air raid shelter, the Britons did not lag behind in committing another ugly crime in Fallujah that is no less outrageous and ugly.[131]

The broadcast, barely discernible in parts, went on to compare the 'crime' with the outcry the British raised over the execution of 'the dangerous spy', Barzoft, which was of course a reminder that the Iraqis considered 'American–Zionist–Atlantic aggression', backed up by old colonial British values, to be the root cause of the war.

On the night of 17–18 February, Baghdad was subjected to one of the heaviest air raids of the entire war, with reportedly 17 cruise missiles striking the city. Coinciding with Iraqi claims now of 20,000 dead and 60,000 wounded, the allies were clearly unshaken in their resolve to prepare as much of the way by bombing for the ground war to begin. This, combined with reports of mounting public hostility within Iraq against the ruling Ba'athist Party (including one report that 10 members had been lynched and hanged by an angry mob[132]), may help to explain why Saddam now appeared to be moving in favour of a diplomatic solution, as we shall see in the next chapter. Or they may simply have been coalition-inspired reports which were attempting to shift the focus of attention away from civilian victims and more on to Saddam's culpability and isolation.

As for Amiriya itself, there remains much that is unknown. If it was an intelligence failure, as seems most likely at the point of writing, then what went wrong? After the war, former American Air Force Chief of Staff General Michael Dugan, fired for his indiscretions about the bombing campaign in the previous autumn, stated that the intelligence information upon which coalition briefers had based their targeting policy 'was not the most current information'.[133] The US military at the time, however, appeared to be convinced that it had monitored signals traffic from the installation and that it possessed supporting intelligence about the movement in and out of the building by military personnel in military vehicles and limousines (presumably taken by spy satellites). This raises the question about when such intelligence had been gathered. If it was derived from an earlier part of the war, it may have been out of date by the time the attack took place. Again after the war, General McPeak stated that many Stealth bombers had been forced to return home with their munitions 'where low cloud cover prevented them from acquiring the target'.[134] Bad weather may have simply forced the Amiriya installation to be placed further down the list of targets on the roster, to be attacked when conditions improved, by which time its function had changed. Finally, there is the additional possibility that the Amiriya raid was part of an unspoken and rigorously denied campaign to kill Saddam Hussein and high-ranking members of his regime, even though, after the war, Tariq Aziz denied that any member of his own family 'was injured, nor were any of those from other members of the leadership'.[135] Again after the war, suggestions were made that the coalition had in fact conducted a 'Get Saddam' operation despite the wartime assertion to the contrary by Washington. Although Secretary Baker had said on 10 February that 'no one would shed any tears' if Saddam went but that 'we're not expanding or enlarging our war aims to include that', it has since been claimed that an intensive search was conducted for Saddam's American-made motor home, his 'Wanderlodge'. Command bunkers were of course a coalition bombing priority right from the start and right to the end. At one point, apparently half way through the war, two patrolling F-16 pilots had strafed a military motorcade carrying Saddam on the Baghdad–Basra road; unwittingly, they hit the front and rear of the convoy while Saddam's vehicle in the middle was left unharmed.[136]

Lastly, another important point that needs to be made about the media coverage afforded to the incident again revolves around the question of context. Avid television viewers of the conflict could be forgiven for remembering the war as a massive allied air offensive in which many civilians died followed by a short ground war, in which comparatively few soldiers were killed. In fact, in terms of deaths, quite the reverse was true. After the war, the BBC's Foreign Affairs Editor, John Simpson, returned to Baghdad and was allowed to travel more than he ever had been during the war itself. He noted that 'there's so little damage in Baghdad that it can take you 15 minutes to drive from one bomb-site to another':[137]

The picture was the same everywhere really, that selected buildings had been damaged – fewer than 30 in Baghdad itself and very very many fewer than that in most of the other cities. There was a little bit of what they called collateral damage, say damage to other buildings and no doubt some people had been killed in those cities, but it wasn't very large. By far the largest number of deaths was caused by the appalling decision, I think, to attack the shelter at Amiriya. Aside from that, if that hadn't happened, I think the casualties in the air war would have been very low indeed.[138]

This was, he felt, true also of other cities, including Basra, Najaf and Mosul, where he found the picture much the same.[139] Other post-war testimonies echoed Simpson's experience. A *New York Times* correspondent spent three weeks in Iraq and reported that 'the area around Baghdad ... has quickly re-emerged into the 20th Century'. Gasoline rationing was abolished on 27 April, and by then electricity had been restored, at least partly, to all main towns, while water quality was improving steadily.[140] On the other hand, four months after the war, Iraq's electricity-generating capacity was said to be at 20–25% of its pre-war level, which would place it in the same position as it had been in 1920 – long before the country's reliance on modern electrical appliances, including medical equipment. This prompted considerable concern amongst a Harvard University medical health team which visited the country after the war and whose members made an important point: that the worst civilian damage occurred not as a result of smart bombs going astray or hitting the wrong target but, conversely, when they hit precisely what they were aimed at in the coalition's attempts to destroy Iraq's generators and electrical grid.

So the Amiriya incident, the exception rather than the rule, distorted the reality of the allied air offensive. It also emerged after the war that, in the entire 43–day war, fewer than 3,000 individual bombs and missiles, 2,800 tons of ordnance, had been dropped on Baghdad. This is a tiny figure when compared with bombing of cities in wars past. Television, in other words, had magnified not only this incident but the entire question of collateral damage. There was such damage, and the allies had never denied that it would be inevitable and always regrettable. Basra, however, was bombed far more intensively than Baghdad, and yet there were no western correspondents transmitting from that city. Even Ramsay Clark had marvelled at the Iraqi clean-up of military sites for his visit, although that was not the point he had been trying to make. One analyst has written:

Some 1,000–3,000 people are estimated to have been killed in cases of known collateral damage from air attacks in these two cities and other towns. It is estimated that some 5,000–15,000 civilians died in 20,000 sorties flown against strategic targets in the war.[141]

It is unclear from these figures how many died as a result of damage to Iraq's infrastructure caused by the loss of water and electricity, for example, to hospitals. Given the nature of the wartime coverage afforded to the air offensive, and when casualty figures from bombing in previous wars are taken into account, it has to be said that what was remarkable about the Gulf War was not the number of civilian casualties which were caused but the number which were not.

This was especially true in view of certain other statistics which came to light shortly after the war had ended. The American Air Force revealed in mid March 1991 that the vast majority of allied bombs used against Iraq were not in fact laser-guided smart bombs but dumb conventional weapons. Much had been made of the high-technology weapons, with one official claiming before the end of the war that 'of the many thousands of precision-guided bombs and missiles launched at Iraqi military targets, fewer than one tenth of one percent had gone astray and fallen in civilian areas'.[142] However, by mid March it was revealed that of the 88,500 tons of bombs dropped on Iraq and occupied Kuwait throughout the war, 70% had actually 'missed their targets'. Of the total, only 6,520 tons had been precision-guided bombs.[143]

Wartime propaganda gave the impression that these types of figures were in reverse. Even though this was not a war in which bombing was used as a weapon for undermining civilian morale, it was one in which bombing would appear to have played a significant role in undermining the morale of Iraqi military personnel, as evidenced in the previous chapter. The record of the precision weapons was nonetheless impressive. It may not have been the 97–98% success rate claimed by General Horner immediately following the cease-fire or even the 90% claimed by

General Peak two weeks later, but even a conservative analyst has written that the success rate 'is believed to average about 80% for all precision-guided weapons'.[144] This was in itself a formidable statistic, although it has to be pointed out that the media were not provided at the time with any indication that as much as 20% of smart bombs were missing their targets owing to weather or other reasons.

Nor should this suggest that the impression of accuracy created by coalition videos was entirely a correct one, given the admission that the vast majority of bombs, some 90% of the total dropped during the war, were conventional and that most of these had missed their targets. The targets for those weapons were mainly the Iraqi ground troops and their supply lines and very few videos were released of that theatre of operations, and even fewer contained any signs of human life. But then, given that only 30% of these were hitting their targets, this might have proved counterproductive. On the other hand, given the enormous amount of tonnage being dropped daily on enemy troop positions as compared with the amount of collateral damage, which goes a long way towards explaining why the ground war was over so quickly, it would have been more profitable from a propaganda point of view for the Iraqis to allow western cameramen to visit the military theatre. We will probably never know the casualty figures caused here – estimates vary between 40,000 and 200,000 – but this was where the main 'killing fields' of the Gulf War were and we have a very inadequate record, visual or otherwise, of a theatre where the war was mainly fought and won.

Indeed, given the attention which coalition air forces were giving to the military theatre of operations by mid February as part of their preparations for the ground offensive, the justification for the Amiriya bombing really revolves around the entire question of whether military signals traffic was emanating from the building. Although the allies said it was, it was virtually impossible to provide the media with substantiating evidence given that this type of detection capability falls into the realm of secret intelligence and counter-espionage. It would also be fair to say that very few journalists possess the kind of specialised knowledge needed to identify modern intelligence equipment. Announcing how the traffic had been intercepted would have been the equivalent of telling the Nazis that the allies had broken their ULTRA secret immediately

221

prior to D-Day. In the short time since the cease-fire, it has been difficult to clear the matter up for precisely the same reason: it might alert terrorist groups and potential enemies alike to the key to avoiding detection. On the other hand, as in all matters concerning necessarily secret activities, it is a terribly convenient way of disguising not just the successes but also the failures of intelligence evaluation. After the war, General McPeak, the highest-ranking officer in the American Air Force, admitted that he 'knew of several' instances where bombing mistakes had occurred and that he had seen photographic evidence of them. When asked when this information would be released, he replied: 'It ain't my call. I made some recommendations about this, [but] it got turned around, quite frankly.'[145] Once again, until the official records are opened we shall simply not know precisely what went wrong, when and why.

It is only in this respect, therefore, that the issue of collateral damage was a propaganda victory for the Iraqis while the war was being fought. As one observer pointed out:

Whatever his primitivism, Saddam knows television, and he knows that the power is in the pictures. All the apologies and explanations and military briefings in the world can't compete with the impact of seeing the bodies of women and children being carted out of rubble.[146]

Such pictures deflected attention away from the real slaughter taking place in the desert, which was good for domestic and wider pro-Iraqi morale, as it played upon anxieties in the West concerning the killing of 'innocent women and children' and it forced the coalition's media managers on to the defensive. Whether or not the destruction of the Amiriya installation was more accident than design in a sense misses this vital point. It was unfortunate, but it was untypical. And it failed to shake public support for the war in any significant way. Besides, much worse devastation was going on every day and every night at the front lines and it was in the interests of both the coalition and the Iraqis to keep that well and truly away from the prying eyes of the media and the 'visible brutality' of television in wartime.

Chapter Five

'Apocalypse where?': the 100 hour land war and 'the highway to hell'

Introduction

The political consequences of Amiriya were potentially very serious indeed. It was not just inflamed or outraged Muslim opinion, even in the coalition's Arab countries, that the Americans needed to worry about. The mood amongst some of their western coalition partners, especially those which were considered anyway to be less than whole-hearted in their support for the entire venture, also wavered. Spain, which housed the Torrejon airbase from which a high percentage of the B52 raids were launched, requested an international enquiry into the tragedy and called for an end to the 'blanket bombing' of Iraq. An Italian spokesman stated that 'we believe that it is dangerous to continue bombing urban centres and the government thinks that this should be avoided'.[1] The outcry at the event itself, however, was short-lived, as the BBC's John Simpson pointed out:

The anger aroused by the deaths of several hundred civilians in the air raid shelter in the Baghdad suburb of Amiriya lasted a shorter time, even in Jordan and other Muslim countries, than the anger of British MPs and the tabloid press over the way the deaths were reported on television.[2]

The air war thus continued as planned; it still offered the best possible military solution with the minimum of casualties to the allied side. That is effectively what Cheney and Powell had told President Bush on their return from meeting Schwarzkopf over the weekend of 9–10 February[3] and, despite the unfortunate Amiriya incident, there was still no military reason for changing the schedule. Politics was another matter but, just as Washington was prepared to leave the military solution to CENTCOM, so also was

223

Riyadh prepared to leave the political ramifications of its actions to the White House.

Originally, the allies had planned for a 30–day air campaign but, according to Lieutenant General Chuck Horner after the war, it needed to be extended to 39 days owing to 'weak battlefield intelligence, clever Iraqi camouflage, mobile targets and bad weather'.[4] Essentially, there were four phases to the coalition's grand strategy. The first was the establishment of 'air superiority' aimed at disrupting Iraq's command and control structure, the destruction of its principal air bases and air defences and the eradication of as much as possible of Iraq's nuclear, biological and chemical storage and production facilities. Greatly aided by the mysterious non-performance of the Iraqi air force, this had taken about a week to ten days to achieve.[5] The second phase was to neutralise Iraq's 'surface to air defences' in both Kuwait and southern Iraq. This was only supposed to take a few days and was again greatly aided by the surprise exodus of much of Iraq's air force to Iran. The third phase, the longest in intention and in practice, was the systematic pounding of the Iraqi army in Kuwait and their supply lines in Iraq to prepare the battlefield for phase four, the actual ground war. Enemy cities, however, were bombed right to the end, with some of the heaviest air raids on Baghdad taking place after Amiriya. As General Powell explained: 'we continued to find targets there worth bombing. They had a very resilient, redundant communications system. I called it the spinal column of this animal and the brain stem. It was a very target-rich environment.'[6]

Despite this, media attention quickly steered away, or was steered away, from the bombing issue after Amiriya. Instead, coalition briefers were keen to downplay the number of raids against the enemy capital by concentrating on what was happening in the KTO (Kuwaiti theatre of operations). Here at least there were enemy soldiers who were 'legitimate' targets for bombing raids. It was likely that they possessed chemical weapons and much was made of their willingness to use them in the build-up to the Ground War: yet one more reason why they must be defeated. Another was the treatment which they were handing out to Kuwaiti citizens. But this, too, was a delicate operation. As a way of deflecting any concern that might be expressed for the safety of the Kuwaiti people, let alone Iraqi civilians, owing to allied bombing, a renewed emphasis was placed by the coalition upon the atrocities being committed at the hands of the Iraqi occupiers rather than the damage being caused to Kuwait at the receiving end of coalition air attacks.

Atrocity propaganda from Kuwait and preparations for G-Day

In the aftermath of Amiriya, therefore, more and more stories about the treatment of Kuwaitis by the Iraqi occupiers began to emerge from various coalition sources. This helped to counter-balance the effects of the bombing tragedy, shifting sympathy to the victims of the Iraqis and away from the Iraqis themselves. The problem, of course, was that there were so few pictures, not to mention the difficulties of verifying the various claims that were being made by Kuwaitis-in-exile and by the Kuwaiti resistance. For weeks, indeed months, stories had been filtering out about the brutality of the Iraqi occupation. The reports, while unconfirmed, were considered to be generally reliable by coalition authorities and, at every opportunity, they were relayed to the media as part of the overall attempt to sustain the impression of a just war being waged on behalf of innocent victims of immoral aggression. Denied momentarily the graphic reinforcement of TV pictures that could illuminate the Kuwaiti tapestry on the miseries of life under the Iraqi occupation, the coalition had to rely principally upon words to weave the picture for them. And although such an impression was difficult to verify in the absence of footage, coalition spokesmen insisted upon the credibility and reliability of their sources by indicating, for example, that they had provided the first news of the massive oil spillage into the Gulf by the Iraqis two days before it was officially confirmed in Riyadh.[7]

It only later emerged how some of these stories leaked out. Initially, some members of the Kuwaiti resistance had actually managed to phone CNN in Atlanta where their impressions were relayed live to the rest of the world. Although these early efforts to keep the plight of the Kuwaitis before world attention served as invaluable reminders as to what this war was ostensibly about, they were designed more for publicity purposes than anything else.[8] But it was in a sense the equivalent of someone phoning London on a BBC phone-in show from inside the Warsaw Ghetto in 1944. The Kuwaiti resistance would also send signals on a secret short wave transmitter to Sweden where Kuwaiti exiles and sympathisers would fax them on to their London office for distribution to the media. Other information was transmitted from Kuwait City to the West 'almost daily' by secret satellite telephones, fax machines 'and other means', stories which portrayed a miserable, grim existence for the ordinary citizens of Kuwait under a repressive military regime, capable of torture and random execution, which had plundered a country and forced its inhabitants to endure a pitiable indoor existence, venturing outside only to queue for depleting food and medical supplies. These messages also contained information about the strength of Iraqi forces and the extent of damage to roads and buildings, which would undoubtedly have been of extreme intelligence value to the coalition as it prepared for the military liberation of the country.[9]

At a press conference in Riyadh on 14 February, a Kuwaiti military spokesman, Colonel Abdullah Al-Kandari, claimed that to date more than 200 Kuwaitis had been executed by the Iraqis, 65 of them in the past week. Moreover, the reported manner of killing sounded like classic atrocity propaganda, with one victim being crucified with nails and having his knees and head skewered with drills.[10] Twelve were said to have had their throats cut and then decapitated. Atrocity stories like these were to increase dramatically over the next two weeks as the Iraqis appeared to clamp down on those very sources of information and, as was demonstrated with the liberation, they turned out to be not as exaggerated as many of those on their guard against propaganda might have thought. A rare video, taken secretly in southern Kuwait, was then played which showed a resistance fighter dropping two Molotov cocktails from a road bridge onto a passing Iraqi truck.[11] This footage, however, had been taken in early January and Al-Kandari pointed to his concern at how recent world attention had moved away from the suffering of the 700,000 Kuwaitis who remained in the country but who were still being systematically and indiscriminately brutalised.

Certainly, by 19 February, human rights activists were complaining of the difficulties of focusing world attention on Iraqi atrocities in Kuwait. At a special all-party press conference at the House of Commons that day, the father of the house Sir Bernard Braine stated that 'we must not forget what the whole grisly business is about. It is the wanton, unprovoked aggression of a brutal dictator against a small neighbouring state'.[12] His fear was that the plight of the Kuwaitis would be overshadowed by the flurry of diplomatic exchanges that were taking place immediately prior to the ground war.[13] Kuwaiti officials also reported that the Iraqi secret police had begun to murder torture victims who, if left alive, would be able to testify to their crimes.[14] Unlike the question of chemical weapons, the end of the conflict did not bring to light much evidence that wartime propaganda concerning atrocities had been unduly exaggerated. If anything, just as pro-Kuwaiti lobbyists had been saying all along, the real horror had been underplayed. It made a nice counterpoint for those who argued that the presence of television magnified the brutality of war. Its absence equally minimised the realities of the Iraqi occupation. Many of those who argued against the presence of western journalists in Iraq were the very same people who demanded that the Iraqis permit them to visit the Kuwaiti theatre. Paradoxically, therefore, they were essentially saying that it was wrong to show the brutality of what the coalition was doing by its bombing campaign but that it was right to see the consequences of Iraqi terror. But if, in wartime, dual standards are the norm, then there was no paradox.

It was a matter of some conjecture whether or not the timing of the ground war, the count-down for which we now know began on 15 February for exactly one week later,[15] was influenced by the growing number of atrocity stories coming out of Kuwait. The commander of the joint Saudi forces, Lieutenant-General Khalid bin Sultan, who was to lead the frontal Arab assault against Iraqi positions in Kuwait, stated that people were being struck on the head with axes, that women were being raped and mutilated and children being killed. 'We hope to stop it soon, 'he said.[16] Reports that the Iraqis had seized 40,000 Kuwaiti men and taken them to Iraq to be used as human shields greeted the eve of the allied attack,[17] while in Britain *Sun* readers on 25 February were taken back to the First World War with a story that 'Iraqis Bayonett Babies ... [while] drunk and high on a concoction of radiator coolant and distilled date juice'.

With the growing involvement of the Soviets in peace moves to end the war, even before 13 February considerable pressure was being brought to bear upon President Bush to begin the land assault sooner rather than later for political reasons.[18] The shelter tragedy may have increased that political pressure still further. But then, two days after Amiriya, with Pentagon officials still worrying about how to explain not only that incident but also the likely recurrence of civilian damage as the air offensive continued on schedule, Saddam launched the first of a series of 'peace initiatives' which were thought to be efforts to capitalise upon any sympathy or nervousness which Amiriya had created for his country's plight and to salvage what he could from what was likely to prove an inevitable defeat. In the early afternoon (local time) of Friday 15 February, Baghdad radio carried a long statement by Iraq's ruling Revolutionary Command Council in which it appeared that Saddam was actually offering to withdraw from Kuwait by complying with UN resolution 660. As news spread from Baghdad to Washington and throughout the world via an Associated Press wire service flash,[19] the news was greeted with a wave of excitement and relief since it appeared that the war was over. CNN and ABC reported celebrations in the streets of the Iraqi capital with citizens firing their weapons into the air. Americans were waking up to the story and NBC's Today show greeted its viewers with 'some stunning news, some very hopeful news', while CBS's This Morning declared that 'this war, for a lot of intents and purposes, is over'.[20]

As it turned out, the event was yet again another illustration of the dangers of breaking news stories live on air before they had been fully analysed. As one observer noted:

Once more, TV viewers were hearing the news develop at the same time that government officials and journalists were, and once more balloons were being floated, only to be burst. The problem isn't just that the news reaches the air unedited; it's that it sometimes reaches the air unverified.[21]

Hours later, President Bush, who had been sharing in the general mood of elation as he watched the cheering crowds in Baghdad on CNN, was describing it all as 'a cruel hoax dashing the hopes of the people in Iraq and, indeed, around the world'.[22] John Major echoed the sentiment, calling it 'a bogus sham'.[23]

The statement was in fact so long and rambling that it took several hours for a valid translation of it to be made.[24] As usual, it began with an appeal both to Arabs and to the wider world: 'Oh dear Iraqis, Oh honest Arabs, Oh Muslims who truly believe in Islam, Oh honest and free men of the world ...' On first hearing, Iraq appeared to be stating that, 'in order to achieve a dignified and acceptable political settlement', it had decided to comply with Resolution 660. Yet, as bullets fired into the air were creating their own collateral damage by injuring several celebrating Iraqis, it further emerged that Baghdad was actually laying down conditions for its withdrawal, namely a full and immediate cease-fire, the abrogation of all other UN resolutions concerning Iraq, Israeli withdrawal from the Golan Heights and other occupied territories, the overthrow of Kuwait's ruling family, reparations for the damage incurred by Iraq, the cancellation of Iraq's £30 billion debt and the withdrawal of US forces from the region within one month. 'The more we look at it,' said Fitzwater at the White House, 'the worse it gets'. As a *Times* leader the next day ran: 'Saddam must be truly divorced from reality if he believed these terms would be accepted.'[25] But, by then, television had created false expectations by its rush to get the story out before it had unfolded fully. For a moment Iraq once again appeared to be a conciliatory victim rather than a brutal aggressor. On the other hand, the story's prominence as news was a godsend for the White House in that it finally pushed the shelter/bunker story further down the media agenda and thus further away from public concern.

One theory for Saddam making an offer that he surely must have known would be refused was that it was designed to show the Iraqi people, increasingly worried by intensive allied bombing (and whose relief at news that the war might be over was plain for all to see), that the Americans in reality wanted to destroy Iraq and expose Kuwait as a pretext for doing this.[26] Reports of growing unrest inside Iraq suggested, according to one coalition official, that Saddam was 'having problems controlling the population'.[27] However, when General Neal stated that Iraqi forces were suffering 'horrendous' casualties, possibly 20,000 dead and 60,000 wounded (as the Iraqis now claimed), Latif Jassem, Iraq's Minister of Information, taunted Schwarzkopf to 'try his luck'.[28] President Bush, clearly angry with what was perceived as another propaganda stunt rather than a genuine peace proposal, added:

There is another way for the bloodshed to stop, and that's for the Iraqi military and the Iraqi people to take matters into their own hands, to force Saddam Hussein the dictator to step aside and to comply with the [UN] resolutions.[29]

229

As allied bombing was kept up, almost as a signal that neither Amiriya nor the 'peace offer' had resulted in a weakening of American resolve, a senior European official was quoted as saying: 'I see this as the beginning of the endgame, but it may be a long and bloody one. It is a sign that Saddam is weakening, and this is his opening bid for a way out.'[30] Alternatively, some saw it as an attempt to postpone a land war, raising once again the spectre of the 'nightmare scenario' in which Iraq's forces would have been depleted but not eliminated as a threat to the region.

This was further complicated by conflicting signals coming out of the USSR, themselves a reflection of divisions within the Soviet establishment, especially since Tariq Aziz was due to visit Moscow on Sunday 17 February. This was the follow-up to Primakov's mission earlier in the week after which he had announced that he had seen 'rays of light'. Almost as if to pre-empt any diplomatic initiative that might result from the Aziz visit, President Bush declared on the Sunday that 'Iraq's takeover of Kuwait will end very, very soon'.[31] The President was reported to be concerned that Saddam might survive the war, but this, like details of the Gorbachev peace proposal handed to Aziz, was rarely elaborated upon in public. As it turned out, the Gorbachev plan was rejected by both Britain and America. 'The goals have been set. I'm not going to give,' said Bush,[32] although the Soviets pointed out that it was up to Iraq to accept the deal, details of which were withheld from the public for several days, and not for the United States to reject it. This placed the Bush administration in a difficult position because if Saddam had decided to accept the Soviet proposals and quit Kuwait suddenly, it would have shifted responsibility for the impending ground war onto the Americans, who might thus be seen to be exceeding their UN mandate and thus jeopardise the unity of the coalition. Saddam, however, was slow in replying, possibly playing for time, as the French and Iranians then entered the diplomatic fray. France, which had been involved in a last-minute diplomatic initiative to forestall the outbreak of the war back on 15 January, urged the Americans to at least wait for an Iraqi reply. Nerves were clearly straining for several days before the Americans decided to pre-empt any possible Iraqi acceptance by declaring on 20 February that Iraq must anyway begin to leave Kuwait by midday, Eastern Standard Time (20:00 Iraqi time) on Saturday 23 February and have completed its full withdrawal by the following weekend. If they did this, coalition forces would not attack withdrawing troops but would 'exercise restraint'.[33]

If the Americans were attempting to force Saddam's hand and expose his real intentions concerning the Soviet peace proposals, they succeeded. The Revolutionary Command Council denounced President Bush as the 'enemy of God' and declared that 'Iraq wants peace and is working seriously to support the Soviet initiative and facilitate its success, but not out of fear of Bush's threats'.[34] Events then began to move extremely rapidly. Details of the Soviet plan began to leak out, showing that it called for a complete and unconditional withdrawal from Kuwait, supervised by the United Nations, and to be completed within 21 days. Some of the conditions laid down by Iraq on 15 February had been dropped but it still called for a cease-fire before any withdrawal would take place and for the dropping of economic sanctions and the other UN Resolutions.

It was just about conceivable that the Iraqis believed the Americans were bluffing, that they would not risk Vietnam-style casualties in a land war, even at this late stage. Once again, Saddam's sheer defiance was an obstacle to genuine progress so far as the coalition was concerned. He announced in a speech on Baghdad radio on Thursday 21 February that 'the Mother of All Battles will be our battle of victory and martyrdom. They want us to surrender, but they will be disappointed'.[35] It was also possible that the Iraqis still believed their old Soviet friends might be able to re-enter a superpower confrontation. Even when the Revolutionary Command Council finally announced late on Thursday the 21st that it was prepared to accept a modified version of the Soviet plan, it still called for a cease-fire before any withdrawal from Kuwait and offered no guarantees concerning the restoration of Kuwaiti sovereignty, the Al-Sabah family, and awarding reparations. No mention of this was made in the Iraqi press. But this was for the Americans too little and, most of all, too late. In announcing his ultimatum the day before, President Bush declared not only that Saddam must begin to withdraw immediately and unconditionally from Kuwait but that he must hear it from Saddam Hussein himself. By making the announcement for him, and with the news that Iraq had begun a scorched earth policy by the firing of Kuwait's oil wells, the Revolutionary Command Council was clearly signifying it would not conform to the coalition's

231

wishes. President Bush may have announced that he 'appreciated' the Soviet initiative, but the die had been cast.

One month into the war, the Pentagon doubled its previous estimates of destroyed Iraqi tanks. It claimed that one-third of Iraq's artillery had been verifiably destroyed by the 70,000 sorties flown up to that point (33% of the 4,200 tanks and 38% of Iraq's 1,200 artillery pieces) and that growing numbers of deserters indicated poor conditions and morale. General Schwarzkopf subsequently admitted that the timing for the final phase of Desert Storm was 'part tactical, part political'. He wondered 'how long would the world stand by and watch the United States pound the living hell out of Iraq without saying, "Wait a minute – enough is enough".[36] Baghdad radio's comment on all the speculation about the timing of the attack was that:

As is the case in all US propaganda that is void of everything but misleading manoeuvering, the matter is being portrayed as a picnic for its male and female soldiers soon ending with few and insignificant casualties ... We tell the evil alliance that all your masters sitting in their holes are hoping for is pure imagination. If US aircraft have managed to fire their missiles from a distance, hitting Iraqi cities and economic and cultural installations, the situation is completely different on the ground, where one million valiant Iraqi fighters are amassed, armed with an unshaken belief in the justice of their cause, as well as the high combat experience enjoyed by each Iraqi soldier which makes him superior to his enemy, no matter what this enemy possesses in terms of weapons, numbers and equipment.[37]

Another broadcast derided US claims by pointing out that the true strength of Iraqi forces was 'an invisible strength of faith in the forces of evil and deception ... [which] makes a mockery of the enemy aircraft and missiles. It also makes us say that victory will inevitably be ours'.[38]

The world waited anxiously to see. Throughout February, as television stations world-wide tried to tease the question of where and when for a ground offensive from the army of pundits, they needed only to have asked their reporters in the allied news pools at the front. Not that the reporters would have been able to answer. The press corps with the various armoured divisions had been fully briefed as to what was likely to be ahead of them, but journalists privy to this information were thereafter forbidden to leave the pools. Kate Adie, with the British 1st Armoured Division, which was to surge forward into southern Iraq and then cut eastwards north of Kuwait City, testified to the fact that British journalists had been briefed 'on the entire battle' by General Rupert Smith a week before the actual assault began.[39] This was an extremely astute move, as Colin Wills of the *Daily Mirror* recognised:

We knew the entire battle plan a week before the land war started. On a professional level, needless to say, it was very frustrating. To be in the know and not be able to file a word was like being given the secret of alchemy and at that same instant being struck dumb.[40]

On the other hand, he continued, 'that kind of censorship was vital for the success of the operation and saving lives, and nobody begrudged it'.

In fact, there was plenty of informed speculation in the public domain not only about the likely shape of the ground offensive but also about its timing. Although the coalition was feeding the media with innumerable clues that a sea-borne assault by an armada of ships would take place, the *Independent on Sunday* was stating as early as 27 January:

The insider's story in Westminster is that the Gulf War of 1991 will end on or around the 4 March: 40 days of aerial bombardment will be followed by a brisk and crushing five day land war in Kuwait. In Washington, there is smart money on a six to eight week war, in which case it would be brought to an end during the first two weeks of March.[41]

Analysing the battle of Khafji several days later, the *Guardian's* Martin Woollacott also wrote an acute piece of analysis, pointing out that Saddam's strategy seemed to invite a battle just in Kuwait rather than allowing it to spill over into Iraq, which would 'blur the distinction between two different wars':

The Iraqis would in other words much prefer to have to deal with an allied right hook than an allied left hook. They may believe that by attacking repeatedly on the seaward side – and it is yet to be seen whether Khafji is the beginning of a series of attacks – they can embroil allied units in a fight that will suck in troops that were destined for the western part of the front. Whether Iraqi defensive capacity is sufficient to achieve such an object and alter either the timing or form of the allied offensive, is another question. But that is what they may well be attempting to do.[42]

Equally, on 7 February in *The Times,* Michael Evans asked how Saddam might possibly be taken by surprise thanks to the coalition's comparatively open policy towards television coverage:

Take, for example, the speculation that American and British forces might be involved in a flanking manoeuvre to the far west, across the Saudi–Iraq border, by-passing the 'Maginot Line' in southern Kuwait and advancing into Iraq to cut off the Republican Guard divisions from the rear. Although no one in authority has outlined such a strategy, enough information *has* been given to add credence to the reports.[43]

By mid February, there was widespread discussion that the allies would attempt 'another Cannae', a reference to Hannibal's defeat of the Romans in 216 BC when he had encircled the enemy forces with low casualty figures. As Edward Luttwak pointed out in *The Times* on 20 February:

For all the heavy hand of censorship, it is now no longer a secret that the decisive action is to be fought by the US Army's armoured and mechanised forces (and one British division) now ready and waiting near the junction of the Iraqi, Kuwaiti and Saudi borders. Moving northeast, they are to by-pass virtually all Iraqi fortifications on their way to the Basra area, thus slicing Kuwait from Iraq without meeting resistance before the heavily bombarded Republican Guards around Basra.[44]

With such detail as this in the public domain, it would be vital for the coalition to step up its disinformation tactics. Even Luttwak's well-informed sources appear to have suggested that an amphibious landing was also on the cards.

Reports of desertions even amongst the Republican Guard stationed in southern Iraq had also begun to seep out, although Marie Colvin of the *Sunday Times*, who was inside Iraq and who encountered various soldiers, found that their morale was high and that they were in fact itching to get on with the fighting.[45] This was certainly the line being adopted by Baghdad radio on 15 February when the Iraqi chief of staff was quoted extensively as saying that 'when the battle occurs, the enemy forces will meet Iraqi men who won their military ranks through fighting, not in luxurious air-conditioned offices', failing to mention that the American volunteer army was as professional as any in the world. The broadcast continued:

He referred to the battles of Khafji, Ar'Ar and other border areas, saying that the enemy forces and agent mercenaries fled like horrified ravens in front of our advancing soldiers. He added: 'Here are the enemy forces, avoiding confrontation with our ground forces and sending their ravens to attack our economic, cultural and religious institutions and residential areas in Iraq's cities and villages ... The heroes of our armed forces will take revenge on the criminals on the battlefield and will return them in coffins to their countries'.[46]

This did not quite seem to square with General Schwarzkopf's pronouncement that the Iraqi army was 'on the verge of collapse' or that 450 Iraqis had deserted in a single day (20 February), the largest single mass surrender of the war since Khafji.[47] As to what was really happening, it clearly depended on where you were and what sources of information you were allowed access to. And, as one observer put it, 'so many different manoeuvres had been leaked that Iraqi intelligence must be hopelessly confused'.[48]

An essential part of the preparations for the ground war was indeed to disorient and confuse the enemy by any and every means, including propaganda and disinformation. Part of the ground attack codenamed Operation Desert Sabre, this deception campaign involved faking amphibious operations, pounding frontline Iraqi artillery, conducting special operations behind enemy lines and deliberately leaking misinformation to the media. Although the real plan was what General Schwarzkopf, somewhat enigmatically, later called the 'Hail Mary Play',[49] various seaborne gestures were being made to provide an indication of preparations for an assault from the sea. The liberation of the island of Qurah had provided one signal and the attacking of the island of Faylakah, 10 miles off the coast of Kuwait City, over the weekend of 2–3 February was another. As Group Captain Irving said of the latter operation, which implied that the coalition had been successful: 'It's very important that it's in our hands. By clearing out the enemy from there, we may open another option that exists from the sea.'[50] The island was essentially an artillery outpost which might harass amphibious operations but it was only marginally more significant than Qurah as a military operation. Besides, almost exactly one month later, on the opening day of the Ground War, Faylakah was again being reported as being attacked, and this time taken, by the coalition (see below). Nonetheless, considerable media attention had already been afforded to the latest allied 'victory', overshadowing the loss of a B52 into the Indian Ocean and the admission that most of the US Marines killed in the previous week's assaults across the border had been by 'friendly fire'. And when the USS's *Missouri* and *Wisconsin* started to pound the coast at the start of February, one American official admitted that 'we wanted to let them know we have a third supporting arm'.[51] To keep this feint up, a flotilla carrying 17,000 US Marines was moved northwards up the Gulf on 6 February.[52] Ashore meanwhile, Rhino Force, a British unit said to be 'made up of the noisiest, most conspicuous troops on the Gulf battle-field', began its part in the deception. Recordings of tank and communications traffic from a previous Anglo-American training exercise were played over and over again while clouds of dust ('coat trailing') were kicked up along the Kuwait–Saudi border. Iraqi signals intelligence, monitoring the traffic, thus heard and saw coalition forces apparently moving east when in fact the British 1st Armoured Division was moving quietly west to join the US 7th Army Corps.[53] As for the actual thrust, *Newsweek* published a highly accurate map on 11 February, almost two weeks before the offensive started. Several days before that, the *Guardian* published a fairly accurate map of the likely main attacks.[54]

Another major area of speculation concerned the possible deployment of battlefield chemical weapons by the Iraqis. The air offensive was reportedly very successful in destroying Iraq's manufacturing capability,[55] but stockpiles remained a worry in the military theatre of operations. Press and pool reports throughout February speculated intensely about this issue, with stories about anthrax and plague vaccines being issued to the coalition's troops. Scores of pool reports depicted troops wearing their chemical protection equipment and rehearsing for such an attack. There are several possible explanations for why these weapons were not used, ranging from the swiftness of the allied thrust, which prevented the Iraqis from deploying chemicals that needed to be carefully handled, bad weather, which would have merely blown the toxins back at their users, fear of retaliation by like means, poor command and communications and even fear of nuclear retaliation. But as General Neal said on 26 February: 'I don't have an explanation of why they haven't used chemicals during the retreat.'[56] He later admitted that Iraqi chemical capability might not have been as great as the coalition had feared, with their equipment leaving 'a lot to be desired'.[57] The French commander-in-chief, General Maurice Schmitt's theory was that the order to use chemicals had been given by Saddam but that the commanders disobeyed because they knew the end of the war was imminent and did not want to be charged with any more atrocities than they had already committed.[58]

Meanwhile, the troops continued their preparations. Colin Wills interviewed soldiers about their feelings concerning bayoneting enemy troops and burning them alive in their tanks and 'I know from seeing the published copy later', he said after the war, 'that nothing was removed for reasons of tone or taste'.[59] A media-conscious military in fact recognised that real war was rarely fought in front of television cameras. The film crews could shoot artillery and rockets firing into the desert horizon or aircraft flying in this or that direction and returning without their bombs, but the actual point of impact was rarely witnessed by the cameras. The Iraqis did not take camera crews to their front lines and so we have no pictures even now of the impact of carpet bombing against the Republican Guard. A BBC editor recognised this to have been a mistake from a propaganda point of view: 'If the Iraqis had shown any sense they would have taken foreign crews down to the front line and filmed the effects of allied bombing.'[60] By implication, however, this was also an admission that the presence of foreign crews in Baghdad did serve the interests of Iraqi propaganda.

Whenever it could find emergency generators, Baghdad radio, together with the Mother of All Battles station in Kuwait, continued to taunt the Americans over casualty figures: 'The battle will be decided on the ground. We will inflict grave human losses in the ranks of the aggressors until they drown in the rivers of their own blood.'[61] Although of limited impact on the troops themselves, American hypersensitivity to the question of casualties was evident in all of their pools. Colin Wills pointed out that the preparations being made to receive battlefield casualties 'were virtually a no-go area' for journalists. 'Pester though we might, they wouldn't put anybody up to talk to us about it, nor arrange visits to field hospitals.'[62] If the battle was to be decided on the ground, clearly neither the Iraqis nor the coalition were prepared to tolerate the intrusion of television cameras which might reveal the 'visible brutality' of modern warfare – just in case the war was in fact to be decided politically on the home front before the military outcome had been decided.

The ground war

On Friday 22 February, President Bush issued his final ultimatum for Iraq to withdraw from Kuwait or face a ground offensive the next day. The press revelled in Washington's show-down at High Noon. As with the launch of the initial air offensive, however, the White House was prepared to wait a little longer than the public deadline before launching the ground war at 04:00 (local time) on Sunday 24 February, just eight hours after the ultimatum had expired. In the United States it was still Saturday the 23rd, 20:00 EST. Two hours later, President Bush announced that the liberation of Kuwait had entered its final phase.

At 10:30 (local time) on the Sunday, Baghdad radio carried a speech by Saddam Hussein stating what his troops had already known for six and a half hours, namely that the mother of all battles had finally begun. In his speech Saddam asserted that 'when the armies of men meet, the technology will be irrelevant and the final result will be decided only by the bravery of the true believers'.[63] In fact, as coalition troops from 11 of the coalition's 31 countries poured through the gaps created in the minefields of the Saddam Line and raced north into southern Iraq and Kuwait, the Iraqi forces appeared to fold before them. Although a news blackout had been imposed by the coalition and the regular daily briefings in Washington and Riyadh suspended temporarily, it quickly became apparent that the attack was going so well for the allies that the news was 'simply too good to suppress'.[64] It was General Schwarzkopf himself who was first prepared to provide some preliminary details later that Sunday: 'we are going to go round, through, on top, underneath and any other way necessary to achieve victory'. He added that 5,500 Iraqi soldiers had already been taken prisoner.[65] In Washington, Dick Cheney also signalled that there too they were unmuzzling themselves when he appeared on television, while in London John Major spoke in general terms on the encouraging early progress from Downing Street. By the next day the number of prisoners had reached 20,000 and the main worry then was how to accommodate what was expected to be 100,000 Iraqi PoWs.[66] 'They jump up like squirrels to surrender,' was how one soldier described it graphically, while another likened the assault to a video-game in which they had 'gobbled up Iraqi divisions like Pac-man'.[67] Even when President Bush cautioned against over-optimism, he knew all was going better than anticipated: 'Kuwait will soon be free ... But we must guard against euphoria. There are battles yet to come and casualties to be borne, but make no mistake, we will prevail.'

Meanwhile the coalition's black radio stations stepped up their offensive. The Voice of Free Iraq greeted the land war as follows:

In the name of God, the Compassionate, the Merciful. Sons of our honourable Iraq people; sons of our valiant army. That which we used to warn against and fear has happened. The land war began this morning following the failure of all sincere efforts by brothers and friends – the leaders – to convince the criminal tyrant of Iraq, Saddam Hussein, to withdraw from Kuwait and save our homeland and army and our beloved people from more catastrophes, defeats and destruction ... As you can see, he is unjustifiably and aimlessly pushing our sons into the deadly incinerator. He will inevitably lose this battle, as he has lost all previous battles ... Honourable sons of Iraq, do you know that Saddam has smuggled his family out of Iraq, and has smuggled out with them the remaining funds and wealth, so that he will leave Iraq in ruins and quite empty? ... Stage a revolution now before it is too late ... Hit the headquarters of the tyrant and save the homeland from destruction.[68]

On the battlefield, the Iraqis did put up some resistance, including the firing of a Scud missile which hit an improvised military barracks in Khobar City, near Dhahran, and killed 27 American soldiers on Monday 25 February – the largest single death toll sustained by the Americans in the entire war. At the time, it was wondered why the Patriots had not intercepted this missile but it later emerged that they had, and that it was the debris of the Scud falling on the building which had caused the damage. Much further to the north, it was reported that 80 Republican Guard tanks had moved out of their hardened bunkers against coalition forces for the first time but had been pounded by American aircraft, and 35 of the T72 tanks were destroyed. The Iraqis also fired their first Silkworm missile at allied ships in the Gulf, but this was safely intercepted by a Sea Dart missile fired by HMS *Gloucester*. But these were really gestures: the traffic was mainly in the opposite direction, with the American marine commander, Lieutenant General Walter Boomer, announcing that victory was a 'matter of days, not weeks'.[69]

Baghdad radio meanwhile was reporting that the enemy forces had been smashed into 'fragments of flesh' and that it had succeeded in 'expelling enemy forces totally from all positions held before the attack and recaptured them'. The coalition, it claimed, had 'retreated in utter defeat'.[70] Claiming massive victories, the radio station declared:

We call on the American people to ask the enemy of God, Bush, to tell it about the fate of these forces and the losses they have suffered instead of spreading lies and fabricátions. The blackout imposed by the US military command on the reports about the battle and the cover-up of the details of the losses suffered by the Bush forces are certain proof of the difficult position the forces of aggression are experiencing.[71]

Other broadcasts had attempted to exploit the coalition's temporary news blackout, citing it as evidence of a desire to hide their real losses, and to undermine initial coalition reports (presumably diversionary tactics) that Faylakah had been retaken – again! – and that an amphibious landing was under way:

They, for example, claimed that they had occupied Faylakah Island. We challenge them to invite the press and television correspondents to go there. They will not be able to do so, for sure, because the heroic Iraqi forces are in Faylakah. They also claimed that tens of thousands of Iraqi troops surrendered to them. We again challenge them to show them on television. We challenge them once again to confirm their claim about their amphibious landing. Our shores are standing fast and our forces are guarding them with all firmness, and woe to those who dare approach them.[72]

Coalition statements indicated that some surrendering Iraqis claimed ignorance of the fact they were fighting Americans and when some Baghdad citizens were shown photographs of surrendering Iraqis marching in long columns they believed they were Egyptians dressed up to look like Iraqi infantrymen. Michael Evans, defence correspondent of *The Times*, concluded:

There is a clear message here. Saddam and his information ministry are succeeding in blinkering the Iraqi people. In spite of the bombing they have suffered and the damage they can see across the country, they probably believe that the Iraqi army is winning the ground war. If Washington and London want the war to end with the overthrow of Saddam, preferably by his own people, they will have to convince the average Iraqi citizen with an intensive publicity campaign that their president is leading them towards a humiliating defeat.[73]

This perhaps highlights one sense in which Saddam Hussein was to win the propaganda war at home. It soon became apparent that he had not lost the faith of the bulk of his elite forces or of his closest circle of henchmen. Nor had he lost that combination of fear and adulation which he, like other charismatic tyrants, depended upon, at least in his Sunni heartland. Time would tell whether a crushing military defeat would affect his image and standing in other parts of the country. The final hours of the war would determine his ability to deal militarily with any such protest and to survive.

The liberation of Kuwait City

In one sense, it was the media who liberated Kuwait City. Or rather it was the unilaterals, whose size had grown greatly in numbers thanks to mounting dissatisfaction with the pool arrangements since the Khafji incident. Shortly before the start of the ground offensive, the Saudi Arabian Ministry of Information had announced that any unescorted journalist found within 100 kilometres of the war zone would be arrested and deported, a decree to which the British authorities in Dhahran had apparently given their 'wholehearted support'.[74] Despite a Pentagon memorandum issued to the American press in Riyadh that journalists attempting 'unilateral coverage' risked arrest and deportation if they ventured within 62 miles of the Saudi–Kuwait border, many were prepared to risk minefields and even being shot by coalition troops to cover what they could of the story. The memorandum had warned that 'unescorted reporters travelling into a battlefield could be mistaken as a threat to the safety of those troops and be brought under fire'. It also banned the use of portable satellite telephones or dishes in any location not approved in writing by the Saudi Ministry of Information and the wearing of military uniforms by non-pool reporters.[75] If the Iraqis could be accused of blinkering their own people, the coalition was also setting itself up for similar charges, especially with a report that a vehicle containing journalists attempting to violate these rules had its tyres shot out and its occupants arrested.[76] However, it was from the pool reporters that all information about the forward thrust was to come and, given that we still know so little about much of what actually happened at the front, this says a great deal about the effectiveness of the pool system at the time from the coalition's point of view.

241

In another sense, however, Kuwait City was never really liberated in the true sense of the word, given that the Iraqis had
already decided to abandon it. Many of their soldiers had started
to leave in the early hours of Tuesday 26 February as they heard
Baghdad radio announce (00:30 local time; 16:30 EST on the
25th) that Saddam had ordered his troops to leave the country in
accordance with UN Resolution 660 and in acceptance of the
Soviet peace initiative 'to put an end to the criminal behaviour of
the United States and its allies'.[77] This sudden announcement
created considerable confusion for all concerned. Saddam may
have declared that his troops were withdrawing, but the coalition
claimed that they were retreating and, as such, were still 'fair
game'. At a Pentagon press conference called at 22:30 EST (still
Monday the 25th in the USA), Marlin Fitzwater announced:

We have no evidence to suggest that the Iraqi army is withdrawing; in
fact, Iraqi units are continuing to fight. Moreover, we remember when
Saddam Hussein's tanks pretended to surrender at Khafji, only to turn
and fire. We remember the Scud attacks today, and Saddam's many
broken promises of the past ... The statement out of Baghdad today says
that Saddam Hussein's forces will fight their way out while retreating. We
will not attack unarmed soldiers in retreat but we will consider retreating
combat units as a movement of war ... The ground-rules are very clear
here. We are not going to attack retreating forces. They should lay down
their arms and leave, and they wouldn't have to worry about that. But if
they are moving as a combat unit they are still subject to the rules of
war.[78]

Was Saddam simply attempting to forestall a massive military
defeat and preserve his armed forces for his own internal survival?
    Much was to rest upon the definition of a withdrawal as
compared with a retreat. Technically, the coalition was let off the
hook by the fact that Saddam had accepted only one of the twelve
UN resolutions against him. If he had accepted all of them at this
stage, it might have been difficult for the coalition to continue
prosecuting the war with continued UN support and the 'nightmare scenario' of potentially having Saddam's forces left intact
would have arrived. As it was, President Bush was in no doubt as
to what Saddam's game was, calling his speech an 'outrage' in a
live interview from the Rose Garden of the White House:

He is not withdrawing. His defeated forces are retreating. He is trying to
claim victory in the midst of a rout, and he is not voluntarily giving up

Kuwait. He is trying to save the remnants of power and control in the Middle East by every means possible and here, too, Saddam Hussein will fail. Saddam is not interested in peace, but only to regroup and fight another day, and he does not renounce Iraq's claim to Kuwait.[79]

In Britain, the House of Commons was informed in the measured – but possibly very revealing – tones of John Major that 'I do not believe that our troops or world public opinion would forgive us if at this stage we permitted the Iraqis to withdraw with their weapons'.[80]

Part of the problem was again Saddam's bravado, telling his troops as they withdrew to 'shout for victory, O brothers, shout for your victory and the victory of all honourable people, O Iraqis. You have fought 30 countries ... How sweet victory is'.[81] In Jordan, where the public tended to follow Iraqi versions of events rather than coalition sources, western journalists reported a belief that Iraq was indeed winning.[82] After the sudden order to withdraw came, even the Iraqi ambassador to the United Nations stated that he was unaware of any such directive.[83] In Baghdad, Peter Arnett showed the morning papers on CNN which were declaring a victory and stated, importantly, that his impression was that the order to withdraw was as units.[84] There was certainly an air of unreality about the whole affair, but it soon became apparent to even the most blinkered that the mother of all battles was looking more and more like the mother of all defeats. Much, as we shall see, was thereafter now to depend on whether the event was in fact being presented as the mother of all retreats.

By daylight on Tuesday the 26th, Kuwait City had been virtually totally abandoned. This left the way clear for reporters not attached to the military units to scoop their colleagues and the race was on to get there first. Two days earlier, ITN's Sandy Gall had revealed the risks to which some journalists were prepared to go when, on the opening night of the ground war, he and his crew had shadowed an Arab thrust 'trying to keep the Saudi tanks in sight so that we knew where we were going, but keeping far enough back so that they could not turn us back'.[85] They witnessed the taking of some Iraqi prisoners and returned with them to file the report, the first eyewitness account of the offensive by a western journalist.

This prompted the scramble for the big scoop: the first to Kuwait City. CNN, in one sense, was there already, having managed to secure a live telephone interview with Abou Fahad, the head of the Kuwaiti resistance, early on 26 February. But the subsequent sprint to secure the first pictures from the Kuwaiti capital has been explained thus:

Until the end, when CBS's Bob McKeown raced to Kuwait City first for a scoop, CBS, NBC and CNN stuck with the pool rules and paid for it. Only ABC, after much internal debate, agreed to let Forrest Sawyer break free of the system. His strategy was to hook up with the Saudi and Egyptian forces, which, ironically for countries with rigid anti-press policies, were far more open to coverage than their American counter-parts. The result was that ABC was the first network with footage of deserters (well before the ground war), the first (and only) to go along on a bombing mission and the first with pictures from the front. As ABC's experience showed, the news media can be trusted to report without exposing their personnel to the hazards of the modern battlefield or interfering with military operations.[86]

It was CBS, however, which was first into Kuwait City. In a rented Toyota, Bob McKeown and his crew drove up the coastal road from Saudi Arabia into Kuwait City without any problems. They passed abandoned Iraqi tanks and other burned-out vehicles and set up their satellite dish near the American embassy. 'As we stand here', McKeown began, 'Kuwait City is a free city.' A crowd of cheering Kuwaiti men waving their national flag surrounded him. Having played a major role in the diplomatic, let alone the pro-paganda, aspects of the war, it was now television's turn to play a part in the military. A US Marine who had been involved in the retaking of the American embassy as part of the advance operation told his comrades when he approached the CBS crew: 'we're waiting for you to come into the city'.[87] Incidentally, this little event tended to take the gloss off the intended coalition perspective that the Arab forces led by the Kuwaiti army should be seen to be first into the liberated city.

One further aspect of this coverage had an important conse-quence for the way in which the horror of what was soon to be discovered north of Kuwait City was to be framed. As other journalists raced to join McKeowan's crew, they found evidence of 'a disorganised army in fearful flight' with abandoned Iraqi military equipment strewn throughout the city.[88] But when jour-nalists actually arrived in the Kuwaiti capital, many were not only overwhelmed by the welcome they received but also appalled by the consequences of what they saw of the Iraqi occupation. 'Nothing', wrote Christopher Walker in *The Times,* 'that one has read or viewed over the past seven months can prepare a new arrival for the horror of what has been perpetrated against its people, their possessions and even its animals'.[89] Kuwaiti resistance fighters told of how the Iraqis had plundered, raped and tortured the population, with one even claiming that the blood had been drawn from victims and their internal organs removed: 'The Iraqi military was short of blood. Maybe they needed body parts too. They were criminals.'[90] Reporters were taken to the Mubarak and Adan hospitals where some victims appeared to have been burned alive, their skulls smashed and their eyes gouged out. The bodies of children had been dumped on rubbish tips.[91] Robert Fisk perhaps put it best:

In the immediate days that followed the liberation of Kuwait, many journalists and it includes myself were struck by the very wicked way, the very wicked and evil behaviour, of the Iraqi military hierarchy in Kuwait itself. The looting was on an extraordinary scale, the killings and the tortures were real. They had shot children in front of their parents, they had used drills to crucify people. This sounds like typical war propaganda; I did not believe it all until I got there and saw bodies in the mortuary with drill holes through their hands and legs and through their eyes. And I think the discovery of how these people had treated the Kuwaitis, how they had oppressed the Kuwaitis, how they had kidnapped thousands of them, I think it hardened the sympathy which we might otherwise have shown to the dead soldiers lying along the road.[92]

The overwhelming impression was that the city had been thoroughly gutted – buildings torched, shops ransacked, museums plundered, homes looted, civic and scientific institutions vandalised and hospitals stripped of their equipment. Press reports in fact varied widely according to where journalists went, and when. For one, the 30 mile drive into the city centre showed that 'shops, businesses and houses ... had been looted and burned'.[93] Yet others noted that Kuwaiti International Airport, the scene of the city's fiercest engagement with remnants of the Iraqi forces, needed little clearing before it was made functional again. A pool reporter for the *Washington Post* maintained that

Throughout the city, destruction was spotty. Windows of some stores, such as jewellery and watch shops, were smashed and the contents looted. Many others were left untouched. Gaping holes yawned in the sides of several posh hotels ... Overall, however, most buildings throughout the city remained undisturbed.[94]

It was certainly difficult to sort out what damage had been caused by whom: by the Iraqis, by the Kuwaiti resistance, by coalition bombing or bombardment. Nonetheless, two scenes in particular were to follow which were to imply precisely where the blame for the destruction should be placed: the firing of 600 or so of Kuwait's oil wells, and the loot found amidst the carnage of the remnants of the occupying army on the road north to Basra out of Kuwait City.

The battle of Mutlah Gap

Meanwhile, with the armed forces, many of the pool journalists were getting their first taste of what it was like to be involved in a battle. The military had finally decided to increase the number of places in the official pools a week before the ground war, but this was not to alleviate criticism of the system, the main flaw of which was still considered to be the speed, or rather the slowness, of getting reports back to the FTUs. After the war, Colin Wills said of his ground offensive experience in the pools:

I lost my temper only once, and then badly, and now I think I was at least half right. When the ground war actually started, the advance was so swift that the system of getting our copy back to the transmission unit's satellite phones 50 kms back broke down completely. It was days before London got the first battle reports from 7th Armoured and by then the war was virtually over and we had to hurriedly compose retrospectives.[95]

Because the advance was so rapid, the FTUs certainly found it hard to keep up, but Wills also complained that the minders with his pool were unwilling to improvise, unlike those with the 4th Armoured Brigade who were themselves prepared to drive back to the FTUs and hand in the copy personally. The 7th Armoured Brigade minders, however, 'relied on pressing bits of paper into soldiers' hands and hoping they would get there'.[96]

Reuters' correspondent Paul Majendie, who was further forward still with the American 1st Armored Division, encountered even worse problems:

The next headache was Major Cook, PR at 7th Corps, who delayed the copy still further. At best the copy took 72 hours to get back to the pool.

At worst it just vanished. To write copy that survived Major Cook you had to steer away from hard news and write feature-style battlefield colour pieces to have any chance of being used. On return to Dhahran, I let rip at Colonel Mulvey, JIB boss. Mulvey had the gall to say my copy must surely have some historical value. I reminded him I worked for a wire service, not Esquire magazine.[97]

This does raise an important additional point. If the military was so concerned – as it frequently maintained – with the press providing some kind of historical record, it might not be too fanciful to suggest that it was attempting to shape not only perceptions about what was actually going on at the time but also the way in which the war would be regarded in the future.

It does have to be remembered that, at the front, the coalition forces sustained remarkably light casualties, so there were few body bags to film. Yet even these shots were subject to restrictions. On one occasion, the British military stopped the filming of a group of fusiliers who had been mistakenly bombed by US planes, while Martin Bell of the BBC said that several hours of front-line footage were returned to him without having been transmitted.[98] The same was true for photojournalists:

The problem with covering an armoured ground war is one of speed. As most photo pool members found out, an M1 tank is faster than a Humvee in the desert. Tanks also fight at night. And if the other guys in the T72s do not or cannot fire back, then there is not much to see or photograph. Some photographers with the armoured divisions shot the whole war on a few rolls of film and they never saw anything of importance.[99]

Or another way of putting it was, as one observer noted, that the technical inability of television 'to tell the truth is mostly out of its control'.[100]

That may well have been true in a conceptual sense, but there was at least one noticeable example of a journalist who refused to fall victim to the military censorship system which had mastered the ability of journalists to report upon the ground war adequately. A freelance cameraman, Vaughan Smith, tricked his way into joining his old regiment disguised in his former captain's uniform. When it became impossible to continue his ruse, he joined the Americans, who actually sent him into battle. From the turret of 'his' Bradley armoured vehicle, Smith was able to film the destruction of Iraqi tanks, footage which John Simpson regarded as 'the best television pictures of the entire war'. They were

247

also uncensored since he managed to smuggle out the footage by a combination of ingenuity and luck.[101]

Despite the efforts of such mavericks, the main problem for the pool reporters was that they found that their reports, especially those from forward US Army units in Iraq, took up to four days to reach Dhahran, arriving long after they could be used for any meaningful news reports on the progress of the war.[102] One consequence of this, wrote one American journalist, was that 'the Army has received little attention for its part in the ground combat, whereas the Marines and the US Air Force – which facilitated transmission of reports – have figured much more prominently'.[103] The major frustration of American reporters with the pool system once the Ground War began was indeed the problem of getting broadcast tapes, photographers' film and reporters' dispatches back from the field. Combat forces were literally moving so fast that they had often left the pick-up points far behind by the time the military courier arrived to take video reports back to Dhahran to the satellite earth stations. They were even moving too fast for the journalists to set up their own portable satellite transmitters. But this was at least a more satisfactory situation than the problems being encountered by the forward British news pools, since no reports at all were getting back from there, from either print or broadcast correspondents.

Kate Adie admitted to a high degree of self-censorship taking place in the field at that time, largely for reasons of combined military–media safety:

On some occasions we held back footage because part of an operation might not have been completed, and transmission could endanger lives; on some, we held footage because the involvement of specific forces would have betrayed the position or thrust of an action. For instance, British artillery alone fired Type 110 guns on the first day of the major ground bombardment. We held the footage 24 hours, until US 110s had fired, so as not to give away the precise location of the British guns, which was central to the deception tactic in the invasion of Iraq.[104]

Such discretion was at least possible with a portable satellite dish. Journalists in other pools enjoyed no such luxury.

Ironically, even when military officials tried to be helpful, the journalistic requirements for speed ran foul of the military's need for taking on board the rapidly surfacing intricacies of coalition politics. When the official Saudi pool to newly liberated Kuwait

City was assembled at 02:00 on 26 February, it managed to leave Dhahran only three hours later with the journalists on a C-130 transport specially laid on for the trip amidst hopes that it would speed up reports. 'It didn't,' wrote one reporter involved, 'and delays included a 40 minute stop so a Saudi TV crew could tape the raising of the Saudi flag at the Saudi Embassy in Kuwait City. Another pause, this time at night on a highway, came when the official heading the pool turned back a 17 car British TV pool heading north on its own'.[105]

While the allied forces were busy attempting to 'cut off and kill' the fleeing Iraqi army to the north, the journalists who had liberated Kuwait City were having a field day with reports which, to some, appeared like Paris 1944 with television. Jubilant Kuwaitis sought out the television crews and testified to their happiness, their gratitude, their relief and their sadness concerning those who had not survived or those who had been taken away. This turned out to be live television's main view of the ground war. The cameras, in other words, were pointed away from the scene of the actual fighting, and at a liberated city which was no longer part of the military action. It made good television to show the Kuwaitis' moment of history and so it became the focus of the world's media attention; this was after all the first time in seven months that English-speaking people in Kuwait had an opportunity to tell their stories, which may have been what western audiences anyway wanted to hear because it justified their support for the war.

Meanwhile, allied forces were finding that the 43 Iraqi divisions facing them were just crumbling before their advance. The 14 front-line Iraqi divisions had been so devastated by allied bombing that they were estimated to be at less than half their combat strengths at the start of the land war.[106] One pool reporter with the American Army's 2nd Armored Division later described the scene as follows:

Most Iraqis just gave up – or tried to. It was a bizarre scene. The advance was like a giant hunt. The Iraqis were driven ahead of us like animals ... They looked like spectators on a demolition-derby circuit.[107]

It certainly seemed that pre-ground-war estimates concerning the size of the Iraqi army in theatre had been exaggerated and that perhaps only two-thirds of the claimed half million men faced the coalition. But despite the coalition's numerical superiority, it also held considerable advantages in so far as technology and skills were concerned. In Washington, General Kelly conceded that it was 'nothing like the fight we thought it would be'.[108]

A major objective of the American ground forces was to take the town of Al-Jahrah, just to the west of Kuwait City at the junction of its sixth ring road and the highway which ran north to Basra. As the departing convoy of Iraqi occupiers fled the city on 26 February in everything from tanks to civilian buses, US Marine aircraft started to lay down an aerial barrage, attacking in 'kill zones' every 15 minutes. 'It was a turkey shoot for several hours,' said one commander, 'then the weather turned sour.' 'Like shooting fish in a barrel,' said a US pilot.[109] The traffic was reported to be bumper to bumper as American Air Force planes and helicopters dropped their cluster bombs and any other types of bomb they could get their hands on as they returned to their ships to rearm.[110] One journalist likened what happened to the escaping convoy to 'a worm when it is chopped by a spade – the segments wriggle, but the creature is already dead'.[111]

The US Army's 2nd Armored Division, moving north rapidly to the west of the convoy, ordered its 2nd Marine Division and its armoured 'Tiger' brigade to race across the desert and block enemy forces from retreating into Iraq. President Bush was meanwhile adamant: 'It is time for all Iraqi forces in the theatre of operations to lay down their arms. That will stop the bloodshed.'[112] Baghdad radio's version of what then happened was that the coalition had 'interfered in the withdrawal of our forces and demonstrated all his cowardly, mean and lowly characteristics while trying to harm our units'.[113]

One final Iraqi effort to retain its armed forces in tact was attempted on Wednesday 27 February with a letter from Tariq Aziz to the United Nations in which he offered to renounce Iraq's claim to Kuwait and to pay reparations in return for a cease-fire.[114] Baghdad radio meanwhile accused the allies of obstructing its 'withdrawal' while insisting that the western 'media trumpets are still repeating their illusions regarding this offensive'. It continued:

By its withdrawal, Iraq has foiled all the pretexts that the aggressors used as a cover. What they have done, and what they are doing now, goes beyond the resolutions which they made themselves and dictated to the world in the name of the Security Council ... They have taken the slogan 'the new world order' as an excuse, not to destroy Iraq only, but also to humiliate the peoples of the world and impose absolute US hegemony on the world. But the scoundrel aggressors must understand that Iraq is something different and the people of Iraq cannot tolerate aggression, humiliation and submissiveness to the aggressors' tyranny.[115]

When a senior Pentagon official was quoted as saying that 'we're out to destroy the myth as much as the might',[116] he was perhaps revealing a clue to why the allies were treating what the Iraqis claimed was a withdrawal as a military retreat. Iraqi statements were undoubtedly directed at Middle Eastern audiences who might indeed have been impressed that, for seven months, Saddam had taken on the world and even now was only withdrawing and not being forcibly ejected by it. However, the reality was that the rout had to be stopped if some of Iraq's military forces were to be retained and so, at the UN, the Iraqi ambassador said that, because the last Iraqi soldiers had now left Kuwait City at dawn that day, Iraq was prepared to comply with all remaining Security Council resolutions.

In view of what pool reporters attached to the 2nd Armored Division were encountering just north of Kuwait City, and which only emerged subsequently, this was hardly surprising. As they approached a 'vast traffic jam of more than a mile of vehicles, perhaps 2000 or more', one wrote:

As we drove slowly through the wreckage, our armoured personnel carrier's tracks splashed through great pools of bloody water. We passed dead soldiers lying, as if resting, without a mark on them. We found others cut up so badly, a pair of legs in its trousers would be 50 yards from the top half of the body. Four soldiers had died under a truck where they had sought protection.[117]

It would later emerge that this was only the start of it, with some reports claiming that the carnage extended many more miles further northwards. The intention had been clear: to cut off the Iraqi forces before they reached the Mutlah Gap and the safety beyond of Iraq. When General Schwarzkopf gave his *tour d'horizon* briefing on Wednesday the 27th, which became an instant best-seller when it was released on video in the United States, he had pointed out that 'the gates are closed ... there are no ways out'.[118] It was also in that briefing that the General, in response

251

to a question about the retreat, stated: 'We're not in the business of killing them. We have PSY OPS aircraft up. We're telling them over and over again, all you've got to do is get out of your tanks and move off, and you will not be killed.'[119]

Realising that the coalition had indeed achieved, as Schwarzkopf put it, 'an absolutely gigantic military accomplishment', and because Iraq had finally agreed to comply with all UN Resolutions, President Bush decided to call a 'unilateral cessation of offensive operations' (not therefore technically a cease-fire) to begin at midnight EST time on Thursday 28 February, exactly 100 hours after the ground war had commenced. In Iraq it was at 08:00 on 1 March. Baghdad radio took three hours to make the announcement, after the allies had suspended their attack, calling it a cease-fire.[120] In his post-war interview with David Frost, Schwarzkopf stated that because the 'back door' had been closed after the third day and that there was thus no way out for the Iraqis, it 'was literally about to become the battle of Cannae: a battle of annihilation'. He therefore discussed with General Powell whether the coalition's military objectives had been achieved. They agreed they had and informed President Bush. 'That was a very courageous decision on the part of the President to also stop the offensive,' said Schwarzkopf. 'Frankly, my recommendation had been, you know, continue to march.' These last ten words were to cause a minor media storm and were often taken out of context, implying a greater gap between Schwarzkopf and Bush than may have existed. Although the general who so often professed to hate war admitted that the decision was responsible for many enemy troops escaping into Iraq, he nonetheless felt that the President's decision was the most 'humane' and 'courageous' in the circumstances, in that it avoided the annihilation of those 'poor fellows that had been all the way down in the front line'. The Republican Guard, further back, 'had pretty much bugged out by then' anyway, he added. It further came to light after the war that some coalition pilots were also reluctant to continue the slaughter.[121]

It was only on Friday 1 March that the first television and other pictures started to come through of the battle which had started to take place north of Kuwait City and south of Mutlah Gap on the night of the previous Tuesday. And it was only on that Friday that the real extent of the carnage was brought home to television viewers around the world. Just after 17:00 (local time), CNN's

Tom Mintier was in Kuwait City reporting live on the victory parade that had been going on for the past five hours when Greg LaMotte joined him, having just returned from the battle site with the first videotape. Mintier introduced the footage with the words: 'You know, we haven't seen much of the war itself ... but the horror of war came home today into a harsh reality of people who have died in this war', whereupon LaMotte was interviewed live on camera:

What happened, Tom, is that the Iraqis tried to flee, given the order that they were given. It was almost like a weekend trying-to-get-to-the-beach traffic jam. What compounded the problem was allied military [attempts to] cut 'em off at the pass, so to speak, before they could get into Iraq and what ensued was this tremendous traffic jam. In the midst of this traffic jam, allied aerial strikes began and what ensued was in essence what you could only describe as a massacre.

They then ran the tapes which the CNN crew had taken through the windscreen of their car as they had approached the rear of this convoy and weaved their way through the back-end of it, with LaMotte adding: 'I should warn you that some of it is somewhat graphic':

What we're seeing is bodies strewn all over the place, body parts [difficult to discern]. We've got cars that have been stolen from Kuwaitis as the Iraqis tried to get out of town. They piled the cars full of booty and they simply didn't make it. There's civilian cars all over the place, there's burned out tanks, there's trucks, you name it ... Some were completely disintegrated, including the people inside of them. What this could be is thousands of people possibly could have died given the number of vehicles involved. The pilots described their mission as shooting fish in a barrel and indeed that's what the case was. It seems that many probably didn't know what hit them given the scenes that we saw. Apparently, what we're told, is that they looted Kuwait City: radios, TVs, VCRs, even things like doorknobs, women's underwear, clothing, children's clothing – you name it, they took it ... This was the most horrific thing I have ever seen in my life: bodies everywhere, body parts everywhere, cars that you know that the person couldn't possibly have known what hit them, disintegration in many cases. In some cases you got the impression that some of them thought that they could get out of their cars and run – not to be ... it's unbelievable.

The footage was certainly unforgettable, although the number of bodies visible was comparatively few and, of those shown, most were covered by blankets. Indeed, given the sheer number of vehicles involved and the extent of the carnage shown, what was surprisingly absent were corpses and bomb craters.

While this report was being transmitted, Britain's BSkyB News began running Kate Adie's taped pool report at 14:10 GMT. It began with a shot of a wounded Iraqi soldier being stretchered to treatment and a statement that he feared the Americans would shoot him. But the reapers of carnage had turned angels of mercy, a theme which predominated in Britain's tabloid press coverage of the battle. Kate Adie's report stated:

He was found amidst a battlefield scene of carnage: hundreds of vehicles burned out and stinking. All had come helter skelter out of Kuwait, trying to escape north to Iraq on the one road. At a police station on the road, though, there was a big battle. The American Second Marine Division had come on tanks round the station when the Iraqis decided to make a fight of it on the road while thousands of people piled remorselessly towards the battle.

An American marine, Major Bob Williams, was then interviewed and described the scene as 'apocalyptic'. Kate Adie continued:

The fighting went on for five hours and in this inferno vehicles exploded and were ripped up by small arms fire and further away the bombers overhead caught the flood of escaping soldiers ... The scene was both devastating and pathetic [over shots of the loot taken by the fleeing army]. Corpses had been laid by the police station. We found more amidst the wreckage. It was an erie and grisly end for a fleeing army.

An hour and a half later, at 15:42 GMT, Sky News ran segments of Robert Moore's pool report. Why Sky chose to leave out the statements identified in the brackets is unknown, although a fuller version of the report including those omissions was shown on that evening's ITN news. Using much of the same footage as Miss Adie's report and some additional shots, he stated:

It was, quite literally, a trap. A ridge to one side; a minefield to the other, (allied armour ahead) – and above them, the bombers. The allies have cleared many of the bodies from the cars and placed them in small groups to one side (many of them too badly charred ever to be identified) ... The Iraqis fought back, but without air power they stood little chance.

Almost 40 minutes later, a journalist at the Riyadh briefings asked for any details which the military may have had. An uneasy British officer replied 'A military convoy was this?' 'Well, evidently civilian vehicles as well.' 'No, I'm sorry you have the advantage on me on that. I have no details at all on that.' Given that the battle had taken place nearly three days earlier, this only served to raise press suspicions about what had actually taken place.

When ITN ran Robert Moore's pool report as its lead item on its 17:30 news, the following section not shown earlier by Sky was included:

Some had tried desperately to hide under the [road] bridges, but even this didn't save them. In the panic of the attack, tanks and cars were crashing into each other. The road is now, in effect, a scrapyard and a burial site. No one knows how many died [at this point there is a slur on the sound-track which implies an – albeit clumsy – edit]. The Americans are quick to point out that the vast majority of those killed here are not refugees, nor civilians, but the scattered remnants of an invading army ... .[122]

This last point was a curious one in light of Kate Adie's report, which was again shown on the 18:00 BBC News but which now contained the additional statement:

And those who fought and died for Iraq here turned out to be from the north of the country, from minority communities persecuted by Saddam Hussein: the Kurds and the Turks. Some were by the roadside, lying with others burned beyond recognition who had been retrieved from vehicles. We found still more among the wreckage.

Why Sky had also chosen to omit this reference is again unknown; it was the only pool report in which a specific reference to the presence of such troops was made.

At almost 19:10 GMT that day, BSkyB News went over live to Christopher Morris in Riyadh to find out about the reaction there to growing criticism that the coalition had massacred the fleeing Iraqi army. Morris had been to the battle site that afternoon and described it as one of the 'worst scenes of carnage I've ever seen in my life':

Now nobody will probably ever know how many people died in that attack but I can assure you that the carnage on the ground is quite terrible. There are many dead bodies still littering the ground three days, or shall I say just under three days after the attack took place ...

He said that 720 Iraqis had been taken prisoner at the scene but that hundreds more had escaped 'by simply running away into the desert'. Although only 40 bodies had been recovered so far, the number was likely to be 'infinitesimal' not least because many had

been 'incinerated into nothing'. Sky then ran a taped report by
Morris in which he described the scene as 'the road to hell'. As
the camera weaved through the carnage from south to north,
Morris's commentary stated:

On a hillside, at a place called Jahra, the sheer horror of what happened
can only be described as like a nightmare from Dante's Inferno: the desert
killing field where Iraq's army in full retreat was halted in its tracks with
all the savagery and yet detachment of high technology warfare ...

Many more bodies than seen before were shown amidst the
wreckage of the vehicles (none particularly graphically) and the
same Marine interviewed by Kate Adie went on record as saying
that the only bodies they had collected were military personnel.
British soldiers who were interviewed were also clearly shaken by
the scene, with various descriptions of it as 'ghastly', 'horrific',
'quite frightening' and a 'nightmare'. One stated: 'I've never seen
nothing like this before in my life, not at all, no, and never wish
to see it again either.'

One thing that was striking about the initial television coverage
at this stage was that it was giving the impression that an ambush
followed by a massacre had taken place. In fact, it had been a
battle. It may have been one-sided owing to the coalition's air
supremacy but it had been a battle nonetheless. Major Bob Williams was quoted more fully in a pooled press dispatch as saying
'they fought harder than we have seen before. It really was apocalyptic'.[123] As we have seen, most of the TV coverage merely
concentrated on the word 'apocalyptic' because that was the most
suitable sound-bite to match the pictures. But it was apparent that
the police station at Jahrah 'had to be stormed room by room by
US infantry'[124] and that considerable other resistance had taken
place.

On BBC1's Nine O'Clock News that evening, Kate Adie's
report was re-shown (complete with the reference to the Kurds and
the Turks), together with another by Brian Barron, who had
travelled even further north to just inside Iraq. He reported on the
firing of hundreds of Kuwaiti oil wells and added the following:

This is the border of Kuwait and Iraq. Behind me is the lead American
tank. We just drove into Iraq for five miles taking pictures. On our way
back, at the border post, we stopped and talked to Iraqi soldiers. It
became very clear they're not happy with the cease-fire and what's

happened in the war. They confiscated our cameras, threatened us with guns and we just got out.

If the effect was to undermine any sympathy which viewers may have been feeling for the massacred Iraqis, on ITN's News at Ten, Jeremy Thompson's report showed some graphic pictures of the dead and then described how Kuwaitis who visited the rear of the column 'came to look at the gruesome wreckage of their oppressors as if to prove to themselves that the nightmare of occupation was at last really over'. One Kuwaiti woman was interviewed: 'I want to smell the freedom of my country, the liberation of my country. I want to smell it, I want to feel it.' Coming three days after the battle and over the pictures of Iraqi bodies, this was an unfortunate analogy. As they came up to where the major scene of carnage was, Thompson's commentary ran:

The spoils of war were spilling from almost every vehicle – evidence of the Iraqis' orgy of looting. They tried to drive home with all the treasures of Kuwait. There were clothes and children's toys, radios and vacuum cleaners, jewellery and china. A musical card still played 'A Happy New Year'. A stolen Koran: the ultimate sacrilege ... For American Marine General Walter Boomer, the shambles summed up his views on Saddam's defeated army: 'In addition to being fairly incompetent, they were thieves as well as murderers'.

So not much sympathy here either for men described by the American troops as REMFs ('Rear Echelon Motherfuckers'). Indeed the whole framing of the story by all the news organisations became such that any sympathy which reporters may have felt for the massacred army evoked by the shocking scenes they had witnessed was more than counterbalanced by the sheer scale of plundering which the Iraqis had clearly undertaken. To consolidate this impression still further came the footage of the burning oil wells which Saddam's escaping army had set ablaze for no apparent reason other than 'Saddam's revenge upon Kuwait before his army's hasty exit' (Thompson).

Tony Clifton of *Newsweek*, attached to the 'Hounds of Hell' battalion which had attacked the tanks and petrol tankers at the front of the column at dusk on 26 February causing the six-lane-wide tailback, described the night fighting as follows: 'you could see the little figures of soldiers coming out with their hands up and it really looked like a medieval hell ... you know, in Bosch, you

257

see the great red flames and these weird little contorted figures.'
The next morning he investigated the battle scene:

I could see a lot of the soldiers really taken aback because there were
bodies all over the place, and I remember at one point looking down at
a car track and I was up to my ankles in blood ... and there were a lot
of very white faced young men going round saying 'Jesus, did we really
do this?'.[125]

At the time, however, the paucity of bodies in the scenes of
carnage filmed by television crews was striking. Given that it was
estimated by some people that as many as 25,000 Iraqis may have
died in the ground war's final phase, where were the corpses?
Well, they were there, at least 400 of them according to John
Simpson,[126] but very few appeared on television. Questions of
taste and decency intervened once more to remove the true horror
from the footage. Some indication of that horror was revealed by
a still photograph taken by Kenneth Jarecke of a charred Iraqi
corpse sitting upright in his burned-out vehicle and published by
The Observer on Sunday 10 March. There were also numerous
press reports, but these (like the television pictures) were published
days after the event itself. One of the first British officers on the
scene, Major Mark Auchinleck, was quoted as saying that a brief
religious ceremony was conducted over each corpse before they
were buried in mass graves away from the main highway.[127] The
Washington Post quoted Pentagon officials as saying that 'heaps
of Iraqi corpses are being buried in mass graves across the desert'[128] and the *Wall Street Journal* reported that 'allied forces used
bulldozers to bury thousands of enemy dead in trenches as the
allies advanced'.[129]

On BBC2's Newsnight on 1 March, the footage from Kate
Adie's pool report of Mutlah Gap was sandwiched into a report
dealing with Saddam's future and the options now open to the
United Nations. Jeremy Paxman took over the commentary with
the words:

Pictures from liberated Kuwait make plain the scale of the Iraqi rout:
1200 vehicles commandeered or highjacked by fleeing Iraqi soldiers
were wrecked in one engagement on the road north alone. If it moved
it got blasted. Many of those who died at allied hands in this engagement were Kurds, Turks and other minorities already victimised by the
Party dictatorship.

Later in the programme, a report by Mark Urban in Kuwait City
was shown about the rounding up of Iraqi soldiers in hiding and
the possible ill-treatment of the Palestinians by the Kuwaitis. Then,
in a live interview, Urban pointed out that many of the Kuwaitis
taken from the city might have died in the attack on the convoy;
he had spoken to two who had escaped from it. Urban subsequently went up to the scene with his crew over the weekend
and filmed the burial of Iraqi soldiers in mass graves for the BBC.
When this was shown on BBC2's Newsnight on Monday 4 March,
his report stated:

Just north of Kuwait City at a place called Al-Mutlah on the road to Basra
there was a slaughter which is already becoming infamous. Hundreds of
Iraqi vehicles were destroyed by allied aircraft. The road became blocked
so people tried to drive around it and they were killed too. While the
world saw the sanitized videos from briefing rooms in Riyadh, this is what
it looked like on the ground. Scattered around the vehicles, cheap loot,
ammunition and war supplies. The flaying of this army of occupation
from the air was so thorough that allied ground forces met little resistance
... The allies exploited high technology to shatter their enemy and now
they use it to inter him. A burial detachment plots the position of its mass
graves by satellite; another one is covered over by engineer tractors. 80
people were buried here. The soldiers doing this thankless work assume
that all of them belong to the Iraqi army, but only one was wearing
identity dog-tags. 79 unknown soldiers. 79 families who will never know
for sure what happened to the men they sent to war or where they lie ...

The pictures were fairly graphic as the bodies were lined up in the
graves before being covered over by bulldozers. A religious ceremony held for the coalition troops ended the item: there was no
concern now for that 'host nation sensitivity' which had so worried the PAOs and the PROs attached to the news pools only days
earlier.

The battle of Mutlah Gap had undoubtedly been a slaughter.
The military rights and wrongs were never properly debated in the
media until after the war was over, and even then not fully. This
was helped considerably by the fact that the first real indication
of the extent of the carnage inflicted by the coalition, the television
pictures of the battle's aftermath, came through after a halt to the
war had been called. John Simpson has since claimed that 'aware-
ness of what the TV pictures of the slaughter at Mutlah Gap might
do to public opinion at home played an important part in Presi-

dent Bush's decision not to pursue the Iraqi troops any further, and certainly not to take the war to Baghdad'.[130] It is possible that the President may have seen the pictures before the rest of the world, but this seems unlikely given the amount of time which footage was taking to reach the FTUs during the Ground War and in light of the timing of his decision to call a halt. The newspool system, itself on the verge of collapse as the battle was under way, had nonetheless held together long enough for the coalition to pursue its military objectives away from the prying gaze of television, which might have introduced political considerations before those objectives had been achieved. But an enormous suspicion remains about the timing of the release of those apocalyptic pictures of the burned-out convoy. Was it mere coincidence that television stations in Britain and the United States received their pictures from the region at about the same time? The 24–hour all-news stations BSkyB and CNN, renowned for breaking stories as they came in, both began transmitting their footage shortly after 5 o'clock local time on Friday 1 March, by which point the story was more about the end of the war than it was about what had happened several days earlier.

As for the firing of Kuwait's oil wells, General Schwarzkopf later recalled his feelings on seeing the scene as he flew to meet Saddam's generals to negotiate the cease-fire agreement:

I was totally unprepared for what we saw. It was getting darker and darker and darker, then all of a sudden, it was black outside. Then I saw the fireballs all over the place, all this senseless destruction. I was angry and disgusted all at once. It was almost terrifying. All I could think of was, 'I'm flying into hell'.[131]

The Iraqis had in fact been preparing for the destruction of Kuwaiti oil fields in the event of evacuation almost as soon as they had invaded back in the previous August. The Al-Wafra oil fields and storage tanks were reported to be on fire as early as 21 January and two further sites were fired the next day.[132] Within days the coalition was releasing aerial photographs of the billowing smoke, which may have been designed to provide some cover from coalition aircraft even though General Neal in Riyadh had stated that 'we are not concerned that it would seriously interrupt any operations now, or in the future'.[133] But the real destruction began in earnest at the end of February just before the ground war began. By 28 February, 580 wells were reported to be on fire, 200 more damaged and a further 220 storage tanks, refineries and related facilities burning.

This kind of wanton destruction once again tended to reduce the level of sympathy afforded to the defeated foe, even though many coalition soldiers had tended to focus their ire against Saddam rather than the conscripted Iraqi troops. When General Schwarzkopf told his men that he did not want his opposite numbers arriving to sign the final cease-fire agreement in a tent at Safwan airbase on Sunday 3 March to be 'humiliated' or 'embarrassed', he did add: 'I'm not here to give them anything. I'm here to tell them what we expect them to do.'[134] One of the things that was urgently needed was to make it clear to all Iraqi forces that a cease-fire had now been agreed upon. Baghdad radio, by insisting that it had already secured a cease-fire, must take its share of responsibility in the deaths of soldiers who died after the 'unilateral cessation' of the coalition's 'offensive operations'. And perhaps the coalition, by indulging in semantics, should also take its share of the blame. A minor clash had occurred at an allied checkpoint on Friday 1 March when two buses carrying Iraqi soldiers heading west were stopped for questioning. Gunfire from the second bus prompted the Americans to return fire, killing 6, wounding 6 and with 9 more taken prisoner.[135] More seriously, on Saturday 2 March, a clash had occurred resulting in the destruction of 187 Iraqi armoured vehicles by the American 24th Mechanised Division – long after the temporary cease-fire/unilateral cessation of offensive opertions had been called.

What had apparently happened in this second incident was that an Iraqi convoy totalling 1,000 vehicles was moving north along highway 8 to the west of Basra in southern Iraq. It encountered the American division and 'opened fire in an effort to clear a path toward a causeway across the Euphrates'.[136] The Americans returned fire and brought in Cobra attack helicopters, whereupon a severe firefight occurred, resulting, according to one source, in 2,000 Iraqi deaths. The whole event received minimal media attention.[137] When one pool reporter attempted to talk to the medics on the spot, he was told: 'no interviews'.[138] If all this was designed to keep real war off the screen, then it was highly effective. Very little of the ground war was actually seen at all. For Philip Knightley, this was one of the main innovations of the Gulf War:

Ever since the British invented military censorship in 1856 ... wartime news management has had two main purposes: to deny information and comfort to the enemy and maintain public support. In the Gulf War the new element has been an effort to change public perception of the nature of war itself, to convince us that new technology has removed a lot of war's horrors.[139]

It would certainly appear that, despite the shocking nature of the Mutlah Gap pictures, that was the closest television viewers were going to be allowed to the real war: a burned-out convoy days after the event. Besides, perhaps Robert Fisk was right when he wrote that 'No film could do credit to this chaos. It was both surreal and pathetic.'[140] However, it soon became clear that even greater carnage had occurred elsewhere, nowhere near the prying gaze of television.

On a coastal road running north east from Jahrah to the Iraqi border city of Umm Quasr, there was an even longer convoy of vehicles than that south of Mutlah Gap. Unlike that scene of carnage, it had not been tidied up when journalists inspected it 10 days after the war. One described what he saw:

For a 50 or 60–mile stretch from just north of Jahra to the Iraqi border, the road was littered with exploded and roasted vehicles. It is important to say that the 37 dead men I saw were all soldiers ... The road was thick with the wreckage of tanks, armoured personnel carriers, 155mm howitzers, and supply trucks ... The explosions had torn tanks and trucks apart ... the heat of the blasts had inspired secondary explosions in the ammunition. Some fires had been fierce enough to melt windshield glass into blobs of silicone.[141]

Here may be a clue to why so few dead Iraqi soldiers were seen, certainly far fewer than the estimated numbers of dead. Even this reporter had seen only 37 bodies in a 50–60 mile stretch of carnage, although he did notice wild dogs and Bedouin scavenging about the wreckage. The fact is that modern weapons, such as fuel-air bombs or soft-tipped uranium shells, leave little evidence of human remains. Perhaps this was the eventual fate of the real butchers of Kuwait City if it was true that Kurds, Turks and Kuwaitis had died in their hundreds, perhaps thousands, on the road to Mutlah Gap. As another journalist pointed out, whereas 450 people may have survived the first convoy,

Not here. Largely unnoticed by the media so far, this tableau stretches for miles. Every vehicle was strafed or bombed. Every windscreen is shattered. Every tank is burned. Every truck is riddled with shrapnel. No looting by the dead soldiers was evident. No survivors are known or likely.[142]

By the time this tale emerged, however, the main story of which it was but a part had moved on. The war was over and attention was rapidly shifting to the rebellion first in southern Iraq and then, more dramatically because of the presence of western journalists, to the plight of the Kurds further to the north. Saddam had not fled to Algeria, as was widely reported at the end of the war;[143] he was still very much in control, with the bulk of his Republican Guard still in tact. If the allies could take comfort from having achieved their avowed war aim of removing Iraq from Kuwait, privately they could only regret that what was widely regarded as their hidden intention of removing Saddam from power had failed.

The ramifications of this became very quickly apparent with Baghdad radio's conclusion on the war. 'The mother of battles was a clear victory for Iraq,' it pronounced. 'We are happy with the cessation of combat operations as this would preserve our sons' blood and people's safety after God made them triumph with faith against their evil enemies.'[144] Moreover, 'Iraq has punched a hole in the myth of American superiority and rubbed the nose of the United States in the dust'.[145] No matter that no one in Britain, France, Kuwait, America or any of the coalition countries believed this. Student protests in Egypt saw four die. In North Africa comparisons were made between Mutlah Gap and the French slaughter in Algeria in 1945. In Jordan, 10,000 people flocked into the streets brandishing models of Scud missiles, portraits of Saddam and intertwined Iraqi and Jordanian flags. 'Saddam is so clever,' said one 'victory marcher'. 'He started to withdraw his troops before the ground war began. Now he has ended the war with much of his army intact.' Another stated: 'Now that Russia is no longer powerful, there is only America. But if the Arabs can come together, they can be a superpower as well.'[146] Ironically, a point that was rarely made was that Saddam had indeed united many Arab states – in opposition to him. And the United States had formed that coalition, with considerable help from Israel whose non-retaliation enabled the Americans to keep the coalition together. Right to the end, however, Baghdad radio was adamant about the conclusion of the war:

263

Just as the sun finally set on Great Britain, a sun which once never set on its imperial possessions, the United States will tumble and fall because of its reckless policy and its practices against the peoples of the world. Bright lights will shine in Asia, Africa and Latin America. The peoples of Europe will reject hegemony. Iraq's great steadfastness will guide the Arab nation to the road to resuming its civilisational march and to expelling the imperialist and Zionist aggressors. The results of the long struggle against the enemies will appear soon.[147]

King Hussein, desperately attempting to salvage something not only from his political situation but also from his badly tarnished world image, put a stop to all this, at least officially, when he described the war as 'one of the greatest disasters our Arab nation has ever endured'.[148]

Conclusion

It was unquestionably one of the most clear-cut and one-sided military victories in the history of warfare. Although the final Iraqi death toll might never be known, at least 40,000 and perhaps as many as 200,000 had died, as compared with fewer than 150 soldiers from the entire coalition who lost their lives in Desert Storm.[1] It is possible that as much as 50% of the Iraqi death toll was sustained during the 100 hour ground war. The Iraqis would concede that only 2,000 of their civilians had been killed. Part of the difficulty in assessing precisely how many of the enemy had died was, as American officials cautioned, 'that even a tally of buried bodies will be highly imprecise because many Iraqi soldiers were dismembered or charred beyond recognition in explosions of deadly US munitions'.[2] The media coverage gave very little indication of this. As Ian Hargreaves, Deputy Editor of the *Financial Times*, said after the war: 'the public in Britain and in America will have had the impression that this was a war involving very little death and very little utter horror'.[3]

It did appear, however, that all those pre-war American anxieties about body bags, a hostile media and a poor American military performance had proved unwarranted. One message which emerged was that modern technology, both military and communications, had changed the face of warfare. Militarily, it was a warning to Third World countries that might be entertaining notions of flexing their muscles that they had better think again before taking on the champions of the New World Order: the United Nations and the First World's leading technologically based military power. The Gulf War had demonstrated that the gap between the world's fourth and first military powers, with only

265

comparatively little help from the latter's 30 friends, was colossal. Not only had the Gulf War exorcised the Vietnam Syndrome from the American psyche, television's coverage of it had revealed the future – and the future belonged, in peace preferably but in war if necessary, to high technology. Moreover, the idea that 'the media are American', that Anglo-American news organisations dominate the international flow of news to the detriment of the Third World, had not only found substantiating support in the war, it had even been underlined by the coalition's media arrangements, with their Anglo-American emphasis. Ever since decolonisation a generation or so earlier, mounting Third World resentment at what was perceived to be the adverse consequences for developing nations of this information and cultural hegemony by advanced countries, of this 'media imperialism', had now found its apogee. The ability of the American-led coalition to drive its military message home and abroad by superior technology and by controlling international communications systems and news organisations had demonstrated for such people that the New World Order and the New World Information Order had merged into one.

The ramifications of this message, particularly in the Muslim world, may take some time to emerge. During the war, Iraqi propaganda had made a great play of the 'vile', 'hypocritical' and 'atheistic' influence of the United States in the region, which was being achieved with the connivance of the oil-rich Gulf Arab states – and this clearly hit a chord in Middle Eastern streets. Interestingly, American black propaganda also exploited these themes as a way of encouraging Iraqis to overthrow Saddam. But this was covert activity, unprovable and unattributable. The extent to which such transmissions were responsible for the Shia and Kurdish uprisings at the end of the war will remain unknown until we learn the Iraqi side of the story. Certainly, a few Kurdish broadcasters, dissillusioned with the initial coalition failure to help the northern uprising, broke ranks and publicly condemned their former employers after the war for not fulfilling their promises.

In so far as the wider world was concerned, polls indicated that western opinion could be relied upon to continue supporting the coalition to outright victory. In Iraq, people had no such choice. To ensure that the Iraqi people were exposed mainly to a coalition version of events, it had been important for its air forces to target enemy radio and television transmitters. It was successful with television but not with radio, which, as we have seen, was transmitting defiant messages right to the end. Like the battle of Khafji, all references in the domestic media to Iraq having been defeated were forbidden and so the scale of the coalition's victory could be witnessed only outside the country. CNN may have been a nuisance occasionally but it was not yet seen extensively in the Arab world, where Iraqi radio still commanded a not inconsiderable audience. The extent to which Iraqi proclamations of defiance and even of victory had a successful impact upon public opinion in Muslim countries cannot as yet be measured.

Saddam Hussein, his Ba'athist regime and its ideology, at the time of writing, were still in power. How long they can remain so waits to be seen. During the war, Saddam had made a great propaganda play of 'winning by losing', that with every day which passed against '30 nations' Iraq had scored a moral victory for the forces of Islam and Pan-Arabism. As long as he remains, some in the West will feel that they may have won the war but lost the peace and that this could have been avoided if President Bush had not called a halt to the fighting when he did. Only time will tell whether they are right.

Being so one-sided a victory, however, should not detract from the fears and anxieties about the outcome which appear to have been genuinely felt by both coalition governments and peoples and which the propaganda of the time also reflected as well as exacerabated. Hindsight can be an extremely valuable tool for understanding but it can also produce myths which hinder that very process of understanding. In other words, just because the war resulted in so one-sided a victory does not mean that that was how it was necessarily regarded before that had been achieved. That the media 'routing of the doom-merchants' and the exposing of the pessimistic pundits after the war[4] were an *ex post facto* indication of relief and should not be allowed to detract from the existence prior to then of genuine anxieties and fears about what a ground war would be like. The media record stands as a lasting testimony to all those fears concerning Iraq's capability of performing more effectively than it did. Just because Saddam did not use chemical weapons or succeed in inciting a larger-scale and more concerted campaign of international terrorism should not suggest that the coalition's expressed fears in these respects were merely

267

propaganda. The two specific propaganda themes that have been exposed as being exaggerated by what has emerged since the war, namely the coalition's success in knocking out Iraq's nuclear programme and the overall accuracy of allied bombing, do not mean either that the remaining aspects of the coalition's propaganda at the time were misleading. In wartime, being economical with the truth is a fourth arm of defence. The problem for journalists is their tradition of acting as 'the fourth estate'. Getting conscripted into military service is one thing; whether the media should voluntarily enlist is quite another.

There are a number of preliminary conclusions which can be drawn about this from the Gulf conflict:

1 Relative unanimity of media coverage

Despite the existence of well over a thousand journalists in the Gulf from a wide variety of news-gathering organisations with differing editorial styles and journalistic practices, they were all essentially dependent upon the coalition military for their principal source of information about the progress of the war. It was monopoly in the guise of pluralism. To continue to be supplied by that source was, rightly or wrongly, regarded as essential to the ability of competitive news organisations to report the war satisfactorily – but from whose point of view? – and this created the need more for co-operation than for conflict with the principal source of information. This was perhaps what Pete Williams really meant when he said after the war that the Pentagon's view was that it had been 'the best war coverage we've ever had'.[5] The media, especially in Britain and the United States, were supportive, largely uncritical and generally reflected the official line. There were exceptions – the unilateralists, the reporters in Baghdad, occasional freelance investigations – but what this newspaper with its editorial approach or that television station with its broadcasting standards said or showed was essentially based upon the same information, which was being tightly controlled at source. It was secrecy disguised as publicity. In other words, the appearance of a pluralistic media reporting in different styles camouflaged this fundamental point and, bearing in mind the definition provided in the Introduction in which the importance of disguise was stressed, this helped official coalition propaganda immeasurably.

There was, however, nothing particularly new in all this. It was for example very similar to the approach adopted by the British and American governments through their Ministry of Information and Office of War Information in the Second World War.[6] The British, for example, had operated a system in which the five independent newsreel organisations were placed on a rotation system whereby one would supply raw footage in turn to the other four which they could then edit in accordance with their own styles. Most of the censorship of sensitive footage took place right at the start of the image-gathering process, although post-censorship would then also take place. In the Gulf, the newspool system, as well as the briefings, operated on the same principle. All material was pooled but only after it had been pre-censored. There are examples of post-censorship having taken place in the Gulf, but so far as we can yet tell, these were largely the exceptions rather than the rule. This was perhaps owing to a feeling on the part of the military that its pre-censorship system, of controlling what came out of the pool before it was distributed more widely, was functioning quite smoothly and effectively.

Mostly, it appears, censorship of *news* was confined largely to matters of operational security. Censorship of *views* was comparatively rare, being confined largely to religious matters. But then, given that most of the media supported the conflict, there was very little need to censor views. Nonetheless, even the unilateralists were able to get their slightly more sceptical and critical copy out of the region, although the coalition possessed the means to prevent it if it had so wished. Censorship of opinions was, of course, much more difficult to implement anyway; there was nothing to stop a critical editor back home from writing a hostile piece, although, again, it has to be remembered that the information upon which such views could be formed was being tightly controlled at source. Besides, censoring opinions would really have been an admission of a bad cause, even though there were several examples in the Gulf War of the military making life difficult for journalists who had written unsympathetic pieces.

Journalists on the spot, in London or in Washington, might occasionally be able to tease a juicy nugget from a briefer, but instances of this are rare. This might have been because journalists were not doing their job effectively because they had been working within the official news machine – as often maintained by those who prided themselves on not having been – or, more likely, it might have been because the briefers were essentially well-trained, media-aware and media-sensitive professionals who understood how journalists operated and how they could be manipulated for the coalition's own purposes. There was anyway the limiting nature of journalism itself, as *Newsday* reporter, Susan Sachs, indicated when she wrote that a pool reporter could 'only get an ant's view of the war. And we're all under the naive impression that by piecing together the pool reports and briefings, we can present a real picture of the war. Yet, all the parts do not make up a whole'.[7] The degree to which coalition arrangements and reporting restrictions recognised and exploited this played a significant part in the outside world's perception of the war.

If all this sounds thoroughly conspiratorial, in some respects it was. After the war, David Beresford of the *Guardian* wondered 'whether a Machiavellian strategy was involved or whether it was merely an exercise in stupidity'.[8] The military, particularly the Americans, believed from their Vietnam experience that the media possessed a power to lose wars on the home front. Planning for and implementing the information war would therefore be every bit as important in the Gulf War as would the remarkable logistical aspects of Operation Desert Storm. Propaganda requires skilful planning, especially if it is to appear as something else, as it must to be really effective. It is therefore by definition a covert activity, just as intelligence is. Although it thus lays itself open to conspiratorial theories and to exposure when mistakes occur, it is nonetheless important to recognise that propaganda is an inextricable part of the modern world, in peace as in war. It is not worse than war – and there remains a consensus that war is still a sometimes unavoidable means of settling international disputes, as was the case in the Gulf conflict. Moreover, this was a war which could not have been fought without propaganda on the coalition's part given that propaganda was being employed extensively by the enemy. Hence the great deal of attention given by coalition politicians to the idea of a 'just war' and the personification of the conflict as being fought against Saddam Hussein and the Republican Guard and not against the Iraqi people as a whole. This was also needed in view of the sensitivities concerning what was seen by some in the Muslim world as an American-inspired civil war fought between various factions of the Arab brotherhood. It was propaganda's role to maintain the perception of a just war and a justified offensive against the Iraqi enemy by largely democratic governments which enjoyed popular support for their actions.

Yet this in turn does bring us back to the question of allied short-term and long-term war aims. Coalition leaders had been strongly denying charges throughout the conflict that the war was about something more than the 'mere' liberation of Kuwait. The British Foreign Secretary, Douglas Hurd, had stressed on 3 February that the implementation of the UN resolutions 'does not mean dismembering Iraq'. Although he conceded that both London and Washington would be happy to see Saddam Hussein go, the war was not about imposing a particular regime upon Baghdad.[9] Or, as General Schwarzkopf stated in his 27 February briefing in Riyadh:

There are a lot of people still saying that the object of the United States of America was to capture Iraq and cause the downfall of the entire country of Iraq. Ladies and Gentlemen, when we were here, we were 150 miles away from Baghdad, and there was nobody between us and Baghdad. If it had been our intention to take Iraq, if it had been our intention to destroy the country, if it had been our intention to overrun the country, we could have done it unopposed, for all intents and purposes .... That was not our intention. We have never said it was our intention. Our intention was truly to eject the Iraqis out of Kuwait *and destroy the military power that had come in here.*[10]

What precisely this meant in the long-term policy sense remains uncertain, but specifically it is clear that only in the coalition's black propaganda, which by definition appeared to be conducted by someone else, was the removal of Saddam Hussein from power an avowed war aim. The coalition's white propaganda stated all along that the intention was simply to remove Iraq from Kuwait.

2 The 'right to know' versus the 'need to know'

Whether the public received the propaganda it deserved and indeed demanded is far too large a question to be answered here. The degree to which public support for the war was the result of a coincidence of views with coalition governments or the spontaneous majority public perception that Saddam Hussein was a man who must be stopped will be debated for a long time. Such coincidence was less apparent in anti-Iraqi Arab coalition partners than it was in the democracies. In the former, one would expect the media to toe the government line. In the latter, however, the

271

degree to which the media were generally supportive of their governments, their involvement and their cause, is striking. Dissenting voices were rare, even though they were seldom found represented proportionally to their size in the media. This was not to be a war in which the 'vocal minority' were to be given a magnified voice. This may well be a testimony more to the effectiveness of democracy, and to the media's responsibility within that, than to the effectiveness of the coalition's propaganda. But it does raise important issues.

The extent to which the perceived lessons of Vietnam were adapted by the Pentagon to ensure that a desired media perspective was being taken was no doubt greatly helped by the fact that the coalface of the information war in the Gulf conflict was in Saudi Arabia, a country whose government had never been noted for its liberal attitudes towards journalists. But, equally, western journalists themselves, more keen to cooperate with the hands that fed them with their tit-bits of vital information, must take their share of responsibility. Above all, however, perhaps the most important lesson to be learned from the Gulf War is the need to redefine the relationship between the media and their audience. When the authorities can speak directly to the audience via live television, rather than indirectly via the interpretations with which journalists have traditionally informed their readers and viewers of what was going on, the gap between government and governed is narrowed substantially. What role is therefore left for the media? In the eighteenth century, the press emerged as an agent of liberty, defining a role for itself as keeper of the public conscience. But when the public and the government are at one, as they were in the Gulf War, what role should the media adopt? The fact that the electronic medium of television – the principal source by which most people derive news and information – has been a major contributor to this uncertainty is ironic, to say the least.

During the war, *The Economist* defended the coalition's arrangements for releasing information in the following terms:

The Pentagon and the British Ministry of Defence have coralled reporters into official groups subject to strict rules of security. No sensible editor should oppose that; journalists swanning around on their own are as likely to be shot by their own side as by the other ... The citizens of a democracy do have a right to know what war is like, and whether its horrors are worse than the alternative. A dutiful press that merely regurgitates what it is told is useless, in the field and at home. The job of the press is to tell the truth, about right and wrong alike. Such reports can force improvements and save lives ... The apparent contradiction in those views disappears in the face of one simple fact. War is an aberration. While it lasts, the practice of democracy is obscured, just as the view of a battle is restricted from any one part of the field ... Editors should, by all means, stake their claim to fair reporting, but not get too upset if the answer comes slowly.[11]

The *Washington Post* went further when it strongly criticised journalists at the Riyadh briefings for making fools of themselves by asking silly questions – and all on television. It suggested that the reasons for the apparent gulf between the media and the military were as follows: the military was closer to Middle America in terms of values than the press; the military demands team play, whereas journalists fight with one another; the military is hierarchical, whereas journalists have no rank; the military values loyalty and confidence in superiors, whereas the press values objectivity and scepticism; the military are 'average guys' valuing anonymity whereas, journalists are striving constantly for recognition; when the military makes a mistake, people die, but when the media make a mistake, 'it runs a correction'.[12]

Walter Cronkite on the other hand argued on 25 February:

The greatest mistake of our military so far is its attempt to control coverage by assigning a few pool reporters and photographers to be taken to locations determined by the military with supervising officers monitoring all their conversations with the troops in the field. An American citizen is entitled to ask: 'What are they trying to hide?' The answer might be casualties from shelling, collapsing morale, disaffection, insurrection, incompetent officers, poorly trained troops, malfunctioning equipment, widespread illness – who knows? But the fact that we don't know, the fact that the military apparently feels there is *something* it must hide, can only lead eventually to a breakdown in home-front confidence and the very echoes from Vietnam that the Pentagon fears the most.[13]

Yet, as Jonathan Alter pointed out: 'At bottom, the military needs TV to build and sustain support for the war even more than TV needs the military to build ratings.'[14] It also needed a rapid war, with minimal casualties, to ensure that the kind of debate suggested by Cronkite could not emerge to undermine public support for the war effort. That the Americans were able to achieve both was due as much to judgement on the part of Central Command's military planners as it was to luck on the part of the Joint Information Bureau. Iraqi incompetence, both militarily and propagandistically, also played its part.

   After it was all over, John Wilson, Controller of Editorial Policy at the BBC, stated:

The Gulf War wasn't just the first CNN war; it was a war where those waging it could coordinate information centrally in the Pentagon, and pump out core texts to briefers and politicians around the world. At the centre, you could shift moods, hail victory or exert glum caution, with unparalleled control. For much of the time the media didn't even realise the scope for manipulation. Access to events was scattered and restricted. The voices of Cheney, Colin Powell and Norman Schwarzkopf dominated. The whole truth came later, if at all. That may be a price the newspaper reader and television viewer will pay for a successful war. But it is not a price that journalists should easily pay. And next time, if there is no brisk success, they will not be thanked by anyone for paying it.[15]

The same situation had in fact been true of the Second World War, a total war which had seen civilians on both sides bombed and which lasted for six years rather than six weeks. In other words, provided a war is perceived as just – and, perhaps even more significantly, winnable – morale would appear to be linked much more directly to the overall perception of the justness of a cause for which lives need to be risked and lost than to media access to bad news or to unpalatable details of specific incidents, battles or blunders.

   As for the role of journalists as custodians of the public's right to know, the Gulf War has presented a new challenge: the public's apparent desire *not* to know beyond the sketchiest details what is going on while it is going on. Whereas journalists see speed as essential to their profession, their readers seemed more than willing to wait until the military could report that a mission had been accomplished before finding out about it.[16] Polls taken during the war in both Britain and the United States indicated a greater sympathy for the arguments of *The Economist* outlined above than for those who were concerned about the extent of the coalition's control over information. So long as the truth comes out in the end, in other words, the democratic publics of Britain and the United States do indeed seem prepared to suspend their right to know, provided they believe the war to be just and the anticipated gains worth the price of the deaths of a certain number of professional soldiers. This, argued Ronald Dworkin after the war, was 'a harmful precedent' because it could be used to justify censorship:

I mean the argument that government may properly manipulate public opinion in order to prevent the public from criticising the war or its conduct. Censorship with that aim is defended not of course on the ground that officials are entitled to protect their own political positions ... but on the more insidious ground that a pleased and supportive public is a great military advantage, that a nation can pursue a war more effectively, win it more quickly, and with fewer of its own soldiers dead and wounded, when the public is on its side.[17]

3 Air power, distance and the distancing role of television

The Gulf War may not have been won solely by the combination of air power and high technology, but it was almost thus. Most of the coalition's casualties were caused either directly by air power or as a consequence of it, owing to 'friendly fire'. The coalition lost 47 planes during the war, 32 of them in combat. Iraq may have been able to amass an army of half a million men in the field – and the Americans and coalition partners to match it in size – but the war belonged primarily to the air force. This had an important consequence for the media coverage of the war. Air power is a notoriously difficult weapon to evaluate for the media. They can interview pilots before and after bombing missions and sometimes – though rarely in the Gulf War – they can accompany crews on their bombing runs. But air power has a unique quality: distance. Once the pilots have released their bombs, the mission has been accomplished and their priority is to return home safely without any undue concern for the consequences of their actions at the receiving end of their weapons. The Gulf War may have appeared to have reduced this distance with the presence of video-cameras in the noses of smart weapons, but the fact remains that, once the bomb impacted, the pictures went blank. One coalition official admitted that the presence of western journalists in Baghdad added a third dimension to the bombing campaign because the damage assessors could see the aftermath of their raids. Or, as one pilot stated:

It certainly was interesting for us to come back and land and watch the [CNN] replays of what it's looking like from another perspective. Knowing where some of the broadcasts were coming from, and seeing the skyline ... we could actually pick out who some of the bombs belonged to ... There was some good in having good old Peter Arnett on the ground.[18]

Nonetheless, the casualties which viewers saw in the Gulf War were mainly Iraqi citizens and, given the historic scale of the air campaign, there were remarkably few of these. And given that the majority of Iraqi military personnel whom viewers saw were surrendering soldiers rather than the remnants of human beings blown apart by smart or, more likely, conventional weaponry, Ian Hargreaves' point made at the start of this Conclusion remains a valid one.

Television not only reinforces this distance, it amplifies it. This is all the more effective as it in fact appears to be doing quite the opposite. This was a war fought by professionals and seen by the public from a distance. On the only occasions when an insight into the real horrors of what occurred at the other end of the bombing was possible, namely at Amiriya and at Mutlah Gap, the images were so horrific that if Iraqi or allied censors did not get to them first then the broadcasters themselves considered the carnage to be too graphic for their audiences to accept, even though the carnage had been wrought on people and soldiers from the enemy side and not from the coalition.

There is considerable evidence to suggest that viewers would not have wanted to see the 'reality' of war anyway so long as the war was going well for the coalition. All the older notions, derived largely from the Vietnam experience, that wars fought before the prying eyes of television cameras were merely bound to alienate audiences and thus undermine the will to fight, might need to be revised. Even the single event which prompted most complaints about British television coverage, the Amiriya bombing, did not shake public support for the war.[19] As Tony Hall, Head of BBC's News and Current Affairs, put it:

Events tend to disprove the idea that if people get to know what happens in a war they would not allow it. Here, viewers, listeners and voters know exactly what's going on and are solidly backing the Government. So if you argue it properly with the viewers, you *can* have a just war and you *can* fight it.[20]

Although there is much to debate in this statement – ie whether viewers knew exactly what was going on and whether the BBC was in fact agreeing that it was toeing the government line and thus serving as its propaganda mouthpiece – an essential point is being made. War is a nasty, brutal business and television viewers know it. That does not mean that they want to see it in full glorious technicolor on their television screens. Liberal intellectuals who instinctively dislike the whole notion of states resolving their international disputes by force may feel that, by showing war in all its horrors, not only will other like-minded people share in their general distaste but other, perhaps not so rational, people may also be exposed to the futility of human beings killing their fellow men and thereby agitate for an end to all war, let alone specific conflicts. Yet the fact remains that this view tends to assume a stance of lofty morality which does not appear to be generally shared outside such circles. The Vietnam War went on for seven more years after the so-called 'turning point' of the Tet Offensive.[21] The Gulf War, as all the polls taken at the time indicated, could well have gone on for longer (though one wonders whether for seven more years) while sustaining overwhelming public support, provided it succeeded not so much in achieving the stated aim of removing Iraq from Kuwait but in actually removing Saddam Hussein from the international scene. The post-war uprising of the Kurds, and the degree of public support and sympathy for those people in that crisis, combined with comparatively open television coverage of living people's suffering, was a major factor in motivating coalition governments to intervene in the establishment of 'safe havens' inside Iraq. This would also suggest that, for most people, the war did indeed end too quickly, in that public aspirations, as distinct from UN goals, were to see the man perceived to have been solely responsible for the war removed from power. Thus a clear distinction was drawn between the Iraqi invasion of Kuwait as a *casus bellum* and the coalition's intervention inside Iraq on humanitarian grounds. In short, the 1970 statement by Sir Robin Day quoted in the Introduction to this book perhaps needs to be reconsidered in this light.

So what kind of war was actually seen? Certainly not the war fought at the point of perhaps its most critical action, namely the front line of Iraqi troops. As the BBC's Mark Urban said after the war:

I think it's undoubtedly true that the greatest failure in the reporting of the war was the impossibility of showing the reality of what the air forces were doing to Saddam Hussein's armed forces, because that really was where the war was won, and that was the reality of probably 90–95% of the killing which went on.[22]

The coalition therefore demonstrated that modern democracies could fight wars, or at least a war of this rather special kind, in the television age without allowing too much of war's 'visible brutality' to appear in the front rooms of their publics. Only that which was deemed acceptable by the warring partners was permitted but, thanks to the presence of western journalists in Baghdad, the illusion was created that war was being fought out in full view of a global audience. However, the absence of cameras in Kuwait or at the Iraqi front line meant that neither the main reason for the war, nor the battlefields where it was mainly won and lost, were being seen. It was in the interests and in the power of neither side to let this happen. Although the Gulf War will undoubtedly be remembered as CNN's war or television's war, it was no such thing. The conflict belonged to the coalition's armed forces, and to the victors went the spoils of the information war.

Notes and references

Introduction

1 *The Independent*, 2/3/91; *The Times*, 2/3/91.
2 R.A. Schroth in the *National Catholic Reporter*, 15/3/91.
3 He added: 'after a while, one gave up suggesting that this was perhaps oversimplifying the situation'. *Reporting the War: a collection of experiences and reflections on the Gulf*, a discussion paper published by the British Executive of the International Press Institute, May 1991 (hereafter *Reporting the War*) p. 18.
4 CNN, 16/1/91, 21:08 EST, University of Leeds, Institute of Communications Studies Gulf War Archive (hereafter ULICS). See also the studio discussion of what one hand tied behind American backs meant – or didn't mean – on ITV, 24/1/91, 00:58 GMT, ULICS.
5 Central Command (hereafter CENTCOM) Briefing, Riyadh, 8/2/91, CNN, ULICS.
6 Cited in Philip M. Taylor, *Munitions of the Mind: War propaganda from the ancient world to the nuclear age* (Patrick Stephens, Wellingborough, 1990) p. 228. Ironically, *Encounter* was to publish its last issue during the Gulf conflict.
7 David E. Morrison and H. Tumber, *Journalists at War: the dynamics of news reporting during the Falklands conflict* (London, Sage, 1988).
8 See, for example, President Bush's statement to American troops made on his Thanksgiving Day visit in November. After the war, the *Bulletin of the Atomic Scientists* (March 1991 issue) published an article by D. Albright and Mark Hibbs entitled 'Hyping the Iraqi Bomb' in which they demonstrated how, just days after a poll on 20 November 1990 indicating that Americans would not be prepared to go to war for oil but they would to prevent Iraq acquiring atomic weapons, President Bush was publicly asserting that Saddam

279

was just months away from this scenario. They concluded that Iraq was in fact 5–10 years away from a usable such device. On 11/7/91 CNN reported that UN officials believed that Iraq possessed enough uranium to develop up to 40 devices. Several days later Iraq disclosed in a 29 page report to the UN and International Atomic Energy Agency that it had 2 kg of enriched uranium: about the size of a golf ball. The US was considering targeting about 100 sites connected with Iraq's secret nuclear programmes if it did not conform to the terms of the cease-fire. On the other hand, Albright and Hibbs seem to have been proved more wrong than Bush in light of what the UN Commission discovered after the war, including the existence of an Iraqi hydrogen bomb project.

9 Saddam, for example, told April Glaspie before the war that 'I do not belittle you but I hold this view by looking at the geography and nature of American society ... Yours is a society which cannot accept 10,000 dead in battle'. Cited by Philip Towle, *Pundits and Patriots: Lessons from the Gulf War* (London, Institute for European Defence and Strategic Studies, 1991) p. 26.

10 *Washington Post*, 19/8/90.

11 See, for example, Saddam's speech to the American people on 25/9/91, ULICS. For a British 'profile' of CNN see BBC2, The Late Show, 22/1/91, ULICS. For an interesting wartime discussion of the media coverage and of Mark Urban's analysis, see also The Late Show, BBC2, 30/1/91, ULICS.

12 Stephen Robinson, 'Fighting for Screen Time', *Spectator*, 12/1/91.

13 This charge was made by Senator Alan Simpson following the Amiriya bunker/shelter incident of 13 February and was based upon alleged Vietcong links through Arnett's ex-Vietnamese wife. In April 1990, during a visit to Iraq, Senator Simpson had informed Saddam that the dictator's main problems were not with the US government but with the western media. *Washington Post National Weekly Edition*, 18–24/2/91. Simpson later apologised.

14 Mark Lawson in *The Independent*, 21/1/91.

15 At the end of June 1991, for example, the American Newspaper Publishers' Association urged Dick Cheney to meet leaders of the media industry to discuss their complaints about the stifling of their wartime coverage. *Guardian*, 1/7/91.

16 John Naughton in the *Observer*, 20/1/91.

17 Cited by Stephen Robinson in the *Spectator*, op. cit.

18 Ibid.

19 Peregrine Worsthorne's profile of Peter Arnett in the *Sunday Telegraph*, 24/2/91.

20 G. Meade, 'Hard Groundrules in the Sand', *Index on Censorship*,

Vol. 20, Nos 4 & 5, April/May 1991, p. 7.

21 Ibid.
22 This phrase is taken from Philip Schlesinger's book of the same title (Constable, 1978) and which is essential reading for an understanding of the making of news.
23 John Simpson, *From the House of War* (London, Arrow Books, 1991) pp. xv–xvi.
24 Cited by Jeremy Paxman on BBC2's Newsnight, 6/2/91, ULICS.
25 CNN's Pentagon correspondent, Wolf Blitzer, was asked why so many anonymous sources were prepared to leak information when it was known Saddam would be watching. His reply was: 'That's a good question and reporters never know why confidential sources reveal certain information ... as a good reporter you try to weigh carefully, you try to weigh the motivations, certainly you try to weigh the information that has been provided by those sources in the past; has that information proven to be accurate in the past? If it hasn't then of course you're not going to trust those sources in the future. In the end it becomes a judgement call'. CNN, 8/2/91, 21:15 GMT, ULICS.
26 Two examples of this could be seen when Charles Jaco for CNN was shown on ITV, 17/1/91, 00:13 GMT, and Alex Thompson was shown on Channel 4 News at 19:00 GMT, 18/1/91. Thompson also admitted he did this on BBC2's The Late Show, 'Tales from the Gulf', 6/6/91, ULICS.
27 By early February, American psychologists were already encountering what they called the 'CNN Complex', *The Times*, 7/2/91.
28 *The Times*, 'Real Time Blues', 22/1/91. The leader was discussing the general relationship of television to politics.
29 *New York Times*, 21/2/91.
30 *Spectrum*, Summer 1991, p. 7.
31 Ibid.
32 For a description of battlefield communications technology, see L. Covens, 'Mobile Radio in the Gulf War', *Global Communications*, May–June 1991, pp. 20–7.
33 Cited by R.A. Schroth, op. cit., 15/3/91.
34 *Newsweek*, 25/2/91.
35 *Independent on Sunday*, 2/9/90.
36 J. Ellul, *Propaganda: the formation of men's attitudes* (London, Vintage reprint, 1973). For democratic propaganda, see also T.H. Qualter, *Opinion Control in the Democracies* (London, Macmillan, 1985).
37 J.C.W. Reith, *Into the Wind* (London, Hodder & Stoughton, 1949) p. 354.

38 The most significant works on the employment of propaganda by inter-war Britain are N. Pronay, 'The First Reality: Film Censorship in Liberal England' in K.R.M. Short (ed.), *Feature Films as History* (London, Croom-Helm, 1981); N. Pronay, 'Rearmament and the British public: policy and propaganda' in J. Curran, A. Smith & P. Wingate (eds), *Impacts and Influences: Essays on Media Power in the Twentieth Century* (London, Methuen, 1987); Philip M. Taylor, *The Projection of Britain, British Overseas Publicity and Propaganda, 1919–39* (Cambridge University Press, 1981); D. Le Mahieu, *A Culture for Democracy: Mass Communication and the Cultivated Mind in Britain between the Wars* (Oxford University Press, 1988); R. Cockett, *Twilight of Truth: Chamberlain, Appeasement and the Manipulation of the Press* (London, Weidenfeld & Nicolson, 1989).

39 Arthur Ponsonby, *Falsehood in Wartime* (London, 1928; Garland reprint 1971) p. 18.

40 There are numerous works dealing with the British Second World War propaganda experience but in particular see Michael Balfour, *Propaganda in War, 1939–45* (London, Routledge & Kegan Paul, 1979); I. McLaine, *Ministry of Morale* (London, Allen & Unwin, 1979); H. Norman Cole, *Britain and the War of Words in Neutral Europe, 1939–45* (London, Macmillan, 1989); and P.M.H. Bell, *John Bull and the Bear* (London, Edward Arnold, 1990).

41 J.A.C. Brown, *Techniques of Persuasion: from propaganda to brainwashing* (Harmondsworth, Penguin, 1963) p. 21.

42 R. Taylor, *Film Propaganda: Soviet Russia and Nazi Germany* (London, Croom-Helm, 1979) p. 25.

43 Taylor, *Munitions of the Mind*, op. cit., pp. 21–3. An NBC Gulf Special carried an item on these comparisons, including this quotation, and concluded: 'Saddam Hussein's rhetoric has a long pedigree – and so does his savagery'. BSkyB carried this item on 20/1/91 at 13:15 GMT, ULICS.

44 *Guardian*, 29/1/91.

45 Samir Al-Khalil, *The Republic of Fear* (London, Hutchinson Radius, May 1991 edition).

46 'News and Propaganda', *The Times,* 21/1/91. Reprinted in Brian MacArthur, *Despatches from the Gulf War* (London, Bloomsbury, 1991) pp. 44–6.

47 *Guardian*, 7/1/91.

48 Barry Flynn, *Television Week,* 28 February–6 March 1991.

49 Ibid.

50 *International Herald Tribune*, 22/1/91.

51 This was Sir Peter de la Billiere's phrase as reported by ITN, 22:12 GMT, 25/1/91, ULICS.

52 Quoted in R. Pyle, *Schwarzkopf: the man, the mission, the triumph* (London, Mandarin, 1991) p. 41.
53 *Financial Times*, 21/1/91.
54 See, for example, *Financial Times*, 9/2/91.
55 W.A. Arkin, D. Durrant and M. Cherni, *On Impact: Modern Warfare and the Environment. A Case Study of the Gulf War* (Washington, Greenpeace, May 1991).

Chapter One

1 For the record, the games were Leeds v Aston Villa (4–1), Chelsea v Spurs (0–0) and Southampton v Manchester United (1–1).
2 ITV stayed with CNN continuously until 00:36 GMT when John Suchet began anchoring that night's uninterrupted programme with Edward Stourton, returning to CNN, as well as carrying items from ABC and CBS, when appropriate, throughout the night.
3 My source for this information is an off-air discussion in ITN's Washington studio, monitored on the Brightstar satellite downlink at 07:45 EST on 18 January 1991 in the Institute of Communications Studies, Leeds University and stored in its Gulf War videotape archive (hereafter ULICS). Many of the subsequent quotations from the television coverage which are not referenced are taken from this archive; only specific references to the television coverage the source of which is not immediately obvious from the text will be footnoted.
4 The BBC began with Marlin Fitzwater's brief statement and also used CNN intermittently throughout the night. BBC1, 17/1/91, ULICS.
5 *Independent on Sunday*, 20/1/91.
6 *Sunday Telegraph*, 20/1/91.
7 *International Herald Tribune*, 18/1/91.
8 *Observer*, 20/1/91.
9 Until ABC resumed after just over one hour of non-stop coverage. NBC held off until 05:10 EST the next morning, CBS until 10:13 EST. *Washington Post*, 18/1/91.
10 *Observer*, 20/1/91.
11 *The Times*, 22/1/91. For an item on French coverage of the war see *The Times*, 6/2/91.
12 Stephen Robinson, 'Fighting for Screen Time', *Spectator*, 12/1/91. For a brief history of US military–media relations and the evolution of reporting restrictions for the Gulf War see Nan Levinson, 'Snazzy visuals, hard facts and obscured issues' in *Index on Censorship*, Vol. 20, Nos 4 & 5, April/May 1991, pp. 27–8.
13. The 12 American rules, listed on a single sheet, prevented the

publication or broadcast of information concerning numbers of troops, aircraft, weapons, equipment and supplies; future land and operations; locations of forces; and tactics. Bob Woodward, *The Commanders* (New York, Simon & Schuster, 1991) p. 368.

14 *The Times*, 7/1/91.

15 Robert Fox in *Reporting the War*, p. 13.

16 P. Knightley, 'A Warrior Race turns a blind eye to battle', *Independent on Sunday*, 13/1/91. Channel 4 News ran an extensive report on these guidelines and the history of censorship in war on 14/1/91 at 19:40 GMT, ULICS.

17 ITN, 15:48 GMT, 17/1/91; BBC1, 15:48 17/1/91, ULICS; *Financial Times*, 24/1/91.

18 This was effectively admitted by John Wakeham, MP, minister responsible for information policy in Britain, when he wrote that 'our experience in the present conflict is that, generally, the media are acting in accordance with the relevant guidelines', *Index on Censorship*, Vol. 20, Nos 4 & 5, April/May 1991, p. 16.

19 *The Independent*, 17/1/91; *Financial Times*, 24/1/91. Certain Conservative Party MPs had already complained about too much television coverage and the dangers of both providing Saddam with clues to allied intentions through speculation and upsetting the families of troops in the Middle East. *The Times*, 22/1/91. Instead of issuing specific warnings, the Prime Minister in the House of Commons merely asked the media to exercise restraint and sensitivity in covering casualties. *The Times*, 23/1/91.

20 For a profile of Craig see *The Times*, 26/1/91. The first wartime MoD briefing was shown live on BBC1 at 12:10 GMT on 17/1/91, ULICS.

21 *Daily Star* 18/1/91. The story was under the headline 'A bunch of tankers – 2'.

22 *The Independent*, 21/1/91. BSkyB carried the teach-in live on 20/1/91 from 15:03 GMT onwards, ULICS. Tom King was joined by Air Vice Marshal Thompson and Sir David Craig. The presentation included slides of aircraft, standard promotional material, and the video, taken in bad weather, which was difficult to view clearly. Even the interviewed pilots were mute.

23 *The Times*, 21/1/91. *Today* also ran a critical leader on the same day.

24 *Daily Telegraph*, 26/1/91. After 25/1/91, MoD briefings were rarely televised live. For the last regular such briefing see BBC1 10:31 GMT on that date, ULICS.

25 *The Times*, 21/1/91.

26 For a profile of Powell, see Martin Walker in the *Guardian*, 11/2/91.

27 Pyle, *Schwarzkopf*, op cit., p. 103.
28 Ibid., p. 164.
29 Stephen Robinson in the *Daily Telegraph*, 5/2/91.
30 See, for example, the *Washington Post* of 21/2/91 in which Henry Allen argued that 'The Persian Gulf briefings are making reporters look like fools, nit-pickers and egomaniacs ... It is a silly spectacle'.
31 CENTCOM Briefing, Riyadh, CNN, 18/1/91, ULICS. Reprinted in Pyle, op. cit., pp. 169–84.
32 Voice of America broadcast, 17/1/91. I am indebted to Mr Gary Rawnsley for letting me have copies of short wave radio broadcasts which he monitored privately during the Gulf War. ITN also stated that the Iraqi air force had been 'decimated' at 05:58 GMT, ULICS. Brian Hanrahan revealed the point about the 100 Iraqi airfields, whereupon David Dimbleby said he didn't know there were so many. BBC1, 17/1/91, 11:39 GMT, ULICS.
33 *International Herald Tribune*, 18/1/91.
34 This was Paul Johnson's phrase in the *Daily Mail*, 19/1/91.
35 See in particular John Swain's pooled despatch in the *Sunday Times*, 18/1/91, reprinted in MacArthur, *Despatches from the Gulf War*, op. cit., pp. 61–3.
36 *Washington Post*, 22/1/91.
37 CENTCOM Briefing, Riyadh, CNN, 18/1/91, 12:07 GMT, ULICS. Reproduced in Pyle, op. cit., p. 169.
38 Ibid.
39 *Washington Times*, 23/1/91; *New York Times*, 23/1/91.
40 As evidenced in Rear Admiral Mike McConnell's briefing with Thomas Kelly at the Pentagon on the first day. Pentagon Briefing, Washington, CNN, 18/1/91, ULICS.
41 28/1/91. CENTCOM announced that this was the first time a cruise missile had been launched from a submarine. BBC, Evening News, 17:00 GMT, 26/1/91, ULICS.
42 *New York Times*, 24/5/91.
43 Ibid.
44 Mathew d'Ancona, 'LOW warspeak', *Index on Censorship*, Vol. 20, Nos 4 & 5, April/May 1991, p. 9. See also the *Guardian*, 23/1/91, in which it was pointed out that 'we have ... press briefings' and 'they have ... propaganda', 'our boys ... are young knights of the sky' whereas 'theirs are ... Bastards of Baghdad', and so on. This was picked up by the BBC2 programme 'What the Papers Say' on 25/1/91, 19:52 GMT. ULICS.
45 CENTCOM Briefing, Riyadh, CNN, 18/1/91, ULICS; *Guardian*, 19/1/91.
46 *Observer*, 20/1/91.

47 *International Herald Tribune*, 21/1/91.

48 *Observer*, 20/1/91.

49 Pyle, *Schwarzkopf*, op. cit., p. 170.

50 Pentagon Briefing, Washington, CNN, 11:00 EST, 17/1/91, ULICS. *International Herald Tribune*, 18/1/91; *Financial Times*, 19–20/1/91.

51 The full text of this statement is printed in the *International Herald Tribune*, 19–20/1/91. See also *The Independent*, 19/1/91. Air Chief Marshal Sir Patrick Hine, overall commander of the British armed forces, also admitted that he had been worried by the initial euphoria when he suggested that the air campaign was falling slightly behind schedule due to bad weather. BBC1, 21:15 GMT, 31/1/91, ULICS. John Major also attempted a similar campaign of cautioning against a quick victory. See *The Independent*, 18/1/91.

52 *Financial Times*, 23/1/91.

53 CNN of course used this filmed statement as part of its self-advertisement for the rest of the war and beyond.

54 *Guardian*, 30/1/91.

55 In America, in a *New York Times*/CBS poll, 79% believed that Bush did the right thing in starting the war, while an ABC News poll showed 83% backing for the war; in the UK, an NOP published in the *Sunday Times*, 20/1/91, showed 84% of people 'satisfied' or 'very satisfied' with the government's performance. See also *Financial Times*, 21/1/91.

56 *The Independent*, 17/1/91; BBC1, 17/1/91 15:55 GMT, ULICS.

57 Complaints about saturation coverage in Britain prompted John Birt, then Deputy Director-General of the BBC, to respond on 25/1/91 at 08:36 GMT, BBC1, ULICS.

58 *The Independent*, 21/1/91. He also repeated these arguments in his report for BBC2's The Late Show, 30/1/91, ULICS.

59 *The Times*, 23/1/91.

60 *Sun*, 16/1/91. Note that this was the day the UN deadline expired but before the war actually started. For the British press reaction to the war see *The Independent*, 17/1/91.

61 Vanessa Redgrave's statement to a peace rally in Barcelona just days prior to the war, which she claimed had been taken out of context, prompted her to place a full-scale advertisement in the press on 8 February outlining her fuller position, while CNN carried an item on 30 January about the nervousness of Hollywood stars in voicing their opposition to the war, with the exception of Ed Asner. This was transmitted at 22:54 EST. It should be pointed out that other Hollywood personalities were prepared to reflect the mood of public support for the troops, with the likes of Meryl Streep, Kevin

Kostner, Whoopi Goldberg and Sissy Spacek taking part in recording a song 'Voices that Care' in the middle of the war. The song however was largely non-political and the incident is discussed in the *Daily Telegraph*, 13/2/91. The Rolling Stones were to release a far more critical song during the war, 'High Wire', which criticised those who had supplied Saddam's arms in the first place.

62 *New York Times*, 24/5/91. In the case of Britain, it was certainly true that anti-war groups were barely represented on the major news bulletins, but they were given more opportunity to air their views on various current affairs programmes, most notably ITV's Midnight Special which regularly interviewed dissenting individuals. However, the scheduling of this through-the-night programme ensured that viewing figures would be much lower. The two most notable programmes about the anti-war movement in the war were 'The Gulf Between Us' and 'Hell No We Wont Go', screened by Channel 4 on 27 & 28 February. See Steve Bell, 'The Presentation of Dissent in the British Media during the Gulf War', M.A. thesis, University of Leeds, Institute of Communications Studies, 1991.

63 Mark Laity in *Reporting the War*, p. 27.

64 As spoken by T.J. Russert, Washington chief of NBC News, *International Herald Tribune*, 19–20/1/91.

65 *Daily Telegraph*, 22/1/91.

66 *International Herald Tribune*, 21/1/91.

67 *Independent on Sunday*, 20/1/91.

68 Pentagon Briefing, Washington, CNN, 19:00 GMT, ULICS; *Financial Times*, 24/1/91.

69 W. Boot, 'The Pool', *Columbia Journalism Review*, May–June 1991, p. 25.

70 *Guardian*, 24/1/91.

71 *Reporting the War*, p. 9.

72 'Tales from the Gulf', The Late Show, BBC2, 6/6/91, ULICS.

73 *Daily Telegraph*, 15/2/91.

74 Originally reported by the *Washington Post*, 26/1/91, the *Independent on Sunday* picked up the item on 27/1/91.

75 Patrick Bishop in *Reporting the War*, p. 19.

76 *Time*, 18/2/91.

77 *The Times*, 8/2/91; Levinson, op. cit., p. 28.

78 Cited in M. Massing, 'Debriefings: what we saw, what we learned', *Columbia Journalism Review*, May–June 1991, p. 23.

79 *The Times*, 4/2/91 and 8/2/91.

80 *Reporting the War*, p. 2.

81 BBC1, 18:12 GMT, 3/2/91, ULICS.

82 *Reporting the War*, p. 6.

83 Ibid, p. 3.
84 Ibid, p. 13. The piece to which Fox was referring was published in the *Daily Telegraph*, 12/2/91. Incidentally, although the point about prison is indeed missing, the printed quotations read: 'I like it out here. I like the space of the desert' and 'Yeah, just one big happy family'.
85 See Morrison and Tumber, *Journalists at War* , op. cit., chapter 6.
86 *Reporting the War*, pp. 1–3.
87 Ibid, pp. 3–5.
88 Ibid.
89 Ibid, p. 7.
90 *Financial Times*, 16/3/91.
91 *Reporting the War*, p. 12.
92 Ibid.
93 *Washington Post Weekly Edition*, 18–24/2/91.
94 *Daily Telegraph*, 22/1/91.
95 *International Herald Tribune*, 22/1/91.
96 This point was made in a discussion between various journalists transmitted live on NBC at 10:00 EST on 13/2/91, shown on BSkyB, ULICS.
97 *International Herald Tribune*, 22/1/91.
98 *Reporting the War*, p. 2.
99 *Financial Times*, 16/3/91, as told by Ed Cody, pool reporter for the *Washington Post*.
100 G. Meade, 'Hard Groundrules in the Sand', op. cit., p. 6.
101 *The Independent*, 6/2/91.
102 *Reporting the War*, p. 11.
103 *Time*, 18/2/91.
104 *Reporting the War*, p. 23.
105 Pinder in Ibid., p. 4.
106 *The Times*, 8/2/91.
107 Fisk's first article which caused such a fuss was carried by *The Independent*'s front page on 23/1/91 under the headline 'Tanks bogged down in unmapped mud and confusion'. Interestingly, even at this early stage, *The Independent* itself received complaints from readers questioning the wisdom of publishing such articles. The letters editor wrote: 'I have found this correspondence disquieting, for it suggests that the urge to censor in wartime is not restricted to the authorities, and that our claim that we wish to print the truth as we find it, on behalf of our readers, is perhaps a little thinner than we might like to contemplate.' See Mathew Hoffman, 'Readers' Revolt' in *Index on Censorship*, Vol. 20, Nos 4 & 5, April/May 1991, p. 7.

108 *Guardian,* 27/5/91.
109 Massing, 'Debriefings', op. cit., p. 23.
110 *The Independent,* 6/2/91
111 Article XIX, *Stop Press: The Gulf War and Censorship,* Issue 2, May 1991, p. 9.
112 *The Times,* 26/1/91.
113 *New York Times,* 12/2/91.
114 *Washington Post,* 2/3/91. Bob Simon was interviewed on CNN on the Larry King Show on 3/7/91 when he described his experience. He said then that the Iraqis were accusing them of being spies, and that they were placed in solitary confinement and beaten. He went back to Iraq in May 1991 and said that locals had told him privately that they felt the war had ended too soon.
115 CNN 14/2/91, 10:30 GMT, ULICS. See also Richard Dowden's piece on this attack in *The Independent,* 14/2/91.
116 *The Independent,* 7/2/91.
117 Dowden in 'Tales from the Gulf', The Late Show, BBC2, 6/6/91, ULICS.
118 Ibid.
119 This observation was made by William Boot who kept a diary throughout his time in the pool which was published after the war in *The Columbia Journalism Review,* May–June 1991, pp. 24–7.
120 *The Times,* 22/1/91.
121 *Reporting the War,* p. 26.
122 Ibid, p. 27.
123 Tony Walker in the *Financial Times,* 6/2/91.
124 *Reporting the War,* p. 27.
125 Con Coughlin in the *Daily Telegraph,* 5/2/91.
126 *The Times,* 14/2/91.
127 *The Times,* 25/1/91 on Henderson.
128 *The Times,* 14/2/91.
129 As quoted in *Time,* 4/2/91.
130 *New York Times,* 17/2/91.
131 *Daily Telegraph,* 19/1/91.
132 *The Independent,* 19/1/91.
133 BSkyB's Review of the War, 1/3/91, ULICS.
134 *International Herald Tribune,* 25/1/91.
135 *The Times,* 23/1/91.
136 *Time,* 4/2/91.
137 *Guardian,* 30/1/91.
138 *The Independent,* 21/1/91.
139 As quoted in the *Daily Telegraph,* 21/1/91.
140 This interview was shown on BSkyB on 20/1/91 at 14:30 GMT,

ULICS; *International Herald Tribune*, 21/1/91.

141 *Daily Telegraph*, 22/1/91.

142 CNN, 21:50 GMT onwards, 20/1/91, ULICS; Daily Telegraph, 21/1/91.

143 *Daily Telegraph*, 21/1/91.

144 *International Herald Tribune*, 22/1/91.

145 BSkyB, 28/3/91, ULICS.

146 *The Independent*, 23/1/91.

147 *International Herald Tribune*, 23/1/91.

148 ITN, 22:20 GMT, 25/1/91; BBC, 17:15 GMT, 26/1/91, ULICS. See the *Independent on Sunday*, 27/1/91 for table of Scud statistics.

149 *The Independent*, 25/1/91. Much emphasis was given to the Australian role in relaying these signals from the Middle East to the USA on BBC1's Evening News, 17:15 GMT, 26/1/91, ULICS.

150 *The Times*, 12/2/91. See also Channel 4's Equinox programme on the high-tech weaponry of the Gulf War, transmitted on 11/8/91, ULICS.

151 *International Herald Tribune*, 29/1/91.

152 *International Herald Tribune*, 23/1/91.

153 Reprinted in *International Herald Tribune*, 24/1/91.

154 CNN, 23:31 GMT, 30/1/91, ULICS.

155 Reprinted in *International Herald Tribune*, 24/1/91.

156 *Daily Telegraph*, 25/1/91.

157 *Daily Telegraph*, 22/1/91. If this was designed to prevent the Iraqis from gathering invaluable information concerning weather conditions, it should be borne in mind that CNN, received in Baghdad, continued to transmit regular bulletins and forecasts.

158 *Daily Telegraph*, 18/2/91.

159 Pentagon Briefing, Washington, CNN, 19:45 GMT, 24/1/91, ULICS; *International Herald Tribune*, 25/1/91; *The Times*, 25/1/91.

160 Ibid.

161 *The Independent*, 25/1/91.

162 *International Herald Tribune*, 26–27/1/91.

163 *The Independent*, 28/1/91. The story made the front page of the *Sun* with the headline 'She's off to Africa with the kids', 19/1/91. *Today* described Sajida Hussein as 'the Imelda Marcos of the Middle East' who 'even while the poor people of Iraq grovelled in the streets for food ... paid £350 million for the Empress of Iran's fabulous jewellery collection', 19/1/91.

164 *The Independent*, 26/1/91; *The Times*, 26/1/91.

165 Although this Interfax agency appears to have been genuine, formed as a result of *glasnost* within the Soviet Union, this was its first major international coup. However, doubts as to its veracity be-

cause of this were raised, especially as its report was monitored by the BBC Monitoring Service at Caversham. See BBC1, 21/1/91 at 11:46 GMT, ULICS. This may indeed have been an elaborate coalition black propaganda exercise, although an Interfax correspondent who appeared to be genuine was interviewed in Moscow, which was carried by BBC1 at 13:03 GMT on 21/1/91, ULICS.

166 For a wartime profile of Saddam, see BBC1's Panorama, 11/2/91, 21:35 GMT, ULICS.

167 ITN, 22:17 GMT, 24/1/91. BBC1's report of this victory was reported – without pictures – at 07:00 GMT on 25/1/91, ULICS; see also the *Daily Telegraph*, 25 and 26/1/91.

168 *Daily Telegraph*, 26/1/91. One amusing footnote to this story was carried in the Peterborough column of the same issue of that newspaper. Because the BBC had no immediate pictures of the island of its own, it snapped at the opportunity of a photograph taken several years earlier by a scuba diver on holiday with his girlfriend and who had tried to breed rabbits on the rock. The part of the picture which showed his girlfriend bending over was airbrushed out by the BBC when it was broadcast.

169 *The Independent*, 26/1/91. For the role of the Kuwaiti forces in the rock's liberation, complete with interviews with officers involved in the operation, see ITV 21:59 GMT, 27/1/91, ULICS.

170 ITN, 22:20 GMT 24/1/91, ULICS. The Qurah story and the Saudi pilot's heroics made the front page of *The Independent*, 25/1/91. *The Times* carried it on page three, 25/1/91.

171 *The Independent*, 26/1/91.

172 CENTCOM Briefing, Riyadh, 27/1/91, CNN, ULICS; *The Times*, 28/1/91.

173 *The Times*, 28/1/91 for Genscher; BBC, 13:00 GMT, 27/1/91 for Boomer.

174 *The Independent*, 28/1/91. Great play of the violation of Islamic law was made by Dr Abdulbar Al-Gain of the Saudi Environmental Agency at a press conference screened in part on BBC, 27/1/91 at 13:00 GMT. It was not until BBC1's Six O'Clock News on 28 January that it became clear to British viewers that there were in fact three separate slicks. ULICS.

175 *The Independent*, 29/1/91; Kelly's statement was given a small paragraph tucked at the bottom of the front page.

176 'Lies, damned lies and military briefings', *New Statesman and Society*, 8/2/91.

177 *The Independent*, 30/1/91.

178 Pentagon Briefing, Washington, CNN, 25/1/91, ULICS.

179 Peter Sharpe's story was transmitted on ITN at 22:12 GMT,

25/1/91, ULICS. Jeremy Thompson's earlier report was shown on ITN, 14:00 GMT, 17/1/91, ULICS.

180 *Reporting the War*, op. cit., p. 20.

181 Arkin, Durrant and Cherni, *On Impact*, op. cit., p. 11.

182 *International Herald Tribune*, 4/2/91.

183 CENTCOM Briefing, Riyadh, CNN, 27/1/91, ULICS. BBC1's Evening News on Saturday 26/1/91 carried a pool report by Brian Barron stating that 'whoever is to blame, the impact of the disaster on the Arabian environment is all too plain' and that because the oil was sinking below the surface 'it shouldn't inhibit any American amphibious operation', ULICS.

184 *The Times*, 28/1/91. The news was released only at the Sunday evening briefings.

185 Arkin et al., *On Impact*, op. cit., pp. 62–3.

186 These were among the disturbing findings of Greenpeace, as reported by ITN at 12:45 GMT, 4/9/91.

187 *The Times*, 31/1/91. For the initial television reports see BBC, 27/1/91, 13:05 GMT, ULICS.

188 *Independent on Sunday*, 27/1/91. See also *The Independent*, 24/1/91.

189 *The Independent*, 29/1/91; *International Herald Tribune*, 29/1/91.

190 *Financial Times*, 29/1/91; *International Herald Tribune*, 29/1/91. BBC1, 18:08 GMT, 28/1/91, ULICS.

191 As reported first by John Sweeney from Riyadh, 04:45 local time, CNN, 17/1/91, ULICS.

192 *The Times*, 23/1/91.

193 *The Independent*, 30/1/91. For an example of the debate within the United States, see the heated exchanges between Robert Grant of the American Freedom Coalition and the Reverend Robert Drinan of the Georgetown University Law Center on CNN, 8/2/91, 22:30 GMT, ULICS. The Pope's anti-war stance was given minimal coverage in the British media.

194 BBC1, 18:16 GMT, 30/1/91, ULICS.

195 *The Times*, 31/1/91.

Chapter 2

1 *The Independent*, 21/3/91.

2 *Independent on Sunday*, 20/1/91; *Newsweek*, 25/2/91.

3 This empirical statement is based upon the findings of the audience survey conducted by Dr David Morrison for the Institute of Communications Studies during the Gulf War, the findings of which will be published shortly. The results of this survey are based upon 10

group discussions carried out in mid-March 1991, consisting of 8–10 respondents per group. The groups were each single-sex – 5 male, 5 female – and were further split by age and social grade as follows: 1. Male C1/C2 (age 16–34); 2. Female C1/C2 (16–34); 3. Male C1/C2 (35–55); 4. Female C1/C2 (35–55); 5. Male C1/C2 (16–34); 6. Female C1/C2 (35–55); 7. Male AB (16–34); 8. Female AB (16–34); 9. Male AB (35–55); 10. Female AB (35–55). The group discussions were carried out in the North (Leeds), Midlands (Birmingham) and South (London) of England.

4 *The Times*, 18/1/91. This point was confirmed at 18:55 EST by Peter Arnett on CNN, 17/1/91, ULICS. John Simpson testified that 'President Bush himself telephoned various American editors to urge them to evacuate their teams. That frightened a lot of people'. John Simpson, *From the House of War*, op. cit., p. 277.

5 Lamis Andoni in the *Financial Times*, 25/1/91.

6 John Simpson, *From the House of War*, op. cit., pp. 281–2. The Iraqi expectation of massive damage to the city in the initial strike would appear to be confirmed by ambassador Al-Salihi's statement the next day that 'I have no details about casualties but they should be very heavy'. See the *Daily Mirror*, 18/1/91.

7 Lamis Andoni in the *Financial Times*, 25/1/91. Marie Colvin also published a graphic account of how journalists coped with the outbreak of war in Baghdad in the *Sunday Times*, 27/1/91.

8 *Observer*, 20/1/91.

9 *Time*, 28/1/91. Simpson also testified to the ferocity of competition between the journalists in Baghdad. See *From the House of War*, op. cit., p. 300.

10 *The Independent*, 18/1/91.

11 *Wall Street Journal*, 7/2/91.

12 *Washington Post*, 18/1/91.

13 CNN, 14:01 GMT, 17/1/91, ULICS.

14 *Observer*, 20/1/91.

15 *Daily Telegraph*, 18/1/91. According to Richard Measham, Editor of World Broadcasting Information, Iraqi radio had closed down for the night, came back on the air normally at 02:30 but made no reference to war's outbreak until 03:30. He also pointed out that it was difficult to monitor Baghdad radio and that jamming was going on. BBC1 17/1/91, 11:50 GMT, ULICS.

16 *Guardian*, 18/1/91. Udai survived the war and was reported resuming his playboy life-style in Baghdad in the summer of 1991.

17 *Sunday Times*, 27/1/91.

18 As carried by BSkyB on 17/1/91, ULICS; *Guardian*, 19/1/91.

19 *Guardian*, 18/1/91.

20 *Guardian*, 19/1/91.

21 *Guardian*, 18/1/91; *International Herald Tribune*, 18/1/91.

22 *Guardian*, 19/1/91. This claim was repeated a week or so later on the Mother of All Battles radio station that began transmitting from Kuwait. *The Independent*, 29/1/91.

23 Sky's Review of the War, an excellent piece of instant television history-montage, transmitted at 18:30 on 1/3/91. Al-Hashimi first made the claim on 19/1/91. When Dan Rather interviewed him for CBS the next day, an interview carried by BSkyB at 09:40 GMT on 20/1/91 he stated: 'Israel has retaliated today because Israeli planes today participated in the raid that took place today ... . They moved yesterday from Israel to Saudi Arabia and participated today,' ULICS.

24 *Daily Telegraph*, 22/1/91.

25 ITN, 17/1/91, ULICS; *Daily Telegraph*, 18/1/91. Richard Beeston of *The Times* kept a diary for the first three days, published on his departure from Iraq on 22/1/91.

26 Beeston in *Reporting the War*, p. 32.

27 *Financial Times*, 25/1/91.

28 Richard Beeston in *The Times*, 9/2/91.

29 *The Times*, 21/1/91; *Daily Telegraph*, 22/1/91.

30 *Daily Telegraph*, 18/1/91; *The Independent*, 19/1/91. See also John Simpson, *From the House of War*, op. cit., p. 302. Towards the end of the war, on 25/2/91 Jeremy Bowen was about to broadcast live from Baghdad to the BBC in London but his minder had yet to turn up. When asked off-air to begin anyway, he refused saying 'It compromises our operation here far too much. They'll simply take it out on us in terms of denying us the chance to do things like this.' The minder then turned up and he began his interview. Visnews feed, 25/2/91, 15:42, ULICS.

31 *Reporting the War*, p. 32. It was also John Simpson's view that the Baghdad administration was caught in total disarray by the attack. BBC1, 17/1/91, 11:20 & 13:23 GMT. For Brent Sadler's report on the order to leave, see ITV, 19/1/91, 13:11 GMT, ULICS.

32 *Observer*, 20/1/91.

33 *Financial Times*, 25/1/91.

34 *Washington Post*, 20/1/91.

35 This could often work extremely overtly, as in the case of a report by John Cookson from Tel Aviv for BSkyB on 20/1/91 at 10:05 GMT. Following a shot of a military convoy the screen went black and a caption stating 'Israeli Army Censor' was placed on screen for several seconds. ULICS.

36 *International Herald Tribune*, 2–3/2/91. Stanger's credentials were

restored several days later, with an apology, after it was ascertained that the offending photograph in the 4 February issue had come from an independent photo agency. *International Herald Tribune*, 7/2/91.

37 *Washington Post*, 20/1/91. John Simpson also described the remarkable accuracy of the initial air strikes on his first broadcast out of Baghdad on the morning of 17/1/91. It was in this report that he described vividly how he had seen a cruise missile flying down the street passing the Al-Rashid hotel. BBC1, 10:10 GMT, ULICS. Simpson again spoke of his observations with a filmed report shown on BBC2, 17:02, 18/1/91, ULICS.

38 *Financial Times*, 25/1/91. John Simpson did the same, taking a cameraman to film damage, only to be arrested briefly. BBC1, 17/1/91, 13:23 GMT. ULICS.

39 *Sunday Telegraph*, 20/1/91.

40 *Observer*, 3/2/91; *Sunday Telegraph*, 10/2/91.

41 CNN transmitted this report by Arnett on Sunday 20/1/91. The BBC crew had actually filmed this incident and the resultant fire but their tape had been confiscated. See Simpson, *From the House of War*, op. cit., pp. 310–11. BBC1 also carried Iraqi TV pictures of a cruise missile soaring towards its target at 21:05 GMT on 21/1/91, ULICS. The dramatic nature of footage of cruise missiles being used for the first time in anger was commented upon by the *Daily Telegraph* on 21/1/91.

42 *The Times*, 21/1/91.

43 CNN, 20/1/91, ULICS. Arnett denied he had said this after the war, saying he had said he was the only western television journalist left, 'Tales from the Gulf', The Late Show, BBC2, 6/6/91, ULICS.

44 Ibid. On 25/1/91, BBC1 had pointed out that Arnett was not the only western journalist left in Iraq and that Rojo was having difficulties in persuading the CNN reporter to use his communications equipment. 07:37 GMT, ULICS.

45 *International Herald Tribune*, 21/1/91; *The Times*, 23/1//91.

46 See the *Observer*, 20/1/91.

47 *Reporting the War*, p. 9.

48 *Financial Times*, 25/1/91.

49 BBC1's 18:00 GMT news on 21/1/91 led on this story, which gave particular emphasis to the question of war crimes. See also *The Independent*, 22/1/91.

50 BBC1, 29/1/91, 13:01 GMT, ULICS. This was the lead story.

51 BBC2's The Late Show, 22:30 GMT, 22/1/91.

52 Sky's Review of the War, 18:30, 1/3/91, ULICS.

53 T.B. Allen, F. Clifton Berry & N. Polmar, *CNN: War in the Gulf.*

From the invasion of Kuwait to the day of victory and beyond
(London, Maxwell–Macmillan International, 1991) p. 143. It
emerged on 2/8/91 that all of the pilots had been tortured and that
the image and the reality were one and the same thing. See the
Sunday Times, 4/8/91. For an account of David Waddington's
experience of torture at the hands of his Iraqi captors, see Charles
Allen, *Thunder and Lightning. The RAF in the Gulf: Personal
Experiences of War* (London, HMSO, 1991) pp. 97–102.

54 See for example the *Daily Star*, 22/1/91, whose front-page headline
ran 'The Bastard is torturing our boys'. The *Sun*'s front page was
the 'Bastards of Baghdad: Hang Saddam long and slow', 22/1/91.

55 *Financial Times*, 24/1/91.

56 *The Independent*, 22/1/91. A week later, the Foreign Office again
protested when it was reported that a coalition pilot had been killed
in a bombing raid while being held in a government building. I have
been unable to find any moving pictures of captured Iraqis before
2/2/91 and therefore remain mystified at the Iraqi ambassador's
response.

57 BSkyB, 28/3/91, interview with David Frost, ULICS.

58 *International Herald Tribune*, 22/1/91.

59 *Daily Telegraph*, 22/1/91.

60 *International Herald Tribune*, 29/1/91.

61 *The Times*, 13/2/91.

62 Pentagon Briefing, Washington, 11/2/91, CNN, ULICS; *The Times*,
13/2/91.

63 *Daily Telegraph*, 23/1/91.

64 *Financial Times*, 26–27/1/91.

65 ITN, 22:27 GMT, 25/1/91, ULICS. ITN then followed this item
with another report utilising Iraqi TV pictures taken from the
previous evening

66 *International Herald Tribune*, 26–27/1/91. The attack on Britain
and John Major, monitored at Caversham, was also covered by
BBC1, 25/1/91, 13:19 GMT, ULICS.

67 Summary of World Broadcasts (hereafter SWB), Part 4. Monitored
19/2/91 after the Fallujah bombing incident (see Chapter 4).

68 *International Herald Tribune*, 2–3/2/91.

69 *Daily Telegraph*, 4/2/91.

70 Ibid.

71 There were too many pool reports on this issue to list here but a
good early example of the preparations being made for a chemical
attack in the future ground war can be found on 29/1/91, BBC1,
13:11 GMT, ULICS.

72 *Washington Times*, 23/1/91.

73 *New York Times*, 23/1/91.
74 ITV, 24/1/91, 09:28 GMT, ULICS.
75 *Guardian*, 28/1/91.
76 CNN's initial report was at 11:38 local time; its first repeat with pictures shot on the previous Monday but not of the plant was at 14:04 and again at 16:23 and the first time the library footage from the previous September was shown was at 18:15 local time *after* the interrupted coalition briefing began at 16:55 local time. 23/1/91, ULICS. For the row it generated see ITN, 24/1/91, 09:45 GMT, ULICS.
77 Although Arnett appeared to have been prevented from completing his report by the Iraqi censors, he resumed seconds later stating he had been cut off for atmospheric reasons. CNN, 18:21 local time (15:21 GMT), 23/1/91, ULICS.
78 Pentagon Briefing, Washington, 14:30 EST, CNN, 23/1/91, ULICS.
79 CENTCOM Briefing, Riyadh, CNN, 27/1/91, ULICS. Also cited in Pyle, *Schwarzkopf* op. cit., pp. 203–4.
80 *International Herald Tribune*, 24/1/91.
81 *Observer*, 3/2/91. See also Brent Sadler's account of this, and of his return to Iraq, in the *Mail on Sunday*, 3/2/91.
82 *International Herald Tribune*, 9–10/2/91.
83 Ibid.
84 *Village Voice*, 5/2/91.
85 CENTCOM Briefing, Riyadh, CNN, 30/1/91, ULICS.
86 CENTCOM Briefing, Riyadh, CNN, 4/2/91, ULICS.
87 *International Herald Tribune*, 9–10/2/91.
88 Ibid.
89 Arkin, Durrant and Cherni, *On Impact*, op. cit., p. 104. The previous point made about the nearby Presidential Grounds is extrapolated from a report made public by *Time*, 22/7/91.
90 *USA Today*, 20/3/91.
91 *The Times*, 25/3/91.
92 *Washington Post*, 3/3/91.
93 *USA Today*, 25/3/91.
94 *International Herald Tribune*, 29/1/91. All sorts of theories were flying around about this, including a front-page story in the *Daily Star* that the Iraqi air force was plotting 'a Pearl Harbour-style sneak attack' on coalition ships in the Gulf. 29/1/91. See also BBC1, 18:00 GMT, 28/1/91, which pointed out that in the Iran–Iraq war Saddam had sent some of his planes to Jordan to keep them safe. ULICS.
95 *International Herald Tribune*, 28/1/91.
96 *Daily Telegraph*, 30/1/91.

97 *Guardian*, 29/1/91.
98 *Daily Telegraph*, 28/1/91. The footage of a Catholic church ceremony, together with graphic shots of dead children, was shown on
   Iraqi television on 25/1/91. These CNN pictures were first carried
   by ITN at 07:06 on 26/1/91 but were dismissed as 'a weapon aimed
   at exploiting civilian damage as a means to influence world opinion'
   in the evening news bulletin that day at 21:55 GMT, ULICS.
   Visnews also had the pictures, as monitored at the ICS on their
   satellite uplink on 27/1/91 at 05:30 GMT.
99 *Daily Telegraph*, 29/1/91.
100 *Daily Telegraph*, 30/1/91.
101 This was monitored by the ICS on the Visnews mobile uplink at
   11:15 GMT on 13/2/91, ULICS.
102 BSkyB, 12:03 and 13:03 GMT, 13/2/91, ULICS.
103 This extract was shown on BBC1, 27/1/91 at 21:11 GMT, ULICS.
104 *Guardian*, 29/1/91. A Reuters report included a statement that there
   was no sign of damage to the Najaf holy shrine, *The Times*, 5/2/91,
   which was confirmed by the pictures shown in Brent Sadler's report
   on ITN, 4/2/91, 22:12 GMT, ULICS.
105 *Guardian*, 1/2/91.
106 *Guardian*, 1/2/91.
107 *Reporting the War*, p. 32.
108 *Financial Times*, 2/2/91.
109 BBC1, 21:16 GMT, 2/2/91, ULICS. On 3 February, the *Independent on Sunday* carried this story under the headline 'Civilian
   deaths rise around missed targets'. Iraqi TV pictures from Basra had
   been shown on BBC1 on 29/1/91 at 18:06 GMT, ULICS. On
   4/2/91, Jeremy Bowen from Jordan did a voice-over report over
   Iraqi TV pictures of a bombed mosque and over NHK pictures
   taken at Diwaniya. This carnage was also supposed to have happened about two weeks earlier. Bowen noted how the vox pops
   'appear to have been prompted by an official'. BBC1, 21:05 GMT,
   ULICS.
110 ITN, 4/2/91, 22:12 GMT, ULICS. This report also showed damage
   on the Baghdad–Basra road.
111 *Daily Telegraph*, 4/2/91. See also Richard Beeston's report of this
   organised visit in *The Times*, 4/2/91.
112 BBC1, 18:02 GMT, 5/2/91, for the point about the schools; ITN,
   7/2/91, 22:20 GMT for his annoyance at Iraqi propaganda. ULICS.
113 *The Times*, 8/2/91; *Financial Times*, 8/2/91; *Guardian*, 8/2/91. See
   also Chapter 4.
114 *International Herald Tribune*, 7/2/91; BBC1, 18:25 GMT, 7/2/91;
   ITN 7/2/91, 22:24 GMT, ULICS. ITN gave the Nasiriyah story

much greater attention, including the 'bloodiest' hospital wards
Brent Sadler had seen.

115 *The Times*, 6/2/91.
116 *The Times*, 9/2/91.
117 *Reporting the War*, p. 32.
118 *The Times*, 9/2/91.
119 *The Times*, 5/2/91.
120 *Daily Telegraph*, 28/1/91.
121 CNN, 13/2/91, 03:20 GMT, ULICS.
122 It was CNN's big story of the day, 29/1/91, with the full interview
     being first shown in the evening. BBC1 carried extensive extracts
     from this interview on 30/1/91 at 00:10 GMT onwards, ULICS.
123 *International Herald Tribune*, 30/1/91; *The Independent*, 30/1/91.
124 *Daily Telegraph*, 5/2/91.
125 *Reporting the War*, p. 34.
126 Ibid., p. 30.
127 Ibid.
128 Jeremy Bowen in Ibid, p. 31.
129 Ibid.
130 *The Times*, 18/2/91.
131 Ibid.
132 *Reporting the War*, p. 33. For a profile of Al-Hadithi, former press
     attaché in London who was responsible for Iraqi policy concerning
     the presence of western journalists, see John Simpson, 'Free Men
     Clamouring for Chains', *Index on Censorship*, Vol. 20, Nos 4 &
     5, April/May 1991, pp. 3–4.
133 Ibid., p. 34.
134 *Financial Times*, 8/2/91.
135 Ibid.
136 Ibid. ITN carried a report on the refusal of the Iraqis to allow the
     Red Cross in to investigate their claims on 8/2/91, 22:25 GMT,
     ULICS.
137 Air Vice Marshal Tony Mason in the *Guardian*, 7/2/91.
138 *The Independent*, 15/2/91. This barrage against the UN Secretary
     General was kept up for several days, with Baghdad radio calling
     him 'the first secretary-general to fail to defend even the Charter of
     the United Nations ... and the first to approve a US decision
     banning the supply of food, medicine and baby milk to the Iraqi
     people'. SWB, Part 4, 18/2/91. These areas had not in fact been
     covered by UN sanctions resolutions.
139 Christopher Dunkley in the *Financial Times*, 6/2/91.
140 *Sunday Telegraph*, 10/2/91.
141 *Daily Telegraph*, 12/2/91.

142 *Daily Telegraph*, 15/2/91.
143 Ibid.
144 Ibid.
145 *Daily Telegraph*, 11/2/91.
146 See also *The Times* of 9/2/91 with its front-page headline 'Iraqis morale wilts under allied onslaught' and the *Guardian*, 11/2/91. It should also be pointed out that the level of popular antipathy towards Saddam inside Iraq is the predominant theme of John Simpson's book, *From the House of War*, op. cit.
147 *Daily Telegraph*, 11/2/91. Several days earlier, the faster medium of television had related similar views when ITN interviewed the departing journalists. See ITN, 8/2/91, 22:20 GMT, ULICS.
148 *Daily Telegraph*, 12/2/91.
149 Pentagon Briefing, Washington, CNN, 12/2/91, ULICS.
150 *The Independent*, 14/2/91. As in most newspapers, these scoreboards of claims were printed regularly.
151 *International Herald Tribune*, 1/2/91.
152 *Daily Telegraph*, 4/2/91; *International Herald Tribune*, 4/2/91.
153 *Daily Telegraph*, 5/2/91.
154 *The Independent*, 15/2/91.
155 *Daily Telegraph*, 6/2/91; *The Times*, 6/2/91. See also ITN, 22:15 GMT, 5/2/91, ULICS.

Chapter 3

1 *New York Times*, 10/3/91.
2 *Newsweek*, 11/3/91.
3 Alan Gropman, *Air Force Times*, 10/3/91.
4 BSkyB, 28/3/91, ULICS. The interview was also shown on the American PBS network on 27/3/91.
5 *Life Magazine*, 18/3/91.
6 *Guardian*, 12/1/91. This poll was a Harris Poll for ITN.
7 *The Times*, 21/1/91.
8 'Cowards', shrieked the *Daily Mirror* across its front page about the Iraqis, 31/1/91.
9 Chris Hedges, 'The Unilaterals', *Columbia Journalism Review*, May–June 1991, p. 28.
10 *International Herald Tribune*, 1/2/91; *The Times*, 2/2/91. The news was first broken by CBS. Pete Williams refused to be drawn on any rescue operation that may have been going on. BBC1, 21:14 GMT, 31/1/91, ULICS.
11 *The Independent* 31/1/91. According to BBC1's 18:00 GMT news on 30/1/91, Baghdad radio had first broken the news of Khafji at

midday that day, according to its monitoring service at Caversham. ULICS.

12 *Guardian*, 31/1/91.
13 *Reporting the War*, p. 20.
14 *Guardian*, 31/1/91.
15 *Guardian*, 2/2/91.
16 *International Herald Tribune*, 1/2/91
17 *Guardian*, 31/1/91.
18 *International Herald Tribune*, 1/2/91.
19 *Guardian*, 31/1/91.
20 *Guardian*, 1/2/91.
21 *Independent on Sunday*, 3/2/91.
22 *The Independent*, 6/2/91.
23 'Tales from the Gulf', The Late Show, BBC2, 20/6/91, ULICS.
24 *Time*, 18/2/91; *Free Press*, No. 63, May 1991.
25 CNN, 07:14 EST, 31/01/91, ULICS.
26 *Guardian*, 31/1/91. That day television analysts were also beginning to consolidate the impression that the entire operation could only have been conceived as a propaganda exercise. See ITV, 31/1/91, 08:10 (Adel Darwish) and 12:37 (Jeremy Thompson) GMT, ULICS.
27 *Daily Telegraph*, 5/2/91.
28 *Guardian*, 2/2/91.
29 Ibid.
30 *The Times*, 1/2/91.
31 Ibid.
32 As reported on Baghdad radio. *Financial Times*, 1/2/91.
33 *Sunday Telegraph*, 3/2/91.
34 Ibid.
35 *Daily Telegraph*, 5/2/91.
36 ITN, 1/2/91, 22:20 GMT, ULICS; *Sunday Times*, 3/2/91; *Daily Telegraph*, 5/2/91. Even so this was nothing as compared to a claim by the Soviet Interfax agency that 1,500 Iraqis had been killed in the fighting. *Guardian*, 2/2/91.
37 *The Times*, 2/2/91.
38 While that enquiry was going on, it was disclosed that a convoy of Marines had been mistakenly attacked by allied planes carrying cluster bombs, killing one and wounding two others. *Sunday Telegraph*, 3/2/91. On Sunday 3 February Marine Major General Robert B. Johnston announced in Riyadh that 7 of the 11 marines who died on 29/1/91 had been killed when their armoured vehicle had been hit by a coalition missile. *International Herald Tribune*, 4/2/91. The British term for 'friendly fire' was 'blue on blue'. Peter Sharpe's explanatory report on the incident in which confused

soldiers at Khafji revealed the difficulties of battle was on ITN at 22:16 GMT, 4/2/91, ULICS.

39 *Time*, 18/2/91.

40 *Guardian*, 2/2/91. The BBC also spotted the discrepancy between the footage and coalition statements. BBC1, 21:08 GMT, 31/1/91, ULICS.

41 *Sunday Telegraph*, 3/2/91.

42 *Guardian*, 1/2/91.

43 Ibid. `

44 *Guardian* 2/2/91.

45 *Daily Telegraph*, 15/2/91.

46 *Sunday Telegraph*, 10/2/91.

47 *International Herald Tribune*, 1/2/91.

48 *Daily Telegraph*, 21/1/91.

49 *The Times*, 13/2/91.

50 On British black propaganda in the Second World War see Balfour, *Propaganda in War*, op. cit.; C. Cruickshank, *The Fourth Arm: Psychological Warfare, 1938–45* (London, Oxford University Press, 1977); Sefton Delmer, *Black Boomerang* (London, Secker & Warburg, 1962); Ellic Howe, *The Black Game* (London, Michael Joseph, 1982).

51 BBC2 Newsnight, 8/5/91. When the BBC Monitoring Service at Caversham first began picking up the Voice of Free Iraq, BBC TV reported that it was 'unclear' who was operating it but implied that it was by opposition groups within Iraq since it was clearly anti-Saddam. BBC1 17/1/91, 11:52 GMT, ULICS. It was also being jammed – but this was presumably by the Iraqis.

52 According to the Voice of Free Iraq on 10 February, 'the Ba'athist clique has undertaken the occupation of Kuwait thus giving a justification for foreign forces to enter our sacred land'. SWB, Part 4, 13/2/91.

53 World Broadcasting Information (hereafter WBI), 1/2/91. Emphasis added.

54 On 12 February the Voice of Free Iraq carried a report from the Saudi news agency, SPA, quoting Ibrahim Al-Zubaydi who was identified as 'the former director of Iraqi Radio and the director of the Voice of Free Iraq Radio'. WBI, 15/2/91.

55 SWB, Part 4, 1/2/91.

56 SWB, Part 4, 31/1/91.

57 SWB, Part 4, 13/2/91. The broadcast was monitored on 10 February.

58 SWB, Part 4, 8/2/91.

59 *Financial Times*, 28/1/91.

60 According to CNN, 05:35 GMT, 14/2/91. ULICS.
61 *Sunday Telegraph*, 20/1/91.
62 *The Times*, 7/2/91.
63 *Guardian*, 7/2/91.
64 *The Times*, 7/2/91.
65 *Newsweek*, 17/6/91, put the final figure at 29 million. To put this in some kind of perspective, even in the final six weeks of the First World War, only 5 million leaflets were dropped by the allies over German lines. See M.L. Sanders and Philip M. Taylor, *British Propaganda in the First World War* (London, Macmillan, 1982) pp. 237–8.
66 Pentagon Briefing, Riyadh (General McPeak), CNN, 15/3/91, ULICS.
67 *International Herald Tribune*, 22/1/91.
68 This entire story was told in *Newsweek*, 17/6/91. At the Saudi briefing in Riyadh on 9/2/91, the news was announced that 7 soldiers, including a Lieutenant Colonel, had defected. It seems likely that this group was the one to which the *Newsweek* story refers. The Saudi briefing was monitored on the Visnews uplink on 10/2/91 at 05:35 GMT, ULICS.
69 *International Herald Tribune*, 24/1/91.
70 *International Herald Tribune*, 28/1/91.
71 *International Herald Tribune*, 30/1/91.
72 Christopher Walker in *The Times*, 29/1/91.
73 *Observer*, 3/2/91.
74 *International Herald Tribune*, 2–3/2/91. BBC2 had shown pictures of the deserted town on 26/1/91 at 19:15 GMT, ULICS. In fact, this accusation about the television pictures tended to be made more by pundits who were groping for an explanation about why the coalition had been caught by surprise. See BBC2, 22:47 GMT, 30/1/91 (Sir John Akehurst) and ITV, 06:15 GMT, 31/1/91 (Mike Dewar), ULICS.
75 *International Herald Tribune*, 5/2/91.
76 *International Herald Tribune*, 4/2/91.
77 Tony Walker in *The Financial Times*, 6/2/91
78 *The Times*, 13/2/91.
79 Ibid.
80 *New York Times*, 13/2/91.
81 *The Times*, 19/2/91.
82 *Daily Telegraph*, 19/2/91.
83 *Sunday Telegraph*, 3/2/91.
84 *Daily Telegraph*, 5/2/91.
85 *Sunday Telegraph*, 10/2/91.

86 *Daily Telegraph*, 7/2/91.
87 *International Herald Tribune*, 7/2/91.
88 *International Herald Tribune*, 4/2/91. Stevens also explained this at the CENTCOM Briefing, Riyadh, 31/1/91, 15:25 GMT, CNN, ULICS.
89 *Guardian*, 7/2/91.
90 *The Independent*, 7/2/91.
91 *The Times*, 5/2/91.
92. *The Times*, 4/2/91.
93 *Guardian*, 9/2/91. This had been revealed by CENTCOM's Briefing in Riyadh. See CNN, 8/2/91, ULICS.
94 *Guardian*, 7/2/91.
95 As far as I have been able to ascertain, this received hardly any publicity in Britain or the United States, even though the press conference at which the King made this claim was relayed by Visnews on its uplinks and monitored by the ICS on 28/1/91 at ·05:48 GMT.
96 *Daily Telegraph*, 5/2/91.
97 SWB, Part 4, 20/2/91. The broadcast, transmitted the previous day, went on to say that Britain, 'the old, collapsing and evil empire, is involved in an escalating civil war which is disturbing its domestic situation, dividing the people, and destroying the government's popularity, just as it is destroying Britain's position abroad and its role in Europe and the world ... Perhaps the British government's objective in these foreign aggressive designs is to try to export its domestic difficulties and to divert the attention of the British citizen to what is taking place abroad. This in addition to its old colonialist, aggressive objectives'.
98 *Daily Telegraph*, 5/2/91.
99 *Sunday Telegraph*, 3/2/91.
100 *Guardian*, 5/2/91.
101 *Financial Times*, 6/2/91.
102 *Daily Telegraph*, 8/2/91.
103 *International Herald Tribune*, 7/2/91.
104 *Guardian*, 6/2/91.
105 *The Times*, 13/2/91. The entire trip was afforded considerable publicity, with Cheney even granting journalists an interview on the plane as he flew to Saudi Arabia in which he talked about an 'amphibious capability' several times. See CNN, 8/2/91, 17:05 GMT, ULICS. Cheney was also interviewed on the return flight by television journalists.
106 *The Times*, 14/2/91.
107 *Guardian*, 7/2/91.

108 *The Times*, 11/2/91.
109 *Daily Telegraph*, 12/2/91.
110 *The Times*, 11/2/91.

Chapter 4

1 *The Times*, 14/2/91.
2 TF1, 20:00 GMT, 13/2/91, ULICS. Interestingly, this inevitability
   was reflected by *Le Monde*, which commented that 'we knew that
   the time of devastating images would come'. *Daily Telegraph*,
   15/2/91.
3 CENTCOM Briefing, Riyadh, CNN, 18/1/91. Reprinted in Pyle,
   Schwarzkopf, op. cit., p. 171.
4 An early favourite with the airmen was 'we walked 10,000 miles to
   smoke a Camel' but this was dropped because of 'host nation
   sensitivity', namely for fear of insulting the Arabs. See *The Times*,
   23/1/91. Troop resentment of local rules and customs was described
   in *The Times*, 5/2/91.
5 *Financial Times*, 24/1/91.
6 *Guardian*, 19/1/91.
7 *Guardian*, 18/1/91.
8 *Daily Telegraph*, 19/1/91.
9 *Observer*, 20/1/91.
10 Pyle, *Schwarzkopf*, op. cit., p. 129.
11 *Guardian*, 19/1/91.
12 *Observer*, 20/1/91.
13 *Guardian*, 21/1/91.
14 *Financial Times*, 25/1/91.
15 Ibid.
16 *The Times*, 24/1/91.
17 *International Herald Tribune*, 25/1/91.
18 Ibid.
19 *International Herald Tribune*, 22/1/91.
20 *Daily Telegraph*, 23/1/91.
21 *Reporting the War*, p. 21.
22 Ibid.
23 CENTCOM Briefing, Riyadh, CNN, 27/1/91, ULICS. BBC1,
   26/1/91, carried a report of the plight of the refugees at 17:20 GMT
   and again at 18:00 GMT bulletin, 28/1/91, ULICS.
24 See, for example, *The Times*, 2/2/91.
25 *International Herald Tribune*, 4/2/91.
26 *International Herald Tribune*, 6/2/91. The Jordanians, for their
   part, argued that they had a 'tacit agreement' with the Iraqis to

continue importing oil which neither the US nor the UN had objected to prior to the war. See BBC1 5/2/91, 18:10 GMT, ULICS.

27 *Guardian*, 9/2/91. When, on 31 January, a daylight raid on a convoy was reported to have killed four Jordanians, there was some speculation as to whether the burning tankers had been mistaken for Scud carriers from the air. BBC1, 21:14 GMT, 31/1/91. CNN carried a report on the departing journalists on 8/2/91 at 17:40 GMT, ULICS. Brent Sadler's report of his journey back to Baghdad was shown on ITN at 22:20 GMT on 31/1/91, ULICS.

28 *Los Angeles Times*, 5/2/91.

29 CENTCOM Briefing, Riyadh, CNN, 11/2/91, 10:00 EST, ULICS. BBC1 showed some of the CNN pictures at 21:05 GMT on 11/2/91. This also contained Jeremy Bowen's report on the latest destroyed bridges and his visit to the 'baby milk plant' – the story that wouldn't go away. Brian Hanrahan also discussed the sudden jump in Iraqi claims on this programme.

30 ITN, 22:10 GMT 24/1/91, ULICS. Peter Arnett's report was broadcast on 23/1/91 at 08:10 GMT. See also the *Guardian*, 26/1/91.

31 ITN showed Iraqi TV pictures of Arnett gathering information amidst the rubble, adding some credence to the Iraqi claims. Happy Iraqis were also shown celebrating in an air raid shelter. ITN, 22:30 GMT 25/1/91, ULICS.

32 *Daily Telegraph*, 29/1/91.

33 CENTCOM Briefing, Riyadh, CNN, 30/1/91. BBC2 made a great play of Schwarzkopf's use of that day's 'sexy' video footage of precision bombing released earlier. See 22:39 GMT, 30/1/91, ULICS.

34 *The Times*, 9/2/91.

35 *International Herald Tribune*, 4/2/91.

36 Ibid. Brent Sadler's report of civilian damage in urban and rural areas the day before was at pains to point out that 'this is a restricted view of the results of allied bombing given that we cannot inspect any military sites'. ITN, 2/2/91, 21:50 GMT, ULICS.

37 ITN, 1/2/91, 22:05 GMT, ULICS. This scene was also witnessed by Alfonso Rojo, *Guardian*, 2/2/91, and by Richard Beeston, *The Times*, 2/2/91, and by CNN, 1/2/91. The day before, as the returning journalists arrived back in Baghdad, they had just failed to catch two cruise missiles passing over the Al-Rashid. ITN, 31/1/91, 22:20 GMT, ULICS. For the next week ITN carried a nightly report on bomb damage.

38 *Daily Telegraph*, 15/2/91. See also CNN, 8/2/91, 16:00 and 17:43 GMT, ULICS. CNN maintained that it had learned of the woman's association with the Iraqi Foreign Minister from 'intelligence sources'.

39 *Financial Times*, 6/2/91.
40 *Guardian*, 2/2/91. The same point had in fact been made in Sadler's report and was also made by Richard Beeston in *The Times* on 4/2/91 and again on 11/2/91.
41 *Guardian*, 4/2/91.
42 CENTCOM Briefing, Riyadh, CNN, 4/2/91, ULICS; *The Times*, 5/2/91
43 Jouvenal's voice interview, and some of his pictures, were shown on BBC1, 8/2/91 at 18:18 GMT, ULICS. Given what was available to the BBC to use, including a close-up shot of a dead boy, very little of the real horror reached British television screens. See Visnews Dawn Feed 05:45 GMT, ULICS. See also Article 19, *The Gulf War and Censorship*, Issue 2, May 1991, p. 3.
44 ITN, 7/2/91, 22:25 GMT, ULICS. ITN showed a long shot of the dead boy omitted by the BBC. See also Chapter 2 on the Nasiriyah visit.
45 *The Times*, 11/2/91.
46 Pentagon Briefing, Washington, CNN, 11/2/91. 16:05 EST. ULICS.
47 The British briefing was described in *The Times*, 8/2/91, and was shown on CNN the previous day. The 'luckiest man in Iraq', which was greeted with laughter by the journalists, was shown in a CENTCOM briefing on 30/1/91, also on CNN at 18:00 GMT onwards. On 8/2/91, the British again showed a video of a bridge exploding behind what was claimed to be a military vehicle. BBC1, 18:08 GMT, ULICS.
48 *Guardian*, 13/2/91. The Brent Sadler report was ITN, 4/2/91, 22:12 GMT, ULICS.
49 I am grateful to Ms Jan Euden of Pan Optic for letting me see a full videotape of this interview, parts of which she included in her Channel 4 programme 'The Information War' in May 1991. I am also grateful to Jon Alpert himself for clearing up a few matters concerning his visit and his film in a telephone interview on 1/8/91.
50 Rojo's account was carried by the *Guardian*, 11/2/91. A week earlier, horrific stories of Basra's bombing were recalled by Indian refugees who had fled the city. *The Times*, 4/2/91.
51 *Guardian*, 8/2/91. CNN carried an interview with Clark on 7/2/91 and BBC1 showed a portion of this interview at 18:26 GMT on 7/2/91, and ITN also showed the press conference. ITV, 7/2/91, 22:27 GMT, ULICS.
52 *Guardian*, 12/2/91.
53 Ibid. The item was tucked into a small paragraph on page 2. However, BBC1 carried items on the Clark mission on 11 and 12 February in its 21:00 and 18:00 GMT bulletins.

54 *Guardian,* 12/2/91.
55 *The Times,* 5/2/91.
56 *Daily Telegraph,* 5/2/91.
57 *Guardian,* 11/2/91.
58 *The Independent,* 15/2/91. Gorbachev's disquiet was reported by ITN at 22:00 GMT on 9/2/91, which showed the headline statement from Moscow television.
59 *Daily Telegraph,* 12/2/91.
60 Fitzwater had said in January: 'I don't think you would ever see Geroge Bush going over targeting charts. He's not involved in that kind of micro-management.' *Los Angeles Times,* 14/2/91.
61 *Daily Telegraph,* 12/2/91.
62 ITV, 06:32 GMT, 13/2/91, ULICS.
63 This footage was widely shown throughout 12 and 13 February; my direct source is BSkyB News, 10:15 GMT, 13/2/91, ULICS.
64 BSkyB News, 10:15, 13/2/91, ULICS.
65 James Fallows (Washington Editor of *Atlantic Monthly*) and Scott Shuger (an editor of *Washington Monthly* and a former naval intelligence officer), 'Technophoria: Weapons Videos vs Weapons Policy', *Washington Post,* 3/2/91.
66 *International Herald Tribune,* 21/1/91.
67 This point was made by CNN at 01:34 GMT on 14/2/91, which also showed a brief clip of the pictures with Arab subtitles.
68 *Daily Telegraph,* 15/2/91.
69 *The Independent,* 15/2/91.
70 WTN's uncut footage was sent via satellite link. The most explicit wartime footage of the carnage at Amiriya that I have seen on British television was on ITV, 17/2/91 at 13:18 GMT, when Brian Walden and Donald McCormick discussed the events of the previous week over some of the most horrific shots of the carnage. ULICS.
71 As seen on BSkyB News at 12:31 GMT, ULICS.
72 *The Times,* 14/2/91.
73 A fuller version of this statement, as revealed by Randall on CNN at 09:04 EST was: 'We have no way of telling from what we have seen so far if this facility was really an air raid shelter, no way of confirming its location and no way of telling if the bodies put on such grisly display are in fact civilian or military casualties ... I would remind you it is not in the American tradition to go after civilian targets and if this attack on a shelter did happen we will feel very badly about it.'
74 CNN carried a segment of this interview at 09:00 EST; BSkyB interviewed Irving live at 13:05 GMT but he gave away nothing

new and made fewer statements that could in retrospect be seen as controversial, possibly because the questions put to him were less searching, or perhaps because Irving had had enough time to sort out his responses, which were kept to generalities.

75 *The Independent*, 14/2/91.
76 The *Daily Star*'s headline ran 'Sacrificed' and added 'Let no one point a finger of blame at the Americans ... There is only one guilty man. Saddam Hussein himself', while *Today* ran the story under the banner 'Entombed by Saddam'. The *Sun* attempted to amass the evidence under a line 'Ten Facts to damn Saddam'. All 14/2/91.
77 The *New York Times* stated that the building 'was one of 25 structures that were initially built as bomb shelters during the Iran–Iraq war. In 1985, at least 10 of them were converted into hardened military command posts'. 14/2/91.
78 *The Independent*, 14/2/91.
79 This point made by *The Observer*, 17/2/91.
80 CNN, 13/2/91, 11:47 and 12:05 GMT, ULICS.
81 CNN, 13/2/91, 13:02 GMT, ULICS.
82 The bombing had taken place at 19.30 EST on 12 February, American time.
83 Richard Dowden visited the pyramid at Ur after the war and found widespread evidence of nearby military activity. See *The Independent*, 7/3/91.
84 *The Times*, 21/1/91.
85 CNN 01:02 GMT, 14/2/91, ULICS.
86 *Sunday Times*, 17/2/91.
87 Stephen Robinson in the *Daily Telegraph*, 5/2/91.
88 CNN, 13/2/91, 23:06 GMT, ULICS.
89 *The Independent*, 14/2/91.
90 The debate concerning whether or not this meeting should be closed was won by 9–2 with 4 abstentions. Coming on a day of such sensitive news, the worry was that the 'wrong message' might be sent to Saddam, ie disunity. Sir David Hannay, British ambassador to the UN, stated that he did not want the presence of the media 'to influence or even distort the course and nature of our debate'. The American ambassador, Thomas Pickering, said that he wanted to be 'free from the glare of instantaneous publicity, and the misinterpretation and misuse to which this meeting might be subject'. Addalla Al-Ashtal, the Yemeni ambassador asked: 'What is there to conceal?' while the Cuban ambassador, Ricardo Alarcon de Quesada, said the 'war is not the property of the 15 states around this table' and felt that the UN was being turned into a Pentagon tool. CNN, 01:15 GMT, 14/2/91, ULICS.

91 CNN, 13/2/91, 17:33 GMT, ULICS.

92 A shorter version was shown on ITV at 20:00 GMT, ULICS.

93 The BBC received 300 complaints from viewers that night about its coverage; ITN received 200.

94 *The Times*, 14/2/91.

95 CNN showed this report at 03:03 GMT on 14/2/91, ULICS.

96 It emerged after the war that Simon and his crew had been subjected to considerable psychological maltreatment, even though the Iraqis denied any knowledge of the whereabouts of him and his crew for a month. On 25/1/91, Alistair Stewart was reporting that the Iraqis had no knowledge of the CBS crew. See ITN, 22:00 GMT, 25/1/91, ULICS. Simon's team was released after the end of the war only after representations from Moscow, although Peter Arnett and other colleagues in Baghdad had been constantly reassuring the Iraqis that the journalists were what they said they were.

97 CNN, 01:35 GMT, 14/2/91, ULICS.

98 CNN, 02:30 GMT, 14/2/91, ULICS.

99 *The Independent*, 14/2/91.

100 *The Independent*, 15/2/91.

101 SWB, Part 4, 18/2/91. The point about the reduction of television signals was made by CNN, 05:35 GMT, 14/02/91, ULICS.

102 *International Herald Tribune*, 15/2/91.

103 *The Times*, 14/2/91. The patriotic tabloids were in no doubt, with the *Daily Star*, whose front page carried a colour photograph of a badly injured little girl beneath the headline 'Sacrificed', stating that 'He even arranged for "grief stricken" relatives to be on hand when the foreign news teams were brought to the bunker ... but none of them wept', 14/2/91. This was also picked up by the *Sun* in its '10 Facts to Damn Saddam' front-page coverage of the incident, 14/2/91.

104 *The Times*, 14/2/91.

105 *Sunday Times*, 17/2/91.

106 *Daily Telegraph*, 15/2/91.

107 This is one of the findings of the Institute of Communications Studies audience research conducted by Dr David Morrison which will be forthcoming in print.

108 *Washington Post*, 14/2/91; *New York Times*, 14/2/91.

109 *International Herald Tribune*, 15/2/91.

110 *New York Times*, 14/2/91.

111 *International Herald Tribune*, 15/2/91.

112 CNN, 06:33 GMT, 14/2/91. ULICS.

113 *New York Times*, 15/2/91.

114 *International Herald Tribune*, 15/2/91.

115 John Simpson, *From the House of War*, op. cit., p. 71.
116 *Washington Post*, 15/2/91; *New York Times*, 15/2/91.
117 *New York Times*, 15/2/91.
118 *New York Times*, 15/2/91; *The Times*, 16/2/91.
119 *The Independent*, 15/2/91.
120 Ibid.
121 *Sunday Times*, 17/2/91.
122 *Observer*, 17/2/91.
123 See *The Times*, 16/2/91.
124 *Observer*, 17/2/91.
125 *Sunday Times*, 17/2/91.
126 *New York Times*, 18/2/91; *Washington Post*, 22/2/91; *Daily Telegraph*, 18/2/91.
127 *The Times*, 18/2/91.
128 *The Times*, 19/2/91.
129 *The Times*, 18/2/91; *Daily Telegraph*, 18/2/91. The *Sun's* uncritical acceptance of this story was carried under the headline 'Saddam's DIY (Destroy It Yourself) Ruins', 18/2/91.
130 *Washington Post*, 22/2/91. This was apparently done 'over the objections of senior Air Force officials'.
131 SWB, Part 4, 20/2/91.
132 *The Times*, 20/2/91; *Daily Telegraph*, 20/2/91; the *Observer*, 24/2/91, reported other signs of internal disaffection with the regime.
133 *The Times*, 25/3/91.
134 Cited in Arkin et al., *On Impact*, op. cit., p. 91.
135 *Washington Post*, 8/5/91.
136 Barton Gellman, 'Allies Sought Wide Damage in Air War', *Washington Post*, June 1991, but reprinted in the *Guardian Weekly*, 30/6/91. In July 1991 the US administration was still insisting that it was adhering to a 1976 Executive Order banning assassination attempts. *Time*, 22/7/91.
137 *Observer*, 28/4/91.
138 'Tales from the Gulf', The Late Show, BBC2, 20/6/91, ULICS. See also John Simpson, *From the House of War*, op. cit., p. 5.
139 John Simpson, *From the House of War*, p. 6.
140 *New York Times*, 2/5/91. See also *The Nation*, 6/5/91, whose reporters found 'a city whose homes and offices were almost entirely intact, where the electricity was coming back on and the water was running. Not a normal place – scarcity, grief, hardship, and apprehension marked it – but post-industrial enough for us to be caught in a lot of traffic jams'.
141 Arkin et al., *On Impact*, op. cit., pp. 46–7.

142 *New York Times*, 26/2/91.
143 *Washington Post*, 18/3/91; *The Independent*, 19/3/91.
144 *On Impact*, p. 80. Some wartime reports put the figure much lower at 60% and 40%, but these could not be confirmed by the authors of the Greenpeace report in discussions with Air Force analysts.
145 *USA Today*, 20/3/91.
146 *Washington Post*, 16/2/91.

Chapter 5

1 *Guardian*, 15/2/91.
2 *Spectator*, 23/2/91. The anger of MPs was summarised by Geoffrey Dickens in G. Dickins, J. Eldridge, G. Mathias, & C. Ferguson, '"The Baghdad Broadcasting Corporation?" How television dealt with the Gulf War' in N. Miller, & R. Allen (eds), *And Now for the BBC* (London, John Libbey, 1991) pp. 73–83.
3 *The Times*, 12/2/91.
4 Quoted by Douglas Jehl in the *Los Angeles Times*, 24/3/91.
5 CENTCOM briefing, Riyadh (General Schwarzkopf and General Buster Glosson), CNN, 30/1/91, ULICS.
6 *USA Today*, 25/3/91.
7 *Guardian*, 2/2/91.
8 CNN, 23:35 GMT, 17/1/91. The caller was identified as 'Ali Salem' and he had also phoned earlier in the day.
9 *The Times*, 28/2/91.
10 *Daily Telegraph*, 15/2/91; *The Times*, 15/2/91.
11 *Guardian*, 15/2/91.
12 *The Times*, 20/2/91.
13 *Daily Telegraph*, 20/2/91.
14 *The Times*, leader, 23/2/91.
15 *Sunday Times*, 30/6/91.
16 *The Times*, 26/2/91. In his masterly briefing on 27 February, General Schwarzkopf announced that the stories had been a decisive factor in the timing of the Ground War, saying 'we made the decision that rather than wait the following morning to launch the remainder of these forces, that we should go ahead and launch these forces that afternoon'. CENTCOM Briefing, Riyadh, CNN, 27/2/91, ULICS.
17 *Daily Telegraph*, 26/2/91; *The Independent*, 26/2/91 & 27/2/91. In this second report, the figure was put at 5,000; the *Sunday Times* put the figure at 20–30,000, 24/2/91.
18 *The Times*, 12/2/91.
19 AP scooped Reuters by 15 minutes with this story, breaking it first

at 11:35 GMT. CNN got it out at 11:41 GMT, quoting both AP
and Agence France Presse. 15/2/91, ULICS.

20 *Washington Post*, 16/2/91
21 Ibid.
22 *The Times*, 16/2/91.
23 *Observer*, 17/2/91.
24 *Sunday Times*, 17/2/91.
25 *The Times*, 16/2/91.
26 *The Times*, 19/2/91.
27 *Daily Telegraph*, 20/2/91 & 21/2/91.
28 *Daily Telegraph*, 21/2/91.
29 *The Times*, 16/2/91.
30 Ibid.
31 *The Times*, 18/2/91; *Daily Telegraph*, 18/2/91.
32 *The Times*, 20/2/91.
33 *The Times*, 23/2/91.
34 Ibid.
35 Ibid. For an analysis of the speech see the *Daily Telegraph*, 23/2/91.
36 *Newsweek*, 11/3/91.
37 SWB, Part 4, 18/2/91. This was transmitted on 16/2/91.
38 Ibid. This was argued on 15/2/91.
39 *Reporting the War*, op. cit., p. 1.
40 Ibid., p. 6.
41 *Independent on Sunday*, 27/1/91. The earliest television *wartime* reference I have found to the serious likelihood of 'possibly the biggest amphibious assualt since the Korean War' was on BBC1, 25/1/91 at 07:04 GMT, repeated at 08:06 GMT the same day. By 29/1/91, the BBC was convinced that an amphibious assault would take place. See BBC1 29/1/91, 06:25 GMT and 08:49 GMT, ULICS.
42 *Guardian*, 31/1/91.
43 *The Times*, 7/2/91.
44 *The Times*, 20/2/91.
45 *The Times*, 21/2/91.
46 SWB, Part 4, 18/2/91.
47 *The Times*, 21/2/91, which ran this item adjacent to Colvin's.
48 *Newsweek*, 25/2/91.
49 The reason why I call this description enigmatic is because the 'Hail Mary' play in American football is usually regarded as a desperation measure on the part of a team which, as a last resort in the final seconds of a game, throws as many of its players forward in the hope and prayer that one of them will catch the ball thrown high and far to them by the quarterback and score a touchdown to

win. The only reason that I can imagine Schwarzkopf used this analogy is that he was referring to the secret build-up of his forces to the west as resembling the group of players who were flexing their muscles immediately prior to the play and the speed with which they would rush forward. He could surely not be implying that this was a desperation measure. The frequency of sporting analogies in the language employed by the coalition during the Gulf War is a topic worthy of further investigation.

50 *The Times*, 4/2/91; *The Independent*, 4/2/91.
51 *The Times*, 5/2/91.
52 *The Times*, 7/2/91.
53 *Sunday Times*, 3/3/91; *Observer*, 3/3/91.
54 Including an amphibious assault, about which there was also an item on the same page along with a story about a book published in America just before the war: *If War Comes ... How to defeat Saddam Hussein* by a military historian, Trevor Dupuy. *Guardian*, 7/2/91, p. 3. This book, laying out the various options open to the coalition, had actually been commended as 'brilliant' by CNN's military analyst, Retired General Perry Smith on 23/1/91. CNN, 13:16, ULICS.
55 CENTCOM Briefing, Riyadh, CNN, 30/1/91; Pentagon Briefing, Washington, CNN, 11/2/91, ULICS.
56 CENTCOM Briefing, Riyadh, CNN, 26/2/91, ULICS.
57 *The Times*, 2/3/91.
58 *The Times*, 28/2/91.
59 *Reporting the War*, p. 6.
60 *Financial Times*, 16/3/91.
61 *The Times*, 5/2/91.
62 *Reporting the War*, p. 6.
63 *The Times*, 25/2/92; *The Independent*, 25/2/91.
64 *Daily Telegraph*, 26/2/91.
65 *The Times*, 25/2/91.
66 *Daily Telegraph*, 26/2/91.
67 *Sunday Times*, 3/3/91. See also John Witherow & Aaidan Sullivan, *The Sunday Times: War in the Gulf: A pictorial history* (London, Sidgwick & Jackson, London, 1991), p. 154.
68 SWB, Part 4, 26/2/91.
69 *The Times*, 26/2/91.
70 Ibid; *The Independent*, 26/2/91. Baghdad radio transmitted Military Communiqué No. 61 on 24/2/91 which stated that 'our victorious forces succeeded in containing the attacks of the US–Atlantic alliance, and foiled their objectives for which the enemy prepared through an extensive media propaganda replete with lies and alle-

gations'. It also stated that 'hundreds' of enemy tanks and vehicles had been destroyed and an airborne force dropped behind enemy lines 'annihilated, with God's help'. The situation in southern Iraq was 'completely under control'. SWB, Part 4, 26/2/91.

71 SWB, Part 4, 26/2/91.

72 SWB, Part 4, 26/2/91. This was transmitted on 24/2/91. BBC1's 18:15 GMT News on 24/2/91 reported the amphibious assault and the retaking of Faylakah, according to Kuwaiti sources, which had first been reported as being retaken on 4/2/91. See above, note 50. It later transpired that Iraqi troops on Faylakah island had surrendered to a drone from the USS *Missouri*. See Allen, Berry & Polmar, *CNN: War in the Gulf*, op. cit., p. 177. But see also p. 197, where it is stated that the island was also taken on 4/2/91.

73 *The Times*, 26/2/91. As for the point about the prisoners being Egyptians, Jeremy Bowen also said that an official he had spoken to had made the same point. Visnews feed, 15:45 GMT, 25/2/91, ULICS.

74 Coughlin in *Reporting the War*, p. 22.

75 *The Times*, 26/2/91.

76 Ibid.

77 CNN reported this at 22:00 EST on 25/2/91; 04:00 26/2/91 local time, ULICS. The speech is reprinted in the *Daily Telegraph*, 27/2/91. It was monitored first at 22:30 GMT on 25/2/91. See SWB, Part 4, 27/2/91. The text of the speech by Saddam Hussein saying that withdrawal would be completed by the end of the day was first monitored at 08:24 GMT on 26/2/91. See SWB, Part 4, 27/2/91.

78 Pentagon Briefing, Washington, CNN, 25/2/91, ULICS.

79 *Washington Post*, 27/2/91; *The Times*, 27/2/91.

80 *The Independent*, 27/2/91.

81 *Daily Telegraph*, 25/2/91; *The Times*, 27/2/91. Even as late as 28 February, Baghdad radio was still maintaining that Iraq's victory was 'clear' because 'all the armies of aggression failed to enter Kuwait before our heroic forces withdrew from it'. SWB, Part 4, 2/3/91.

82 *Daily Telegraph*, 26/2/91.

83 As reported by CNN's Jeanne Moos at 00:06 EST on 26/2/91, ULICS.

84 01:34 EST, CNN, ULICS.

85 *The Times*, 25/2/91.

86 Jonathan Alter, *Newsweek*, 11/3/91.

87 *The Independent*, 27/2/91.

88 *Washington Post*, 27/2/91.

89 *The Times*, 1/3/91.

90 *The Times,* 2/3/91.
91 *Daily Telegraph,* 28/2/91.
92 'Tales from the Gulf', The Late Show, BBC2, 20/6/91; Fisk's report at the time was printed under the headline 'Something Evil has Visited Kuwait City' on the front page of *The Independent,* 28/2/91. One of the most extensive descriptions of the torture and brutality of the Iraqi occupation was made by Tim Kelsey in the *Independent on Sunday,* 10/3/91.
93 *Washington Post,* 27/2/91.
94 *Washington Post,* 28/2/91.
95 *Reporting the War,* p. 6.
96 Ibid, p. 7.
97 Ibid.
98 *Financial Times,* 16/3/91.
99 P.T. Benic in *Reporting the War,* p. 10.
100 Hugo Young, *Guardian,* 5/2/91.
101 This entire story is told by Simpson in *From the House of War,* op. cit., pp. 345–6 and 351–2.
102 See, for example, Richard Kay's pooled dispatch about the 1st Armored Division's push, published in the *Daily Telegraph* four days later on 28/2/91.
103 Alexander Higgins, AP writer, wire report entitled 'Military Pools Give Spotty Coverage', 28/2/91.
104 *Reporting the War,* p. 2. Kate Adie had managed to get a pool report back to London in time for BBC1's 18:15 GMT News on 24/1/91, but it was filmed in daylight and couched in such terms that it might have been recorded before the land attack began or at least very soon after at first light. There was little else from her over the next few days.
105 Higgins, 'Military Pools Give Spotty Coverage', op. cit., 28/2/91.
106 *New York Times,* 1/3/91.
107 *Newsweek,* 11/3/91.
108 *Washington Post,* 27/2/91.
109 *The Independent,* 27/2/91.
110 Ibid.
111 Martin Woollacott, *Guardian,* 1/3/91.
112 *The Times,* 27/2/91.
113 *The Times,* 28/2/91.
114 The text is published in the *Daily Telegraph,* 28/2/91. The letter was transmitted on Baghdad radio and its explanation is contained in SWB, Part 4, 28/2/91.
115 SWB, Part 4, 28/2/91. This broadcast was monitored at 08:28 GMT on 27/2/91.

116 Ibid.
117 *Newsweek*, 11/3/91.
118 *The Times*, 28/2/91; *The Independent*, 28/2/91.
119 The full text is reprinted in the *Daily Telegraph*, 28/2/91, and in M.E. Morris, *H. Norman Schwarzkopf: Road to Triumph* (London, Pan Books, 1991).
120 *The Times*, 1/3/91.
121 John Simpson, *From the House of War*, op. cit., p. i.
122 Channel 4 News that evening also ran the report in full at 19:00 GMT. ULICS.
123 *The Times*, 2/3/91.
124 Ibid.
125 'Tales from the Gulf', The Late Show, BBC2, 20/6/91, ULICS. See also Stephen Sackur's account of the battle published in *The London Review of Books*, 4/4/91 and reprinted in MacArthur, *Despatches from the Gulf War*, op. cit., pp. 261–6.
126 *From the House of War*, op. cit., p. 7.
127 The Times, 4/3/91.
128 *Washington Post*, 28/2/91.
129 *Wall Street Journal*, 2/3/91.
130 *From the House of War*, op. cit., p. 7.
131 *Life Magazine*, 18/3/91.
132 *New York Times*, 23/1/91. CNN on 23/2/91 carried a regular report of still photographs released by the coalition of the burning wells. ULICS.
133 *The Times*, 23/2/91.
134 *The Times*, 4/3/91; *Daily Telegraph*, 4/3/91.
135 *The Times*, 2/3/91.
136 *Washington Post*, 18/3/91
137 See, though, the *Sunday Times*, 3/3/91.
138 Arkin et al., *On Impact*, op. cit., pp. 111–13.
139 *Guardian*, 4/3/91.
140 *The Independent*, 2/3/91. It might be added that some combat footage of the battle of Mutlah Gap, taken by the Joint Combat Film Unit, emerged after the war and was shown on Channel 4's Equinox programme at 19:00 GMT on 11/8/91.
141 *Guardian*, 11/3/91.
142 Ibid.
143 *The Times*, 2/3/91. This report appeared first in *Le Monde*, was denied by the Algerian government, which then stated that it would be prepared to offer Saddam political asylum – a good example of how a rumour can become a fact. The story might once again have been the result of the coalition's black propaganda which was

317

attempting to expose Saddam as a coward as it stepped up its broadcasts to the rebels inside Iraq. Georges Marion, the *Le Monde* correspondent who first broke the story from Algeria, had his accreditation removed by the Algerian Foreign Ministry on 2 March. See Article XIX, *Stop Press*, op. cit.

144 *Daily Telegraph*, 1/3/91; SWB, Part 4, 2/3/91.
145 Ibid.
146 Ibid.
147 SWB, Part 4, 4/3/91. Transmitted 1/3/91.
148 *Observer*, 3/3/91.

Conclusion

1 This is a higher death toll, achieved in six weeks, than even the highest estimates of Iraqi dead sustained during the eight-year Iran–Iraq war. See P. Hiro, *The Longest War: the Iran–Iraq military conflict* (New York, Routledge, 1991) p. 250, which puts that figure at 105,000 Iraqis. The first coalition post-war estimates were put at only 25,000–50,000 Iraqi dead and, although the White House apparently ordered an investigation into the death toll, the administration has been reluctant to release figures up to the time of writing this book. See *New York Times*, 1/3/91. Even a month after the cease-fire, an official in Riyadh was not responding to questions about casualties 'because that gets us into the business of enemy body counts, and we have said we are not going to do that', *Washington Post*, 26/3/91. The coalition's figures for both Desert Shield *and* Desert Storm at time of writing were: 266 US dead (105 before the war began), 357 wounded, 6 missing; 44 British dead (25 in action, 19 in non-combatant accidents), 43 wounded; 2 French dead, 28 wounded; 1 Italian dead; 29 Saudis dead, 43 wounded, 9 missing; 9 Egyptians dead, 74 wounded; 6 UAE killed; 8 Senagalese wounded. By 13 March, all 47 of the coalition forces held by the Iraqis had been repatriated.

2 *Washington Post*, 26/3/91.

3 'The Information War', Channel 4, 21/5/91, ULICS.

4 See the *Sunday Times*, 3/3/91 and Philip Towle, *Pundits and Patriots*, op. cit.

5 Cited by William Boot, 'The Pool', op. cit., pp. 24–7.

6 On Britain see P.M. Taylor, 'Censorship in Britain in the Second World War: an Overview' in A.C. Duke and C.A. Tamse (eds), *Too Mighty to Be Free: Censorship and the Press in Britain and the Netherlands* (Zutphen, De Walberg Pers, 1987) pp. 157–78; N. Pronay, 'The News Media at War' in N. Pronay and D.W. Spring

(eds), *Propaganda, Politics and Film, 1918–45* (London, Macmillan, 1982) pp. 173–208; Allan M. Winkler, *The Politics of Propaganda: the Office of War Information, 1942–45* (New Haven, Oxford University Press, 1977).

7 Cited in Nan Levinson, 'Snazzy visuals, hard facts and obscured issues', op. cit., p. 27.

8 *Reporting the War*, op. cit., p. 16.

9 *Guardian*, 4/2/91.

10 CENTCOM Briefing, Riyadh 27/2/91, CNN, ULICS, my italics.

11 *The Economist*, 19/1/91.

12 *Washington Post*, 21/2/91.

13 *Newsweek*, 25/2/91.

14 *Newsweek*, 11/3/91.

15 *Reporting the War*, p. 40.

16 This is amongst the preliminary findings of the Institute of Communications Studies' survey into audience reactions to the war, to be published by Dr David E. Morrison in 1992.

17 R. Dworkin, 'A Harmful Precedent', *Index on Censorship*, Vol. 20, Nos 4 & 5, April/May 1991, p. 2.

18 Cited in Allen, Berry and Polmar, *CNN: War in the Gulf.* , op. cit., p. 236.

19 See the *Sunday Times* survey of 17/2/91 in which 71% were said still to be in favour of bombing military targets in or near cities, even if this resulted in civilian casualties; in the United States, a *Washington Post*/ABC poll indicated that 81% of people believed it was a military bunker.

20 *Daily Telegraph*, 28/2/91.

21 For a more detailed treatment of this point see the concluding essay in Morrison and Tumber, *Journalists at War*, op. cit.

22 'Tales from the Gulf', The Late Show, BBC2, 6/6/91 & 19/7/91, ULICS.

Chronology of the Gulf War

1990

17 July: Saddam Hussein accuses America of conspiring with Gulf states to cut oil prices.

27 July: OPEC raises oil target price.

2 August: Iraqi invasion of Kuwait at 02:00 local time; the Emir, Sheikh Jaber Ahmed Al-Sabah, flees to Saudi Arabia; emergency session of UN Security Council passes Resolution 660 which condemns invasion and demands immediate Iraqi withdrawal; Iraqi and Kuwaiti assets in UK and USA frozen; Margaret Thatcher and George Bush make parallel tough statements from their joint meeting.

3 August: Iraq moves troops in Kuwait to Saudi border; puppet government established in Kuwait and Iraq claims it is helping a Kuwaiti uprising against Al-Sabah family; US Navy ordered to Gulf; Shevardnadze–Baker joint declaration in Moscow calling for arms embargo on Iraq.

5 August: President Bush announces 'this will not stand'.

6 August: UN Resolution 661 imposes trade embargo against Iraq (medical and humanitarian food supplies exempted).

7 August: 4,000 American troops from 82nd Airborne Division sent to Saudi Arabia; Turkey turns off Iraqi pipeline.

8 August: Iraq declares formal annexation of Kuwait; President Bush announces American foreign policy objectives in televised address.

9 August: UN Resolution 662 declares Iraqi annexation of Kuwait null and void.

10 August: Arab League in Cairo votes to send Pan-Arab force to Saudi Arabia.

11 August: Douglas Croskery, a British citizen, shot by Iraqis while trying to escape Kuwait.

12 August: Saddam links any withdrawal from Kuwait with Israeli withdrawal from occupied territories, together with US withdrawal from Saudi Arabia and Syrian withdrawal from Lebanon.

15 August: Formal end to Iran–Iraq war announced.

18 August: Iraqi announcement of 'hostage' policy; UN Resolution 664 demands that all foreigners be allowed to leave Iraq and Kuwait.

23 August: Saddam meets hostages and footage shown on Iraqi TV's 'Guest News'.

25 August: UN Resolution 665 authorises naval blockade to enforce sanctions; BBC and CNN crews enter Iraq.

27 August: Austrian President Kurt Waldheim arrives in Baghdad for mercy mission and takes 80 Austrian hostages home to Vienna.

28 August: Iraq declares Kuwait to be its 19th Province.

1 September: 200 British women and children permitted to leave Iraq on mercy flights to London.

9 September: Helsinki summit: Presidents Bush and Gorbachev call upon Iraq to leave Kuwait.

13 September: UN Resolution 666 authorises humanitarian food shipments if distributed through international aid agencies.

14 September: Britain announces it is sending its 7th Armoured Brigade to Gulf.

15 September: 4,000 French troops ordered to the Gulf.

16 September: UN Resolution 667 condemns Iraqi raids on diplomatic premises in Kuwait; Iraqi TV transmits, unedited, President Bush's speech to Iraqi people warning of dangers of war.

24 September: UN Resolution 669 asks Security Council to assist other nations affected by the embargo.

25 September: UN Resolution 670. All cargo flights to Iraq banned.

27 September: Britain and Iran renew diplomatic relations.

8 October: 21 Palestinians killed and more than 100 wounded on Temple Mount in Jerusalem, renewing linkage issue.

23 October: Iraq releases 330 French hostages. Edward Heath brings home 33 British hostages.

25 October: Dick Cheney announces that a further 100,000 American troops are being sent to join the 210,000 Americans already in Saudi Arabia; US active duty service for combat reservists doubled from 180 to 360 days.

29 October: UN Resolution 674 demands that Iraq stops taking hostages and calls for reparations and redress for war crimes in Kuwait.

3 November: James Baker begins seven-nation tour to start forming grand coalition.

8 November: President Bush announces that he will double the size of the US forces in the Gulf by despatching a further 200,000 US troops.

9 November: Willi Brandt leaves Baghdad with 180 West European hostages.

10 November: General Schwarzkopf (secretly) draws up preliminary plan to envelop Iraqi forces in Kuwait by a flanking movement.

28 November: John Major replaces Margaret Thatcher as British Prime Minister.

29 November: UN Resolution 678 sets deadline of 15 January for with-

321

drawal and approves use of 'all necessary means' to expel Iraq thereafter.

30 November: Bush tell US 'this will not be another Vietnam'.

1 December: Saddam visits his front-line troops and puts Palestine linkage on agenda.

6 December: Iraq announces impending release of all hostages.

22 December: Bush meets Major in Washington.

1991

9 January: Geneva: Baker and Aziz fail to agree. Aziz refuses to take to Saddam a letter from President Bush.

12 January: Perez de Cuellar visits Baghdad in last-ditch attempt to persuade Saddam to adopt UN resolutions; both US Senate and House of Representatives back Bush.

13 January: Iraqi parliament endorses Saddam's rejection of UN deadline.

14 January: Guidelines issued to the media.

15 January: European Community concedes failure of last ditch peace plan and a final French initiative also collapses; Bush signs National Security Directive that formally authorises military action.

16 January: Deadline expires at midnight EST and Cheney orders Schwarzkopf to execute the Directive.

16–17 January: War! Allied aircraft and cruise missiles strike Iraq; first British Tornado lost; CNN broadcasts for 17 hours live from enemy capital before having its plug pulled; Iraqi Voice of the Masses Radio combined with Radio of Iraqi Republic; NOP poll in Britain shows 71% support for sending troops to Gulf.

18 January: 8 Scuds fired at Israel, injuring 12 civilians; 1 fired at Saudi intercepted successfully by first ever combat launch of Patriot missile; 6 mobile launchers destroyed by 'Scudbusting' coalition aircraft; Turkey allows coalition use of its bases; first Iraqi PoWs taken on raids against Kuwaiti oil platforms; President Bush warns against unwarranted optimism by media.

19 January: Most western journalists expelled from Iraq (but not CNN); 3 Scuds fired at Israel, one landing in Tel Aviv and injuring 17 people; Sea Island terminal starts leaking oil; 7,000–10,000 stage peace demonstration in London.

20 January: Bombing missions from Turkey begin; disastrous briefing at MoD prompts series of media attacks in the days that follow; captured coalition pilots paraded on Iraqi TV for first time; alleged 'baby milk plant' bombed.

21 January: CBS crew go missing on the Kuwait–Saudi border; MoD

imposes black-out on Met Office's release of Middle East weather forecasts; first Kuwaiti oil fields, at Al-Wafra, reported to have been fired by Iraqis.

22 January: Momentary euphoria in the streets of Baghdad as a rumour spreads that President Hosni Mubarak of Egypt had been assassinated.

23 January: Iraqi government stops sale of petrol to civilians without warning; Cheney and Powell deliver most forthcoming briefing to date in which General Powell announces that coalition will 'cut off and kill' the Iraqi army; island of Qurah liberated; CNN reports on destruction of Iraqi 'baby milk plant'; Iraqi papers start publishing photographs of civilian damage.

24 January: French air force starts bombing missions against Iraqi targets, reversing a previous decision to attack only targets in occupied Kuwait; Saudi pilots shoot down two Iraqi planes; reports that Saddam had his air force commanders executed; Iraqi tankers start leaking oil into Gulf; Iraq opens border with Jordan, temporarily releasing flood of refugees; Peter Arnett escorted to civilian damage sites.

25 January: Reports of Saddam's 'environmental terrorism' confirmed; Iraqis cease parading captured PoWs.

26 January: Mina Al-Ahmadi oil refinery complex bombed by coalition precision bombs to stem oil flow.

27 January: Start of exodus of Iraqi planes to Iran.

28 January: Baghdad radio warns it will extend war through terrorist attacks throughout the world; President Bush tells National Religious Broadcasters' Convention that it is a 'just war'; Iraqis announce that captured pilot injured in coalition bombing raid; first reports of border clashes.

29 January: French defence minister Jean-Pierre Chevenement resigns, stating 'the logic of war risks driving us further every day from the objectives fixed by the United Nations'; President Bush's 'State of the Union' address; Khafji occupied by Iraqis.

30 January: Coalition declares 'total air superiority'; CNN starts transmitting pictures live from Baghdad.

31 January: Khafji retaken by coalition.

1 February: Coalition–media relations turn sour over Khafji.

2 February: Western journalists in Iraq escorted to Diwaniya; Ramsay Clark mission enters Iraq; Faylakah Island retaken by coalition.

3 February: new coalition media arrangements announced; first Iranian peace offer coolly received at White House.

4 February: Iraqis continue to escort journalists to sites of alleged civilian damage.

5 February: Voice of the Gulf begins transmitting black propaganda.

6 February: 4 Iraqi soldiers surrender to unilateral journalists; Iraq accuses coalition of trying to 'expel Iraq from the 20th Century' and severs diplomatic relations with the USA, Britain, France, Italy, Egypt and Saudi Arabia; French claim 30% of Republican Guard destroyed.

7 February: Physicians for Human Rights report on Iraqi atrocities in Kuwait published.

8 February: Iraq invites UN fact-finding mission to investigate 'baby milk factory' episode; coalition bombing of Nasiriyah; Ramsay Clark leaves Iraq.

9 February: Dick Cheney and Colin Powell begin visit to Central Command in Riyadh; Primakov arrives in Baghdad as Gorbachev expresses worries that coalition is going beyond UN mandate.

11 February: Iran denounces Iraq for failing to take up its peace initiative; Iraq announces that thousands, not hundreds, have been killed by coalition bombing and that it will never accecpt a cease-fire.

12 February: Non Anglo-American journalists write open letter complaining to King Fahd; Saddam informs Primakov he is prepared to consider pulling out of Kuwait under certain conditions; Tom King in Washington visiting Bush.

13 February: Primakov leaves Baghdad; Amiriya bombing; Security Council meets behind closed doors.

14 February: Iraqis launch Scud attack at Hafer Al-Batin; RAF mistakenly bombs market in Fallujah; renewal of campaign concerning Iraqi atrocities in Kuwait.

15 February: Saddam's 'cruel hoax'; ground war count-down begins.

16 February: Americans announce that Iraqis have decapitated mosque and that it was not bombed by coalition.

17 February: RAF admits mistake at Fallujah; Baghdad endures one of heaviest air raids of war; Tariq Aziz visits Moscow.

18 February: Aziz–Gorbachev meeting in Moscow.

19 February: French TV crews temporarily boycott covering the war; another massive air raid on Baghdad.

20 February: US announces that Iraq must withdraw by 23 February, 20:00 local time; 450 Iraqis desert.

21 February: Gorbachev telephones Bush with details of peace plan; Saddam's defiant speech on Baghdad radio.

22 February: Moscow announces that Iraq has accepted its eight-point peace plan. Bush says it does not go far enough and warns Iraq to comply with all UN resolutions by 12:00 EST on 23 February.

23 February: UN deadline for Iraq to withdraw expires with no sign of withdrawal.

24 February: Land War begins at 04:00 local time; News blackout imposed.

25 February: Scud missile kills 27 US servicemen and injures 98 in Dhahran; allies reveal that more than 600 oil wells burning in Kuwait; Iraqis start to evacuate Kuwait.

26 February: Iraq announces it is withdrawing from Kuwait; Kuwait City liberated; UN Security Council goes into closed session at the request of the Soviets; start of battle of Mutlah Gap.

27 February: Tariq Aziz's letter to UN offering to comply with all UN resolutions; President Bush announces victory and end to offensive allied operations and declares a cessation of hostilities to begin at 00:00 EST, 05:00 GMT, 08:00 local time.

28 February: 580 Kuwaiti oil fields reported on fire.

1 March: First television pictures of devastation on road north to Basra come through.

3 March: General Schwarzkopf and staff meet Iraqi commanders to agree permanent cease-fire.

4 March: Sheikh Saad Al-Sabah, Crown Prince of Kuwait, returns home.

14 March: Emir Sheikh Jaber Ahmed Al-Sabah returns to Kuwait

Appendix

Countries considered part of the coalition

Argentina**, Australia**, Bahrain*, Bangladesh, Belgium**, Britain*, Canada, Czechoslovakia, Denmark**, Egypt*, France*, Germany, Greece**, Italy, Kuwait*, Morocco, Netherlands**, New Zealand, Niger, Norway**, Oman*, Pakistan, Poland, Qatar*, Saudi Arabia*, Senegal, Spain, Syria*, Turkey, UAE*, USA*.

(* military involvement in Ground War)

(** naval contributions only)

Countries making economic, humanitarian or other contributions to the coalition

Afghanistan, Austria, Bulgaria, Finland, Honduras, Hungary, Iceland, Japan, Luxembourg, Malaysia, Philippines, Portugal, Sierra Leone, South Korea, Sweden, Taiwan, Turkey, USSR.

Bibliography

MEDIA SOURCES (January–March 1991)

Newspapers

1 British
Daily Express
Daily Mail
Daily Mirror
Daily Telegraph
Financial Times
Guardian
The Independent
Independent on Sunday
Observer
Star
Sun
Sunday Times
The Times
Today

2 American
New York Times
Washington Post
International Herald Tribune

Television

Gulf War Archive, University of Leeds, Institute of Communications Studies:

BBC1
BBC2
ITV
Channel 4

BSkyB (containing NBC and CBS)
CNN

Others
Sky's Review of the War, 1/3/91. ULICS.
'Tales from the Gulf', The Late Show, BBC2, 6/6/91 & 19/7/91. ULICS.
ITN's video compilation, 'Operation Desert Storm: Gulf War: the Complete Story', 1991.
'The Information War', Channel 4, 21/4/91.
'In the Eye of the Storm', Panorama, BBC1, 2/9/91.

Radio

Summary of World Broadcasts, Part 4: East Africa and Latin America (BBC Monitoring Service, Caversham, 1991).
World Broadcasting Information: Broadcasting News and Transmission Schedules (BBC Monitoring Service, Caversham, 1991)

Other works

Al-Khalil, Samir, *Republic of Fear* (London, Hutchinson Radius, May 1991 edition).
Allen, Charles, *Thunder and Lightning. The RAF in the Gulf: Personal Experiences of War* (London, HMSO, 1991).
Allen, T. B., Berry, F. Clifton & Polmar, N., *CNN: War in the Gulf. From the Invasion of Kuwait to the Day of Victory and Beyond* (London, Maxwell–Macmillan International, 1991).
Arkin, W. A., Durrant, D. Cherni, M., *On Impact: Modern Warfare and the Environment. A Case Study of the Gulf War* (Washington, Greenpeace, May 1991).
Article XIX, *Stop Press: The Gulf War and Censorship*, Issue 1, February 1991; Issue 2, May 1991 (London, International Centre on Censorship, 1991).
Badsey, Stephen, 'The Media War', in Pimlott, J., McKnight, S. & Sibbald, R., *A Line in the Sand: The Gulf War Assessed* (London, Arms and Armour Press, 1992).
Covens, L., 'Mobile Radio in the Gulf War', *Global Communications*, May–June 1991, pp. 20–7.
Dickins, G., Eldridge J., Mathias, G. & Ferguson, C., ' "The Baghdad Broadcasting Corporation?" How television dealt with the Gulf War' in N. Miller, & R. Allen (eds), *And Now for the BBC* (London, John Libbey, 1991) pp. 73–83.
Index on Censorship, Vol. 20, Nos 4 & 5, April/May 1991.

Bibliography

International Press Institute, *Reporting the War: a collection of experiences and reflections on the Gulf*. A discussion paper published by the British Executive of the International Press Institute, May 1991.

MacArthur, Brian (ed.), *Despatches from the Gulf War* (London, Bloomsbury, 1991).

Massing, M., 'Debriefings: what we saw, what we learned', *Columbia Journalism Review*, May–June 1991, pp. 23–4.

Morris, Capt. M. E., *H. Norman Schwarzkopf: road to triumph* (London, Pan Books, 1991).

Morrison, David E., and Tumber, H., *Journalists at War: the dynamics of news reporting during the Falklands conflict* (London, Sage, 1988).

Parrish, Lt Col. Robert D., *Schwarzkopf: an insider's view of the Commander and his victory* (London & New York, Bantam Books, 1991).

Pyle, Richard, *Schwarzkopf: the man, the mission, the triumph* (London, Mandarin, 1991).

Ridgeway, James (ed.), *The March to War* (New York, Four Walls Eight Windows, 1991).

Robinson, Stephen, 'Fighting for Screen Time', *Spectator*, 12/1/91.

Simpson, John, *From the House of War* (London, Arrow Books, 1991).

Taylor, Philip M., *Munitions of the Mind: War propaganda from the ancient world to the nuclear age* (Wellingborough, Patrick Stephens, 1990).

Towle, Philip, *Pundits and Patriots: Lessons from the Gulf War* (London, Institute for European Defence and Strategic Studies, Occasional Paper No. 50, 1991).

Western, Bruce W., 'The Issue of Media Access to Information', in Bruce W. Western (ed.), *Military Lessons of the Gulf War* (London, Greenhill, 1991).

Witherow, John & Sullivan, Aidan, *The Sunday Times: War in the Gulf: A pictorial history* (London, Sidgwick & Jackson, 1991).

Woodward, Bob, *The Commanders* (New York, Simon & Schuster, 1991).

Index